Towards Corporate Liability in International Criminal Law

SCHOOL OF HUMAN RIGHTS RESEARCH SERIES, Volume 38.

A commercial edition of this dissertation will be published by Intersentia under ISBN 978-94-000-0024-7.

The titles published in this series are listed at the end of this volume.

Cover illustration © Danny Juchtmans.

Typesetting: Wieneke Matthijsse, Willem Pompe Institute for Criminal Law and Criminology, Utrecht University, the Netherlands.

Towards Corporate Liability in International Criminal Law

Naar de strafbaarheid van rechtspersonen in het internationaal strafrecht
(met een samenvatting in het Nederlands)

Proefschrift

ter verkrijging van de graad van doctor
aan de Universiteit Utrecht
op gezag van de rector magnificus, prof. dr. J.C. Stoof,
ingevolge het besluit van het college voor promoties
in het openbaar te verdedigen
op vrijdag 26 februari 2010 des middags te 12.45 uur

door

Desislava Emanouilova Stoitchkova
geboren op 29 januari 1981
te Pernik, Bulgarije

Promotoren: Prof. dr. C.H. Brants-Langeraar
Prof. dr. G.G.J. Knoops

This thesis was accomplished with financial support from the Netherlands Organisation for Scientific Research (NWO).

ACKNOWLEDGEMENTS

In seeing this book come to fruition, I benefitted greatly from the guidance and encouragement of Professor Chrisje Brants and Professor Alexander Knoops. Their constructive comments and stimulating insights into a vast array of themes, ranging from international criminal law through criminology to legal philosophy, enriched my views and the research put forward hereafter. I would also like to thank Professor Fried van Hoof, Professor François Kristen, Professor Héctor Olásolo, Professor Elies van Sliedregt and Professor Harmen van der Wilt for their thorough reading and perceptive advice on the final manuscript. They have been a tremendous source of inspiration to me and I am honoured to have them on my board of examiners. The assistance which I have received in practical matters from my colleagues at the Willem Pompe Institute for Criminal Law and Criminology of Utrecht University has been indispensible over the past years. I am most grateful to Wieneke Matthijsse for scrupulously generating the layout of this book. Special thanks also to my dear friends, Jill Coster van Voorhout, Tsvetelina Petrunova, Lorna Pope, Jovanka Bestebroer, Alberdina Kregel and Werner Lycklema, who have stood by me and have been a welcome distraction from solitary academic work. I am particularly indebted to Antony James Botting for his patience and moral support in moments of dire need. To my parents – Slava and Emanouil – whose unconditional love and faith in me have invariably accompanied the current and all my other endeavours, I dedicate this book.

Utrecht, January 2010 Desislava Stoitchkova

Table of Contents

List of abbreviations

AC	Appeal Cases
A Crim R	Australian Criminal Reports
ATCA	Alien Tort Claims Act
CEO	Chief Executive Officer
Cir.	Circuit
CLR	Common Law Reports
Cr App R	Criminal Appeal Report
CSR	Corporate Social Responsibility
DRC	Democratic Republic of the Congo
EC	European Council
ECHR	European Court of Human Rights
ECJ	European Court of Justice
ESCOR	United Nations Economic and Social Council Official Records
EU	European Union
F 2d	Federal Reporter (Second Series)
F 3d	Federal Reporter (Third Series)
F Supp	Federal Supplement
ICC	International Criminal Court
ICJ	International Court of Justice
ICTR	International Criminal Tribunal for Rwanda
ICTY	International Criminal Tribunal for the former Yugoslavia
ILM	International Legal Materials
ILO	International Labour Organisation
IMT	International Military Tribunal
JCE	Joint Criminal Enterprise
MNC	Multinational Corporation
NGO	Non-governmental Organisation
NW 2d	North-Western Reporter (Second Series)
OECD	Organisation for Economic Cooperation and Development
OTC	Oriental Timber Company
RS	Rome Statute
SATRC	South African Truth and Reconciliation Commission
SCR	Supreme Court Reports
TWC	Trials of War Criminals
UK	United Kingdom
UN	United Nations

UNITA	National Union for the Total Independence of Angola
UNWCC	United Nations War Crimes Commission
US	United States
USC	United States Code
USMT	United States Military Tribunal
VCLT	Vienna Convention on the Law of Treaties

CHAPTER 1
INTRODUCTION

I CORPORATIONS, CONFLICTS AND HUMAN RIGHTS

With the advent of globalisation and the growing influence of multinational corporations (MNCs)[1] in recent decades, there have been mounting concerns about the implications of the corporate lack of accountability on human rights protection worldwide. Business enterprises, whose activities transcend state borders, wield tremendous financial and political power. Albeit instrumental in promoting socio-economic development worldwide, corporate might has a dark side as well. From oppressive working conditions[2] and environmental pollution[3] to intrusion in domestic political processes[4] and 'complicity' in egregious international crimes, MNCs can, and some reportedly do, encroach on human dignity and existence.

As their commercial activities expand in response to market demands, many corporations have come to operate in precariously volatile regions of the world. Even in circumstances of war or widespread violence against civilians, MNCs find it hard to resist opportunities for financial gain. Cognisant of existing regulatory deficiencies, enterprises increasingly venture into business which constitutes or borders on criminal behaviour. Some are known to have been directly involved in gross human rights violations, including forced labour, torture, killings and the displacement of

---

1 The term 'multinational corporation' (and also 'multinational enterprise' and 'transnational corporation') is generally defined as 'an economic entity, which owns (in whole or in part), controls and manages income generating assets in more than one country' (P.T. Muchlinski, *Multinational Enterprises and the Law*, Oxford: Blackwell, 1995, p. 12). A similar definition has recently been embraced by the *UN Norms on the Responsibilities of Transnational Corporations and Other Business Enterprises*, UN Doc. E/CN.4/Sub.2/2003/12/Rev.2 (2003). Although a strict reading of the designations 'multinational', 'transnational', 'corporation' and 'enterprise' may warrant some differentiation in meaning, such terms will be used interchangeably throughout this study (for an overview of various definitions, see Muchlinski, *supra*, pp. 12-15).

2 Allegations of sweatshop production have been documented against companies operating in various industry sectors. See generally S. Prakash Sethi, *Setting Global Standards. Guidelines for Creating Codes of Conduct in Multinational Corporations*, New York: John Wiley & Sons Inc., 2003.

3 Frequently cited in this regard are the effects of Shell's oil extraction activities in the Nigerian Delta. Oil spills have caused extensive environmental damage, killing wildlife, ruining water supplies and destroying food sources. See e.g. J. Eaton, The Nigerian Tragedy, Environmental Regulation of Transnational Corporations, and the Human Right to a Healthy Environment, 15 *Boston University International Law Journal* 261 (1997) at 264-271.

4 For example, in 1970 ITT, an American MNC, allegedly engineered the attempted overthrow of the democratically elected government of Salvator Allende in Chile. See 53 UN ESCOR (1822nd meeting), pp. 19, 22, UN Doc. E/SR, 1822 (1972).

populations in Africa, Asia and South America.[5] Others help sustain – advertently or inadvertently – the infrastructure necessary for the commission of international crimes, being a source of arms, military equipment, raw products and money to violent governments and opposition rebel groups alike.[6]

The circumstances surrounding the exploitation of natural resources in conflict-ridden regions of the world are but an illustration of MNCs' involvement in serious human rights abuse and serve to highlight the pressing need for increased regulation and accountability.[7] The war in Sierra Leone, for instance, was to a large degree financed through the sale of diamonds. It is estimated that, for the duration of the conflict, and apart from the funds accumulated through sales effectuated by the government itself, the Revolutionary United Front rebels raised from $25 million to $125 million per year through the sale of diamonds.[8] The profits were mostly used for the purchase of arms and other military equipment. Throughout the conflict, rebel and army forces as well as different militia groups uniformly and indiscriminately killed, tortured and mutilated civilians. Tens of thousands were abducted and forced to slave in diamond mines. In 2000, the UN Security Council prohibited trade in Sierra Leone rough diamonds, concerned about the role played by diamonds in fuelling the civil war.[9] Despite the embargo, dealers and jewelers in Africa, Europe and the Middle East continued to buy Sierra Leone diamonds, while air and water cargo transportation companies ensured that diamond parcels reached their final destinations.[10]

Strategic control of diamond-rich areas has been a driving force in the ongoing conflict in the Democratic Republic of the Congo as well. In 2001, a panel of experts requested by the UN Security Council to report on the exploitation of natural resources in the DRC, uncovered that in an effort to secure the supply of weapons, the DRC government signed mining contracts with a number of foreign companies, worth

5 See hereunder and also section III.2 below.

6 *Ibidem.*

7 Although not the only avenue for MNCs' involvement in human rights abuse, documented allegations pertaining to corporate participation in violations amounting to international crimes have frequently revolved around MNCs' exploitation of natural resources. The term 'international crimes' in the present study is used to refer to the 'core crimes' currently punishable under international criminal law, namely genocide, war crimes and crimes against humanity. In order to make easier reading and unless explicitly specified otherwise, references to 'grave human rights violations' and 'serious human rights abuse' hereunder should be read to designate the international crimes that fall within the jurisdiction of the International Criminal Court. It must be noted here, however, that not all of the examples mentioned in this illustrative section relate to international crimes *per se*.

8 Report of the Panel of Experts appointed pursuant to Security Council Resolution 1306 (2000), paragraph 19, in relation to Sierra Leone, UN Doc. S/2000/1195, 20 December 2000, para. 78, at <www.un.org/Docs/sc/committees/SierraLeone/SLselectedEng.htm>.

9 UN Security Council Resolution 1306 on the situation in Sierra Leone, UN Doc. S/RES/1306, 5 July 2000, at <www.un.org/docs/scres/2000/sc2000.htm>.

10 UN Panel of Experts Report, *supra note 8*.

several million US dollars each.[11] Recently, in its decision confirming charges against Germain Katanga, the International Criminal Court also referred to the competition over control of Ituri's natural resources as a major reason for the continued conflict in the region.[12]

Angola's devastating civil war was also largely financed through the exploitation of the country's vast mineral reserves.[13] Investigation reports by non-governmental organisations have alleged that foreign oil corporations paid approximately $1 billion in signature bonuses to the Angolan government in order to obtain supplementary drilling licenses.[14] The Angolan government is also believed to have largely financed its military spending through mortgaging crude oil in order to secure credit lines with major international investment banks. Banks have, in turn, been accused of over-subscribing loans and thus effectively freeing up funds for the government to use against rebels threatening to disrupt mortgaged oil production.[15]

Oil extraction companies operating in Nigeria, Sudan and Colombia have also allegedly assisted the training and maintenance of military forces and private security companies charged with guarding oil pipes and terminals.[16] Some of these MNCs have been further linked with the import of high-tech weapons into Nigeria,[17] while others have been criticised for transporting soldiers with company helicopters to offshore drilling platforms where unarmed protestors have been subsequently killed.[18] Still others are reported to have supplied weapons and vehicles to the Myanmar military

11 Report of the Panel of Experts on the Illegal Exploitation of Natural Resources and Other Forms of Wealth of the Democratic Republic of the Congo, UN Doc. S/2002/1146, 16 October 2002, at <www.nisat.org/sanctions%20reports/DR%20Congo/UN%202002-10-16%20DR%20Congo.pdf>.

12 *Prosecutor v. Germain Katanga and Mathieu Ngudjolo Chui*, Decision on the confirmation of charges, ICC-01/04-01/07-717, 30 September 2008, para. 3, referring to UN Security Council Special Report on the Events in Ituri, January 2002 – December 2003, UN Doc. S/2004/573, 16 July 2004.

13 For an overview of corporate involvement in 'sanction-busting' for the benefit of UNITA, including the sale or delivery of arms, military equipment and petroleum as well as the purchasing of diamonds, see Final Report of the Panel of Experts established by the UN Security Council pursuant to Resolution 1237 (1999), UN Doc. S/2000/203, 10 March 2000, at <www.un.org/News/dh/latestangolareport_eng.htm>.

14 E.g. Human Rights Watch, *Some Transparency, No Accountability*, 12 January 2004, pp. 29-30, at <www.hrw.org/sites/default/files/reports/angola0104.pdf>; Global Witness, *A Crude Awakening: The Role of the Oil and Banking Industries in Angola's Civil War and the Plunder of State Assets*, 1 December 1999, p. 7, at <www.globalwitness.org/reports/show.php/en.00016.html>.

15 Global Witness Report, *supra note 14*, pp. 15-16.

16 See e.g. R. Dufresne, The Opacity of Oil: Oil Corporations, Internal Violence and International Law, 36 *New York University Journal of International Law and Politics* 331 (2004) at 337; C. Forcese, Deterring 'Militarised Commerce': The Prospect of Liability for 'Privatised' Human Rights Abuses, 31 *Ottawa Law Review* 171 (2000) at 173-177.

17 W. Reno, *Warlord Politics and African States*, London: Lynne Rienner Publishers Inc., 1998, p. 207.

18 A. Gedicks, *Resource Rebels: Native Challenges to Mining and Oil Corporations*, Cambridge: South End Press, 2001, pp. 49-50.

junta[19] or have been accused of complicity with the Indonesian army in massacres perpetrated during the Suharto regime.[20]

The trade in Cambodian timber, in violation of UN prohibitions on exports, enabled the Khmer Rouge regime to hold onto power and perpetuate for more than twenty years one of the most brutal civil wars in human history.[21] Timber played a role in the perpetuation of the conflict in Liberia too. Despite UN Security Council sanctions, imposed in 2002 and prohibiting the selling of arms to Liberia,[22] weapons continued to find their way into the country, mostly on the logging vessels of multinational timber companies with links to the black arms market. The Oriental Timber Company's security force, for instance, has also been accused of serious human rights violations including torture, forced labour, sexual abuse, looting and destruction of private property.[23]

The list of allegations against MNCs grows every year, although not all pertain to the commission of international crimes. The majority of business enterprises implicated for their participation in human rights abuse, and particularly in genocide, war crimes and crimes against humanity, have not however had their activities legally challenged. Attempts at prosecution have been sporadic and largely ineffective; corporations have been allowed to continue unabated on the quest for financial gain, perpetuating many a cycle of violence. This study, therefore, explores the desirability and feasibility of subjecting business enterprises *per se* to regulation through international criminal law as a means of narrowing the existing regulatory gap. It inquires into the permissibility and inherent challenges of extending criminal law provisions, and in particular the Rome Statute, beyond natural persons. Given the unique features of MNCs, it questions traditional models for constructing the criminal responsibility of economic entities. Furthermore, it discusses the appropriateness of extending liability beyond the

---

19 Dufresne, *supra note 16*, at 337.

20 On 27 August 2008, the US District Court of Columbia found that a case against Exxon under the Alien Tort Claims Act should be submitted to a jury for trial. See <ecf.dcd.uscourts.gov/cgi-bin/show_public_doc?2001cv1357-365>. The plaintiffs allege that Exxon has been complicit in human rights violations committed by Indonesian security forces. For an outline of the Alien Tort Claims Act, see section III.2 below.

21 R.S. Salo, When the Logs Roll Over: The Need for an International Convention Criminalising Involvement in the Global Illegal Timber Trade, 16 *Georgetown International Environmental Law Review* 127 (2003) at 131-132.

22 UN Security Council Resolution 1408 on the situation in Liberia, UN Doc. S/RES/1408, 6 May 2002, at <www.un.org/Docs/scres/2002/sc2002.htm>.

23 In 2006, the Dutch District Court in The Hague convicted Guus Kouwenhoven, owner of the Royal Timber Corporation (and linked to the Oriental Timber Company), for selling arms to Liberia in violation of the UN embargo. Two years later the conviction was overturned on appeal due to lack of sufficient evidence. See LJN: BC7373, 10 March 2008 (at <www.rechtspraak.nl>). Although witness statements confirmed that the OTC security had been comprised and managed by (former) army members, the Appeals Court did not find conclusive evidence that the defendant himself had any control over the security staff. Accordingly, Kouwenhoven was acquitted of charges pertaining to war crimes too.

material perpetrators – not only to the organisation comprising the individuals who physically carry out the impugned conduct but also to parent corporations for their contribution to harm suffered in the course of their subsidiaries' activities.

II The rise of corporate social responsibility

The debate about the responsibilities of business towards society is not a novel phenomenon. Agitation about the ethical implications of commercial activities predates the industrialisation era[24] but it was not until the mid-twentieth century that corporate social responsibility (CSR) began to truly gain momentum. As an organised movement, CSR was largely spurred by increased consumer activism and advances in communication technologies, which brought awareness of the broadening development divide in the modern world to the fore.[25] While campaigners were becoming increasingly vocal about the perceived failures of inter-governmental efforts to design and implement an adequate framework for the regulation of MNC activities,[26] the business community was growing acutely conscious of the importance of fostering a socially responsible image. It gradually came to be realised that a good social record is not only attractive to consumers but also furthers business sustainability in more general terms.[27] Corporate reputation was openly recognised as 'a fragile, intangible asset that complements – and sometimes surpasses – the value of more tangible material and financial' benefits.[28]

As pointed out by Zerk, the rise of the corporate social responsibility movement prompted the gradual displacement of the traditional 'state-centred' perspective on corporate regulation (focusing mainly on issues such as investor protection and taxation) by a more 'people-centred' approach to evaluating company performance.[29] CSR is nowadays generally understood as a need, as well as a duty, to integrate a wide range of social and environmental concerns in business strategy and operations. Although business groups tend to emphasize its voluntary character and equate it to corporate governance, definitions espoused via international forums regard the social responsibility of companies as an integral part of fulfilling legal expectations.[30] Apart from any binding or 'soft law' obligations in relation to reporting and transparency,

24 J. Hood, *The Heroic Enterprise: Business and the Common Good*, New York: Free Press, 1996, p. xv.
25 J. Zerk, *Multinationals and Corporate Social Responsibility*, Cambridge: Cambridge University Press, 2006, p. 21.
26 *Ibidem*, p. 18.
27 C. Avery, Business and Human Rights in a Time of Change, in: M.T. Kamminga and S. Zia-Zarifi (eds.), *Liability of Multinational Corporations under International Law*, The Hague: Kluwer Law International, 2000, pp. 26-29, referring to studies indicating that a socially responsible image has the propensity to encourage productivity, boost workers' moral and attract qualified personnel.
28 C. Fombrun, *Reputation: Realising Value from the Corporate Image*, Cambridge: Harvard Business School Press, 1996, quoted in Avery, *supra note 27*, p. 25.
29 Zerk, *supra note 25*, p. 23.
30 *Ibidem*, pp. 29-32.

CSR thus implies responsibility to not only operate ethically in relation to the environment, society and human health but also in accordance with the law.[31]

Compliance with international human rights standards, espoused in treaty and customary law, has become widely accepted as falling within MNCs' sphere of responsibility.[32] The precise meaning and scope of the requisite compliance, however, remain contentious.[33] The primary duty to protect, respect and fulfill the enjoyment of human rights and ensure their horizontal application in relationships between individuals and business enterprises remains vested in nation states. Nonetheless, having gained (limited) international legal personality, corporations are now seen as direct addressees of human rights obligations too. Although not all of international law is extendable to MNCs, there is now a broad consensus that companies are bound by certain 'core' rules pertinent to all actors within the international domain.[34] Prominent among these generally applicable international principles is the prohibition to engage directly or indirectly in violations of *ius cogens* norms, including genocide, war crimes and crimes against humanity.[35]

Despite increased attention towards the human rights impact of corporate activities worldwide and the growing recognition of MNCs' responsibilities under international law, regulation – as will be seen below, remains piecemeal and largely deficient. While domestic jurisdictions have been reluctant to vigorously pursue mandatory enforcement despite the availability of avenues for regulatory supervision, the international system has not yet put in place any effective compliance mechanism directed at private enterprise delinquency. Flagging the legitimacy of business transactions and the self-proclaimed moral neutrality of their profit endeavours, corporations at the same time have been adamantly resistant to any attempts to regulate their conduct.

---

31 *Idem*, p. 32.

32 In this regard, see also S. Joseph, *Corporations and Transnational Human Rights Litigation*, Oxford: Hart Publishing, 2004; N. Jägers, *Corporate Human Rights Obligations: In Search of Accountability*, Antwerp: Intersentia, 2002; A. Clapham, *Human Rights in the Private Sphere*, Oxford: Clarendon Press, 1993.

33 For an overview of substantive human rights norms deemed applicable to corporations through international instruments and in domestic systems, see e.g. P.T. Muchlinski, *Multinational Enterprises and the Law*, Oxford: Oxford University Press, 2007, pp. 507-536.

34 M.T. Kamminga and S. Zia-Zarifi, Liability of Multinational Corporations under International Law: An Introduction, in: M.T. Kamminga and S. Zia-Zarifi (eds.), *Liability of Multinational Corporations under International Law*, The Hague: Kluwer Law International, 2000, p. 8.

35 *Ius cogens* comprises non-derogable legal prohibitions of peremptory nature. The following international crimes have generally been accepted to comprise *ius cogens*: genocide, crimes against humanity, war crimes, piracy, slavery and torture. See in this regard M.C. Bassiouni, *Crimes against Humanity in International Criminal Law*, The Hague: Kluwer Law International, 1999, also discussing the contentious status that some legal scholars insist on according to crimes against humanity as *ius cogens* (p. 210 et seq.)

III Regulation at the domestic level

Domestic enforcement methods aimed at ensuring corporate accountability for harm caused to others include a range of procedures and sanctions: criminal, civil and administrative. Such mechanisms may be invoked against MNCs in both host and home states and have come to increasingly target also parent companies for the injurious conduct of their foreign subsidiaries.

III.1 Criminal liability

The last century has witnessed a gradual but definite erosion of the traditional principle of *societas delinquere non potest*.[36] As a result, most national jurisdictions nowadays recognise legal persons, corporations in particular, as capable of incurring culpability in terms of criminal law.

Common law countries, such as England, the United States and Canada, were among the first to impose corporate criminal liability. Initially applied to regulatory offenses only, the concept was later extended to *mens rea* crimes.[37] By the 1970s, civil law traditions in continental Europe were beginning to follow suit. The Netherlands, Belgium, Switzerland, France, Denmark, Finland, Norway and Portugal are some of the states to have put in place domestic legislation prescribing the criminal responsibility of corporations in varying degrees of comprehensiveness.[38] Outside of Europe, the notion has been embraced by a variety of legal systems, including Australia, Japan, South Africa and India.[39]

There are a few countries, such as Germany, Italy and Argentina, which continue to resist the inclusion of corporate liability into their criminal codes on conceptual grounds, invoking concerns pertaining to the legal-philosophical underpinnings of subjective culpability.[40] However, even in those jurisdictions that have traditionally opposed the idea of corporate criminal responsibility, there has been a gradual shift of

---

36 Literally 'corporations cannot commit crimes'. The essence of this principle postulates that moral and criminal responsibility cannot be vested with legal entities but fall upon the human beings who have agreed to perform the illegal action.

37 M. Wagner, *Corporate Criminal Liability: National and International Responses* (background paper for the Reform of Criminal Law 13th international conference 'Commercial and Financial Fraud: a Comparative Perspective', Malta, 8-12 July 1999), at <www.icclr.law.ubc.ca/publications/reports/ corporatecriminal.pdf>.

38 See generally S. Sun Beale and A.G. Safwat, What Developments in Western Europe Tell Us About American Critiques of Corporate Criminal Liability, 8 *Buffalo Criminal Law Review* 89 (2002). Also FAFO Report, A. Ramasastry and R.C. Thompson, *Commerce, Crime and Conflict. Legal Remedies for Private Sector Liability for Grave Breaches of International Law. A Survey of Sixteen Countries*, 2006, at <www.fafo.no/pub/rapp/536/ 536.pdf>.

39 *Ibidem*.

40 The legal-philosophical debate surrounding the topic of corporate criminal responsibility, and in particular contentions in relation to the moral agency and moral responsibility of corporations, are further discussed in Chapter 2.

attention over the past decade to the question of how to construct the liability of 'fictitious' entities. Corporations in such states are being increasingly subjected to quasi-criminal sanctions.[41] Argentina has enacted a specific law establishing the liability of legal persons for certain categories of crimes,[42] while Germany imposes heavy administrative penalties subject to appeal in a criminal court. In many other legal systems, administrative penalties are increasingly being substituted for direct criminal provisions.[43]

National jurisdictions generally tend to criminalise serious human rights violations, including the egregious acts of genocide, war crimes and crimes against humanity. In many countries corporations can be held liable for breaches of such provisions not only when committed within the domestic legal system, but also when perpetrated abroad.[44] In some instances and on the basis of universal jurisdiction, a state may undertake the prosecution of international crimes committed anywhere in the world and irrespective of the nationality of the perpetrator or the victims.[45]

Despite the potential for domestic criminal prosecution of MNCs for human rights violations committed abroad, attempts at transnational human rights litigation by means of criminal law have been sporadic. Although corporations are prohibited under international law from engaging in, *inter alia,* genocide, crimes against humanity, forced labour, torture and extrajudicial murder, states have generally been averse to the strict regulation of MNCs' extraterritorial activities. On the one hand, the failure to prevent or punish corporate human rights transgressions does not give rise to state responsibility, although the duty to horizontally apply human rights has been affirmed in international jurisprudence.[46] On the other hand, fears of the adverse effects that over-regulation might have on competitiveness, innovation and productivity continue to fuel resistance to non-voluntary systems for appraising corporate conduct.[47]

---

41 For an overview of the applicable regulatory regimes in a number of European countries, including Germany and Italy, see Sun Beale and Safwat, *supra note 38.*

42 FAFO Report, *supra note 38.*

43 C. Wells, *Corporations and Criminal Responsibility*, Oxford: Oxford University Press, 2001, p. 140.

44 On 2 April 2007, a Dutch Court of Appeal sentenced Frans van Anraat to 17 years imprisonment for his complicity in war crimes. Van Anraat's company, *FCA Contractor*, had commercially sold large quantities of Thiodyglicol (TDG) to the Iraqi regime of Saddam Hussein. At trial it was found that chemical weapons containing the TDG supplied by Van Anraat were subsequently deployed against the Kurdish population in Iraq and in the war against Iran. The Dutch Prosecution justified its choice to indict the individual businessman, not the company, by reference to the company's liquidation in 1992. See LJN: BA4676, 9 May 2005 (at <www.rechtspraak.nl>).

45 States, which have adopted universal jurisdiction with respect to breaches of international criminal law, include the United Kingdom, Canada, Australia and the Netherlands. Before amending its relevant law in 2003, Belgium sought the prosecution of the French energy company TotalFinaElf for its alleged complicity in forced labour in Myanmar. See S. Smis and K. van der Borght, Legislation, Belgium: Act Concerning the Punishment of Grave Breaches of International Humanitarian Law, 38 *International Legal Materials* 918 (1999).

46 Joseph, *supra note 32*, p. 9.

47 Zerk, *supra note 25*, p. 36-37.

Litigation prospects are further often impeded by an array of political and socio-economic factors of significant impact on domestic regulatory regimes. Generally 'host states', i.e. the states where MNCs operate, especially in the developing world, lack the legal resources, technical expertise and financial means to effectively monitor and enforce corporate compliance. Given their dependency on foreign investment, often coupled with conditions of poor governance and corruption, host states are rarely eager to seek the accountability of MNCs (in particular where the host government is itself involved in human rights abuse). 'Home states', i.e. the states of incorporation, are usually better placed to effect mandatory regulation. Domestic courts in home states, however, face a different set of challenges relating to MNCs' propensity to shift their form and hence avoid liability.[48]

III.2 Liability through civil courts

Tort-based litigation against MNCs for violations of human rights obligations abroad has been particularly popular in the US over the past decade. The Alien Tort Claims Act (ATCA) grants federal courts jurisdiction over civil lawsuits initiated by foreign citizens for torts committed by US corporations in violation of 'the law of nations.[49] The torts concerned have been consistently interpreted as encompassing violations of international human rights and humanitarian law norms of an obligatory and universal nature, including genocide, war crimes and crimes against humanity.[50] In order to be actionable, however, the claims must generally allege foreign government involvement in the human rights breaches giving rise to the harm impugned. Only a few of the lawsuits brought under the ATCA have sought to assert direct human rights violations by private companies themselves.[51] In the absence of state involvement in the abuses alleged, a plaintiff's claim stands a chance of success only if it is established that the norm breached is of direct application to non-state entities.[52] Thus far, US courts have declared such directly applicable norms to include the prohibitions of genocide,[53] piracy,[54] slave trading[55] and forced labour.[56] International law violations such as torture

48 For a discussion of separate legal personality and limited liability in relation to corporate accountability, see Chapter 6, section II.1: The intrinsic protections of the corporate form.

49 28 USC § 1350.

50 B. Stephens, The Amorality of Profit: Transnational Corporations and Human Rights, 20 *Berkeley Journal of International Law* 45 (2002) at 86. See also e.g. Estate of Marcos, 25 F 3d 1475-6 (1994); Kadic, 70 F 3d 246 (1995); Abebe-Jira, 72 F 3d 844 (1996); Unocal, 963 F Supp 880, 891-2 (1997).

51 C. Forcese, ATCA's Achilles Heel: Corporate Complicity, International Law and the Alien Tort Claims Act, 26 *Yale Journal of International Law* 487 (2001).

52 Tel-Oren v. Lybian Arab Republic, 726 F 2d 774 (1984), 794-5.

53 Kadic, 70 F 3d 232 (1995), 242-3.

54 Unocal, 963 F Supp 880 (1997), 891.

55 Unocal, 395 F 3d 932 (2002), 946-7.

56 Unocal, 963 F Supp 880 (1997), 892.

and summary execution give rise to corporate liability under the ATCA only where the private entity is demonstrated to have acted in complicity with state authorities.[57]

The list of MNCs against whom class action lawsuits have been filed under the ATCA has grown exponentially in recent years. Among the defendants is Exxon Mobil, alleged to have provided logistical and material support to the Indonesian army in exchange for protection of its local operations and in the knowledge that the support was used to effectuate the commission of human rights abuses.[58] Proceedings are currently underway also in the case of Talisman Energy for allegedly abetting genocide by the government of Sudan.[59] No ATCA lawsuit, however, has yielded a merits decision as yet. Most cases have been delayed or dismissed on jurisdictional or procedural grounds. Those that survive the preliminary stage of examination, generally tend to be settled out of court.

The most formidable obstacle to ATCA-based claims has been the doctrine of *forum non conveniens*. It provides a ground for dismissal if the court establishes that there is an alternative, more adequate, forum to hear the case.[60] *Forum non conveniens* has also been a hurdle in cases involving claims of human rights violations through negligence or similar causes of action. Some of the earliest complaints against US corporations by human rights litigants – *Union Carbide* and *Aguinda v. Texaco* – were struck on *forum non conveniens* grounds. The difficulty in surviving this preliminary jurisdictional threshold does not, however, detract from the inherent value of human rights litigation based on ordinary tort principles. As Joseph explains, the option of having resort to such principles is particularly important where the claims fall outside ATCA's scope of application.[61]

Tort law as a cause of action against MNCs for violations of human rights norms abroad is also employed in other common law jurisdictions, including the United Kingdom, Australia and Canada. Transnational tort litigation for breaches of human rights in the courts of civil law countries is also a possibility[62] although such cases are generally rare and tend to focus on injuries or other harm suffered through poor

57 See e.g. Kadic, 70 F 3d 245 (1995); Beanal, 969 F Supp 374-80 (1997); Unocal, 963 F Supp 890-1.

58 Doe v. ExxonMobil, Complaint, 11 June 2001. See also *supra note 20.*

59 Presbyterian Church of Sudan v. Talisman Energy Inc., 244 F Supp 2d 289 (2003).

60 Although confirmed as a valid jurisdictional threshold in a succession of cases (for an overview see K. Boyd, The Inconvenience of Victims: Abolishing Forum Non Conveniens in US Human Rights Litigation, 39 *Virginia Journal of International Law* 41 (1998)), US courts have recently adopted a more lenient approach to the application of *forum non conveniens.* Indications of willingness to realign the evaluation of the public interest in providing a forum for the adjudication of international human rights abuses have recently been demonstrated in *Wiwa v. Royal Dutch Petroleum, Bowoto v. Chevron* and *Presbyterian Church v. Talisman.* For further discussion, see Joseph, *supra note 32*, p. 147.

61 Joseph, *supra note 32*, p. 146.

62 For a discussion of tort-based transnational litigation in the Netherlands, see G. Betlem, Transnational Litigation against Multinational Corporations before Dutch Courts, in: M.T. Kamminga and S. Zia-Zarifi (eds.), *Liability of Multinational Corporations under International Law*, The Hague: Kluwer Law International, 2000.

working conditions, breaches of safety standards and environmental damage. A European Union Council Regulation[63] further allows the courts of Member States to hear tort-based claims against MNCs registered within the EU for damage that occurred in third states. The Regulation, however, does not require the application of international law and it is left to the discretion of domestic courts to decide on the direct application of human rights norms to MNCs.

III.3 Non-mandatory mechanisms

Although increasing numbers of states around the world have introduced legal sanctions for corporate breaches of human rights norms, self-regulation continues to dominate as the preferred option over mandatory techniques. Although compulsory regulation may have some drawbacks, particularly in terms of its cost-effectiveness and propensity to lag behind changing social expectations,[64] self-regulation through corporate codes of conduct is hardly a viable approach. The policy statements and social responsibility reports of most, if not all, MNCs today feature some sort of human rights commitments. Endorsements of international human rights instruments, however, do not generally translate into open recognition of the treaties' legally binding nature with regard to business enterprises. There are ample reasons to doubt the efficacy of codes adopted within the framework of trade associations, multi-stakeholder groups or inter-governmental organisations as well. They vary considerably in the scope of their human rights coverage and also often differ in their respective treatment of business relations (e.g. suppliers).[65] Such codes of conduct, furthermore, do not always make provisions for independent monitoring and their implementation is relatively limited.[66] Despite some evidence that they may have certain leverage on corporate behaviour, codes of conduct generally lack rigorous enforcement mechanisms and, therefore, cannot ensure effective compliance with human rights norms.

---

63 Council Regulation (EC) nr. 44/2001, 22 December 2000 on jurisdiction and the recognition and enforcement of judgments in civil and commercial matters, *O.J.* 2001, L12/1. See also Council Regulation (EC) nr. 864/2007, 11 July 2007 on the law applicable to non-contractual obligations, *O.J.* 2007, L199/40.

64 Zerk, *supra note 25*, p. 37.

65 R. Jenkins, *Corporate Codes of Conduct: Self-Regulation in a Global Economy*, United Nations Research Institute for Social Development, 2001, p. 39, at <www.natural-resources.org/minerals/cd/docs/other/jenkins.pdf>.

66 *Ibidem.*

IV International regulation

IV.1 'Soft-law' initiatives

At the international level, attempts to regulate MNCs' operations have been of a predominantly non-binding nature. The idea of enforceable corporate accountability for human rights violations, however, has been gaining recognition.

The most notable guidelines for ethical business behaviour include the *OECD Guidelines for Multinational Enterprises*,[67] the *ILO Tripartite Declaration of Principles concerning Multinational Enterprises and Social Policy*,[68] and the UN Secretary General Kofi Annan's *Global Compact*[69] launched in 1999. A revision to the OECD Guidelines, introduced in 2000, extended existing provisions to include express references to human rights norms. The revised recommendations urge multinationals to 'respect the human rights of those affected by their activities'[70] and to contribute to the elimination of forced labour.[71] Mention of the need to abide by international human rights instruments and ILO Conventions pertaining to compulsory labour, and in particular child labour,[72] was also introduced in the ILO Tripartite Declaration by an amendment in 2001. The UN Global Compact – although a platform for multilateral discussion rather than a code of conduct – sought to extend previously recognised guiding principles for corporate behaviour. Principle 2 in particular discerned a responsibility on the part of businesses to avoid complicity in human rights abuses. Since the launch of the Global Compact, the question of corporate complicity and accountability has become a recurrent theme in UN efforts to devise an effective regulatory mechanism for MNC conduct.

In 2003, the Sub-Commission on the Promotion and Protection of Human Rights adopted the UN *Norms on the Responsibilities of Transnational Corporations*.[73] Unlike the OECD Guidelines and the ILO Tripartite Declaration, which put forward non-binding sets of standards, the UN Norms seek to impose on MNCs direct and legally-binding obligations under international human rights law. Such obligations relate to the respect, protection and fulfillment of internationally-recognised human rights, including the right to security of person,[74] within the corporations' respective spheres of activity and influence.[75] MNCs are, furthermore, impressed with a duty to 'use due diligence in ensuring that their activities do not contribute directly or

67 (1976) 15 ILM 969.
68 (1978) 17 ILM 422.
69 See <www.globalcompact.org>.
70 OECD Guidelines, Part II (General Policies), para. 2.
71 OECD Guidelines, Part III (Employment and Industrial Relations), paras. 1(b) and (c).
72 ILO Tripartite Declaration, paras. 36 and 58.
73 UN Doc. E/CN.4/Sub.2/2003/12/Rev.2.
74 *Ibidem*, Articles 3, 4.
75 *Idem*, Article 1.

indirectly to human rights abuses'[76] and 'that they do not directly or indirectly benefit from abuses of which they were aware or ought to have been aware'.[77] In contrast to the other existing international initiatives to promote responsible corporate behaviour, the UN Norms also feature a supervisory mechanism with a goal transgressing awareness-raising. MNCs are thus subjected to 'periodic monitoring and verification by the United Nations and other international and national mechanisms already in existence or yet to be created regarding the application of the Norms'.[78] At the UN level, such mechanisms include the various human rights treaty monitoring bodies, specialised agencies, country rapporteurs and the Sub-Commission on the Promotion and Protection of Human Rights. In 2005, the UN Secretary-General also appointed a Special Representative on the Issue of Human Rights and Transnational Corporations[79] with a mandate to, *inter alia*, identify and clarify standards of corporate responsibility and accountability with regard to human rights.

By invoking reliance on UN monitoring mechanisms, the Norms signal a shift in regulatory approach: from mere oversight of implementation to identification and supervision of non-compliance. The problem of how to ensure the effective enforcement of directly applicable human rights standards with regard to MNCs, however, remains unresolved.

IV.2 The International Criminal Court

A concerted effort to introduce a sanctioning mechanism at the international level as a means to address corporate wrongdoing relating to gross human rights violations was made in the mid-1990s. In fact, the idea to make provisions in international criminal law not only for capturing the individual culprits of mass crimes but also for securing the liability of groups (i.e. organised entities), which direct, perpetrate or collaborate in genocide, war crimes and crimes against humanity, is not novel. The initial attempt to criminalise collectives was made at Nuremberg. The momentum was, however, subsequently lost, as the principles expounded by the military tribunals were insufficiently clear and largely inconsistent.[80] The difficulty of how to square group liability with the premise that guilt must be personal has been the most significant stumbling block in the way of developing a doctrine of criminal responsibility for legal persons at the international level. A number of other issues have also contributed to

76 *Idem.*
77 *Idem.*
78 Commentary on the Norms on the Responsibilities of Transnational Corporations and Other Business Entities with Regard to Human Rights, UN ESCOR (55th session), p. 16, UN Doc. E/CN.4/Sub.2/2003/38/Rev.2 (2003), Article 16.
79 John Ruggie was appointed as Special Representative in July 2005 on the basis of Resolution 2005/69 (UN Doc. E/CN/4/RES/2005/69) issued by the UN Commission on Human Rights. By Resolution A/HRC/RES/8/7, adopted on 18 June 2008, the UN Human Rights Council renewed the Special Representative's term for a period of 3 years.
80 For an extended discussion of the Nuremberg model of collective criminality, see Chapter 3.

the ongoing contentious status of the idea. These all came to the fore in the process of the drafting of the Rome Statute of the International Criminal Court.

Already in 1995, an informal working group was created whose objective was to identify a number of general principles of criminal law to be included in the Statute.[81] By mid-1997, under the chairmanship of Per Saland, it had prepared drafts of proposed articles, thus laying the ground for the work of the Preparatory Committee. Reaching agreement on the draft articles, however, was no easy task. One of the more divisive issues concerned the Court's jurisdiction over legal persons.[82]

The draft Statute, which emerged from the Preparatory Committees' negotiation rounds and was tabled at the beginning of the Rome Conference in July 1998, did contain, albeit bracketed, a provision granting the Court jurisdiction over legal persons. Draft Article 23, paragraphs 5 and 6, provided that:

> [23(5) The Court shall have jurisdiction over legal persons, with the exception of States, when the crimes committed were committed on behalf of such legal persons or by their agencies or representatives.
>
> 23 (6) The criminal responsibility of legal persons shall not exclude the criminal responsibility of natural persons who are perpetrators or accomplices in the same crimes.] [83]

Corporate criminal responsibility as part of the Rome Statute was from the very beginning of the preparatory draft process a French conception and revolved around the recognition of criminal liability for *personnes morales* in the French legal system.[84] As Clapham explains, several considerations suggested the inclusion of legal persons within the jurisdiction of the Court.[85] First, from a moral perspective, there was a perceived need to ensure the penalisation and corresponding censure of *any* entity, natural or legal person, involved in the perpetration of international crimes. Second, criminal responsibility of corporations was thought of as a practical mechanism for assuring compensation in instances where the individual perpetrator would not have the assets to pay reparations ordered by the Court. Last but not least, there were hopes that corporate liability would serve a deterrent purpose, engendering greater caution in profit-motivated decision-making processes of potential criminal impact.

---

81 P. Saland, International Criminal Law Principles, in R.S. Lee (ed.), *The International Criminal Court. The Making of the Rome Statute. Issues, Negotiations, Results*. The Hague: Kluwer Law International, 1999, p. 191.

82 *Ibidem*, pp. 193-194.

83 UN Doc. A/CONF.183/2/Add.1.

84 A. Clapham, The Question of Jurisdiction Under International Criminal Law Over Legal Persons: Lessons from the Rome Conference on an International Criminal Court, in: M.T. Kamminga and S. Zia-Zarifi (eds.), *Liability of Multinational Corporations Under International Law*, The Hague: Kluwer Law International, 2000, p. 146.

85 *Ibidem*, p. 147.

Despite a general agreement on the potential benefits of corporate criminal responsibility, a deep divergence of views as to the advisability of including an explicit provision in the Rome Statute permeated the discussions around the French proposal. Although the notion of the criminal responsibility of legal persons was far from unknown to most national systems around the world, the approaches to imposing liability and the type of legal persons affected varied greatly. Many delegates called attention to the involvement of private businesses in ongoing or recent conflicts worldwide, e.g. the radio stations urging the killing of Tutsis during the Rwandan genocide and multinational oil corporations involved in forcible population transfers and acts of violence.[86] Others pointed to ongoing Holocaust-related litigation in some domestic systems, most notably in the United States against Swiss banks and German companies. They contended that the exclusion of jurisdiction over corporate entities would be a step back in light of Nuremberg and subsequent related trials at the national level.[87] At the same time, some delegations discarded the French proposal as immature or unfeasible in view of the ongoing debates surrounding the Nuremberg precedents and the lack of relevant consolidated developments in international law and practice. Others were prepared to compromise but only to the extent of providing for civil or administrative liability of legal persons.[88] In addition, many expressed concerns about procedural problems relating to who would represent corporations before the Court and how assets would be taken without affecting the rights of third persons.[89]

A few delegations opposed the proposal because their domestic legal traditions did not provide for the criminal responsibility of legal entities, while still others were predominantly concerned about the impact that the inclusion of jurisdiction over juridical persons would have on the principle of complementarity.[90] The latter envisages the ICC as supplementing, rather than supplanting, national systems; it expounds the inadmissibility of cases before the Court where they are being genuinely investigated or prosecuted by states with jurisdiction over them.[91] States' insistence on complementarity as a cornerstone of the Rome Statute regime was primarily motivated by concerns about safeguarding state sovereignty but had pragmatic undertones too. The Court would have only limited resources and would be critically dependent on

---

86 *Ibidem*, p. 148.

87 Saland, *supra note 81*, p. 199. For an overview of ATCA-based litigation and Nuremberg case law pertaining to the banking sector, see e.g. A. Ramasastry, Secrets and Lies? Swiss Banks and International Human Rights, 31 *Vanderbilt Journal of Transnational Law* 325 (1998).

88 UN Doc. A/CONF.183/2/Add.1, 14 April 1998, Article 23, para. 6, note 3.

89 Clapham, *supra note 84*, p. 157.

90 Some legal commentators have also contended that the inclusion of corporations within the Court's jurisdiction would undermine, and even be irreconcilable, with the ICC complementarity regime. See in this regard e.g. M. Frulli, Jurisdiction Ratione Personae, in: A. Cassese et al., (eds.), *The Rome Statute of the International Criminal Court: a Commentary*, Oxford: Oxford University Press, 2002, pp. 532-533; A. Eser, Individual Criminal Responsibility, in Cassese et al. (eds.), *supra*, p. 779; W.A. Schabas, General Principles of Criminal Law in the International Criminal Law Statute (Part III), 6 *European Journal of Crime, Criminal Law and Criminal Justice* 84 (1998) at 94.

91 Article 17(1)(a) RS.

states for their cooperation; domestic jurisdictions would thus be better equipped to undertake investigations and enforce sentences. With regard to economic entities, the complementarity objection translated into concern about the implications of a possible inclusion of MNCs in the ICC jurisdiction *ratione personae* for domestic systems whose legal tradition did not recognise corporations as subjects of criminal law. Could such non-recognition render cases admissible pursuant to the 'inaction', 'inability' and 'unwillingness' stipulations of the complementarity regime?

The question could not be easily detached from policy considerations. There was the realisation that the Rome Statute could not oblige states to subject business enterprises to compulsory criminal regulation, although it could be argued that permitting the differential treatment of classes of offenders (natural as opposed to legal persons), would contravene the very goals expounded by the regime. Ideally corporate criminal responsibility would encourage States Parties to subject corporations to penal sanctions at the domestic level with regard to at least the offences falling within the jurisdiction of the ICC.[92] Some might perceive this as affording the principled objectors to the idea of corporate criminality middle ground to align with the purpose of the Rome Statute while continuing to adhere to their favoured legal principles in general. Others could argue – not implausibly – that apart from unlikely in practical terms, such an arrangement would in essence entail such states departing from certain fundamental precepts of their legal traditions. The opposite effect of embracing corporate criminal liability was not inconceivable either: states withdrawing from the Statute or slowing down the ratification process due to their inability to accept criminal liability for (their) corporations, whether on legal-philosophical or other grounds.

Each round of negotiations, attempting to tackle the (perceived) impediments outlined above, resulted in the initial French proposal being reshaped and increasingly compromised.[93] The definition of a 'legal person' in the final draft text was specifically limited to only certain types of organisations. Apart from excluding states from the jurisdiction of the Court, as the initial proposal already envisaged, the revised version also ruled out jurisdiction over inter-governmental and non-governmental organisations as well as domestic public bodies. Eventually, after several weeks of intensive negotiations and far-reaching concessions on the part of the French delegation, no general agreement allowing for the text to be adopted by consensus, could be reached. Faced with substantial controversy and realising that the subject was not yet ripe for international agreement, the French delegation withdrew its proposal.

The question remains, however, as to whether a consensual adoption of the text was indeed strictly necessary. Admittedly, adopting the proposal setting out the criminal responsibility of corporations by consensus, would have contributed to the smooth

---

92 Despite resistant to the notion of corporate criminal liability in principle, Argentina, for example, has enacted special enabling legislation with regard to the prosecution of business entities for war crimes. See section III.1 above and FAFO Report, *supra note 38*, pp. 13, 31.

93 See also Chapter 5, section IV.1.2: Liability along vicarious lines.

acceptance and subsequent ratifications of the Rome Statute, and by extension enhanced the Court's legitimacy. Nonetheless, ICC jurisdiction could have been extended to profit-oriented business entities by majority vote – an attainable objective considering that the suggestion of regulating corporate conduct had strong support among the delegations and was not unknown to the various legal traditions represented.

IV.3 Some post-Rome developments

More than a dozen multilateral international instruments, adopted since the Rome Statute negotiations, have sought to reconcile the reality of organised functional criminality with the divergent legal regimes underpinning approaches to corporate accountability at the national level.[94] While embracing corporate criminal responsibility as a matter of principle, they allow states parties a margin of appreciation in establishing the liability of corporations. Thus states can determine the responsibility of business entities – be it criminal, civil or administrative – in a manner consistent with their legal systems as long as the sanctions imposed are 'repressive', and comply with the obligations enshrined in the respective conventions.[95] Repressive is understood to denote sanctions which are effective, proportionate and dissuasive, even where such sanctions do not amount to a criminal penalty in the domestic legal order. According to Swart, this middle-ground approach to resolving the tension between the growing realisation of the need for stricter regulation of corporate conduct and the array of domestic positions favoured, is indicative of 'a new international standard' emerging.[96] The acceptance of states' margin of appreciation in relation to corporate liability and sanctions for illegal misconduct is detectable at the level of the United Nations, the European Union and the Council of Europe.[97] It must be noted, however, that none of the relevant conventions and decisions in this regard concern the 'core' international crimes *per se*.

Nevertheless, the aforementioned developments merit careful consideration. On the one hand, there is the uncertainty as to whether or not the prospect of an effective non-criminal prosecution and sanctions could, and should, preclude the admissibility of a case against a corporate defendant before the ICC. While some national legal systems

---

94 E.g. UN Convention for the Suppression of the Financing of Terrorism, UN Convention against Transnational Organised Crime, UN Convention against Corruption, 1997 Second Protocol to the European Convention on the Protection of the European Communities Financial Interests. In addition, several Council of Europe conventions have introduced the notion of corporate criminal liability at the international level since the Rome Statute negotiations, e.g. Convention on the Protection of the Environment through Criminal Law, and Convention on the Protection of Children against Sexual Exploitation and Sexual Abuse.

95 K. Haigh, Extending the International Criminal Court's Jurisdiction to Corporations: Overcoming Complementarity Concerns, 14 *Australian Journal of Human Rights* 199 (2008) at 206.

96 B. Swart, Discussion: International Trends towards Establishing Some Form of Punishment for Corporations, 6 *Journal of International Criminal Justice* 947 (2008) at 953.

97 *Ibidem*, at 948-953.

may object to the notion of corporate criminal responsibility on conceptual grounds, they may however – and usually do – recognise the civil or administrative liability of economic entities. Thus, in Germany – the most vehement opponent to criminal liability for legal persons – corporations are subject to non-reparatory sanctions which in many respects are similar to criminal responsibility.[98] Entertaining the idea of effective, proportionate and dissuasive civil or administrative sanctions, precluding the admissibility of a case before the ICC, may certainly spark the interest also of states which do not have principled objections to the concept of corporate criminal responsibility. Although domestic legal systems in recent decades have increasingly subjected business entities to criminal sanctions, they have been hesitant to undertake proceedings involving allegations of human rights violations committed abroad.[99] At the same time, national jurisdictions which have been most forthcoming in their prosecution of MNCs, and particularly for international crimes, have opted for tort law litigation.[100] Not inconceivably, governments may be faced with significant pressure on the part of business to restrain prosecutorial initiative and refrain from initiating criminal proceedings. Given the hurdles typically associated with bringing up civil action, MNCs are bound to lobby for the non-extension of corporate criminal responsibility to international crimes at the national level. On the other hand, and closely related to the previous point, is the question of the comparative advantages of criminal as opposed to civil or administrative liability for corporations (particularly in relation to international crimes). This naturally leads into the discussion of what the goals of international criminal justice are and to what extent the notion of corporate criminal responsibility would align with them.

V Central Question

The issue of extending ICC jurisdiction to legal persons, in particular corporations, is expected to resurface at future review conferences of the Rome Statute.[101] During the first such review conference, convened by the UN Secretary-General for 2010, corporate criminal liability is unlikely to feature prominently on the agenda. The attention of States Parties is currently preoccupied with the possible inclusion of the crime of aggression in the Statute and the need to consolidate already existing provisions.

Presumably there are good reasons to insist on the inclusion of corporate criminal responsibility within the *ratione personae* jurisdiction of the Court, even if the

98 T. Weigend, Societas Delinquere Non Potest? A German Perspective, 6 *Journal of International Criminal Justice* 927 (2008) at 930-932.

99 See section III.1 above.

100 See section III.2 above.

101 Pursuant to Article 123 RS, seven years after the Statute's entry into force, a review conference shall be held to consider possible or necessary amendments. At any time thereafter, at the request of a State Party, the UN Secretary-General can convene a review conference upon the approval by a majority of States Parties.

necessary amendment does not materialise during the forthcoming statutory review. The concentrated efforts, which brought the issue to the fore more than a decade ago, are still awaiting fruition. The involvement of business in international crimes and its role in the fuelling of many ongoing conflicts entailing egregious human rights abuse is a parallel reality demanding attention. As Stephens cogently points out, the transnationality and power of MNCs has created 'a disconnect between international corporate structures and the law'.[102] On the one hand, states' ability to effectively regulate corporate activities, particularly in the human rights domain, no longer matches MNCs' economic and political influence. On the other hand, and as a consequence of this ever-deepening imbalance, domestic systems have 'increasingly relinquished their control over business.'[103] The inherent difficulties of prosecution at the national level – by host or home states – and the propensity of the MNC form to disperse, exploiting the principles of separate legal personality and limited liability, serve to further expand the existing enforcement gap. The International Criminal Court arguably presents a unique opportunity for the introduction of an international sanctioning mechanism to offset – at least partially – regulatory deficiencies with regard to business entities and human rights.

The purpose of the present study is to explore the underlying issues and possible contours of corporate criminal responsibility at the international level as a means of addressing corporate wrongdoing. Implicit in the discussion of (legal) feasibility is also the issue of desirability. The study thus revolves around the question of whether penal liability under the Rome Statute could, and should, attach to profit-oriented legal persons – not only for crimes physically committed by individuals operating within their organisational structures but also for crimes that materialise through the activities of affiliate entities. There is the uncertainty as to what purpose penal sanctions by the ICC would effectively serve and how to adequately reconcile collective criminality with personal guilt. An international enforcement mechanism, such as the ICC, might help constrain corporate evasion of compliance standards applicable to grave human rights violations and function as a compensating system for the reluctance or incapacity of states to rigorously regulate corporate behaviour. This, however, gives rise to questions pertaining to the relevance of regulation and prosecution at the national level as well.

The outlines of this research endeavour are inevitably pre-determined by the Rome Statute as the primary frame of reference. Thus, while regulation of corporate transgression within the human rights domain is lacking in many respects, especially in relation to socio-economic and environmental conditions in less developed countries, the focus of the study is on the 'core crimes' which currently fall within the jurisdiction of the International Criminal Court. The discussion, moreover, revolves around business enterprises whose inherent goal is profit maximisation. The

102 Stephens, *supra note 50*, at 54.
103 *Ibidem*, at 58.

propositions explored in this study have been formulated primarily with view to the challenges posed by legal incorporated entities that conduct legitimate cross-border activities but nevertheless become involved in the commission of international crimes. It is, therefore, not concerned with single-owner companies, especially where such businesses exist outside of the law. Neither is it intended to apply to entities behind whose facade repressive governments hide corrupt and illegitimate accumulations of personal wealth. The scenario of states acting as entrepreneurs and suppositions as to the necessity or viability of state (criminal) responsibility in this regard also fall outside the scope of the present research.

VI Method and structure

In exploring the multiple facets of corporate criminal responsibility in the context of the ICC, the study will make use of a variety of legal sources, primary and subsidiary in nature. While Article 21 RS prescribes that the Court is to apply, first and foremost, the stipulations of the Statute, provisions laying down the liability of legal persons, as discussed above, are lacking altogether. This necessitates recourse to other sources of law as a means of delineating the possible construction, and in particular the constitutive elements, of MNCs' responsibility under international criminal law. References will, therefore, be made to pertinent provisions of other treaties and relevant findings of international courts and tribunals, including the ICJ. Such references will serve to appraise the consolidation of judicial opinion and complement understanding of contentious points of law. Special attention will be given to Nuremberg, ICTY and ICTR case law, as authoritative, albeit not binding on the ICC, sources of international law. Jurisprudence in this regard will be used to demonstrate that, while there are no precedents in international (criminal) law that concern corporate criminal responsibility *per se*, past judgments and established principles for the ascription of culpability nevertheless befit legal persons.

The existence of general principles derived from national legal systems will also be explored as a means of outlining the recognition of corporate criminal liability at the level of domestic jurisdictions. Furthermore, national case law and doctrine will be discussed in order to illustrate the applicability of internationally accepted precepts in domestic practice. The underlying research approach is not comparative in nature; it does not seek to provide an exhaustive overview of the corporate liability avenues favoured by States currently party to the Rome Statute. However, it does draw upon a comparative analysis on a more theoretical level with a view to demonstrating caveats, uncovering common denominators and highlighting developing trends in existent or proposed approaches to corporate criminal responsibility. Considering the lack of directly relevant provisions in the Statute and international law in general, the inquiry into national legislation is dictated by the need to explore the possible deduction of general principles of law as an auxiliary mechanism to address the issue of the criminal liability of corporations at the ICC level.

Existing provisions of the Rome Statute, including Articles 25, 28(b) and 30, will be scrutinised as they are not only pertinent to individual corporate officials who might stand trial before the Court but also espouse certain underlying liability notions which are potentially operative with regard to MNCs too. Interpretation of the law in this regard will follow established principles.[104] It will seek to accord with the ordinary meaning given to terms and with the object and purpose of the Rome Statute, also taking into account the intention of the drafters. In delineating the scope of Articles 25, 28(b) and 30 RS, references will, moreover, be made to relevant judgments and decisions of the *ad hoc* tribunals as well as the writings of legal commentators so as to illustrate certain areas of contention. Although non-binding on the ICC, in its early case law the Court has relied upon such supplementary sources to support its reading of statutory provisions.

Although existing literature abounds with works linking human rights in general to the ethical obligations of business entities to refrain from their violation, there is currently no comprehensive treatise on the subject of corporate responsibility for international crimes. Efforts to survey the feasibility of subjecting MNCs to criminal prosecution at the international level and with regard to the 'core' crimes, have been sporadic and only limited in scope. This study is an attempt to systematise academic writings and utilise the experience of domestic legal systems with a view to critically discussing possible avenues for constructing the liability of corporations in the context of international criminal law and the Rome Statute in particular. It strives to draw upon recognised concepts in both national and international law in order to determine whether concerns about extending jurisdiction beyond natural persons can effectively be reconciled with the goals of (international) criminal justice. While exploring the viability of less traditional approaches to corporate criminal responsibility, the study nonetheless resorts to notions that are already present in international law (although with respect to individuals) for the purpose of providing a controversial topic with a theoretical and legal framework that is not entirely alien to either scholars or practitioners.

The study begins by tracing the evolution of the 'collective criminality' concept and the inherent challenges in reconciling the impact of the group context with individual culpability. Chapter 1 outlines existing regulatory mechanisms for addressing corporate criminality at the national and international level, and in particular the stumbling blocks before the inclusion of corporations within the jurisdiction of the International Criminal Court. Chapter 2 scrutinises the legal philosophical under-pinnings of the debate surrounding the notion of corporate criminal liability. It also explores the appropriateness of domestic criminal law rationales in relation to the ascription of responsibility to collective entities *per se*, such as business enterprises,

---

104 Vienna Convention on the Law of the Treaties, Articles 31 and 32, *United Nations Treaty Series*, Vol. 1155, p. 331.

in international criminal law. Chapter 3 delineates the contentious Nuremberg attempt to introduce a model of collective criminality at the supranational level and to apply it – for the first time in the history of international prosecutions – to the business domain. Chapter 4 subsequently examines the continued difficulties on the part of the international criminal tribunals with the notion of group liability and the 'collective criminality' remnants discernible in the Rome Statute. The remaining chapters of the study centre on the need for, and the feasibility of a *sui generis* model for ascribing direct criminal liability to corporations involved in the commission of international crimes. To this end, Chapter 5 discusses the approaches considered during the drafting of the Rome Statute and the inherent limitations of existing provisions. Drawing upon both theoretical methods and domestic techniques for the attribution of culpability to legal (business) entities, a model of liability is developed which seeks to capture the nature of corporate participation in mass crimes without impinging on the Statute's overall frame. Chapter 6 explores the extension of direct criminal liability to companies for the criminal transgressions of their suppliers and to parent corporations for harm caused by their subsidiaries. It further discusses the utility of Article 28(b) RS for the prosecution of individual corporate agents for their contribution to organisational wrongdoing. Finally, Chapter 7 highlights the relevance and limitations of effectuating corporate criminal liability at the international level against the backdrop of persistent collective criminality, organisational deviance, regulatory deficit and the goals of international criminal justice.

CHAPTER 2

CRIMINAL RESPONSIBILITY AND THE CORPORATE ENTITY

I INTRODUCTION

International crimes constitute a form of collective criminality which grossly transgresses common individual wrongdoing in design, scale and impact. The various institutions for international criminal justice have struggled with the underpinnings and legal complexities of group violence. Their jurisdictional focus, however, has remained exclusively on the individual. In this regard, many legal commentators have postulated that collective criminality – whether pertaining to mass crimes or on the part of organised groups – is not only quantitatively but also qualitatively different from individual deviance. Hence, it may warrant an approach premising culpability on distinct sets of modalities.

While the international criminal tribunals have given some leeway to the development of doctrines which recognise the systemic nature of genocide, war crimes and crimes against humanity, any attempt to shift the liability lens onto collective entities *per se* has thus far been effectively stalled. With regard to MNCs in particular, the question arises as to whether or not embracing subjectivism and moral guilt as the ground stones of criminal responsibility – which have traditionally been adopted with regard to the individual – is also requisite for corporate liability. Such a construction seemingly fails to recognise the inherent divergence in nature between natural and legal persons. It also tends to promote the indirect implication of corporations in international crimes through individual convictions, which may or may not be attainable. The need to adequately differentiate between corporate fault and individual mental states is, furthermore, reflected in growing municipal recognition of the significance of organisational facets in constructing the culpability of business enterprises.

Since it constitutes a form of collective criminality, in which individual action cannot be isolated from the group context, corporate crime bears a certain analogy to international crimes. The inner dynamics of organised structures – military, political or commercial – engaged in the commission of grave human rights abuse share certain characteristics. Irrespective of their nature and goals, groups have the propensity to legitimise immoral, or even illegal, decisions and actions. They feature a 'culture of normality', which routinises decision-making, rationalises choices and serves to defuse the moral connotations of deviant practices.[1] The phenomena of corporate crime and mass atrocity, however, also retain some apparent differences. The state-induced or mob violence often typifying mass crimes is not comparable to the functional criminality of legitimate economic entities to the extent that the latter are rarely, if ever, ideology-motivated.

In order to foster understanding of why institutional idiosyncrasies cannot be easily divorced from the discussion pertaining to organisational culpability as well as moral blameworthiness and collective guilt, this chapter explains how corporate crime transpires. It examines the legal philosophical considerations that have hindered the recognition of business entities as subjects of criminal law – at the national and international level – and highlights some due process concerns pertaining to the prosecution of corporate offenders (natural and legal persons).

II The criminology of international corporate crime

The expansion of global economy, the diversification of business activities and the existing regulatory challenges in that regard have spurred heightened interest on the part of criminologists in the phenomenon of international corporate crime. The scale of business-related violence resulting in the death, injury or harm of large numbers of victims though industrial disasters, occupational accidents, product defects and managerial failures is well established.[2] Efforts have centred on identifying the causes and the inner-working mechanism of such violence, as well as clarifying the apparent difficulty faced by the law in crafting an adequate response. Although empirical studies of corporate crime have predominantly been concerned with domestic regulatory offences, attempts have recently been made to also apply criminological terminology to business involvement in occurrences of mass criminality.

II.1 Conceptualising corporate crime

The notion of corporate crime has evolved significantly since Sutherland first introduced its ambiguous original definition as a 'white-collar crime'. Perceiving it as a type of crime 'committed by a person of respectability and a high social status in the course of his occupation',[3] Sutherland failed to differentiate between white-collar criminals who abused their position for personal gain and transgressions committed on behalf of the corporation. It was not until several decades later that the focus shifted

---

1 See e.g. C.H. Brants, Gold Collar Crime: The Peculiar Complexities and Ambiguities of War Crimes, Crimes against Humanity and Genocide, in: H.N. Pontell and G.L. Geis (eds.), *International Handbook of White-Collar and Corporate Crime*, New York: Springer, 2006.

2 M. Punch, Suite Violence: Why Managers Murder and Corporations Kill, 33 *Crime, Law and Social Change* 243 (2000), referring to numerous studies documenting corporate violence.

3 E.H. Sutherland, *White Collar Crime: The Uncut Version*, New Haven: Yale University Press, 1983, p. 7.

from the 'social status' to the 'occupational position' of the criminal[4] and eventually fixated on the organisation itself. Group criminality in relation to business activities thus became the focal point of attention. Corporate crime is now generally understood as a type of organisational deviance.[5] It is defined as 'any act committed by corporations that is punishable by the state, regardless of whether it is punished under administrative, civil or criminal law'.[6] The emphasis is thus placed on the nature of the crime and how it comes to be rather than the notion of corporate personhood.

In criminological literature on organisational deviance, the incentives and means for corporate crime are analysed in the context of organisational characteristics.[7] In this regard, Punch for instance explains the collective nature of the deviance by reference to corporate paraphernalia, including structure and culture.[8] He perceives the hesitancy to recognise corporations as actors in their own right as a legal and institutional defence against facing up to the consequences of death and suffering among victims.[9] Studies on corporate crime are generally premised on the distinction between individual and organisational criminality. While the motivation of individuals is important, their behaviour is regarded as largely dependent on the organisational context in which they operate. The group settings and institutional environment play a major role in shaping individual choices. Organisational goals, structure, culture and processes, furthermore, serve to both encourage and conceal individual acts of potential criminal impact, which becomes apparent only when considered against the backdrop of the organisation's overall actions.

The existing theoretical models for the explanation of corporate crime typically centre on the elements of opportunity, motivation and lack of control as the factors underlying deviance.[10] Motivation pertains to internal competition and corporate

---

4 R. Quinney, The Study of White-Collar Crime: Toward a Reorientation in Theory and Research, in: G. Geis and R.F. Meier (eds.), *White-Collar Crime*, New York: Free Press, 1977.

5 The concept of 'organisational deviance' was formally introduced by Ermann and Lundman. See E.D. Ermann and R.J. Lundman, *Organisational Deviance*, cited in Diane Vaughan, *Crime Between Organisations*, Columbus: Ohio State University Press, 1979, p. 61. It was subsequently built upon by Sherman and Shover who clearly distinguished between individual deviance within the organisation and deviance on the part of the organisation itself. See L. Sherman, *Scandal and Reform*, Berkeley: University of California Press, 1978 and N. Shover, Defining Organisational Crime, in: M.D. Ermann and R.J. Lundman (eds.), *Corporate and Governmental Deviance: Problems of Organisational Behaviour in Contemporary Society*, New York: Oxford, 1978.

6 M.B. Clinard and P.C. Yeager, *Corporate Crime*, New York: Free Press, 2000, p. 16.

7 See e.g. R.C. Kramer, Corporate Crime: an Organisational Perspective, in: P. Wickman and T. Daley (eds.), *White-Collar and Economic Crime. Multidisciplinary and Cross-National Perspectives*, Lexington: Lexington Books, 1982.

8 Punch, *supra note 2*, at 243-280.

9 *Ibidem*, at 243.

10 See generally W. Huisman, *Between Profit and Morality. Background Factors of Regulatory Compliance and Violation by Corporations*, The Hague: Boom Legal Publishers, 2001; Clinard and Yeager, *supra note 6*; D.V. Cohen, Ethics and Crime in Business Firms: Organisational Culture and the Impact of Anomy, 6 *Advances in Criminological Theory* 183 (1995).

strategy and is closely associated with the size, complexity and fragmentation of corporations. Like the factor of control, motivation is also connected to the inadequacies of existing regulatory frameworks and monitoring mechanisms for constraining corporate behaviour. Opportunity, in turn, relates to the availability of means to achieve corporate goals, and may be linked to profit considerations. Although some scholars have argued that the pursuit of profit generates sufficient incentive to indulge in illegal behaviour,[11] and is hence inherently criminogenic, this view has not been devoid of criticism.[12] The profit-centred view largely fails to account for, *inter alia*, the element of corporate culture. As Punch explains, behind the apparently coherent and rational facade of corporations, there is a hidden world of segmentation, power-struggles, and political strategising.[13] While the idiosyncrasies of the established corporate culture may well promote the unethical pursuit of profit, profit in itself does not explain why some corporations engage in crimes while others do not.

The criminogenic factors that tend to foster illegal or risky behaviour encompass organisational characteristics pertaining to institutional functionality or structure. Deficient internal processes (e.g. relating to supervision) and structural difficulties arising out of complex communication networks often facilitate deviance. Bureaucratic routines,[14] cognitive limitations[15] and group socialisation[16] also serve to promote behaviour which would be erratic when considered outside the context of the collective. The peculiarities of organisational existence thus may – and sometimes do – lead to irrational decision-making as a result of which corporations engage in conduct contrary to their self-interest. This stands somewhat at odds with the conventional rational choice model, which postulates that the accumulation of benefit is at the heart of business enterprises' choice to transgress the law, particularly where enforcement is weak and the likelihood of detection is only minimal.[17] As stipulated earlier however, the threat of reputational loss has been growing in significance with the rise of the CSR movement.[18] While profit maximisation remains central to corporate endeavours, it is no longer regarded, by social scientists or MNCs themselves, as the sole manifestation of corporate self-interest. Studies of organisational behaviour have, moreover, increasingly suggested that criminal misconduct on the part

---

11 E.D. Helihy and T.A. Levine, Corporate Crisis: The Overseas Payment Problem, in: E. Bittner and S.L. Messinger (eds.), *Criminology Review Yearbook*, Vol. II, Beverly Hills: Sage, 1980.

12 E.g. K. Jamieson, *The Organisation of Corporate Crime*, Thousand Oaks: Sage, 1994.

13 Punch, *supra note 2*, at 245, referring to M. Dalton, *Men Who Manage*, New York: John Wiley & Sons, Inc., 1959.

14 Punch, *supra note 2*, at 259.

15 Note, Organisational Irrationality and Corporate Human Rights Violations, 122 *Harvard Law Review* 1931 (2009) at 1934-1937.

16 On the phenomenon of 'groupthink', see generally I.L. Janis, *Victims of Groupthink*, Boston: Houghton Mifflin Company, 1972.

17 See *supra note 15*.

18 See Chapter 1, section II: The rise of corporate social responsibility.

of economic entities may follow rational calculations about financial gain as well as irrational decision-making detached from profit considerations. In both instances, the criminogenic factors relate to organisational paraphernalia that may or may not advance legal transgressions for the sake of revenue accumulation only.

II.2 Corporate crime in international context

While various empirical studies have sought to corroborate existing theoretical models explaining corporate deviance in general, similar data with regard to organisational transgressions in the context of international crimes has thus far never been systematised. Nevertheless, as Huisman points out, the trigger factors of corporate crime, already identified in criminological literature, are discernible in instances entailing business involvement in mass atrocity as well.[19]

Corporate participation in genocide, war crimes and crimes against humanity requires the coincidence of several factors on the macro level, i.e. the environment in which the entities operate.[20] In this regard, motivation and opportunity are both present in the political and socio-economic conditions of volatile conflict zones, where grave human rights violations mostly occur. As illustrated earlier,[21] the abundance of timber, crude oil, diamonds, and other minerals in many parts of the underdeveloped world, coupled with a lack of sufficient regulatory enforcement, has the propensity to coax corporations into the grey area of the law and even beyond. The continuous need of governments and rebel movements engaged in protracted violence to finance their military spending, often places the exploitation of natural resources upfront on the agenda. This, in turn, is a strong incentive for MNCs to engage in business with either side. The existence of avenues for lucratively expanding business activities, possibly resorting to illegal means with the acquiescence or participation of violent and corrupt local authorities, may conceivably encourage corporate transgression. This is only compounded by the ineffectiveness of existing control mechanisms at the domestic and international plane. At the same time and at the level of the organisation, the pressures of internal competition, or more generally the peculiarities and deficiencies of the institutional structure and culture, are prone to affect the choice between deviance and compliance in the same manner as postulated above in relation to corporate crime in general. While profit is by and large the driving force behind corporate existence, it alone cannot account for organisational misconduct, even where serious human rights abuse is concerned. It is the meso analysis, i.e. the interplay of organisational characteristics, that serves to explain differences in the likelihood of criminal involvement amongst corporations sharing external settings.[22] In this regard, the

19 W. Huisman, Corporations and International Crimes, in: A. Smeulers and R. Haveman (eds.), *Supranational Criminology: Towards a Criminology of International Crimes*, Intersentia, 2008, p. 197.

20 *Ibidem*.

21 Chapter 1, section I: Corporations, conflicts and human rights.

22 Huisman, *supra note 19*, p. 198.

existence (and adequacy) of internal systems for supervision and control is an important factor for gaining insight into the dynamics of transgression in a collective (corporate) context. Formal or informal policies and practices have certain propensity to induce – but also restrain – wrongful behaviour.

Understanding how institutional idiosyncrasies influence personal deviance and how such deviance – seemingly innocuous – can develop into collective criminality enables us to distil a set of underlying principles pertaining to the construction of corporate liability. These principles will be discussed elsewhere.[23] Suffice it here to emphasise that the corporate *modus operandi* often serves to conceal the criminal nature of rational business decisions or promote irrational choices of potential criminal impact. Separated from the organisation, individuals do not generally have the same incentives, opportunities and means to engage in harmful activities. Neither can those activities reach the scale and impact that collective action and access to organisational resources bring about, particularly in the circumstances of the 'core' international offences. Corporate crime materialises through collective action or blameworthy inaction and cannot be detached from the institutional framework in which it takes place. Appropriate models for constructing the criminal liability of corporations must, therefore, reflect the peculiarities of organisational deviance.

III The morality paradigm and corporate liability

Many national legal systems have traditionally revolved the issue of corporate responsibility around the individual and moral guilt, thus seeking to equate corporate fault to individual *mens rea*. A few jurisdictions object to the idea of making legal persons subject to criminal law more generally, conceiving of business enterprises as fictional entities with 'no soul to damn, no body to kick'.[24] The focus on individualism, which largely typifies domestic criminal law, has been historically and politically determined. It is predominantly, if not exclusively, the result of the Enlightenment and the ideology of liberalism which shaped the development of modern Western societies. The heritage of liberal political thought, with its emphasis on the individual as the basis of law and society and its denunciation of collectivism, explains how we have come to construct and attribute responsibility.[25] So engrained has individualism become in our thought and custom, that we rarely question the precept of the human being as the common starting point in both law and ethics. We tend to overlook the fact that in some systems of thinking 'the community would be the axiom, an individual man the derivative'.[26] We also frequently neglect to notice that even

23 See Chapter 5.

24 J.C. Coffee, No Soul to Damn, No Body to Kick: an Unscandalised Inquiry into the Problem of Corporate Punishment, 79 *Michigan Law Review* 386 (1981).

25 C. Wells, *Corporations and Criminal Responsibility*, Oxford: Oxford University Press, 2005, p. 73.

26 R. Williams, *The Long Revolution*, Harmondsworth: Penguin, 1965, p. 94.

liberalism did not dispense with the concept of sovereignty as the expression of a collectivity, whose preferences and choices of action depend on cultural, economic and other contexts. Within this collectivity, which is not reducible to its single constitutive human units, individuals are organised in – and fundamentally influenced by – social institutions. By recognising the limits of individualism as the only prism, through which we view the organisation of life and attribute blame, we can gain a more complete and accurate perspective of human existence, regularity and deviance.

The pre-occupation of Western philosophical and legal thought with the individual as the cornerstone of organised society, has persisted till modern times, shaping and solidifying the traditional approach of criminal law towards blame allocation. Guilt, moral responsibility, and therefore liability in criminal law have been conventionally perceived as resting on the individual, as it is the individual who is generally regarded as being endowed with the natural capacity to rationalise his actions and the autonomy to causally control them.[27] This emphasis on the subjective mental state, i.e. the ability to reason and hence act with intention as the basis of criminal culpability, embedded as it is in legal theory and practice, has not gone unchallenged. Both the meaning of the mental state and the human ability to divine it have been contested by different schools of thought.[28] However, the intricate nuances of their ongoing discussions are not directly relevant to the present study and therefore will not be explored in further detail here. Instead the argument will revolve around the question of whether or not moral agency and moral responsibility are necessary preconditions for constructing the criminal liability of corporations.

III.1 Can corporations be regarded as persons?

The answer depends partially on how corporations are perceived. The tendency to focus on the individual as the primary object and subject of law has invariably compelled scholars to compare corporate to human characteristics. This comparison has been at the bottom of attempts to determine whether corporations may indeed be regarded as persons.

The descriptive approach, even when detached from any considerations pertaining to the morality paradigm, has generated contrasting conclusions as to the nature of the corporate entity. The anthropocentric view associates personhood with the human being exclusively, and hence expounds that corporations cannot be seen as persons (in the sense of indivisible wholes).[29] Corporations are thus regarded as the mere collection of individuals and as lacking a separate metaphysical existence of their own. This view, however, has been increasingly contested by scholars of collectivist orientation. The latter have sought to establish the reality of distinct corporate

---

27 M. Moore, The Moral and Metaphysical Sources of the Criminal Law, in: J.R. Pennock and J.M. Chapman (eds.), *Criminal Justice*, New York: New York University Press, 1985, p. 23.

28 For a condensed overview, see Wells, *supra note 25*, pp. 66-67.

29 Wells, *supra note 25*, p. 77.

personhood by reference to the organic nature of organisations. In their perception, corporations constitute entities which, by virtue of some unique characteristics, are different from the sum of their individual members and at the same time comparable to human beings in their indivisibility.[30] However, even those who agree that corporations possess certain unique attributes, which justify regarding them as persons, differ as to whether corporations can be morally blameworthy.[31]

III.2 Moral agency and moral responsibility

Fault ascription in criminal law generally presupposes a breach of moral responsibility.[32] This fixation on morality has dominated much of the debate around the legal implications of collective behaviour – guilt, responsibility and punishment. Remarkably, both proponents and opponents of the notion of corporate criminal liability lapse into the moral agency mire which is in itself a never-ending source of contention.

It has long been contended that business and ethics are entirely separate domains, incompatible with each other.[33] As corporations do, and should, make profit-maximising decisions irrespective of their ethical implications, business is perceived by those who subscribe to the 'separation thesis' as amoral per definition. While rejecting the notions of moral agency and moral responsibility in relation to corporations, Friedman nevertheless concedes that businesses must seek the maximisation of profit within a certain framework of morality.[34] He perceives this framework as consisting of legal rules, social norms and ethical criteria. De George in his turn, attributes to corporations a certain degree of moral responsibility, at the same time maintaining that corporations cannot be moral persons.[35] In this sense corporations are regarded as moral actors whose moral obligation is to refrain from causing harm but who cannot be accorded the same consideration and treatment as humans. At the end of the morality discourse continuum is French, who not only views corporations as the bearers of moral responsibility but also as analogous to moral

30 E.g. P. French, *Collective and Corporate Responsibility*, New York: Columbia University Press, 1984.

31 Wells, *supra note 25*, p. 75.

32 Legal responsibility, however, is not invariably equivalent to moral blameworthiness. As Hart points out, 'the coincidence of legal responsibility with moral blameworthiness may be a laudable ideal, but it is not a necessary truth nor even an accomplished fact' (p. 223). While liability for punishment and moral blame are inter-related, they can also exist independent of one another (for instance, in cases of strict liability or vicarious responsibility). H.L.A. Hart, *Punishment and Responsibility. Essays in the Philosophy of Law*, Oxford: Clarendon Press, 1968.

33 For an overview and critique of the 'separation thesis', see R.E. Freeman and P.H. Werhane, Business Ethics: The State of the Art, 1 *International Journal of Management Reviews* 1 (1999).

34 M. Friedman, *The Social Responsibility of Business is to Increase its Profits* (1970), reprinted in: T.L. Beauchamp and N.E. Bowie, *Ethical Theory and Business*, Englewood Cliffs: Prentice-Hall, 1993.

35 R.T. De George, *Business Ethic*, New York: Macmillan, 1986.

persons.[36] According to French, corporations possess their own identity and intentionality, not reducible to the individual level without remainder. The corporate identity and intentionality are, in his view, reflected in the internal decision-making structure. Gilbert offers a similar account of collective intentionality. She argues that the intentionality of collectives can operate at a level higher and different from the intentions of individual group members and therefore collectives possess responsible, moral agency of their own.[37]

Intentionality, therefore, is seen as the basis of moral agency and thus the starting point for ascribing both blame and liability. In this regard, the proponents of methodological individualism contend that the attribution of responsibility to corporate collectives is meaningless, as statements about such responsibility are reducible to the moral responsibility of individual agents within the corporation.[38] This reductionist view draws upon the conviction that it is only individuals who can act rationally and autonomously, and therefore intentionally. Corporate criminal responsibility is thus rejected, for corporations are not deemed to possess the agency to act with reason on their own. Collectivists challenge this view, arguing that groups organised around common goals and acting with the purpose to further these goals exhibit collective intentionality, which exceeds the intentions of individual members and is dependent on the interests and norms of the group itself. With regard to corporations, French asserts that 'when the corporate act is consistent with, an instantiation or an implementation of established corporate policy, then it is proper to describe it as having been done for corporate reasons, as having been caused by a corporate desire coupled with a corporate belief and so, in other words, as corporate intentional'.[39]

How corporate collectivists deduce intentionality and ascribe responsibility has generally been criticised by individualists and mentalists alike.[40] Apart from the question of whether corporate policy indeed reflects agency rather than merely collective goals realised through individuals, there is also the objection to linking collective intentionality and moral responsibility. It has been contended that, even if

---

36 P. French, The Corporation as a Moral Person, in: L. May and S. Hoffman (eds.), *Collective Responsibility: Five Decades in Debate in Theoretical and Applied Ethics*, New York: Rowman and Littlefield, 1991.

37 M. Gilbert, *Sociality and Responsibility: New Essays in Plural Subject Theory*, Oxford: Rowman and Littlefield, 2000.

38 For a description of methodological individualism, see J.A. Corlett, Collective Punishment and Public Policy, 11 *Journal of Business Ethics* 207 (1992); M.J. Zimmerman, Sharing Responsibility, 22 *American Philosophical Quarterly* 115 (1985); and D.E. Cooper, Collective Responsibility, 43 *Philosophy* 258 (1968).

39 French, *supra note 36*, p. 145.

40 While individualists refute the idea that the whole is greater than the sum of its parts and that intentionality can attach to any other entity but the individual, mentalists question whether intentionality is indeed the defining characteristics of the mental. E.g. R. Marres, *In Defence of Mentalism: a Critical Review of the Philosophy of Mind*, Amsterdam: Rodopi, 1989, pp. 17-19.

we accept the existence of a kind of intentionality on the part of corporations which is not reducible to the intentionality of individual members or merely the sum thereof, this would still not justify our regarding them as morally responsible agents.[41] In response to this criticism Isaacs argues that the moral significance of certain group actions cannot be captured by the description of acts at the individual level.[42] Thus, for instance, an act of genocide bears moral significance different from, if not greater than, the moral significance attached to individual acts that contributed to the genocidal act as a whole. Isaacs' view has not, however, gone unchallenged for it has been perceived as prescriptive rather than descriptive, and therefore as falling short of establishing that groups *are* morally responsible.[43] Silver, on the other hand, concedes that groups, and in particular corporations, might be deficient in agency, but this deficiency does not negate the existence of their moral responsibility.[44] Interestingly, his conclusion is based on the same argument which has been put forward by some scholars, Strawson in particular, explaining the moral responsibility of human beings. This argument revolves around the question of how the attitudes expressed in holding persons morally responsible affect our judgments about responsibility.[45]

The debate between individualists and collectivists has thus gone back and forth, with no prospects of abating. Irreconcilable as they may be with regard to the question of whether or not corporations possess agency and whether agency is a necessary precondition for moral responsibility, both sides generally agree that corporations should meet the same criteria of moral responsibility as humans do. So deeply embedded in both philosophical and legal thought is the notion of the individual as the epitome of ethics, that we often mechanically seek to transpose distinctly human qualities to manifestly non-human entities. The discourse on corporate liability thus becomes fixated on the morality paradigm. However, to what extent is this fixation warranted?

III.3 Legal personhood and moral responsibility

Corporations are not human beings, neither do they act or think according to the models of culpability on which criminal law has been traditionally premised. Entirely divorcing legal personality from morality considerations is, however, neither feasible nor

41 B. Lawson, *Collective Intentionality and Agency*, p. 4 (a paper presented at the 'Agency and Identity' conference held at the University of Toronto on 18-20 May 2007), at <www.chass.utoronto.ca/gpsu/conference/2007/papers/lawson.pdf>.

42 T. Isaacs, Collective Moral Responsibility and Collective Intention, in: P. French and H. Wettstein (eds.), *Shared Intentions and Collective Responsibility*, Boston: Blackwell Publishing, 2006, p. 63.

43 Lawson, *supra note 41*, pp. 7-9.

44 D. Silver, A Strawsonian Defence of Corporate Moral Responsibility, 42 *American Philosophical Quarterly* 279 (2005), also at <copland.udel.edu/~dsilver/Publicat/corporate.doc>.

45 For a complete overview of the argument, see P.F. Strawson, *Freedom and Resentment and Other Essays*, Oxford: Methuen & Co. Ltd., 1974, pp. 1-25.

desirable. Opponents of corporate liability have often contended that the status accorded to corporations in law is an artificial, fictitious construction, which fails to answer key questions about the attribution of blame to non-human entities.[46] More importantly, eliminating moral considerations altogether from our perception of corporations having a separate existence would make it easier for the entities to evade the implications of their responsibility.[47]

Legal personhood, therefore, cannot – and neither should it – be detached from the morality paradigm. This paradigm, however, need not be applied to corporations in the same manner as is customary in relation to individuals. As Wells suggests, instead of revolving the debate of corporate criminal responsibility around the issues of moral personhood and moral blame, focusing respectively on moral responsibility and accountability may be a better suited approach to pave the way forward.[48] Such an approach would open the door for the adoption of a liability theory that takes into account existing differences while acknowledging the uniform applicability of certain moral precepts.

Corporate criminal responsibility need not be grounded on the entity's realisation of the moral wrongfulness of a given act. Culpability and liability may well flow from a different set of principles than those applicable to individuals, without however detracting from the importance of moral responsibility. Since corporations are simply not comparable to individuals, attempting to identify or attribute a subjective mental state to the organisation itself detracts from the culpability criterion in terms of outcome,[49] just as does the question of whether corporations can exercise independent moral judgment. Business enterprises can – and reportedly do – become engaged in wrongful acts.[50] This engagement transgresses the mere sum of individual wrongful acts and is largely influenced by the peculiarities of corporate existence.[51] The contention pertaining to the ascription of moral reasoning to corporations, on the other hand, does not eliminate the fact that we generally tend to perceive the corporation as the one committing the transgression, not a group of individuals within, and it is the entity itself we subject to moral judgment.

IV Guilt and Punishment of Collectivities

Favouring the adoption of methods which do not focus exclusively on subjectivity in constructing the criminal responsibility of corporations, does not dispense with the

46 Wells, *supra note 25*, p. 76.

47 *Ibidem*, pp. 82-83. See also W.S. Laufer, *Corporate Bodies and Guilty Minds: The Failure of Corporate Criminal Liability*, Chicago: University of Chicago Press, 2006, discussing the importance of maintaining the 'moral stature' of criminal law even with regard to corporations (pp. 93-95).

48 Wells, *supra note 25*, pp. 78-81. Wells finds French's position, which relies on moral blame while at the same time expounds that corporations are unlike human beings, unconvincing.

49 *Ibidem*, p. 155.

50 Punch, *supra note 2*. See also Chapter 1, sections I and III.2.

51 See section II.1 above: Conceptualising corporate crime.

requirement of culpability. Seeking to uncover criminal fault – a subjective notion in itself – with recourse to a (partly) objective approach, should not be perceived as equating to liability for a breach of a purely objective standard.[52] Neither could grounding corporate criminal responsibility on an examination of the attitude displayed towards the prospect of a harmful outcome rather than the traditional approach of identifying a subjective mental state, be viewed as an attempt to impose a form of strict liability. The legal responsibility of business entities for their perpetration of, or more frequently, facilitation of international crimes must be premised on some form of fault. Such fault must reflect culpability or else we run the risk of detracting from the very essence of criminal law. Culpability, however, is not necessarily derived from intentional conduct. It can, and does, also encompass morally responsible *culpa* behaviour.

The morality paradigm with regard to any attempt to extend criminal liability to corporations thus entails two separate but inter-related questions. On the one hand, there is the problem of where to fix the culpability threshold with regard to economic entities *per se* under criminal law and whether this threshold can be constructed without recourse to individual mental states.[53] On the other hand, and directly relevant to the legal-philosophical debate espoused here, are concerns pertaining to the (perceived) propensity of corporate criminal responsibility to promote collective guilt and collective punishment, and compromise the position of the individual in penal law.

While corporate criminal liability is a form of collective responsibility, it need not be understood as presupposing (at least legally speaking) the collective guilt or punishment of individual members. Confusion in this connection tends to stem from the ambiguity surrounding the terms collective guilt and collective punishment. They may be interpreted as referring to the entity itself or they may be construed to designate the moral and legal effects that individuals come to bear as a result of a wrongdoing committed by the entity. In the first instance, guilt and punishment would be ascribed to the corporation following deviance on the part of some, but not necessarily all, corporate agents. The justifiability of punishing a collective for the wrongdoings of only a few of its members is bound to underpin the discussion in this regard. Such a discussion cannot be divorced from the criminological perspective on corporate crime without risking becoming entirely detached from actual reality.[54] In line with the second interpretation of the collective responsibility claim referred to above, the liability of the corporation would give rise to the guilt and punishment of all individuals comprising it, irrespective of whether or not they have been involved in any wrongful activities.

---

52 For further discussion in this regard, see Chapter 5, section IV.2.4: Constructive corporate fault.

53 Arguments pertaining to the requisite culpability threshold with regard to corporations involved in the commission of international crimes, and the various existing avenues for constructing corporate fault, are extensively dealt with in Chapter 5.

54 See section II above.

Both philosophy and law differentiate between responsibility that attaches to a collective *per se* and responsibility on the part of individuals by virtue of their belonging to a collective.[55] Each category encompasses one or more types of collective responsibility potentially giving rise to moral and legal implications at the level of the individual. In the corporate context, collective responsibility can manifest in two different forms. On the one hand, it can refer to the responsibility of an individual or a plurality of individuals who are held liable on behalf of the organisation as a whole (e.g. the executive board members of a business enterprise). On the other hand, it can denote the responsibility that attaches to the organised entity itself. It is this second variant of collective responsibility that is contained in the notion of corporate criminal responsibility as espoused in the present study. There is also a third category of collective responsibility, the so called 'group responsibility', which relates to the responsibility of individuals by virtue of their membership in a group. This form of collective responsibility is contentious and has been recognised as acceptable in philosophical and legal doctrine in only limited circumstances.[56] As will be seen below, concerns about the possible moral and legal effects that holding an organised entity liable might have on individual members, are not easy to disperse. However, such concerns tend to somewhat unnecessarily compound the notion of group 'membership' responsibility with the responsibility of the corporation as a legal person.

IV.1 The moral guilt contention

With regard to the ascription of moral guilt to the corporation, the difficulty once again relates to the disputed moral position of 'fictitious' entities. Perceived as attaching to the violation of moral norms, guilt has traditionally been assigned to individuals, regarded as the epitome of moral agency and responsibility. Jaspers has thus contended that political guilt – envisaging co-responsibility for how society (i.e. the state) is organised and functioning – is the only type of collective guilt that may legitimately be attributed to a group.[57] Deviating from the liberal school of thought, Fletcher has more recently put forward a strong case for collective guilt arising out of collective action. Taking the holistic approach, which views groups as organic wholes, he has sought to justify the meaningful attribution of collective guilt by virtue of its

55 For a concise overview of collective responsibility variants in philosophical as juxtaposed to legal writings, see E. van Sliedregt, *The Criminal Responsibility of Individuals for Violations of International Humanitarian Law*, The Hague: T.M.C. Asser Press, 2003, pp. 349-352.

56 See section IV.2 below: Collective legal guilt and the position of the individual.

57 K. Jaspers, *The Question of German Guilt* (translated by E.B. Ashton with a new introduction by W. Koterski, New York: Fordham University Press, 2000), pp. 25-26. Jaspers expounds a four-fold categorisation of guilt. He distinguishes between criminal and moral guilt in that the latter rests with human conscience exclusively while the former relates to the violation of legal norms. Metaphysical guilt arises out of 'a solidarity among men as human beings that makes each co-responsible for every wrong and every injustice in the world'.

associative (rather than aggregate) nature.[58] Fletcher, however, remains among the few radical pioneers of the idea that collective guilt is 'a plausible and sometimes healthy response to collective wrongdoing'[59] and his position has not gone unchallenged.[60]

It may also arguably be contended that the legal responsibility of a collective need not be considered to impose guilt on individual agents in the moral sense at all. Guilt within the meaning accorded to it by moral philosophy is an internal feeling arising out of the acknowledgement that the individual concerned has transgressed a certain moral norm. Although some individuals may feel guilty because they have come to identify with the collective entity, which has been pronounced legally responsible, this does not imply that they are actually morally guilty themselves. Moral guilt would follow only if they were personally involved in the wrongdoing that gave rise to the liability of the entity. In this sense, guilt sentiments are not comparable to – and should not be regarded as symptomatic of – actual guilt. It must be acknowledged however that, generally, moral guilt pertaining to individuals in the context of deviant collectives has often been interpreted differently. It has been understood to designate blameworthiness and responsibility (albeit not in the legal sense) because of group membership and acquiescence to behaviour which, in hindsight, should not have been tolerated.

Albeit insightful, the ongoing philosophical debate between liberal methodologists and collectivists does little to further in any practical terms the question of the criminal liability of corporations *per se*. At the same time, domestic jurisdictions have long overcome the theoretical considerations pertaining to the question of how, if at all, guilt may be attributed to a collective entity. Although the moral condemnation contained in charges of collective guilt can, and often is, employed for political needs,[61] collective guilt as giving rise to legal consequences has largely been refuted in modern legal science and practice.

IV.2 Collective legal guilt and the position of the individual

The collective responsibility undertones of corporate criminal liability understandably also give rise to questions pertaining to the permissibility of drawing inferences from the legal guilt of the collective to the culpability of individual members. Despite the appeal that the notion of guilt by association has for prosecutors of collective crimes,

58 G.P. Fletcher, Liberals and Romantics at War: The Problem of Collective Guilt, 111 *Yale Law Review* 1499 (2002) at 1540-1544.

59 G.P. Fletcher, Collective Guilt and Collective Punishment, 5 *Theoretical Inquiries in Law* 163 (2004).

60 See e.g. H. Morris, George Fletcher and Collective Guilt: a Critical Commentary on the 2001 Storrs Lectures, 78 *Notre Dame Law Review* 731 (2003).

61 S. Darcy, *Collective Responsibility and Accountability under International Law*, Leiden: Martinus Nijhoff Publishers, 2007, p. xxi. For a discussion of the collective guilt contention in the context of the Second World War as well as the Balkan and Rwanda conflicts, see respectively D.J. Goldhagen, *Hitler's Willing Executioners: Ordinary Germans and the Holocaust*, London: Abacus, 1996; N. Eltringham, *Accounting for Horror; Post-Genocide Debates in Rwanda*, London/Virginia: Pluto Press, 2004; A. Jokic (ed.), *War Crimes and Collective Wrongdoing: a Reader*, Oxford: Oxford University Press, 2001.

attempts to employ this notion at either the domestic or international level have been sporadic and ultimately unsuccessful.[62] The proponents of both methodological liberalism and collectivism also generally agree that the attribution of individual responsibility for participation in group crimes must be circumscribed if it is to be regarded as legitimate. Thus, in order to establish the guilt (in a legal sense) of a member of the collective, mere membership of the collective would not suffice. Some personal wrongdoing, connected to the role of the individual within the group, would need to be ascertained before the individual can incur legal responsibility. In this regard, liberals and 'Romantics' appear to share a common perspective.[63] They both align with traditional criminal law, which grounds individual liability on proof of personal fault.

The peculiarities of group crimes dictate recourse to liability modes that can capture individual participation in collective deviance and even the culpability of the group where identifiable entities, having a separate existence of their own, are concerned. This should not, however, be allowed to unjustifiably detract from the importance of safeguarding personal culpability as a basic assumption in criminal law at the national or international level. While renouncing subjectivism as the cornerstone of culpability with regard to corporations is dictated by their distinct nature, there is no reason to depart from the moral stature of criminal law in relation to individuals. Some reasonable concessions inevitably have to be made in order to accommodate for the collective aspect of group deviance. However, we must be careful not to stray too far and punish innocent individuals merely by virtue of their association with a collective.

In this regard, as will be demonstrated in the following chapters, the position of the individual in international criminal law and in the context of system criminality has at times been compromised. The institutions for international criminal justice from Nuremberg to The Hague have grappled with the challenge inherent in the collective aspect of mass atrocity and the phenomenon of group deviance. They have crafted and repeatedly resorted to collective responsibility doctrines while trying to uphold the basic assumption that nobody can be held criminally responsible for acts or transactions in which he has not personally engaged or in some other way participated.[64] Their practice, however, has not been devoid of controversy. Criticism pertaining to modes of individual liability that seek to accommodate for the collective element of group crimes, is however not particular to international criminal law. It is a recurring theme in domestic legal systems as well, in relation to efforts to criminalise and punish mob violence and participation in criminal organisations. The fundamental issues underlying such criticism warrant consideration in the context of corporate criminal responsibility too.

---

62 For a critical discussion of the approach adopted at Nuremberg with regard to liability for membership in a criminal organisation, see Chapter 3.

63 Fletcher, *supra note 58*, at 1504-1513.

64 See in this regard also *Prosecutor v. Tadic*, ICTY Case No. IT-94-1-A, Appeal Judgment of 15 July 1999, para. 186.

There are understandable concerns about the effects that the penalisation of corporations may have on individuals. The dispersed impact of corporate sanctioning, in terms of job losses and investors having to bear (part of) the financial burden of MNCs' closure of premises or suspension of operations, may be perceived as a type of collective punishment. Nevertheless, this should not be confused with guilt in the legal sense, and especially with reference to individuals. Corporate liability and individual responsibility are two distinct concepts whose construction is reasonably warranted on the basis of different sets of principles. Fears that collective responsibility – whether as a method for establishing the liability of natural persons or an accountability avenue targeting group entities *per se* – may dilute the principle of personal culpability are nevertheless legitimate. The appropriate form of (potentially) expansive participatory modes for establishing individual responsibility in international criminal law, and also applicable to corporate officials, will be discussed elsewhere.[65] Views on how to adequately demarcate the permissible limits of individual liability modes in group context are prone to diverge. Suffice it here to note that the notion of corporate criminal responsibility need not – and does not in itself – preclude the prosecution and sanctioning of individuals to the extent of their personal contribution to collective wrongdoing. The liability of individuals, however, must remain firmly grounded on established principles of criminal law, irrespective of how differently the criminal responsibility of corporations may be constructed.

IV.3 Accountability, culpability and due process

Attempts to circumscribe corporate criminal liability so that it does not give rise to collective legal guilt are inevitably bound to also stumble over questions pertaining to due process. Apart from the argument that collective criminality should not compel us to 'dispense too quickly with the protections of the criminal law that seeks to ensure that an individual is convicted for his own wrongdoing', there are also fears that 'concern for symbolic vindication of victims' human rights [may prove] a more potent influence than worries over potential violations of defendants' rights.'[66] Such fears assume an added dimension in light of the proposition, entertained by Rome delegates in 1998, envisaging the extension of the Court's jurisdiction to corporations as a means of ensuring reparations for victims.[67] While this should not be read to imply scepticism about the judicial ability to safeguard the fairness of proceedings and the rights of corporate defendants, it must be acknowledged that defence counsel representing legal persons before the ICC are likely to raise many of the same issues frequently invoked in relation to individual accused.

---

65 See Chapter 4.

66 Amicus Curiae Brief of the Association of Defence Counsel in *Prosecutor v. Brdjanin*, ICTY Case No. IT-99-36-A, para. 49 (filed on 5 July 2005).

67 See Chapter 1, section IV.2: The International Criminal Court.

The right to an effective defence is an essential corollary of the right to a fair trial. In international criminal proceedings, in particular, defence counsel face certain unique challenges.[68] The complexity and scale of international trials exert considerable pressure on legal representatives, which often leads to contentions about the equality of arms tenet and the expeditiousness of proceedings. In order to circumvent, for instance, proportionality arguments related to the (limited) capability of the defence to collect sufficient evidence, the Rome Statute espouses an obligation on the part of the prosecution to investigate incriminating and exonerating circumstances equally.[69] However, this cannot dispense with the importance of defence conducting its own investigations and the obstacles it may be confronted with in this regard. As a matter of fact, the prosecution remains better placed to conduct on-site inquiries and obtain the cooperation of states. Disclosure issues may also arise in connection with the scope of the prosecution's obligation and ability to disclose exculpatory or other evidence. The effects of prosecutorial 'recklessness' in the light of certain confidentiality agreements on defence rights pertaining to disclosure and the efficiency of proceedings have already been evidenced in early ICC case law.[70] Defendants' right to a fair and expeditious trial may additionally be compounded by victims' participation in the proceedings. Although victim participation *per se* is a desirable development in principle, reflecting the long-standing experience of many domestic legal systems and aimed at addressing the broader goals of international criminal justice, the scope of that participation at the international level is a matter of considerable controversy.[71] Overly expansive participatory modes for victims have the propensity to put additional pressure on the defence. Participation is warranted by the need to enhance the legitimacy of international courts at the macro level and bring justice closer to victims. At the same time, however, the legitimacy of international criminal law is at risk of becoming compromised at the micro level by perceptions as to how justice is administered in individual cases. Compromises with fairness – whether in relation to procedural defence rights or the excessive extension of personal culpability – harbour the danger of 'discounted' convictions. This may in turn 'diminish the didactic

---

68 See generally J.T. Tuinstra, *Defence Counsel in International Criminal Law*, The Hague: T.M.C. Asser Press, 2009.

69 Article 54(1)(a) RS.

70 *Prosecutor v. Thomas Lubanga Dyilo*, Decision on the consequences of non-disclosure of exculpatory materials covered by Article 54(3)(e) agreements and the application to stay the prosecution of the accused, together with certain other issues raised at the Status Conference on 10 June 2008, ICC-01/04-01-06/1401, 13 June 2008.

71 See e.g. *Victim Participation at the Case Stage of Proceedings*, Report of the War Crimes Research Office, American University Washington College of Law, 2009, at <www.wcl.american.edu/ war-crimes/icc/documents/WCROReportonVictimParticipationattheCaseStageofProceedingsFebruary 2009.pdf?rd=1>. E. Baumgartner, Aspects of Victim Participation in the Proceedings of the International Criminal Court, 90 *International Review of the Red Cross* (2008) at 409-440.

significance' of judgments and infringe upon 'the historical legacy' of the institutions for international criminal justice.[72]

The due process issues outlined above have repeatedly surfaced in international trials and are as pertinent to corporate officials who might in future stand trial before the ICC as they are to political and military figures. Similar, albeit not necessarily identical, concerns are likely to arise in relation to the prosecution of corporate entities *per se*. Subjecting corporations to penal regulation at the international level is, however, bound to also prompt additional considerations. The requirement of clarity and predictability of the law where human rights violations, and the scope of MNCs' duty of care, are concerned may pose certain difficulties. As stipulated earlier, the prohibition on genocide, crimes against humanity and war crimes is generally accepted as falling within the corporate sphere of responsibility.[73] However, domestic jurisdictions vary in how they apply this prohibition and in the requirements that they attach to it, such as, for instance, linking justiciability to the need to establish government involvement in the abuses alleged.[74] At the international level, the concept of corporate complicity in the 'core' crimes is vaguely formulated and widely interpreted. This leads to uncertainty as to its precise scope and the obligations that it gives rise to.[75]

The prohibition on the *ex post facto* application of the law is unlikely to be problematic since the possible penalisation of corporations under the Rome Statute for their involvement in international crimes cannot be applied retroactively. This does not, however, detract from the relevance of other legality concerns, namely the justifiability and permissibility of lowering the culpability threshold for corporations to *culpa* and the need to avoid the semblance of strict liability being imposed.[76] Nor does it solve the problem of the ICC possibly attempting the prosecution of business entities incorporated in states, which do not recognise legal persons as subjects to penal provisions on legal-philosophical grounds. Discussions pertaining to the higher standard of requisite proof in criminal law *vs* the lower evidentiary barriers in civil law and the symbolic value of penal sanctions *vs* the erosion of criminal law's moral stature through broad interpretations of culpability, particularly in relation to international crimes, are likely to surface in this regard. Arguments concerning the comparative advantages of criminal and private regulation, as well as the ability of (international) criminal law to adequately address corporate wrongdoing through

72 W.A. Schabas, Mens Rea and the International Tribunal for the former Yugoslavia, 37 *New England Law Review* 1015 (2003) at 1033.

73 See Chapter 1.

74 In the US, for instance, international law violations such as torture and summary execution give rise to corporate liability under the ATCA only where the private entity has acted in complicity with state authorities. See Chapter 1, section III.2: Liability through civil courts.

75 See Chapter 5, section III.2: The notion of complicity as an avenue for corporate accountability.

76 For further discussion in this regard, see Chapter 5, section IV.3.1b: *Culpa* as a benchmark for corporate criminal responsibility.

individual convictions, have primarily a bearing on complementarity rather than due process.[77] The latter is, nonetheless, central where the double jeopardy rule is concerned. As this study postulates, the criminal prosecution of a corporation at the national or international level cannot preclude the penalisation of individual agents or subsidiary companies by either domestic or international courts since they are generally regarded as separate persons.[78] *Ne bis in idem* contentions do not arise in this regard. An exception might be cases in which affiliate entities are so closely related to the parent enterprise that they cannot be deemed to have an independent existence.[79] The rule of double jeopardy does not furthermore exclude the possibility of private parties initiating civil actions for damages following a criminal conviction, at the national or international level. Debates about *ne bis in idem* might, however, surface in relation to complementarity, where international crimes are defined as tort or corporations are subjected to repressive civil or administrative penalties by domestic jurisdictions rather than criminal regulation.[80] Determinations in this regard are nevertheless inevitably bound to be casuistic in character.

V Conclusion

Collective responsibility and collective guilt are notions of somewhat convoluted meaning and often used misleadingly as interchangeable.[81] Hence, the controversy that surrounds corporate liability as an avenue for securing accountability for international crimes. Criminal responsibility in the sense of legal guilt (following a court's finding to that effect) does not necessarily entail moral guilt. Jurisdiction over the latter emanates from human conscience, not judicial institutions. Nevertheless, this does not negate corporate moral responsibility for grave human rights abuse. The morality paradigm is thus at the bottom of attempts to seek the accountability of business enterprises, although it is rendered inoperative in relation to the actual construction of culpability. Criminal law cannot, and should not, become completely detached from subjectivism, even in relation to corporations. However, there are good reasons to resist regarding individual mental states as the only reasonable and permissible ground for the imputation of liability to economic entities. By endowing them with a formal legal status and increasingly subjecting them to criminal law provisions, national legal systems have acknowledged not only that corporations can commit crimes but also that their facades often serve to disguise or even conceal harmful activities. In approaching corporate criminal liability, a growing number of domestic jurisdictions have furthermore come to recognise the idiosyncrasies of organisational existence and their

77 See also Chapter 7, section II: Prospects along the regulatory continuum.
78 See Chapter 6.
79 *Ibidem.*
80 See further Chapter 7, sections II.1 and II.2.
81 D. Cooper, Collective Responsibility, 'Moral Luck' and Reconciliation, in: Jokic (ed.), *supra note 61*, p. 205.

role in the realisation of collective wrongdoing. At the same time, although corporate crime materialises through collective action, and hence cannot be entirely divorced of perceptions of collective guilt, it does not necessarily imply group responsibility in the legal sense. Such collective responsibility might be detectable in the dispersed effects of sanctioning or the shared (internalised rather than externally imposed) moral responsibility of the individuals comprising the group. However, collective legal responsibility for mere membership in a group falls outside the scope of corporate criminal liability envisaged in the present study.

At the international level, the controversy surrounding collective responsibility and collective guilt has revolved around the phenomenon of mass violence in the context of the 'core' crimes, and has only marginally been concerned with organisational culpability. Since its inception international criminal law has been cognisant of the peculiarities of collective action and struggled to reconcile them with the notion of individual guilt. The unusual interpretation and application on the part of the Nuremberg tribunals of the doctrine of conspiracy and the concept of criminal organisations exemplified this struggle at an early stage. At present, the continuing attempts to overcome the existing tension are illustrated by the contentious and changing approaches to the liability theories of common purpose and superior responsibility. To a certain extent the same tension underlies the failure to extend the jurisdiction of the International Criminal Court to corporate entities. As the subsequent chapters will demonstrate, the biggest challenge in addressing culpability in the context of collective criminality – mass violence as well as corporate crimes – is the inherent difficulty in prosecuting indirect perpetrators and facilitators while respecting traditional tenets of fault ascription and the requirements of due process.

CHAPTER 3
CORPORATE ACCOUNTABILITY *À LA* NUREMBERG

I INTRODUCTION

The post-Second World War trials exemplified an early attempt to prosecute business for its contribution to international crimes. In scale, cruelty and effectiveness the Nazi atrocities were unprecedented in human history. They were made possible by the keen participation or silent compliance of not only Germans soldiers and government officials but also a wide-spanning network of industrialists and civilian collaborators. In 1945, the principal Allied Powers established an *ad hoc* International Military Tribunal (IMT) in Nuremberg to bring the major Nazi war criminals to trial.[1] Mindful of the substantial role played by the munitions, heavy industry and chemical corporations in the sustenance of German war efforts and the pursuit of a pure Aryan race, the Allies' original intention was to include business executives in the list of indictees. The plan was eventually abandoned for political reasons. Nevertheless, corporate officials later stood trial before US, British and French domestic military tribunals.

This chapter explores the controversies surrounding the application of the Nuremberg 'collective criminality' model, based on the doctrine of conspiracy and the notion of criminal organisations. It outlines the key principles of individual criminal responsibility that emerged from the IMT's interpretation of the approach adopted. Those principles were subsequently relied upon – albeit inconsistently – by the Allies' domestic military courts in relation to the prosecution of corporate officials for their involvement in Nazi crimes. Offshoots of this 'collective criminality' model became subsequently integrated in contemporary international criminal law, and pertinent to the discussion about the possible liability of corporations and their individual agents for involvement in 'core' crimes.[2] Although the IMT and domestic military tribunals had no jurisdiction over legal persons, they sought to address the pressing need for business accountability within the legal constraints of their constitutive documents. In this regard, the following provides a critical overview of the attempt made at Nuremberg to delineate culpable criminal conduct in an organisational context. Such an outline is furthermore relevant in that individual prosecutions could serve – as evidenced by Nuremberg trials – as an indirect avenue for pronouncing on the

1 London Agreement establishing the IMT, published in *Trial of the Major War Criminals before the International Military Tribunal*, Nuremberg Germany (1947), Vol. I (hereafter 1 *IMT*), at 8-9.

2 Contemporary liability concepts aimed at capturing the relative contribution of individual group members to collective criminality are extensively discussed in Chapter 4.

responsibility of corporations. Should jurisdiction over legal persons be lacking, as was the case in Nuremberg, convictions of individual corporate agents might, moreover, be the only path available for securing the accountability of business for its contribution to international crimes. In addition, the notion of criminal organisations was not only potentially applicable to economic ventures in Nuremberg but also resurfaced some fifty years later during the negotiations of the Rome Statute in relation to the proposed criminal responsibility of MNCs.[3] Therefore, the interpretation of 'criminal organisations' by the IMT warrants some consideration.

II THE NUREMBERG 'COLLECTIVE CRIMINALITY' MODEL

The conspiracy doctrine and the concept of criminal organisations sparked great controversy at the London Conference where the Nuremberg Charter[4] was negotiated. Cognisant of the need to preclude the perception of 'victors' justice', but also aware of the pressure to punish those responsible for the crimes committed, the delegates sought to meld two disparate systems of criminal justice. Fundamental differences between the common law and civil law traditions, however, could not be easily resolved. Neither could the expansion of already controversial principles into entirely novel legal approaches be easily accepted.

II.1 The doctrine of conspiracy

Conspiracy, being a notion of common law origin, sat uncomfortably with the representatives of civil law countries. On the one hand, unlike the common law tradition, continental systems tended to differentiate between non-punishable preparation of a plan to commit a crime and criminal attempt.[5] On the other hand, the interpretation and application of conspiracy as an inchoate crime in common law countries themselves had been somewhat vague and not entirely consistent.[6] Despite such problems, the concept of conspiracy was eventually incorporated in Article 6 of the Nuremberg Charter. Its formulation and interpretation, however, reflected a troubled compromise.

---

3 UN Doc. A/CONF.183/C.1/L.3, 16 June 1998, in *Official Records of the United Nations Diplomatic Conference of Plenipotentiaries on the Establishment of an International Criminal Court*, Vol. II: Summary Records of the Plenary Meetings and of the Meetings of the Committee of the Whole, New York: United Nations, 2002.

4 Published in 1 *IMT*, *supra note 1*, at 10-18.

5 S. Pomorski, Conspiracy and Criminal Organisations, in: G. Ginsberg and V.N. Kudriavtsev (eds.), *The Nuremberg Trial and International Law*, Dordrecht/Boston: Martinus Nijhoff Publishers, 1990, p. 218.

6 *Ibidem*.

> **Article 6**
> The following acts, or any of them, are crimes coming within the jurisdiction of the Tribunal for which there shall be individual responsibility:
> a) *crimes against peace*: namely planning, preparation, initiation or waging of a war of aggression or a war in violation of international treaties, agreements, or assurances, or participation in a common plan or conspiracy for any of the foregoing;
> b) *war crimes*: namely, violations of the laws or customs of war. [...]
> c) *crimes against humanity*: [...]
>
> Leaders, organisers, instigators and accomplices participating in the formulation or execution of a common plan or conspiracy to commit any of the foregoing crimes are responsible for all acts performed by any persons in execution of such plan.

Article 6 thus delineated conspiracy as an anticipatory crime, punishable *per se*, in relation to crimes against peace only. The liability of conspirators in relation to war crimes and crimes against humanity was limited to complicity in crimes committed by others in furtherance of a common plan.[7] Participation in a conspiracy to commit war crimes and crimes against humanity was not criminalised as such.[8]

On the one hand, the reluctance on the part of both the drafters of the Nuremberg Charter and subsequently the IMT to employ the doctrine of conspiracy in a broader context is understandable. It was a vague liability theory with unsettled status even in common law countries which had championed its application. At the heart of the controversy lay the propensity of the doctrine to allow for collective punishment. On the other hand however, the compromise struck in Nuremberg in relation to the application of the conspiracy doctrine was somewhat arbitrary. Concerns about possible infringements of the *nullum crimen sine lege* dictum and the desire to safeguard the principle of criminal liability based on personal fault, cannot provide an entirely satisfactory justification of Nuremberg's choice to criminalise conspiracy to wage an aggressive war but not conspiracy to commit war crimes or crimes against humanity. The status of both crimes against peace and crimes against humanity in international law was contentious at the time.[9] Furthermore, the Nuremberg Charter did not provide a definition of conspiracy. It also fell short of indicating whether conspiracy as an inchoate crime ought to be prosecuted cumulatively with the substantive offence.

---

7 *Ibidem*, p. 223.

8 Despite the Prosecution's attempt to plead conspiracy with regard to war crimes and crimes against humanity as well, the Tribunal ruled that the Charter did not define as a separate crime any conspiracy except one to commit acts of aggressive war. It therefore decided that '[it will] disregard the charges in Count One [alleging] that the defendants conspired to commit War Crimes and Crimes against Humanity, and will consider only the common plan to prepare, initiate, and wage aggressive war'. 1 *IMT*, *supra note 1*, at 226.

9 See e.g. M. Lippman, Nuremberg: Forty Five Years Later, 7 *Connecticut Journal of International Law* 1 (1991).

In its judgment, the IMT did not directly address either of these issues.[10] Yet, all of the defendants convicted of conspiracy were simultaneously convicted of substantive crimes against peace.[11] As to the scope of conspiracy, the Tribunal adopted a restrictive approach requiring evidence of a concrete plan on the part of a clearly defined group of individuals to commit crimes against peace.[12] The participants in the common plan would incur liability if they partook in the preparation of specific acts of aggression with knowledge of Hitler's aims.[13] Moreover, the execution of the plan had to be not too far removed from the time of the plan's formulation.[14] The Tribunal sought to hold criminally liable only those individuals who cooperated with Hitler in or after 1937 – the year in which Germany's actual acts of aggression against foreign nations commenced.[15]

As a consequence of the restrictive interpretation of the requisite level of knowledge adopted by the IMT in relation to conspiracy to commit crimes against peace, only a few government officials in the immediate circle of Hitler were eventually convicted. Culpability was based on a rather strict *mens rea* standard. The Tribunal refused to accept that awareness of Hitler's plans of aggression was widespread, even amongst senior staff of the administration. There was insufficient direct evidence and it refrained from drawing inferences about actual knowledge of aggressive goals unless such inferences were established beyond reasonable doubt.[16]

II.2 The concept of criminal organisations

Given the applicability of conspiracy to crimes against peace only, a failure to penalise participation in groups with a common plan to commit other criminal acts would have allowed many culprits of Nazi system criminality to go unpunished. The drafters of the Nuremberg Charter acknowledged the moral and political significance of bringing to trial not only the masterminds of Nazi crimes but also those rank and file members whose acquiescence in criminal activities ensured the smooth running of the German war machine. At the same time, however, they also faced the predicament of how to bring a multitude of second-level defendants within reach of the Tribunal. The concept of 'criminal organisations' provided the solution they needed. It was an offshoot of the

---

10 Judgment of 1 October 1946, in: 1 *IMT, supra note 1.*

11 The convicted offenders included: Goering, Hess, Ribbentrop, Keitel, Rosenberg, Raeder, Jodl, and Von Neurath. 1 *IMT, supra note 1*, at 279-336.

12 1 *IMT*, at 225 reads: 'Conspiracy is not defined in the Charter. But in the opinion of the Tribunal the conspiracy must be clearly outlined in its criminal purposes. It must not be too far removed from the time of decision and of action. The planning, to be criminal, must not rest merely on the declarations of the party programme, [...] announced in 1920, or the political affirmations expressed in Mein Kampf in later years. The Tribunal must examine whether a concrete plan to wage war existed, and determine the participants in that concrete plan.'

13 *Ibidem*, at 226. See also Pomorski, *supra note 5*, p. 233.

14 See *supra note 12.*

15 Pomorski, *supra note 5*, p. 233.

16 *Ibidem*, p. 234.

conspiracy doctrine and as such it was not devoid of contention. Acutely conscious of its drawbacks, the drafters nonetheless recognised that at the time the conspiracy doctrine was the only powerful tool at their disposal for solving evidentiary and procedural problems.[17] Such barriers were bound to arise in the attempt to prosecute large numbers of individuals who had operated at different positions and levels of authority within the Nazi hierarchy.

The United States proposal delineating the scope of application of the concept in the context of the IMT, envisaged a power on the part of the Tribunal to declare major Nazi groups and organisations criminal, based on the Tribunal establishing that they had been drawn together by common criminal objectives.[18] On the basis of these predetermined declarations of criminality and in secondary proceedings against individual members of the groups or organisations concerned, national courts would be able to issue convictions on proof of membership alone.[19] Membership would be interpreted as evidence of conspiracy and individual convictions would be imposed not only for the crime of conspiracy itself, but also for any substantive offence committed by other members of the group in furtherance of its conspirational objectives. Moreover, voluntary membership and knowledge of the group's criminal objectives would be presumed, the burden of proof thus being shifted onto the defendant.[20]

Not surprisingly the far-reaching implications of the United States proposal did not appeal to delegates at the London Conference.[21] Motivated by the pressing need to find a workable means for the prosecution of a multitude of Nazi defendants but at the same time anxious to preserve the principle of criminal liability based on personal fault,[22] the drafters of the Nuremberg Charter eventually adopted the United States proposal in a restricted form.

> **Article 9**
> At the trial of any individual member of any group or organisation the Tribunal may declare (in connection with any act of which the individual may be convicted) that the group or organisation of which the individual was a member was a criminal organisation. […]

---

17 *Ibidem*, p. 245.

18 Minutes of Conference Session, 26 June 1945, reprinted in Report of Robert H. Jackson, United States Representative to the International Conference on Military Trials, Washington 1949 (hereafter Jackson Report), Doc. XIII, at 71-72. Also Minutes of Conference Session, 29 June 1945, reprinted in Jackson Report, Doc. XVII, at 97, 111.

19 Minutes of Conference Session, 2 July 1945, reprinted in Jackson Report, Doc. XX, at 129, 133.

20 Revision of American Draft of Proposed Agreement, 14 June 1945, in Jackson Report, Doc. IX, at 59. See also Revised Draft of Agreement and Memorandum Submitted by American Delegation, 30 June 1945, in Jackson Report, Doc. XVIII, at 125.

21 *Supra note 19*, at 129.

22 *Ibidem*, at 132-133.

Article 10
In cases where a group or organisation is declared criminal by the Tribunal, the competent national authority of any Signatory shall have the right to bring individuals to trial for membership therein before national, military or occupation courts. In any such case the criminal nature of the group or organisation is considered proved and shall not be questioned.[23]

The provisions of the Charter deviated from the original United States proposal envisaging a presumption of guilt and a reversed onus of proof. Thus, the ambition to ensure the expeditious prosecution of a large number of defendants did not prevail over concerns about the implications of detaching liability from personal guilt. Articles 9 and 10 of the Nuremberg Charter, however, failed to provide a definition of the concept of 'criminal group or organisation' and did not specify the requisite link between the criminal act of a convicted individual and the criminal nature of the organisation.

In its judgment, the IMT partially rectified the Charter's deficiencies in this regard. The Tribunal held that a criminal organisation was in essence analogous to a criminal conspiracy.[24] The group had to be bound together and organised for a common purpose, and in order to be declared criminal it had to be formed or used for the commission of crimes punishable under the provisions of the Charter.[25] Cautious to avoid mass punishment, the Tribunal rejected the possibility of convictions based on membership only. Proof of knowledge of the criminal purpose or acts of the group would be required before an individual could be convicted for being a member of a criminal organisation.[26] Sufficient knowledge would be inferred when the criminal purpose or activities that bound the group together, were so widespread and well-known that it could in all fairness be assumed that, in general, its members were aware of them.[27] Naturally those who had been conscripted into membership by the state would not be subject to liability unless they voluntarily continued their membership in the organisation after finding out about its criminal objectives or acts.[28] Last but not

---

23 The Tokyo Charter of the International Military Tribunal for the Far East did not contain similar provisions with regard to criminal organisations. The judgments eventually rendered relied extensively upon the doctrine of conspiracy. Its interpretation and application, however, were not as circumscribed as the approach adopted by the Nuremberg Tribunal. Although a few of the decisions are notable, particularly in relation to the notion of superior responsibility, they did not set endurable precedent. Accordingly, the Tokyo Tribunal's practice will not be discussed in the present study.

24 1 *IMT, supra note 1*, at 256. For an extended discussion of the IMT judgment with regard to 'criminal organisations', see S. Darcy, *Collective Responsibility and Accountability under International Law*, Leiden: Martinus Nijhoff Publishers, 2007.

25 *Trial of the Major War Criminals Before the International Military Tribunal*, Nuremberg Germany (1948), Vol. XXII, at 500 (hereafter 22 *IMT*).

26 *Ibidem*.

27 *Idem*, at 516.

28 1 *IMT, supra note 1*, at 262, 268, 273.

least, a group or organisation would be declared criminal only if its size did not render separate trials of its members possible.[29] Thus the notion of group criminality, relied upon in Nuremberg, was relatively well safeguarded against mass convictions of innocent persons.

Guided by the aforementioned cumulative conditions, the IMT declared the Gestapo, the Sicherheitsdienst des Reichfuehrer (SD) and the Schutzstaffel (SS) to be criminal organisations.[30] Remarkably, the Tribunal did not convict any natural persons for membership thereof.

However, in subsequent secondary proceedings before national courts and tribunals, the concept of criminal groups and organisations was extensively relied upon.[31] Some domestic judicial organs even went so far as to consider certain collective entities (e.g. concentration camps) criminal, although they were not formally declared such by the IMT.[32]

National courts strived not to base individual convictions on membership alone. Like the IMT, domestic judiciaries fixed the requisite *mens rea* at the level of 'knew' or 'must have known'. Despite efforts to remain mindful of the principle of personal culpability, their application of the subjective standard was far from straightforward. The United States tribunals did not differentiate between principals and accomplices in the commission of crimes, and attributed liability on the basis of the functional position of defendants within the criminal organisation.[33] Individuals who did not physically participate in the commission of crimes, incurred criminal responsibility by virtue of their membership in the group and their position in it. Awareness was inferred from the official capacity and associated functions of the accused. In the absence of direct evidence of actual knowledge, liability could be based on a 'must have known' standard. Such an approach had the inherent danger of slipping into negligence-type liability. 'Must have known' by virtue of a functional position and in the absence of other indications of awareness, closely resembles a 'should have known' level of *mens rea*. The British courts also employed the doctrine of common

---

29 *Ibidem*, at 275-6, 279.

30 *Idem*, at 262, 268, 273. In declaring the organisations criminal, the Tribunal once again emphasised that the declarations were effective only with regard to persons who had become, or remained, members with knowledge of the organisations' criminal goals or acts.

31 Secondary proceedings at the national level were conducted pursuant to Allied Control Council Law No. 10 (adopted on 20 December 1945), enforcing Article 10 of the Nuremberg Charter. T. Telford, *Final Report to the Secretary of the Army on the Nuernberg War Crimes Trials under Control Council Law No. 10*, Washington, 1949.

32 Relying on a domestic concept of membership responsibility, Polish courts declared the staff of the Auschwitz concentration camp to have formed a criminal organisation. The case of *Rudolf Hoess,* in: *Law Reports of Trials of War Criminals (UNWCC)*, Vol. VII, London: His Majesty's Stationary Office, 1949, pp. 20-24.

33 E.g. The case of *Altstötter et al.*, in *Trials of War Criminals Before the Nuremberg Military Tribunals Under Control Council Law No. 10, Nuremberg (TWC)*, Washington 1949-1953, Vol. III, pp. 954-1201.

design in establishing culpability and did not differentiate between those who physically committed the crime and those who aided and abetted in its commission.[34] Liability would, however, rest on the Prosecution establishing beyond reasonable doubt that the defendant knew of a crime and with his conduct wilfully contributed to its commission. On the other hand, the French tribunals relied on the doctrine of complicity in adjudicating jointly committed crimes and made a clear distinction between instigators, perpetrators and accomplices.[35] Unfamiliarity with the concept of conspiracy, however, did not deter other continental national courts from employing the Anglo-American approach in dealing with Nazi group criminality. Some even deviated from their own national criminal law, prescribing complicity as the applicable doctrine to the adjudication of collective crimes, and went on to treat perpetrators and facilitators equally.[36]

II.3 A missed opportunity *vis-à-vis* corporate accountability?

The 'collective criminality' model, outlined above and applied by the Nuremberg judiciary with regard to military and political groups, was also potentially applicable in the corporate context. The issue of business involvement in Nazi crimes arose during the Nuremberg Charter negotiations. The German policy of aggressive territorial expansion during the Second World War and the Holocaust provided ample opportunities for enrichment to many profit-oriented entities. Several thousands of German companies relied heavily on the slave labour of concentration camp inmates, deportees and prisoners of war.[37] It is estimated that some 8 to 10 million people were exploited as forced labourers in the factories of German companies during the war, many of them dying as a result of dire working and living conditions.[38] The growth and prosperity of many renowned multinational firms nowadays is alleged to have resulted to a large extent from the profits they accumulated in the course of the Second World War through the exploitation of slave labour.[39] Pharmaceutical companies supplied the drugs used in Nazi medical experiments and chemicals for the concentration camp gas chambers.[40] Technological advances were utilised to organise and maintain Nazi records

---

34 E.g. The case of *Otto Sandrock et al.*, in *Law Reports of Trials of War Criminals (UNWCC)*, Vol. I, London: His Majesty's Stationary Office, 1949, pp. 40-43.

35 E.g. The case of *Franz Holstein et al.*, in *Law Reports of Trials of War Criminals (UNWCC)*, Vol. VIII, London: His Majesty's Stationary Office, 1949, pp. 26-33.

36 E. van Sliedregt, *The Criminal Responsibility of Individuals for Violations of International Humanitarian Law*, The Hague: T.M.C. Asser Press, 2003, p. 31.

37 A. Zuppi, Slave Labour in Nuremberg's I.G. Farben Case: The Lonely Voice of Paul H. Herbert, 66 *Louisiana Law Review* 495 (2006) at 496.

38 M.J. Bazyler, Nuremberg in America: Litigating the Holocaust in United States Court, 34 *University of Richmond Law Review* 1 (2000) at 191-192.

39 See e.g. Iwanowa v. Ford Motor Co., 67 F. Supp. 2d 424, 432-34 (1999), discussing allegations about Ford's use of slave labour and the impact of that labour on the company's profitability.

40 Bazyler, *supra note 38*, at 207.

of plunder, spoliation and slave labour.[41] Banks and insurance companies financed the construction of concentration camps, insured their facilities and made profit by retaining the assets of those killed or interned by the Nazis.[42]

The Nuremberg Charter did not preclude the prosecution of corporate officials. In fact it was intended to provide the legal basis for such prosecution either before the IMT or otherwise before national military tribunals which were to conduct subsequent trials. The IMT, however, did not prosecute German industrialists for their substantial contribution to Nazi crimes. The indictment was limited to a small group of political and military leaders. The decision not to engage corporate officials as defendants was politically pre-determined shortly before the IMT trial commenced. It was primarily motivated by expediency considerations rather than unwillingness to hold industrialists criminally responsible for their involvement in Nazi crimes.[43] Cognisant of the major involvement of the German business sector in the crimes committed by the Hitlerites, the Allied Powers actually forged a plan to hold a second, separate, IMT trial later to deal with corporate executives only.[44] The plan was however eventually abandoned as the Allies became preoccupied with the post-war reconstruction of Germany. Instead it was decided to leave the prosecution of industrialists to national military tribunals.[45]

Whether business executives would have been convicted had they stood trial before the IMT, is a matter for speculation only. As discussed in the preceding sections, the Tribunal adopted a very restrictive standard for the requisite level of knowledge with regard to crimes against peace. It did not consider Hitler's plan to wage an aggressive war privy to anyone outside the immediate circle of his closest aids. Moreover, re-armament in itself was not viewed as a precursor to such a war. Accordingly, ownership and control over factories in the munitions industry would hardly have constituted sufficient evidence of corporate officials' contribution to crimes against peace. National military tribunals asserted the latter point subsequently in proceedings against German industrialists.[46] The same would have likely been maintained by the IMT as well.

---

41 E. Black, *IBM and the Holocaust: The Strategic Alliance Between Nazi Germany and America's Most Powerful Corporation*, New York: Crown Publishers, 2001.

42 See Bazyler, *supra note 38*, at 31-39, for a discussion of Holocaust claims against Swiss banks. *Ibidem*, at 93-136, for claims against European insurance companies.

43 M. Lippman, War Crimes Trials of German Industrialists: The Other 'Schindlers', 9 *Temple International and Comparative Law Journal* 173 (1995) at 176-177.

44 For a complete discussion, see W.A. Zeck, Nuremberg: Proceedings Subsequent to Goering et al., 26 *North Carolina Law Review* 350 (1948).

45 *Ibidem*.

46 The *Farben* judgment established that accessorial liability in the planning and waging of a war of aggression could not be deduced solely from a company's participation in the re-armament of a state, no matter how substantial that participation might have been. In the absence of any specific knowledge that the munitions supplied were intended to be deployed in the course of an aggressive war, corporate executives could not be held criminally responsible. See *Law Reports of Trials of War Criminals (UNWCC)*, Vol. X, London: His Majesty's Stationery Office, 1949 (the case of *I.G. Farben*), at 36-40.

With regard to war crimes and crimes against humanity, the Nuremberg Charter would have allowed the prosecution of industrialists as either direct perpetrators or accomplices to a common plan to commit such crimes. Convictions, however, would have been difficult to obtain and an IMT trial of business executives would have presumably resulted in fewer guilty verdicts than were later delivered by national military tribunals. The assumption here is that the requisite *mens rea* with respect to civilians (i.e. industrialists) would not have been any lower than that required by the IMT *vis-à-vis* the Nazi military and political leaders. Thus the IMT would probably have refrained from imposing liability in the absence of sufficient evidence of industrialists' direct engagement in the planning, ordering, inciting or commission of crimes. As in the cases of high-ranking military and political officials, mere knowledge of criminal acts, communication of orders or a failure to prevent the commission of crimes, would not have been sufficient to sustain convictions.[47] The trials of industrialists by national military tribunals applied slightly more lenient liability criteria, albeit far from consistently.

The Nuremberg Charter furthermore did not preclude the making of declarations of criminality with regard to corporations as well as political and military groups. It is, however, unlikely that the IMT would have extended the scope of such declarations to encompass economic ventures. The Tribunal was very cautious in applying the concept of criminal organisations and refrained from bringing within its scope even organisations of an obviously criminal nature.[48] On the one hand, it is improbable that the Tribunal would have ventured to declare profit-oriented entities criminal where their purpose and activities did not present a clear-cut case of groups existing to commit crimes. On the other hand, the small size of the corporate governing bodies would, in any case, have permitted individual prosecutions, and hence the IMT would presumably have refrained from making declarations as to the groups' criminal character. Yet, the approach adopted by the Tribunal does not detract from the fact that corporations could, in principle, have been declared criminal organisations had industrialists stood trial before the IMT. The concept of criminal organisations was interpreted and applied with care so as to curtail the probability of arbitrary convictions. It is an entirely different matter to what extent declaring corporations or their governing bodies to be criminal organisations would have served a useful legal purpose.[49]

---

47 Lippman, *supra note 9*, at 33.

48 The following organisations were indicted: the Reich Cabinet, the Leadership Corps of the Nazi Party, the SS, the Gestapo, the SA and the General Staff and High Command of the German Armed Forces. 1 *IMT*, *supra note 1*, at 28. Concentration camps were not part of the indictment. Although such camps could be regarded tangible enough to satisfy the criteria for 'a group' or 'an organisation', the Tribunal would probably have held that their administrations were merely weapons in the hands of the conspirators. The latter was the Tribunal's conclusion with regard to the General Staff and the High Command of the German Army, and accordingly neither was declared 'a criminal organisation' within the meaning of Article 9 of the Nuremberg Charter. 1 *IMT*, *supra note 1*, at 278.

49 The utility of the 'criminal organisations' concept to corporate liability is further discussed in Chapter 5. More generally, for an argument in favour of the application of the concept in contemporary context,

III The Nuremberg prosecution of industrialists

The IMT did not deal with the contribution of German companies to the crimes committed during the Nazi era. Individual corporate agents were, however, held accountable before various national military tribunals. The trials were conducted in the context of Control Council Law No. 10, which the Allied Powers adopted in 1945 in order to create a uniform legal basis for the prosecution of 'war criminals and other similar offenders'.[50]

III.1 An overview of domestic military trials

In 1946, the British Military Tribunal indicted the owner and two employees of *Tesch and Stabenow* for selling the highly toxic gas Zyklon B to German concentration camps. Declaring the laws and customs of war applicable not only to combatants and members of state or other public authorities but also to 'anybody who is in a position to assist in their violation',[51] the tribunal convicted the defendants for they either 'knew' or 'must have known' of the use to which Zyklon B was put by the Nazis. It was deemed that in the absence of direct evidence, knowledge could be construed from a person's position within the organisation.[52]

Two years later, the French Military Tribunal convicted the directors of the iron and steel *Roechling Company* for crimes against peace and war crimes. It was deemed that they knew of the atrocious working conditions in the *Roechling* plants but failed to do anything to alleviate them.[53] In some instances, they even actively sought to obtain slave labour from the Nazi government.[54]

In 1947, the United States Military Tribunal (USMT) indicted several top executives of the *Flick Concern* for the deployment of slave labour in the company's

---

see N.H.B. Jørgensen, A Reappraisal of the Abandoned Nuremberg Concept of Criminal Organisations in the Context of Justice in Rwanda, 12 *Criminal Law Forum* 371 (2002).

50 Control Council Law No. 10: Punishment of Persons Guilty of War Crimes, Crimes Against Peace and Against Humanity, at <avalon.law.yale.edu/imt/imt10.asp>.

51 *Law Reports of Trials of War Criminals (UNWCC)*, Vol. I, London: His Majesty's Stationary Office, 1949 (the case of *Zyklon B*), at 103.

52 *Ibidem*, at 97, 99-100, 102.

53 H. Lauterpacht (ed.), *Annual Digest and Reports of Public International Law Cases 1948*, London: Butterworth & Co., 1953 (the case of *Roechling et al.*), p. 411. Liability followed not only from active participation in the commission of a crime but also from a failure to prevent a crime provided that the defendant knew about it and was in a position to interfere. The same approach was adopted by the British Military Tribunal when prosecuting employees of the Japanese *Nippon* Mining Company on charges of forced labour and mistreatment of prisoners of war. The tribunal refused to uphold a fiduciary duty with regard to corporate superiors. For a discussion of the *Nippon* trial, see A. Ramasastry, Corporate Complicity: From Nuremberg to Rangoon. An Examination of Slave Labour Cases and Their Impact on the Liability of Multinational Corporations, 20 *Berkeley Journal of International Law* 91 (2002) at 113-117.

54 Roechling et al., *supra note 53*, pp. 410-412.

coal, iron and steel plants, the spoliation of public and private property in the occupied territories, and accessorial liability for crimes committed by the SS. Liability for the charges of slave labour and property spoliation was incurred by those defendants who knew of concrete criminal acts and voluntarily contributed to their commission.[55] Those individuals who by virtue of their subordinate position, could neither prevent nor otherwise oppose the crimes being committed were exonerated from responsibility. With regard to the count of aiding and abetting the criminal activities of the SS, the tribunal settled for a 'must have known' standard of knowledge. Two of the defendants were convicted for extending financial support to the SS, despite the lack of evidence that either of them had approved of or condoned the organisation's criminal activities.[56] Although liability was not based on membership alone, the tribunal equally did not require knowledge on the part of the defendants that the monetary contributions made would be used by the SS to further its criminal goals.

The following year the USMT convicted Alfred Krupp and other executives of the *Krupp* munitions corporation for supplying Nazi Germany with armament during the war. They were held liable for plunder, spoliation, and labour exploitation of prisoners of war as well as of civilians under inhuman conditions. The tribunal refused to extend a fiduciary duty to corporate officials. Liability was imposed only on those defendants who either personally committed criminal acts or knowingly instigated or authorised the commission of such acts.[57] The tribunal inferred knowledge from direct as well as circumstantial evidence, provided it was convincing beyond reasonable doubt. With regard to the charge of slave labour, the USMT re-iterated the conclusion reached in the *Flick* judgment, holding that the defence of necessity was not applicable in cases where the defendants had purposefully taken advantage of, or actively sought after, free labour.[58]

The same approach was applied in the *Farben* Case. In 1948, the USMT convicted all members of the governing body of the largest chemical and pharmaceutical manufacturer at the time, I.G. Farben, for having acted 'through the instrumentality of Farben' to commit crimes justiciable under the Nuremberg Charter.[59] Like many other German companies during the war, Farben perceived the Nazi policy of aggressive territorial expansion as an opportunity to enhance its economic power. The members of its governing body were not motivated by a desire to persecute the civilian

55 *Law Reports of Trials of War Criminals (UNWCC)*, Vol. IX, London: His Majesty's Stationary Office, 1949 (the case of *Flick*), at 7-10.

56 *Ibidem*, at 14-16, 28-30.

57 *Law Reports of Trials of War Criminals (UNWCC)*, Vol. X, London: His Majesty's Stationary Office, 1949 (the case of *Krupp*), at 150.

58 *Ibidem*, at 146-149.

59 Farben, *supra note 46*. The charges included allegations of deportation, slave labour, torture, killings, plunder and spoliation of property in the occupied territories, and the production and supply to concentration camps of poison gas and medication for experimental and extermination purposes.

population of the occupied territories. Nevertheless, those of them who knowingly authorised, approved of, or participated in, acts of plunder and spoliation, were eventually convicted.[60] With regard to the charges pertaining to the supply of poison gas and drugs to concentration camps for experimentation and extermination purposes, the tribunal concluded that the evidence presented did not establish knowledge on the part of the defendants as to what use Farben's production was put by the Nazis.[61] As to the allegations of involvement in the enslavement, deportation and maltreatment of civilians and prisoners of war, it was conceded that knowledge could be inferred from the evidence presented, and in particular the scale of the slave labour utilised in Farben's plants.[62] However, the tribunal refused to attribute liability without concrete proof of direct engagement in the alleged criminal acts.[63] Thus, those members of the governing body who did not actively seek the procurement of slave labour from the Nazis managed to evade criminal responsibility by successfully invoking the defence of necessity. The tribunal refused to impose a fiduciary duty to stay apprised of corporate conduct at all times and, likewise, was reluctant to deduce knowledge from the defendants' positions of power and influence.

Legal scholars have put forward several justifications for the lenience of the *Farben* judgment. On the judicial side, the general unease about the application of the doctrine of conspiracy to international crimes and the corresponding concern about possible mass punishment, presumably motivated the tribunal to offset any perceptions of it imposing strict liability by basing convictions on a rather narrow interpretation of personal fault. Some authors have furthermore argued, not implausibly, that by focusing on establishing a conspiracy of Farben to assist the German war machine in crimes against peace, the prosecution somewhat neglected the charges of war crimes and crimes against humanity.[64] Should the prosecution have concentrated on uncovering sufficient and credible evidence establishing Farben's involvement in such crimes, the outcome of the judgment might have been different. Stokes has also contended that the judgment is in line with the US judicial tradition to impose relatively light sentences for white-collar crime.[65] On the political side, authors have, moreover, maintained that the growing tensions of the Cold War gradually detracted

---

60 *Ibidem*, at 49-53.

61 *Idem*, at 57.

62 *Idem*, at 25-28.

63 In his dissenting opinion (*Idem*, at 61-62), Judge Herbert opposed limiting liability to only those individuals who 'exercised initiative' in the utilisation of slave labour. In his view, liability had to be borne by those members of the Vorstand who knowingly authorised the participation of *Farben* in criminal activities. As the use of slave labour had been approved as a matter of corporate policy, according to Judge Herbert all Vorstand members had to share criminal responsibility. His view was further re-enforced by the absence of any credible evidence that any of the defendants opposed the use of slave labour and did not cooperate willingly with Nazi plans.

64 E. g. R.G. Stokes, *Divide and Prosper: The Heirs of the I.G. Farben Under Allied Authority, 1945-1951*, Berkeley: University of California Press, 1988, p. 153.

65 *Ibidem*, p. 153.

attention from Nazi crimes and speeded up the adjudication process.[66] By the late 1940s – with the IMT trials of the major political and military leaders already completed, and the geo-political climate in Europe rapidly changing – going after the German industrialists was no longer a priority on the political agenda.

III.2 Synthesising the Nuremberg principles of individual criminal responsibility in relation to corporate officials

The national military tribunals based individual convictions of industrialists on disparate standards of knowledge. The *Tesch and Stabenow* Case signalled an inclination to allow for convictions even in the absence of any knowledge on the part of the defendants of criminal acts. However, the outcomes of subsequent trials (and in particular those of *Farben* and *Krupp*) revealed overwhelming judicial reluctance to impose a duty on business executives to stay invariably aware of their subordinates' conduct. The tribunals nevertheless failed to establish with sufficient clarity and consistency what the requisite level of knowledge for incurring criminal responsibility was. In *Roechling*, defendants were held liable on the basis of direct evidence of knowledge on their part of concrete criminal acts. By contrast, in both the *Tesch and Stabenow* and the *Flick* Case some of the accused came to bear criminal responsibility because the tribunals considered that, by virtue of their positions within the organisational structure or the societal reputation of the political group they supported, they 'must have known' that criminal activities were taking place. The presumed knowledge did not have to concern specific crimes. While in *Farben* the tribunal refused to apply a 'must have known' standard, requiring instead evidence of direct engagement in concrete criminal activities on the part of each individual defendant, in *Krupp* the broader context was more readily taken into consideration and knowledge was deduced from circumstantial evidence. In any event, it had to be established beyond reasonable doubt that the defendant participated in, authorised, instigated, or approved of the criminal acts alleged.

Other cases involving corporate officials likewise resulted in individual liability being imposed (or not) on the basis of rather inconsistent thresholds of knowledge and participation. Karl Rasche – the chairman of the German *Dresdner Bank* – was, for instance, acquitted of all charges against him.[67] The USMT refused to extend criminal responsibility to bank officials who by virtue of their professional activities had become indirectly involved in the financing of crimes. Karl Rasche also managed to

66 J. Borkin, *The Crime and Punishment of I.G. Farben: The Unholy Alliance between Hitler and the Great Chemical Combine*, New York: Barnes & Noble Books, 1979, pp. 187-188.

67 The USMT indictment charged Karl Rasche with facilitating the Nazi slave labour programme by providing loans to entities, which made use of such labour. See *Trials of War Criminals before the Nuremberg Military Tribunals under Control Council No. 10, Nuremberg*, Washington (1949-1953), Vol. XIV (the case of *Weizsaecker et al.*).

evade liability for the donations he had made to Himmler's Circle of Friends. According to the tribunal, the evidence presented did not establish knowledge on his part that the fund to which Dresdner Bank made contributions was intended to be or was ever used by Himmler for unlawful purposes.[68] In this regard the judgment differs significantly from the USMT's earlier decision in the *Flick* Case. As will be recalled, two of the *Flick* defendants were convicted for financially supporting the SS, albeit with blank checks. Evidence of Rasche's active participation in the SS and Himmler's Circle of Friends was not as forthcoming as in *Flick*. The tribunal, nevertheless, did point out that, as a bank official whose responsibility it was to obtain and ascertain information as to the purpose for which a loan was sought, it would have been inconceivable to assume that Rasche did not possess knowledge as to where and for what the bank loans were utilised.[69] Yet, in the absence of any direct evidence the tribunal refused to draw incriminating inferences.

The Karl Rasche trial was a feeble attempt to implicate the private banking sector for its possible complicity in international crimes. The judgment rendered was disappointing in its failure to properly discuss the effect that the knowledge element might have on constructing accomplice liability. Although it seemed to overturn the earlier decision in the *Flick* Case, the inadequate and unclear arguments pertaining to the requisite level of knowledge left the door ajar for further judicial interpretation. Several decades later the controversy around this particular judgment was revived as Holocaust survivors and their heirs sought to implicate Swiss banks for their complicity in Nazi crimes under the Aliens Tort Claims Act in the United States.[70]

It is difficult to deduce from the Nuremberg 'corporate' trials clear and coherent standards for the attribution of individual criminal responsibility. A general pattern is discernible nevertheless. Eager to avoid (the perception of) mass punishment, the tribunals were in principle cautious not to lapse into strict liability. Unfortunately, good intentions did not always translate into equitable outcomes. Some of the verdicts rendered precariously compounded the 'must have known' with the 'should have known' mental state. While the former generally designates subjective knowledge inferred from circumstantial evidence as the only reasonable conclusion, the latter presumes knowledge objectively on the basis of a legal duty and a criminal outcome. In this regard the tribunals allowed culpability to flow from a functional status only or a breach of a fiduciary relationship in a number of instances. In most cases, however, constructive knowledge was based on the existence of indications pointing in the direction of awareness with regard to criminal acts or the criminal nature of an organisation. Furthermore, some form of personal dereliction on the part of corporate officials was generally required in order for them to incur criminal responsibility.

68 *Ibidem*, at 622.

69 *Idem.*

70 See e.g. A. Ramasastry, Secrets and Lies? Swiss Banks and International Human Rights, 31 *Vanderbilt Journal of Transnational Law* 325 (1998).

Dereliction would follow from either the intentional commission of a criminal act or a wanton failure to fulfill a legal duty. In most cases, therefore, the tribunals effectively maintained the required level of knowledge above the 'should have known' threshold. The *mens rea* element was, moreover, coupled with a requirement for active participation – through ordering, authorising, approving or joining – in the crimes alleged.

Striving to ensure that guilt was attributed on a personal rather than collective basis, the tribunals also permitted extensive reliance by corporate defendants on a defence of necessity. The terms 'necessity', 'duress' and 'compulsion' were often used interchangeably, although their application in case law was far from uniform. Generally, the tribunals applied the traditional common law test. It provided that a defence of necessity/duress could be successfully invoked when the criminal act was carried out in order to avoid a grave and irreparable physical harm, on a scale strictly proportionate to the evil sought to be prevented and only when there was no viable non-criminal alternative. Mere moral pressure emanating from within or outside the corporate structure did not provide an exemption to criminal responsibility; the danger faced had to be real, imminent and inevitable. It could emanate from either men, circumstances or the repressive political system of the Third Reich. It also had to pose a threat to life and could not relate to the mere loss of assets.

In the context of corporate superior-subordinate relationships, the tribunals acquitted most low-level defendants. They considered that, by virtue of the subordinate positions occupied by the accused, they could not have refused to comply with policies effectively emanating from the government without running a substantial risk. In relation to superior orders stemming from within the corporation, the defence was deemed unavailable to those responsible for the existence or execution of the orders. This approach was connected to the recognition and application of superior responsibility by the IMT and subsequently domestic military tribunals, although the concept was not explicitly provided for in the Nuremberg Charter. Even with regard to senior executives, however, the defence of necessity/duress was refused to only those defendants who clearly took the initiative to commit criminal acts exceeding what was strictly required of them by Nazi officials.

III.3 The implicit denunciation of corporations as accessories to Nazi crimes

The principles for attributing individual criminal responsibility, particularly with regard to civilian superiors such as corporate officials, have evolved considerably since Nuremberg.[71] The Nuremberg attempt at securing some form of corporate accountability is, however, instructive in that it illustrates the inherent pitfalls in

---

71 For an extended discussion, see Chapter 4, section III: The concept of superior responsibility and Chapter 6, section IV: The superior responsibility of corporate officials.

ascribing liability in the corporate context. It also reflects an early understanding of the effects of the organisational context on individual wrongdoing.

The domestic military tribunals had jurisdiction over natural persons only and therefore no corporation was ever convicted for its contribution to Nazi crimes during the Second World War. Nevertheless, the judgments eventually rendered implicated a number of business entities as accessories in the commission of war crimes and crimes against humanity. Some decisions even went so far as to regard the company as the prime perpetrator – albeit not in a legal sense. It was the individuals who had acted 'through the instrumentality' of the organisations concerned, who were held criminally liable. Remarkably, at the same time corporations were deemed to possess their own intent, not necessarily equivalent to the intent of individual members.

The *Farben* judgment has frequently been read as implying that the corporate entity itself had committed the crimes with which its directors were charged.[72] Individual defendants were in fact found guilty on the basis of the USMT pronouncing that Farben, as a legal entity, was capable of violating the customs and laws of war[73] and in fact did so through its governing body, whose members used legal incorporation as an instrument to knowingly and wilfully engage in unlawful acts. It is important to note that the *Farben* judgement was not explicitly based on a declaration of criminality, as permitted under the Nuremberg Charter. In the context of Farben, both the indictment and the conviction were formulated pursuant to Article 2, paragraph 2e of Control Council Law No. 10, which stated that:

> 'Any person without regard to nationality or the capacity in which he acted, is deemed to have committed crimes as defined in paragraph 1 [...] if he ... (e) was a member of any organisation or group connected with the commission of any such crimes.'

Despite their different legal bases, the judgements rendered by the IMT on criminal organisations, and by the USMT in *Farben*, are in essence very similar. Both rest on the recognition that organisations, public or private, are bound by international criminal law to refrain from engaging in the commission of war crimes and crimes against humanity. Neither tribunal had jurisdiction over legal persons, nor sought to convict organisations *per se*. Rather, both the IMT and the USMT aimed to implicate individuals for their wilful and knowing involvement in juridical entities carrying out unlawful activities. In either case, however, the implicit outcome had been to indirectly condemn the legal entities concerned for transgressing international law through their

72 See e.g. A. Clapham, The Question of Jurisdiction Under International Criminal Law Over Legal Persons: Lessons from the Rome Conference on an International Criminal Court, in: M.T. Kamminga and S. Zia-Zarifi (eds.), *Liability of Multinational Corporations under International Law*, The Hague: Kluwer Law International, 2000, pp. 166-171.

73 Farben, *supra note 46*, at 50-52.

activities. While the IMT did so by declaring political and military organisations 'criminal', the USMT opted for the less explicit strategy of regarding corporate ventures as 'criminal instrumentalities'.

The importance attached in Nuremberg to the implication of legal persons in the commission of international crimes, was also clearly reflected in the *Krupp* Case. Throughout its judgement, and particularly with regard to the charges of plunder, the USMT persistently centred on the Krupp corporation as such, rather than the actual defendants. The evidence presented was, for instance, considered to show that:

> '... the initiative for the acquisition of properties, machines and materials in the occupied territories referred to above, was that of the Krupp firm, [which utilised] the Reich government and Reich agencies whenever necessary to accomplish *its* [emphasis added, *DS*] purposes.'[74]

As in the *Farben* Case, the tribunal concluded that it was the company itself that committed violations of the Hague Regulations pertaining to the inviolability of private property in the territories under occupation.[75] Individual defendants were then convicted for having acted 'though the instrumentality' of the firm[76] to commit criminal acts, whose prime perpetrator, nevertheless, was the corporation itself. The USMT in fact went to great lengths to identify the collective purpose and intent of the enterprise, along with the motives and actions of its directing minds. The actual effect of the tribunal's judgment was thus to position the Krupp firm at the heart of convictions, although Alfred Krupp and the other leading executives, as the actual defendants over whom the tribunal had jurisdiction, were sentenced in lieu of the legal entity.

The Control Council Law No. 10 did not require an explicit declaration of criminality *vis-à-vis* a group or an organisation in order for the national tribunals to be able to prosecute individuals for membership thereof. It sufficed for the group or organisation to be 'connected with' the commission of crimes to have the mechanism for the determination of individual criminal responsibility triggered. Eventually, although no declarations of criminality were made, corporations were implicated in the commission of international crimes and individual 'members' did incur liability. However, the mere fact that a defendant was a member of a group (i.e. a corporation or a company's governing body) that had been implicated in criminal activities, did not in itself give rise to criminal responsibility.[77]

74 Krupp, *supra note 57,* at 92.
75 *Ibidem,* at 49-50.
76 *Idem,* at 52.
77 *Idem,* at 52.

IV The legacy of Nuremberg

As regards the trials of industrialists, Nuremberg is notable in that it sought to implicate legitimate, profit-oriented, entities in the commission of crimes and it succeeded, albeit only indirectly. The judgments are largely devoid of detailed reasoning and at times inconsistent in the interpretation and application of legal principles. Nevertheless, their value is significant. They not only documented historical reality but also evidenced the business side of system criminality. The prosecution of industrialists revealed how individual crimes can reach unprecedented scale when committed through the instrumentality of an organisation and how economic entities can exhibit an organisational mind transcending the mental states of individual members. It further established that legal persons, not only their agents, might incur liability for criminal acts committed in the pursuit of profit. The trials upheld the pertinence of addressing cooperation between business actors and repressive governments as well as the justifiability of attaching some legal consequences to the corporate facilitation of international crimes.

On a more general note, Nuremberg's legacy is not devoid of contention. The set-up of the IMT and the streamlined procedures it adopted in order to cope with the prosecution of a multitude of defendants, have preoccupied critics for decades on end. It has been contended – not entirely warranted as will be posited below – that the Nuremberg trials exemplify victors' justice, or revenge masked behind a thin veil of legality. The Allied Powers' control over the entire process as well as the selective prosecution of defendants and the crafting of legal doctrines to suit the needs of the trial, have re-enforced such perceptions. The Charter's arguable *ex post facto* character and the novelty of some of its provisions, in particular those pertaining to aggressive war, crimes against humanity and organisational criminality, continue to raise the same concerns as expressed at the time of Nuremberg more than fifty years ago.[78] These concerns relate to the violation of the principle of *nullum crimen sine lege*, the resulting amalgam of the melding of the common law and civil law systems, the heavy reliance on the doctrine of conspiracy and the controversy surrounding the notions of strict liability and collective guilt. Admittedly, the Nuremberg critics could be justified, at least to a certain extent, in their denigration of the tribunals' legacy. Both the Charter's formulation and subsequently the tribunals' unclear and sometimes inconsistent approach to the application of innovative provisions left much to be desired. Trials *in absentia* and the politically determined choice of defendants blurred the image of a just and fair judicial process.

However, critics have frequently been too harsh on the Nuremberg tribunals, failing to fully appreciate the broader context in which the trials took place and their historical, political and ideological significance. As succinctly put by Borgwardt,

78 Lippman, *supra note 9*, at 19.

Nuremberg was an attempt 'to express moralistic ideas in a legalistic manner, and as such it teemed with internal contradictions'.[79] The legal basis of the trials, their set-up and *modus operandi* were the outcome of complex political negotiations mixed with procedural considerations, and the judges were well aware of the framework within which they were positioned. Against this background, it cannot be denied that they made an honest effort to compensate for the drawbacks of the process while serving much needed – on the societal level – justice. Although instated by the victorious powers, the tribunals sought to rise above the taint of vindictiveness and should be credited for their homage to procedural fairness and transparency. Nuremberg was not merely about retribution. The prosecution of Nazi war criminals served a much larger expressive goal; it endorsed the intransience of fundamental human values and conveyed a didactic moral narrative.

While the judiciary accepted and relied upon novel legal notions, they also moved cautiously in imposing criminal liability[80] rationally debating evidence and the underlying precepts of blameworthiness.[81] It substantially delimited the scope of application of the conspiracy charge and narrowly interpreted the requisite elements for responsibility incurred for membership in a criminal organisation and for complicity in war crimes and crimes against humanity. The tribunals further refused to entertain arguments pertaining to the collective guilt of the German people[82] and were conscious of the importance of avoiding collective punishment or strict liability. Although a multitude of defendants could have easily been imprisoned or executed without resort to complex judicial procedures, those who stood trial were given due access to law.[83] At the same time, from a moral perspective, the innovative (and potentially expansive) approach adopted at Nuremberg with a view to securing accountability in the context of group criminality is understandable. Liability doctrines giving the semblance of collective punishment are a natural offshoot of the predicament posed by collective responsibility.

Perhaps Nuremberg was not as successful as it could have been – or should have been – in compensating for the legal shortcomings of the Charter and the streamlined trial procedures. However, it set the beginning of a new era in the development of international law by sustaining the notion of individual responsibility for international crimes and the denunciation of the acts of state and superior orders defences. The tribunals' interpretation and application of innovative legal theories should not be easily dismissed as arbitrary and self-serving; they should rather be appreciated for

79 E. Borgwardt, Re-Examining Nuremberg as a New Deal Institution: Politics, Culture and the Limits of Law in Generating Human Rights Norms, 23 *Berkeley Journal of International Law* 401 (2005) at 452.

80 Lippman, *supra note 9*, p. 19.

81 D.J. Luban, War Crimes: The Law of Hell, in: L. May (ed.), *War. Essays in Political Philosophy*, Cambridge: Cambridge University Press, 2008, p. 286.

82 Lippman, *supra note 9*, at 20. See more generally R. Arens, Nuremberg and Group Prosecution, *Washington University Law Quarterly* 329 (1951).

83 Borgwardt, *supra note 79*, at 34.

being a reflection of the 'living' nature of international law and for setting a distinctive trend in the development of international standards of legal conduct.

V Conclusion

The Nuremberg 'collective criminality' model was aimed at capturing a multitude of defendants while reflecting the idiosyncrasies of system criminality. Pragmatic rather than dogmatic, it could not be easily divorced from concerns pertaining to group responsibility, mass punishment and strict liability. As evidenced above, despite the tribunals' caution in imposing criminal responsibility, some judgments distorted the contours of individual culpability and rendered the link with personal guilt tenuous. As a whole, the decisions concerning economic actors were, nonetheless, notable in that they reflected a unique, and at the time pioneering, outlook on organised entities as organic collectives transgressing the mere sum of the individuals comprising them. This did not signal a shift in the traditional focus on the individual as the object and subject of criminal law. The international legal system was not ripe for such a fundamental change in perspective; the system had barely come into being.

The Nuremberg trials took place in exceptional circumstances and in many respects they did not set endurable precedent. Nevertheless, Nuremberg remains an important frame of reference. It serves as a cautionary tale of the inherent complexities of seeking to construct liability in a group context. Insight into the judgments and their rationale is thus a useful starting point for any discussion of the subject of corporate criminal responsibility. The (envisaged) prosecution of economic actors – natural or legal persons – brought to the fore several key matters that are still relevant today. The decisions rendered served as an express recognition of the reality of corporate involvement in international crimes. They exemplified a broad-base readiness to address the criminality of organised entities and the realisation that such criminality is qualitatively different from individual deviance, and hence, warrants a distinct approach. At the same time, the judgments reflected certain unease with the idea of moving the jurisdictional focus away from the individual and with the implications in terms of (moral) responsibility and mass punishment of legal pronouncements targeting institutionalised entities *per se*. More generally, Nuremberg also illustrated the prospects and challenges that have epitomised successive efforts in more recent years, to develop viable liability doctrines in international criminal law that are capable of capturing collective (as opposed to organisational) criminality without infringing upon the tenet of personal fault. Many of the principles underlying individual criminal responsibility nowadays, and pertaining also to civilians – not only political and paramilitary figures but also corporate officials – can be traced back to the Nuremberg trials.

Chapter 4
Collective criminality and the Rome Statute

I Introduction

The 'collective criminality' model developed at Nuremberg served its purpose in the immediate aftermath of the Second World War but did not persist in time. Despite its usefulness in addressing system crimes and the tribunals' efforts to compensate for its possible shortcomings, the model turned out to be too controversial to warrant its lasting inclusion in international law doctrine. Nevertheless, the notions of conspiracy and group-member criminality, which formed the core of the Nuremberg model, can be found in contemporary international law, albeit in a different guise. The modern successor to the 'collective criminality' model is the 'common purpose' doctrine, otherwise known also as 'common design' or joint criminal enterprise.[1] The post-Second World War case law also drew the contours of the concept of superior responsibility, which expanded beyond political and military leaders and is nowadays applicable to business executives as well.

This chapter traces the development of 'common purpose' and superior responsibility as modes for establishing individual liability in international criminal law. Both theories extend culpability beyond the physical perpetration of crimes and are geared towards the reality of criminality in group settings. They thus serve to encompass the multitude of individuals who order, instigate, direct, fail to prevent or otherwise collaborate in the commission of mass crimes. Given their propensity to detect blameworthiness in indirect contributions, effectuated in the absence of volition or even knowledge, the application of the 'common purpose' doctrine and superior responsibility has not been devoid of contention. The troubled efforts on the part of the *ad hoc* tribunals to circumscribe the theories' scope and the restraint evidenced in the codification of both concepts in the Rome Statute illustrate the ongoing struggle to effectively reconcile manifestations of collective responsibility with the principle of personal guilt. As previously discussed, the tension between safeguarding the position of the individual in criminal law and the need to acknowledge the impact of the group context, underpins also the discussion of corporate crime as a form of organisational

1 Hereafter 'common purpose' and 'common design' will be used interchangeably, although a differentiation will be made between 'joint criminal enterprise' (within the meaning of the *ad hoc* tribunals' case law) and 'common purpose' within the meaning of the Rome Statute.

deviance, in which the individual conduct is intertwined with, and influenced by, collective thinking and behaviour.[2]

The limitations adopted with regard to the aforementioned doctrines in the context of the *ad hoc* tribunals and the ICC also delineate the outer bounds for the permissible ascription of punishable individual culpability in contemporary international criminal law. This is particularly relevant with regard to corporate officials. The Rome Statute contains express provisions pertaining to 'common purpose'[3] and superior responsibility[4] and these provisions are capable of potentially capturing the contributions of individual business actors to the commission of international crimes. The Court's chief prosecutor has already publicly announced his intentions to investigate corporate involvement in the exploitation of natural resources in Africa, and in particular the 'blood diamond' trade.[5] No cases alleging the responsibility of business 'war criminals' have materialised as yet. For the time being, the capacity of Articles 25 and 28 RS to effectively enclose within their reach the individual corporate facilitators of mass criminality remains untested.

The following exposition will therefore be only marginally concerned with economic actors (natural persons) *per se*. Post-Nuremberg case law, particularly in the context of the international criminal tribunals, on the liability of businessmen for their involvement in grave human rights abuse, is exceedingly scarce.[6] Understanding the scope of existing provisions – thus far employed predominantly with respect to political and military figures – is however a necessary pre-condition for assessing their transposibility to the corporate context. Regardless of whether ICC jurisdiction is extended to MNCs in the future, Articles 25 and 28 RS remain operative in relation to individual agents of such organisations. While such agents can directly commit, order or instigate international crimes, in most instances their participation is likely to be limited to indirect forms of facilitation. In this respect, the 'common purpose' and superior responsibility provisions of the Rome Statute draw the contours of punishable culpability with respect to corporate officials.

---

2 See Chapter 2, section II.1: Conceptualising corporate crime.

3 Article 25(3)(d) RS.

4 Article 28(b) RS.

5 Firms Face 'Blood Diamond' Probe, 23 September 2003, at <news.bbc.co.uk/2/hi/business/3133108.stm>.

6 On 3 December 2003, the ICTR found Ferdinand Nahimana and Jean-Bosco Barayagwiza (founders and programme directors of the RTLM radio station in Rwanda) guilty of public and direct incitement to genocide, conspiracy to commit genocide and crimes against humanity. Nahimana and Barayagwiza were not only held liable for their own acts but also incurred superior responsibility. See *Prosecutor v. Nahimana et al.*, Case No. ICTR-99-52-T, Judgment of 3 December 2003. Four years earlier, the ICTR had convicted Alfred Musema – the director of the Rwandan Gisovu Tea Factory – for genocide and crimes against humanity. See *Prosecutor v. Musema*, Case No. ICTR-96-13-A, Judgment and Sentence, 27 January 2000. Musema was found individually responsible on the basis of Article 6(1) ICTR for ordering, committing and aiding and abetting crimes. He was further held liable as a superior pursuant to Article 6(3) ICTR for crimes perpetrated by his subordinates.

II The 'common purpose' doctrine

Contemporary international criminal law does not recognise a crime of membership in a (criminal) organisation *per se.* However, the gist of the Nuremberg concept and conspiracy as a method of establishing individual liability are discernible in the crime of contributing to the activities of a group with a common criminal purpose. The latter has been extensively relied upon as a participation mode by the *ad hoc* tribunals for the former Yugoslavia (ICTY) and Rwanda (ICTR), and has also been incorporated in the Rome Statute of the International Criminal Court.

II.1 Joint criminal enterprise: doctrinal overview

The joint criminal enterprise (JCE) doctrine is the most complex and controversial liability theory recognised in international criminal law. First developed in the case law of the ICTY, it sought to address the challenge of attributing liability in a way that accurately reflects the relative responsibility of individuals for their contribution to group crimes.[7] Other existing liability modes at the time, e.g. complicity, conspiracy, criminal organisations and superior responsibility, had already recognised the reality of collective deviance and expanded individual responsibility beyond the physical perpetration of crimes. However, none appeared to adequately capture the culprits of system criminality. The Nuremberg legacy and their common law origins rendered the theories of conspiracy and group membership liability unsuitable for application at the international level.[8] Complicity did not recognise the principal liability of non-physical perpetrators who nevertheless dominated the commission of the crimes. Superior responsibility in turn failed to encompass scenarios in which the offences materialised outside the parameters of hierarchical relationships. JCE established a conceptual framework which was intended to fill the gap in legal accountability.

The *Delalic et al.* judgment pioneered the first explicit reference in modern jurisprudence to what the Trial Chamber called 'the common purpose doctrine'.[9] Since then, JCE has undergone unprecedented growth in scope and significance. With international prosecutors increasingly relying on JCE in their indictments,[10] stretching its application to the verge of what is acceptable in criminal law, concerns about the theory's implications have also intensified.

---

7 In its judgments, however, the ICTY has struggled with clearly defining the correct form of participation (principal and/or accessorial liability) to which JCE belongs. See section II.1.2 below.

8 For an extended discussion of the Nuremberg 'collective criminality' model, see Chapter 3.

9 *Prosecutor v. Delalic et al.*, ICTY Case No. IT-96-21-T, Judgment of 16 November 1998, para. 322.

10 See A.M. Danner and J.S. Martinez, Guilty Associations: Joint Criminal Enterprise, Command Responsibility, and the Development of International Criminal Law, 93 *California Law Review* 75 (2005) at 107-108. In the period 25 June 2001 (when the first indictment to explicitly rely on JCE was confirmed) and 1 January 2004 alone, between 64% and 81% of ICTY indictments (percentage varying depending on whether JCE was explicitly or implicitly employed by prosecutors) incorporated JCE as a mode of liability.

II.1.1 The elements of joint criminal enterprise as a mode of liability

The formal elements of JCE were comprehensively elaborated by the ICTY Appeals Chamber in *Tadic*.[11] Relying on the customary international law status of the common purpose doctrine – a rather controversial observation in itself[12] – the Bench determined that there were three different categories of JCE: basic, systematic and extended.[13]

The *actus reus* for each of the three categories is the same, namely: (1) a plurality of persons, (2) the existence of a common plan, design or purpose that amounts to or involves the commission of a crime provided for in the Statute, and (3) participation of the accused in the common design.[14]

The participants in the JCE need not be formally organised in a structure, be it political, military or administrative. Likewise, the common plan need not be pre-arranged or explicitly formulated but may materialise extemporaneously and be inferred from the fact that a plurality of persons acts in unison to carry out a common criminal objective.[15] The participation of the accused need not involve the commission of a specific crime and may take the form of assistance in, or contribution to, the execution of the joint criminal enterprise. The contribution may comprise encouragement or even omission,[16] and although it must have some causal significance, it need not be substantial to the extent that it must have been a necessary condition for the accomplishment of the crime.[17]

The *mens rea* elements, in their turn, are different for each of the three categories of JCE. Basic JCE concerns cases of co-perpetration and thus the requisite *mens rea* entails shared criminal intent among all participants in the common design to commit a crime. In order to be held liable the accused need not have physically perpetrated the crime; it would suffice that he voluntarily participated in one aspect of the common design with the intent that the crime be committed.[18]

---

11 *Prosecutor v. Tadic*, ICTY Case No. IT-94-1-A, Appeal Judgment of 15 July 1999. The earlier *Delalic et al.* judgment defined 'common purpose' liability as the liability of members of a group with a common purpose who knowingly participate in, and directly and substantially contribute to, the realisation of the group's purpose (*supra note 9*, para. 328). The Trial Chamber in *Delalic et al.*, however, failed to sufficiently elaborate on the elements of what subsequently became known as joint criminal enterprise.

12 See section II.1.2 below: Jurisprudential attempts at counteracting the drawbacks of the JCE doctrine.

13 Tadic, *supra note 11*, para. 195. See also *Prosecutor v. Kvocka et al.*, ICTY Case No. IT-98-30/1-A, Appeal Judgment of 28 February 2005, paras. 82-83.

14 Tadic, *supra note 11*, para. 227.

15 *Ibidem*, para. 227.

16 *Prosecutor v. Brdjanin*, ICTY Case No. IT-99-36-T, Judgment of 1 September 2004, para. 355.

17 *Prosecutor v. Brdjanin*, ICTY Case No. IT-99-36-T, Decision on Motion for Acquittal Pursuant to Rule 98bis, 28 November 2003, para. 26.

18 Tadic, *supra note 11*, para. 196.

Systematic JCE is a variant of the first category and relates to organised military or administrative units, which function as systems of ill-treatment (e.g. concentration camps). The *mens rea* elements include knowledge of the nature of the system and intent to further the common design of ill-treatment. Both participation and intent may be inferred from the accused's position of authority within the organisational hierarchy.[19] Systematic JCE, however, may also apply to persons from outside the system who knowingly and purposefully contribute to its objectives.[20]

Extended JCE applies to cases where crimes occur outside of the common design but are nevertheless a result of the JCE execution. The *mens rea* requirements for this third category of JCE comprise: (1) intent on the part of the accused to participate in a joint criminal enterprise and to further its objectives, (2) the crime committed, although not a part of the common plan, was a natural and foreseeable result of the attempt to carry out the common plan, and (3) the accused, aware that other members of the JCE might commit the crime in the course of the JCE execution, willingly took that risk.[21] What is required of the accused is *dolus eventualis*, i.e. knowledge that a given consequence may occur and acceptance of that risk. The meaning accorded to *dolus eventualis* by the tribunal positions it on the fault line between *dolus* and *culpa* and is of the same scope as that accorded to advertent recklessness in some common law systems.[22]

All participants in category one (basic) and category two (systematic) JCE may be held liable for any of the crimes committed within the common criminal design, even those of them who did not physically perpetrate the crimes. The third category (extended) JCE envisages liability for criminal acts committed by others even when these acts fell outside of the common plan and the accused neither knew of nor fully intended their commission.

Among legal scholars and practitioners, the low threshold of the requisite *mens rea* in category three JCE has spurred vigorous criticism of the direction in which the ICTY-contrived doctrine of joint criminal enterprise has been developing. The implication made by the ICTR Trial Chamber in *Kayishema* to the effect that individuals may be held responsible under extended JCE for crimes that were objectively foreseeable even if the accused did not himself foresee the crimes,[23] has only further exasperated critics. Some legal commentators have suggested that the

19 *Ibidem*, para. 228.

20 See *Prosecutor v. Kvocka et al.*, ICTY Case No. IT-98-30/1-T, Judgment of 2 November 2001, para. 610, where a civilian who entered the camp regularly to physically abuse detainees was also found to have acted within the systematic JCE.

21 See e.g. Kvocka et al., *supra note 13*, para. 83; *Prosecutor v. Vasiljevic*, ICTY Case No. IT-93-32-A, Appeal Judgment of 25 February 2004, para. 101; *Prosecutor v. Stakic*, ICTY Case No. IT-97-24-T, Judgment of 31 July 2003, para. 436; Tadic, *supra note 11*, paras. 220, 228.

22 Tadic, *supra note 11*, para. 220.

23 *Prosecutor v. Kayishema*, ICTR-95-1-T, Judgment of 21 May 1999, paras. 203-204.

adoption of such reasoning may effectively lower the requisite level of *mens rea* for category three JCE even further – from recklessness to negligence.[24]

II.1.2 Jurisprudential attempts at counteracting the drawbacks of the JCE doctrine

The Statutes of the *ad hoc* tribunals do not contain any express references to joint criminal enterprise as a mode of criminal responsibility. In their case law, however, both tribunals have come to consider JCE a form of individual liability, falling within the scope of existing statutory provisions. These provisions are Articles 7(1) and 6(1) of the ICTY and ICTR Statutes respectively, stipulating that:

> A person who planned, instigated, ordered, committed or otherwise aided and abetted in the planning, preparation or execution of a crime referred to in [...] the present Statute, shall be individually responsible for the crime.

The interpretation of participation in a joint criminal enterprise as a form of 'commission' was first expounded in *Tadic*[25] and subsequently affirmed as giving rise to principal liability in a succession of judgments.[26] In *Ojdanic*,[27] the Appeals Chamber stated that even if JCE could be considered not to amount to commission, it would still fall under Article 7(1), which provides for the liability of individuals who 'otherwise aided or abetted' crimes within the jurisdiction of the Tribunal. At the same time, however, it also expounded that JCE constituted a form of commission 'insofar as a participant shares the purpose of the JCE [...] as opposed to merely knowing about it'.[28]

II.1.2a The customary law origins of JCE

Early debates about the JCE doctrine centered on its origins and the contentious determination by the ICTY that JCE was 'firmly established in customary international law'.[29] Many legal scholars have challenged this sweeping statement, pointing out that

---

24 Danner and Martinez, *supra note 10*, at 109.

25 Tadic, *supra note 11*, paras. 188-189.

26 E.g. *Prosecutor v. Gacumbitsi*, Case No. ICTR-2001-64-A, Appeal Judgment of 7 July 2006, para. 158; *Prosecutor v. Ntakirutimana*, Case No. ICTR-96-10-A, Appeal Judgment of 13 December 2004, para. 462; *Prosecutor v. Milutinovic*, Decision on Dragoljub Ojdanic's Motion Challenging Jurisdiction, ICTY Case No. IT-99-37-AR72, 21 May 2003, para. 20.

27 Milutinovic, Decision on Dragoljub Ojdanic's Motion Challenging Jurisdiction, *supra note 26*, para. 19.

28 *Ibidem*, para. 20. Some Trial Chambers have previously accepted the distinction between co-perpetrators and aiders and abettors in the context of JCE (e.g. Kvocka et al., *supra note 20*, para. 284; *Prosecutor v. Krstic*, ICTY Case No. IT-98-33-T, Judgment of 2 August 2001, paras. 643-645). For a critique of the Appeal Chamber's refusal to 'distinguish among defendants according to the weight of each defendant's contribution' to the JCE, see K. Ambos, Joint Criminal Enterprise and Command Responsibility, 5 *Journal of International Criminal Justice* 159 (2007).

29 Tadic, *supra note 11*, para. 220.

only some of the cases cited in *Tadic* are indicative of liability being based on a theory of a 'common plan or design'.[30] Moreover, there is very little, if any, evidence suggesting that JCE in its extended form was employed by national courts and tribunals in the immediate aftermath of the Second World War. In their case law, however, the *ad hoc* tribunals have accepted the *Tadic* judgment as *obiter dictum* and refrained from revisiting the findings related to the customary status of JCE.[31] Attempts to contest the definition of JCE as a form of principal liability under customary international law have also been unsuccessful. Despite some inconsistencies in case law,[32] the Appeals Chamber has expressly rejected assertions that JCE gives rise to the responsibility of individuals as accessories to crimes.[33] In *Ojdanic*[34] and *Karemera*,[35] the Appeals Chamber furthermore affirmed that, under customary international law, liability attached to all three forms of participation in a joint criminal enterprise.

Some may argue that, despite its controversial genesis, JCE (and in particular its extended variant) has nowadays attained customary status since it has been generally accepted and extensively utilised by the *ad hoc* tribunals in the past decade. However, this does not alleviate concerns pertaining to the possible infringements of the *nullum crimen sine lege* principle in the context of category three JCE cases. Neither does it find confirmation in the Rome Statute of the International Criminal Court. While the Statute appears to codify modalities of participation reflecting the scope of basic (and also arguably systematic) JCE, a similar recognition of the extended form is lacking. In any case, the inclusion of the 'common purpose' notion within the Rome Statute renders the ongoing debate about its customary status only marginally relevant to the ICC. As will be seen below, Article 25(3)(d) RS explicitly provides for 'common purpose' liability, already interpreted by Pre-Trial Chamber I as 'a residual form of accessorial liability'.[36] In a recent decision concerning the scope of Article 25, the

---

30 See e.g. Danner and Martinez, *supra note 10*, at 110-113; S. Powles, Joint Criminal Enterprise. Criminal Liability by Prosecutorial Ingenuity and Judicial Creativity?, 2 *Journal of International Criminal Justice* 606 (2004) at 614-617; E. van Sliedregt, *The Criminal Responsibility of Individuals for Violations of International Humanitarian Law*, The Hague: T.M.C. Asser Press, 2003, pp. 96-99.

31 For a critical appraisal of the *ad hoc* tribunals' reliance on Nuremberg case law as a source for regarding JCE a form of principal liability, see H. Olasolo, *The Criminal Responsibility of Senior Political and Military Leaders as Principals to International Crimes*, Oxford: Hart Publishing, 2009, pp. 55-57.

32 The contention pertaining to the interpretation of the common purpose doctrine as a form of accessorial liability was first introduced in *Prosecutor v. Brdjanin*, Decision on Motion by Momir Talic for Provisional Release, ICTY Case No. IT-99-36-T, 28 March 2001, paras. 40-45 and subsequently affirmed in Kvocka et al. (*supra note 20*, paras. 250-253).

33 Milutinovic, Decision on Dragoljub Ojdanic's Motion Challenging Jurisdiction, Joint Criminal Enterprise, *supra note 26*, paras. 20, 31.

34 *Ibidem*, paras. 21, 29.

35 *Keremera v. Prosecutor*, Appeals Chamber Decision on Jurisdictional Appeals: Joint Criminal Enterprise, Case No. ICTR-98-44-AR72.5, 12 April 2006, para. 13.

36 *Prosecutor v. Thomas Lubanga Dyilo*, Decision on the confirmation of charges, ICC-01/04-01/06-803-tEN, 29 January 2007, para. 483.

Court has furthermore emphasised the primacy of the Statute over other sources of law.[37] Lack of recognition in customary international law is, therefore, unlikely to preclude the application of a participation mode expressly codified in the Rome Statute.

II.1.2b The inherent complexities of extended JCE

Presently, the principal controversy surrounding the JCE doctrine in the context of the *ad hoc* tribunals concerns the broad scope of application of category three (extended) JCE. The latter has the propensity to encompass within its reach crimes extending over great geographical distances, lengthy periods of time and persons far removed from both the place and time of the crimes committed.[38] This in turn has prompted criticism that the doctrine strays dangerously far from the principle of personal culpability. Not only are there no restrictions on the scope of joint criminal enterprises that prosecutors may allege, there is also no requirement of a substantial contribution for a person to be convicted as a JCE participant. In this regard Danner and Martinez have contended that, because the doctrine has been interpreted and applied too broadly, it may slip into guilt by association, threatening the legitimacy of international criminal law.[39] From the perspective of the individual defendant, the fluidity of JCE dangerously blurs the imperative requirements of due process. As pointed out by Van der Wilt, it also detracts from the principle of legality.[40] Similarly to the Nuremberg 'collective criminality' model, the doctrine of joint criminal enterprise creates the impression of unfairness for its endorsement of what might be perceived as collective responsibility and punishment.

In *Brdjanin*,[41] the ICTY sought to restrict the scope of application of JCE in a way which, according to some, amounted to 'misguided overcorrection' of the doctrine's

---

37 *Prosecutor v. Germain Katanga and Mathieu Ngudjolo Chui*, Decision on the confirmation of charges, ICC-01/04-01/07-717, 30 September 2008, para. 508: '[U]nder article 21(1)(a) of the Statute, the first source of applicable law is the Statute. Principles and rules of international law constitute a secondary source applicable only when the statutory material fails to prescribe a legal solution.' Pre-Trial Chamber I, therefore, concluded that the (lack of) customary status of specific modes of liability was irrelevant where the modes concerned had been incorporated in the Rome Statute. The particular determination was made in relation to objections raised by the Defence on the issue of 'indirect co-perpetration' and the permissibility of its inclusion within the scope of Article 25(3)(a) RS.

38 Van der Wilt, for instance, questions the operative value of JCE as an avenue for holding accountable political and military leaders in particular. See H. G. van der Wilt, Joint Criminal Enterprise. Possibilities and Limitations, 5 *Journal of International Criminal Justice* 91 (2007).

39 Danner and Martinez, *supra note 10*, at 79.

40 Van der Wilt, *supra note 38*, at 100.

41 Brdjanin, *supra note 16*.

extensive reach.[42] The Trial Chamber focused on the *actus reus,* and in particular the requirement of a common plan that amounts to or involves the commission of a crime. It interpreted the prerequisites set out in *Tadic* narrowly. The Bench re-affirmed that it was not necessary to prove that every JCE member intended each of the enterprise's criminal objectives. However, it also held that the prosecutor had to prove the existence of an agreement to commit at least that particular crime between the person physically committing the material crime and the individual held responsible under the JCE.[43] In this connection it furthermore required membership of the material perpetrators in the JCE and ruled that JCE was an inappropriate mode of liability in large cases.

The implications of the Trial Chamber's approach taken in *Brdjanin* were manifold. It appeared that JCEs could no longer include unidentified individuals as the physical perpetrators of crimes since proving the existence of a common criminal plan required evidence of direct mutual agreement between the accused and the material perpetrator. Although the agreement did not need to be explicit and pre-arranged and could be inferred from the circumstances,[44] the physical perpetrator and his link to the defendant had to be identifiable. Furthermore, the existence of the agreement could not be deduced exclusively from evidence pointing in the direction of shared criminal intent between the accused and the physical perpetrator's superior[45] or from general strategic plans.[46] Conclusions about the existence of the agreement could be inferred only if it was 'the only reasonable inference available from the evidence'.[47] The Trial Chamber in *Brdjanin* thus interpreted JCE somewhat along conspiracy lines.

However, the categorisation of JCE participants into 'physical perpetrators' and 'others' appeared to obscure the true extent of the responsibility of those individuals who, although far removed from the site of crimes, are nevertheless the masterminds behind their commission. It threatened the reduction of extended JCE into a form of

---

42 A. O'Rourke, Joint Criminal Enterprise and Brdjanin: Misguided Overcorrection, 47 *Harvard International Law Journal* 307 (2006). Also K. Gustafson: The Requirement of an 'Express Agreement' for Joint Criminal Enterprise Liability: a Critique of Brdjanin, 5 *Journal of International Criminal Justice* 134 (2007). For a different point of view, see Van der Wilt, *supra note 38*, contending that 'it would be incorrect to blame the ICTY for this restrictive approach. Rather it should be considered an honourable effort to save the ICTY from relapsing into the earlier errors of the Nuremberg Tribunal' (at 99-100).

43 Brdjanin, *supra note 16*, para. 264. A similar conclusion was reached earlier by the Trial Chamber in *Prosecutor v. Krnojelac*, ICTY Case No. IT-97-25-T, Judgment of 15 March 2002. Unlike the *Brdjanin* Case, *Krnojelac* concerned category two (systematic) JCE. The Trial Chamber required proof of an agreement between the accused and the physical perpetrator for each specific crime charged within the joint criminal enterprise (paras. 170, 187).

44 Brdjanin, *supra note 16*, para. 262.

45 *Ibidem*, para. 347.

46 *Idem*, para. 351. The Trial Chamber considered that merely espousing a strategic plan could not suffice to prove mutual agreement as the criminal objectives of the plan could be intended 'independently' by different persons, without an understanding or an agreement between them to that effect.

47 *Idem*, para. 353.

mere accomplice liability. Although this might have appeased critics of extended JCE in that accomplice liability requires a slightly higher level of proof,[48] the value of JCE for capturing those individuals whom other modes of perpetration could not encompass, would have been largely lost.

Brdjanin sought to furthermore effectively restrict the size of JCEs that prosecutors could allege. It thus partially addressed valid concerns on the part of those critics who have contended that the doctrine had overexpanded to apply to atrocities on a nation-wide scale involving thousands of participants.[49] At the same time, the ruling threatened to diminish the intrinsic value of the JCE doctrine, whose flexibility was what prompted the ICTY to adopt it in the first place.

The *Brdjanin* trial judgment did not remain standing on appeal. Recognising the reality of JCEs that exist at the leadership level (comprising masterminds who use material perpetrators as 'tools' to carry out a criminal plan),[50] the Appeals Chamber refused to affirm the requirements expounded by the lower division. While acknowledging the inappropriateness of imposing liability on a person where the link to the physical perpetrator is too tenuous, it nevertheless considered the requisite existence of an additional agreement between the accused and the actual perpetrator unnecessary. In response to the Defence contention that JCE constituted an open-ended concept allowing convictions by mere group association, the Appeals Chamber emphasised that criminal responsibility pursuant to JCE always entails some form of participation in a criminal plan.[51] As long as there was a shared criminal plan at the JCE level, acting by means of a person (i.e. the material perpetrator) under the control of another member of the JCE would give rise to liability even where the accused is structurally removed from the actual perpetrator.

I.1.2c Critical appraisal of the *ad hoc* tribunals' approach to JCE

Although the risk of unjustifiable extension of liability may not materialise in any given circumstances, the joint criminal enterprise doctrine, particularly in its extended

---

48 Complicity as aiding and abetting in the jurisprudence of the *ad hoc* tribunals requires that an individual carry out acts specifically directed to assist, encourage or lend moral support to the perpetration of a crime (Tadic, *supra note 11*, para. 229). By contrast, for JCE liability it is sufficient for the participant to perform acts that in some way are directed at the furthering of a common plan or purpose. The distinction between aiding and abetting and JCE has recently been upheld in *Prosecutor v. Krajisnik*, ICTY Case No. IT-00-39-T, Judgment of 27 September 2006, para. 885.

49 D. Robinson, *The Identity Crisis of International Criminal Law* (working paper), 2008, p. 24, at <papers.ssrn.com/sol3/papers.cfm?abstract_id=1127851>.

50 *Prosecutor v. Brdjanin*, ICTY Case No. IT-99-36-A, Appeal Judgment of 3 April 2007, p. 113. For a critical discussion of the 're-conceptualisation' of joint criminal enterprise, from a concept applicable to group crimes at the execution level to a liability theory interlinking JCEs at the execution and policy levels, see E. van Sliedregt, System Criminality at the ICTY, in: A. Nollkaemper and H.G. van der Wilt, *System Criminality in International Law*, Cambridge: Cambridge University Press, 2009.

51 Brdjanin, *supra note 50*, para. 424.

form, remains prone to abuse. In order to offset the tension between the elastic nature of JCE and the principle of personal guilt, various trial chambers have made an effort to extend the level of the requisite contribution to 'significant',[52] while accepting that it need not amount to a *conditio sine qua non* for the commission of the crime. Such attempts, however, have invariably faltered on appeal. The repeated failure to define the element of participation more narrowly is regrettable. It conceals a danger of implicating by means of 'guilty association' a multitude of individuals far removed both physically and in terms of involvement from the crimes being prosecuted. This in turn has perpetuated criticism that JCE has the propensity to expose to principal liability even the most insignificant contributors and can better be described as a 'just convict everyone' stratagem.[53] In this connection, Olasolo has contended that raising the participation threshold would have no real practical value, as it would fail to address the reality of interrelations between senior leaders as the masterminds of crimes and the physical perpetrators of those crimes.[54] This is true to the extent that the traditional JCE doctrine indeed appears ill suited for the prosecution of political and military leadership. The *ad hoc* tribunals have recognised and sought to overcome shortcomings in that regard by adopting the notion of joint criminal enterprise at the leadership level.[55] However, this does not negate concerns about the possible implications of extended JCE for individuals in non-leadership positions.

Also disturbing is the *ad hoc* tribunals' leniency in allowing prosecutors to plead JCE, particularly in its extended form, in relation to specific intent crimes such as genocide and persecution.[56] In this regard, the Appeals Chamber in *Brdjanin* contended that the *mens rea* requirement of the crime of genocide ought not to be conflated with the mental element of the JCE mode of liability.[57] Judge Shahabuddeen's unsound interpretation of the Chamber's equally flawed conclusion maintains that, rather than eliminating the need to prove intent, the third category of JCE provides a mode of proving intent in particular circumstances, i.e. by proof of foresight in those circumstances.[58] In effect, however, the tribunals have dispensed with the requirement that *dolus specialis* be established if the accused is to incur liability for specific intent offences. The *mens rea* that attaches to the definition of a crime is an inseparable component of that crime. In this connection, as pointed out by

52 E.g. *Prosecutor v. Simic et al.*, ICTY Case No. IT-95-9-T, Judgment of 17 October 2003, para. 159; Kvocka et al., *supra note 20*, para. 309.

53 M.E. Badar, Just Convict Everyone!: Joint Perpetration from Tadic to Stakic and Back Again, 6 *International Criminal Law Review* 293 (2006).

54 Olasolo, *supra note 31,* pp. 193, 231.

55 Brdjanin, *supra note 50.*

56 For a criticism of the adopted approach, see D. Robinson, *supra note 49*; Ambos, *supra note 28*; D.L. Nersessian, Whoops, I Committed Genocide! The Anomaly of Constructive Liability for Serious International Crimes, 30 SUM *Fletcher Forum of World Affairs* 81 (2006).

57 *Prosecutor v. Brdjanin,* Decision on Interlocutory Appeal, ICTY Case No. IT-99-36-A, 19 March 2004, para. 10.

58 Separate Opinion of Judge Shahabuddeen, Brdjanin, *supra note 57*, para. 2

Olasolo, principals in the context of JCE ought to incur liability only if it can be established that they possessed the specific mental state required by the crime.[59]

In their jurisprudence, the *ad hoc* tribunals have sought to contain the JCE doctrine and ensure that it does not translate into strict liability or mass punishment. As seen above, however, the requirements affirmed necessitate additional safeguards, such as e.g. restricting the type of crimes to which JCE applies and more narrowly defining the element of 'participation'. Nevertheless, the existing drawbacks of the doctrine do not entirely negate its value. The idiosyncrasies of the crimes adjudicated by the international tribunals undoubtedly call for creative legal approaches to prosecution. Mass atrocities are typically characterised by the distribution of criminal activity among numerous perpetrators with distinct but interrelated functions. As cogently put by Van der Wilt, 'a one-sided emphasis on personal guilt may obscure the collective dimension of system criminality'.[60] The decentralised structure of collective criminality, the scale of the offenses committed, the physical distance between the agents of crime, and the corresponding evidentiary barriers pose furthermore considerable challenges for prosecutors. In this regard, the JCE doctrine is better equipped than other modes of liability to capture those individuals outside of formal chains of command who, through multifaceted relationships amounting in essence to mutual connivance, perpetrate international crimes.

With the tribunals set to close down in a few years, concerns about the possible overexpansion of the joint criminal enterprise doctrine become of predominantly theoretical significance. This is not to deny the difficulties faced by defence teams in numerous trials involving JCE as a mode of principal liability in the past. Neither does it refute the doctrine's shortcomings. There are, however, indications that JCE as interpreted and applied by the *ad hoc* tribunals will not persist in international criminal law. The ICC in particular already seems bound on a different path.

II.2 The 'common purpose' concept in the Rome Statute

The Rome Statute appears not to recognise JCE in its extended form. The notion of 'common purpose' liability, however, is present and operative in Article 25(3)(d) RS, which reads:

> [A] person shall be criminally responsible and liable for punishment for a crime within the jurisdiction of the Court if that person:
> [...]

59 Olasolo, *supra note 31*, p. 180. For a more nuanced perspective on constructing the culpability of JCE members in relation to genocide, see E. van Sliedregt, Joint Criminal Enterprise as a Pathway to Convicting Individuals for Genocide, 5 *Journal of International Criminal Justice* 184 (2006).

60 Van der Wilt, *supra note 38*, at 108.

> In any other way contributed to the commission or attempted commission of such a crime by a group of persons acting with a common purpose. Such contribution shall be intentional and shall either:
> (i) Be made with the aim of furthering the criminal activity or criminal purpose of the group, where such activity or purpose involves the commission of a crime within the jurisdiction of the Court; or
> (ii) Be made in the knowledge of the intention of the group to commit the crime.

Article 25(3)(d) thus provides for the liability of natural persons, who are 'accessories' or 'secondary participants in acts of complicity'.[61] While the *ad hoc* tribunals have adopted a predominantly subjective approach to the distinction between principals and participants in crimes,[62] the ICC bases its understanding of liability for group crimes on the notion of control of the crime.[63] According to that notion, only those individuals who make essential contributions to the objective elements of the crime and hence control the realisation of the crime, will incur principal liability. As a result, and unlike the *ad hoc* tribunals, the ICC favours the interpretation of 'common purpose' liability as a form of complicity in collective criminal activities through which persons may be held culpable as accessories only.

In itself, sub-paragraph 3d of Article 25 establishes the lowest objective threshold for individual participation,[64] as it criminalises 'any other way' that contributes to the commission of a crime within the jurisdiction of the Court and is not already covered in the remaining provisions of the particular article. It is thus a subsidiary means for imposing criminal responsibility.[65] In this regard Pre-Trial Chamber I in the *Lubanga* Case has held that:

> [A]rticle 25(3)(d) of the Statute provides for a residual form of accessory liability which makes it possible to criminalise those contributions to a crime which cannot be characterised as ordering, soliciting, inducing, aiding, abetting or assisting within the meaning of article 25(3)(b) or article 25(3)(c) of the Statute, by reason of the state of mind in which the contributions were made.[66]

Sub-paragraph 3d differs from other liability modes set out in Article 25 RS in that its application is confined to individuals who further the criminal activities of a group with

61 K. Kittichaisaree, *International Criminal Law*, Oxford: Oxford University Press, 2001, p. 234.

62 See section II.1.2b above.

63 *Prosecutor v. Thomas Lubanga Dyilo*, *supra note 36*, para. 338. See also Olasolo, *supra note 31*, who argues that recourse to the control of the crime approach on the part of the ICC has been a natural and desirable consequence to the *ad hoc* tribunals' extended jurisprudential struggle with the doctrine of joint criminal enterprise, particularly in relation to senior political and military leaders.

64 K. Ambos, Article 25: Individual Criminal Responsibility, in: O. Triffterer (ed.), *Commentary on the Rome Statute of the International Criminal Court*, Baden-Baden: Nomos, 1999, p. 484.

65 *Ibidem*.

66 Lubanga, *supra note 36,* para. 337.

a common purpose. Although the accused need not share the criminal plan, nor aim at the implementation of that plan, the contribution must be made at least in the knowledge that it will assist in the commission of a crime that falls within the common purpose.

It will ultimately be within the discretion of the ICC judiciary to delineate the conditions under which an individual will incur liability for furthering the execution of a common criminal plan by a collective as stipulated by Article 25(3)(d). Presumably the Court will take relevant ICTY and ICTR jurisprudence on the JCE doctrine into consideration when interpreting the precise scope of the *actus reus* and *mens rea* of the crime encompassed by the 'common purpose' provision of the Rome Statute. The Appeals Chamber in *Tadic* has in fact noted that its rendition of complicity in group settings reflects 'substantially similar notions' to those stipulated in sub-paragraph 3d of Article 25 RS.[67]

II.2.1 The divergent nature of Article 25(3)(d) RS

Legal commentators, however, have expressed doubts as to the compatibility of interpretations regarding the 'common purpose' provision in the context of the ICC with the case law of the *ad hoc* tribunals. In particular, the scope of the term 'intentional' in Article 25(3)(d) appears to give rise to some controversies.

The overarching *mens rea* provision in the Rome Statute – Article 30 – stipulates 'intent' in the traditional sense, i.e. including volition and knowledge. This has prompted Van Sliedregt to contend that Article 25(3)(d) will have to be interpreted strictly.[68] She regards sub-paragraph 3d of Article 25 as excluding the possibility of liability based on *dolus eventualis*. As stipulated earlier, *dolus eventualis* as employed by the *ad hoc* tribunals designates the mental state of a person who does not specifically intend to bring about a certain consequence but is aware of the likelihood of that criminal consequence and is willing to accept the risk. Interestingly, however, in the *Lubanga* Case, Pre-Trial Chamber I of the ICC has recently interpreted Article 30 to encompass not only *dolus directus* (in the first and second degree)[69] but also *dolus eventualis* to the extent that the accused must be shown to have reconciled himself with the causation of the objective elements of a crime that may foreseeably follow his intended action or omission.[70]

Similarly to Van Sliedregt, Ambos perceives the additional subjective requirements stipulated in sub-paragraphs (i) and (ii) and defining the term 'intentional' in more concrete terms, as rendering Article 25(3)(d) of a somewhat different scope of applicability than that adopted by the *ad hoc* tribunals in relation to JCE.[71] The ICTY

67 Tadic, *supra note 11*, para. 222.
68 Van Sliedregt, *supra note 30*, pp. 50-52.
69 For an extensive discussion of Article 30 RS and the distinction between various degrees of *dolus*, see Chapter 5, section II: The ambit of *actus reus* and *mens rea* in the Rome Statute.
70 Lubanga, *supra note 36*, paras. 352-355.
71 Ambos, *supra note 64*, p. 485.

and ICTR understand the *mens rea* of participation in a joint criminal enterprise as general intent to further a criminal purpose and awareness that a crime may be committed. Article 25(3)(d) RS expounds a narrower definition of the requisite subjective element. It requires that the accused acted in pursuance of the strictly specific objectives of the group whose activity he or she sought to further. It also stipulates that the accused be proven to have been aware of the specific crime intended by the group.[72] Thus, although the Court has ruled that *dolus eventualis* falls within the scope of Article 30 RS, such a standard of *mens rea* does not appear applicable to sub-paragraph 3d of Article 25. The 'common purpose' provision in the Rome Statute embraces positive knowledge as the mental element of the crime of participation in a group with a common purpose.

In this regard, the 'common purpose' concept, enshrined in the Rome Statute, does indeed appear to deviate from established interpretations of the requisite *mens rea* in relation to JCE as applied in the case law of the *ad hoc* tribunals. This may have been partially motivated by the controversies surrounding JCE's application by the ICTY and ICTR and the perceived need to circumscribe the doctrine's overexpansive reach. The scope of the 'common purpose' provision in the Rome Statute, however, raises some questions of its own.

II.2.2 A redundant provision?

The distinction between 'common purpose' (Article 25(3)(d)) and complicity as aiding and abetting (Article 25(3)(c)) is not clear-cut in the Rome Statute. In essence, aiding and abetting as a liability mode in international criminal law encompasses any assistance, physical or psychological, that has a substantial effect on the commission of a crime.[73] It may consist of either an act or an omission[74] and there is no requirement that the aider or abettor is present at the time of the commission of the crime or that the main perpetrator is aware of the aider or abettor's contribution.[75] What constitutes a 'substantial effect' is determined subjectively, on a case-to-case basis.[76]

Despite both being a form of complicity, Article 25 RS expounds 'acting pursuant to a common criminal purpose' and 'aiding and abetting' in two separate provisions. In the case of aiding and abetting within the meaning of Article 25(3)(c), no proof is required of the (pre-) existence of a common concerted plan. The requisite mental element is knowledge that the assistance facilitates the commission of a specific crime. This requirement goes beyond the principles developed by the *ad hoc* tribunals, which

72 *Ibidem*, p. 486.

73 *Prosecutor v. Aleksovski*, ICTY Case No. IT-95-14/1-A, Appeal Judgment of 24 March 2000, para. 162; *Prosecutor v. Furundzija*, ICTY Case No. IT-95-17/1-T, Judgment of 10 December 1998, paras. 235-236, 249, 199-209, 217-226; *Prosecutor v. Kambanda*, Case No. ICTR-97-23-S, Judgment of 4 September 1998, paras. 39(v), (viii), (xi).

74 *Prosecutor v. Blaskic*, ICTY Case No. IT-95-14-T, Judgment of 3 March 2000, para. 284.

75 Kittichaisaree, *supra note 61*, p. 243.

76 Furundzija, *supra note 73*, paras. 217-225.

set forth that the aider and abettor must only know that his acts contribute to the commission of a crime, but not its particular nature. At the same time, however, aiding and abetting in the context of Article 25(3)(c) deviates from the corresponding provisions in the Statutes of the *ad hoc* tribunals and established case law, in that substantial assistance is not explicitly stipulated as a prerequisite for incurring accomplice liability.[77] Thus Article 25(3)(c) provides for a lower objective, but a higher subjective, threshold in comparison to the corresponding provisions on aiding and abetting of the ICTY and ICTR Statutes.[78]

Given the wide scope of liability for an aider and abettor according to Article 25(3)(c), it is conceivable that a case that entails individual criminal responsibility under sub-paragraph 3d will accordingly also entail liability in the sense of aiding and abetting.[79] Similarly to sub-paragraph 3c, sub-paragraph 3d of Article 25 stipulates a rather strict subjective threshold, namely that the assistance extended facilitates a specific criminal objective. Sub-paragraph 3d, however, features a higher *mens rea* requirement. It envisages an intentional contribution to a group crime, supplemented by the additional criteria in sub-sections (i) and (ii).[80] Thus, sub-paragraph 3d could be considered to encompass the notion of aiding and abetting in collective settings.

The existing overlap between aiding and abetting and the 'common purpose' provision of the Rome Statute has prompted Ambos, for instance, to regard Article 25(3)(d) as 'simply superfluous'.[81] Schabas, on the other hand, perceives it as a failed attempt by 'exhausted drafters' to incorporate into the Statute the crime of conspiracy to commit genocide while avoiding the controversy surrounding the conspiracy doctrine since Nuremberg.[82]

The propensity of sub-paragraph 3c to subsume, in given circumstances, liability for assisting the commission of a collective crime may nevertheless have a constructive function. In cases where both complicity modes are applicable, it would enable the selection of that liability form that better describes the role played by the accused. Moreover, as will be recalled, contribution to a group crime has already been construed by the ICC as a mere subsidiary mode of participation yielding the weakest

---

77 In *Furundzija* (*ibidem*, paras. 217, 233-234), the Trial Chamber did not consider a causal relationship in the sense of *conditio sine qua non* necessary but held that the acts of assistance on the part of the aider or abettor must 'make a significant difference to the commission of the criminal act by the principal'. With regard to the Rome Statute, the Chamber noted that the notion of aiding and abetting contained therein was less restrictive, as it was not limited to acts which 'directly and substantially' assisted the perpetrator (para. 231).

78 Ambos, *supra note 64*, p. 384.

79 *Ibidem*, p. 401.

80 *Idem*.

81 K. Ambos, General Principles of Criminal Law in the Rome Statute, 10 *Criminal Law Forum*, Dordrecht: Kluwer Academic Publishers, 1999, p. 13.

82 W.A. Schabas, *Genocide in International Law: The Crime of Crimes*, Cambridge: Cambridge University Press, 2000, pp. 259-266.

form of accessorial liability.[83] This in turn may be invoked to justify differences in sentencing outcomes. Should prosecutors seek to abuse the broad scope of Article 25(3)(c), for it would not require proof of the existence of a group with a common purpose and may presumably entail a higher sentence, the power of the judiciary to request amendments to the charges enshrined in Article 61(7)(c)(ii) RS may provide a balancing check.[84]

The restricted formulation of the 'common purpose' provision in the Rome Statute partially reflects the unease of drafters, legal scholars and defence counsel with the never-ending controversies surrounding the application of the joint criminal enterprise doctrine in the case law of the *ad hoc* tribunals. It further seeks to circumvent the negative connotations inherent in employing conspiracy as a mode of establishing individual liability for group crimes. Some may argue that by eliminating its extended variant and adopting stricter requirements in general, the Rome Statute overly restricts the intrinsic value of the 'common design' theory. In this sense, Pre-Trial Chamber I's interpretation of Article 25(3)(d) as residual form of accessorial liability may be perceived as unfortunate. Such concerns are, however, largely unwarranted. The limitations underlying sub-paragraph 3d of Article 25 dispense with criticism targeting the (potentially) overexpansive reach of liability for low-level participation in collective criminality, and corresponding arguments pertaining to the dangers of guilt by association. As for the involvement of leaders in collective criminality, the Rome Statute enables prosecution without recourse to the troubled JCE doctrine. While superiors who are involved, albeit not physically, in the commission of crimes may be prosecuted as either direct or indirect (co-)perpetrators under Article 25(3)(a), those who assist the commission of crimes by their subordinates through a failure to exercise duty of control properly, run the risk of incurring responsibility pursuant to Article 28.

---

83 Lubanga, *supra note 36,* para. 337.

84 See *Prosecutor v. Jean-Pierre Bemba Gombo*, Decision Adjourning the Hearing Pursuant to Article 61(7)(c)(ii) of the Rome Statute, ICC-01/05-01/08-388, 3 March 2009. In the *Bemba* Case, Pre-Trial Chamber III interpreted the notion of 'a different crime' within the meaning of Article 61(7)(c)(ii) of the Rome Statute as encompassing also the various modes of liability referred to in Articles 25 and 28. Expounding the view that the evidence submitted appeared to establish the applicability of a different mode of liability than the one pleaded in the indictment, the Chamber requested the Prosecutor to consider submitting an amended charging document. While emphasising that, by adjourning the hearing it did not purport to impinge on the Prosecutor's discretion as to the formulation of the charges, the Chamber in effect advised the Prosecutor to review his strategy and base his allegations on the mode of liability deemed by the judges to most adequately reflect the nature of the suspect's participation in the crimes alleged.

III The concept of superior responsibility

The doctrine of superior responsibility[85] constitutes the second pillar of the post-Nuremberg 'collective criminality' model. The rationale behind its inception and development is very much the same as that behind the theory of common purpose. Both recognise the multifaceted collective nature of mass crimes and seek to capture those individuals who, albeit removed from the scene of physical perpetration, contribute to the commission of crimes by others. Just as they have attempted to interpret the concept of JCE participation, international prosecutors have sought to stretch the limits of application of the doctrine of superior responsibility, especially when faced by evidentiary barriers. Accordingly, the development of the doctrine has not been immune to criticism.

III.1 Brief historical survey of the development of the doctrine

The superior responsibility concept was established in principle by the 1907 Hague Conventions IV and X, explicitly stipulating the affirmative duties of military commanders in relation to the conduct of their subordinates.[86] The Leipzig proceedings, instituted by the Allied Powers after the end of the First World War against German officers for their failure to prevent the commission of crimes by their subordinates, constituted the first practical affirmation of the doctrine in concrete terms.[87] However, it was not until several decades later that, as a result of the Second World War, superior responsibility became applicable to all persons with *de facto* or *de jure* power above others, whether in a military context or not.

The International Military Tribunal of Nuremberg did not explicitly rely on the concept of superior responsibility in its judgments against German government officials although it invoked the notion indirectly. The IMT held that criminal responsibility could be established if the defendants had had knowledge of the crimes committed by their subordinates and the crimes had been committed under their authority. No superior-subordinate relationship was required, however, and in fact convictions were based on a type of participatory responsibility.[88] Subsequently, the Nuremberg national tribunals developed the doctrine of superior responsibility even

85 As this study is concerned with the liability of civilians (in the corporate context) as opposed to the individual criminal responsibility of military commanders, the following will explore primarily the scope of the notion of superior responsibility and the critiques it has been subjected to. References to the interpretation of command responsibility (i.e. the liability of military commanders) will be made only on a more general level for clarification and comparison purposes. Hereafter, the term 'command responsibility' will be used in relation to military commanders while the term 'superior responsibility' will be utilised to designate the responsibility of civilian superiors.

86 I. Bantekas, The Contemporary Law of Superior Responsibility, *93 American Journal of International Law* 573 (1999) at 573.

87 *Ibidem*.

88 Van Sliedregt, *supra note 30*, p. 124.

further, upholding its applicability outside the context of military or political structures. In the *Roechling* Case, for instance, German industrialists were held responsible for acts of slave labour, murder and ill-treatment of civilians and prisoners of war occurring in their corporation, because they had the power to prevent those crimes, or at least reduce their scale, but failed to do so.[89] Similarly, in *Flick*, a leading German industrialist was convicted for failing to prevent the criminal acts of subordinates, which included plans to deport and enslave prisoners of war and civilians in the *Flick* industrial enterprise.[90]

Despite the significance of these developments, it was not until 1977 that the concept of superior responsibility was recognised as a positive legal norm in Additional Protocol I to the Geneva Conventions.[91] In the early 1990s, it re-emerged in full blast and was tailored to meet the exigencies of modern warfare. Eventually, the ever-growing relevance of the doctrine and the ICTY and ICTR's experience in dealing with both military and civilian superiors influenced the inclusion of Article 28 in the Rome Statute.

III.2 Superior responsibility under the Rome Statute

The specific rule on superior responsibility, contained in Article 28(b) RS, supplements the broad range of liability modes set forth in Article 25. Like the theory of 'common design', it expands the attribution of individual liability beyond physical involvement as well as knowledge and full intent. It also establishes responsibility for omission, as superiors may be penalised for failing to prevent the commission of crimes by their subordinates and/or to punish the subordinates involved once established that they have committed crimes.

The doctrine of superior responsibility may thus be regarded as a form of accomplice liability.[92] However, it is noteworthy that, under this doctrine, superiors incur individual responsibility (albeit indirectly) for the actual crimes committed by their subordinates, not merely for a dereliction of duty.[93] Although a certain degree of the latter is necessary to trigger the criminal responsibility of superiors, it does not give rise to vicarious or strict liability.

The extension of superior responsibility to civilians caused some controversy during the Rome Conference. From the very beginning, a broad majority supported the idea of subjecting civilian superiors to criminal liability. However, a number of contentious

89 See in this regard Chapter 3, section III.1: An overview of domestic military trials.
90 *Ibidem*.
91 Article 86(2).
92 W.J. Fenrick, Article 28: Responsibility of Commanders and Other Superiors, in: O. Triffterer (ed.), *Commentary on the Rome Statute of the International Criminal Court*, Baden-Baden: Nomos, 1999, p. 517.
93 For an extended discussion of the nature of superior responsibility, see also Chapter 6.

considerations stood in the way of agreement on the draft text of Article 28. These considerations pertained to whether civilians should incur the same degree of criminal responsibility as military commanders, since normally they would not have the same degree of control over subordinates and would not be in the same position to prevent crimes from occurring.[94] At the same time, differentiating the liability requirements for military and civilian superiors and thus effectively implying varying degrees of culpability, was not entirely acceptable either. It had the propensity to blur and underrate the blameworthiness of *de facto* civilian commanders of military and para-military groups.[95]

III.2.1 The components of superior responsibility as a mode of liability

The section of Article 28 RS eventually adopted and expounding the criminal responsibility of superiors other than military commanders, reads:

> 'With respect to superior and subordinate relationships [outside the context of military structures, *DS*], a superior shall be criminally responsible for crimes within the jurisdiction of the Court committed by subordinates under his or her effective authority and control, as a result of his or her failure to exercise control properly over such subordinates, where:
> (i) The superior either knew, or consciously disregarded information which clearly indicated, that the subordinates were committing or about to commit such crimes;
> (ii) The crimes concerned activities that were within the effective responsibility and control of the superior; and
> (iii) The superior failed to take all necessary and reasonable measures within his or her power to prevent or repress their commission or to submit the matter to the competent authorities for investigation and prosecution.'[96]

Thus, there are four requisite elements that must be established before an individual can incur superior responsibility under Article 28(b): (1) the existence of a superior – subordinate relationship; (2) the superior's knowledge, or conscious disregard of, information indicating that a criminal act was about to be or had been committed; (3) the superior's effective responsibility for and control over the acts of his subordinates; and (4) the superior's failure to take all necessary and reasonable measures to prevent the criminal acts or punish the perpetrators thereof.[97]

---

94 P. Saland, International Criminal Law Principles, in: R.S. Lee (ed.), *The International Criminal Court. The Making of the Rome Statute. Issues, Negotiations, Results*. The Hague: Kluwer Law International, 1999, p. 203.

95 *Ibidem.*

96 Article 28(b) RS.

97 As per 1 September 2009, the ICC has rendered only one decision on the scope of Article 28 RS and it pertains to military commanders (Article 28(a)). Therefore, in order to define the content of superior responsibility within the meaning of Article 28(b), recourse must be taken to the jurisprudence of the

III.2.1a The existence of a superior – subordinate relationship

The notion of 'civilian superiors' encompasses individuals in positions of authority outside of military structures, e.g. political leaders, business executives and senior civil servants.[98] The existence of a superior – subordinate relationship between the superior and the actual perpetrator of a crime (who is also the superior's subordinate) can be established in two independent ways – *de jure* and *de facto*.

A *de jure* relationship arises from the assumption of officially delegated authority emanating from a given position or office in a hierarchical structure. Such authority must evince command over other persons not only by virtue of the formal office it is originating from, but also due to the actual right to control enjoyed by those with superior status. In this sense, *de jure* power confines one's competence to take action or intervene in the acts of one's subordinates to a pre-defined field beyond which there exists no competency and, subsequently, no liability. A *de facto* relationship, on the other hand, does not require the existence of a formal superior status in an organised institutional hierarchy. Rather, in order to invoke the doctrine of superior responsibility, it is sufficient to establish that an individual is part of a chain of command within which he has the power to exercise actual and effective control over those situated lower in the hierarchical structure.[99] Thus, even if an individual does not occupy a formal position of superior authority within a given organisational unit, as long as he functions within the unit evidence of subjugation to his orders and respect for his informal authority will indicate a superior – subordinate relationship.

Even in cases where overwhelming evidence exists of the *de jure* authority of a person in a superior position, the *ad hoc* tribunals have also sought to consistently establish *de facto* control over those with subordinate status.[100] *De jure* authority cannot in itself give rise to criminal responsibility. Deriving culpability from an individual's formal position or status in the absence of any actual power or ability on his part to exercise effective control over subordinate behaviour, would amount to strict liability. Hence, a determination of the scope of *de facto* authority is critical for the imposition of superior responsibility.

---

ad hoc tribunals. Given the extent to which ICTY and ICTR case law has been instrumental in fixing the applicability of the superior responsibility doctrine in more precise terms, the ICC judiciary would presumably take into account the precedents thus set. There are also no compelling reasons for the Court to substantially deviate from existing case law, considering the overlap between Article 28(b) RS and the provisions enshrined in the Statutes of the *ad hoc* tribunals. Albeit authoritative, ICTY and ICTR precedents however remain non-binding on the ICC.

98 *Prosecutor v. Delalic et al.*, ICTY Case No. IT-96-21-A, Appeal Judgment of 20 February 2001, para. 195; Aleksovski, *supra note 73*, para. 76; Musema, *supra note 3*, para. 135; Delalic et al., *supra note 9*, paras. 355-363.

99 Delalic et al., *supra note 9*, para. 370.

100 E.g. *Prosecutor v. Akayesu*, Case No. ICTR-96-4-T, Judgment of 2 September 1998, para. 76; Delalic et al., *supra note 98*, paras. 205-206.

The ICTY Appeals Chamber in *Hadzihasanovic* has held that there must be a temporal coincidence between the crime for which the superior is held responsible and the existence of a superior-subordinate relationship between the superior and the actual perpetrator.[101] The judgment has generated considerable debate.[102] In his dissenting opinion, Judge David Hunt opined that the Appeals Chamber's decision left a 'gaping hole in the protection that international humanitarian law seeks to provide.'[103] According to him, it effectively precluded the prosecution of superiors who, albeit aware of crimes that had been committed by their subordinates before they assumed effective control, chose not to act with view to the subordinates' punishment. Indeed, this may result in complicity after the fact[104] where the superior's passive attitude had an encouraging effect on subordinates and thus substantially contributed to the commission of the crimes. It may also foster future criminal conduct, for subordinates will be aware of the superior's lenient disposition. At the same time, however, extending culpability beyond personal fault and imposing liability for crimes which occurred without the superiors' knowledge and prior to their assuming effective authority, is a dangerous approach. As will be recalled, (successor) superior responsibility for a failure to punish entails responsibility not only for a dereliction of duty but also for the actual crimes committed.

The *Hadzihasanovic* and *Halilovic* appeal judgments are of particular interest since Article 28 RS does not specify what the responsibility of military commanders or civilian superiors would be for crimes committed by their subordinates before they effectively took office. Although the issue was identified and discussed during the negotiations at the Rome Conference, there was not enough time to formulate and agree on a text to be included in the article eventually adopted.[105] In this regard, legal commentators have contended that the causality requirement enshrined in Article 28 precludes the liability of successor superiors for crimes committed prior to their assuming control over the actual perpetrators.[106] Recently, in its first-ever decision on

---

101 *Prosecutor v. Hadzihasanovic et al.*, Decision on Interlocutory Appeal in Relation to Command Responsibility, ICTY Case No. IT-01-47-AR72, 16 July 2003, paras. 37-51. The position was later upheld in *Prosecutor v. Halilovic*, ICTY Case No. IT-01-48-A, Appeal Judgment of 16 October 2007, para. 59.

102 See e.g. G. Mettraux, *International Crimes and the Ad Hoc Tribunals*, Oxford: Oxford University Press, 2005, p. 301; C. Greenwood, Command Responsibility and the Hadzihasanovic Decision, 2 *Journal of International Criminal Justice* 598 (2004).

103 Judge David Hunt Separate and Partially Dissenting Opinion in: Hadzihasanovic et al., *supra note 101*, para. 22.

104 Complicity after the fact has been recognised in ICTY case law as part of Article 7(1) of the ICTY Statute (Tadic, *supra note 11*, para. 692). In *Hadzihasanovic et al.*, the Trial Chamber opted for superior responsibility within the meaning of Article 7(3) and did not explicitly rely upon complicity after the fact as a mode of liability in its own right. However, the effect of the judgment was to hold a superior criminally responsible as an accessory after the fact for crimes committed by his subordinates before he assumed command. See *Prosecutor v. Hadzihasanovic et al.*, Decision on Joint Challenge to Jurisdiction, ICTY Case No. IT-01-47-PT, 12 November 2002.

105 Saland, *supra note 94*, p. 204.

106 E.g. Van Sliedregt, *supra note 30*, p. 170.

the scope of Article 28, Pre-Trial Chamber II of the ICC has held that superiors would incur individual responsibility if they had effective control *at least* when the crimes were about to be committed and hence had the material possibility to prevent them from occurring.[107]

III.2.1b The cognitive requirement for superior responsibility

Article 28(b) RS further stipulates the individual liability of non-military superiors when they either 'knew' or 'consciously disregarded information' clearly indicating that their subordinates had committed or were about to commit an international crime but failed to act. In this regard, the provision differs from that on command responsibility, enshrined in paragraph (a) of the same article. While Article 28(a) RS requires proof that a superior 'knew' or 'should have known' about the (intended) activities of his subordinates, Article 28(b) RS substitutes the element of 'should have known' for the stricter requirement of 'consciously disregarded information'. Thus Article 28(b) marks a higher *mens rea* threshold for superior responsibility in a non-military context, requiring proof of not merely negligence but rather wilful blindness.[108]

Actual and constructive knowledge

The element of knowledge in Article 28(b) RS is intended to denote awareness as to the existence of a given circumstance, or awareness that a circumstance will occur.[109]

---

107 *Prosecutor v. Jean-Pierre Bemba Gombo*, Decision pursuant to Article 61(7)(a) and (b) of the Rome Statute on the Charges of the Prosecutor against Jean-Pierre Bemba Gombo, ICC-01/05-01/08-424, 15 June 2009, paras. 418-419.

108 It is worth noting that both Article 7(3) ICTY and Article 6(3) ICTR set forth a 'knew or had reason to know' standard of knowledge. There have been attempts in the case law of the *ad hoc* tribunals to lower the applicable standard to the level of 'should have known' (see, for instance, *Prosecutor v. Blaskic*, ICTY Case No. IT-95-14-T, Judgment of 3 March 2000, paras. 322, 328). Such attempts, however, have been controversial and have not led to a drastic change in judicial interpretation although there has been a slight shift in perspective. Thus, superiors do not incur liability under the ICTY and ICTR Statutes for failing to seek and obtain information, which would have put them on notice that crimes had been or were about to be committed (see, in this regard, Delalic et al., *supra note 98*, paras. 226, 232-238, and also Kvocka et al., supra *note 20*, para. 317). The accused must be shown to have had *in their possession* sufficiently clear and alarming general information to put them on notice that crimes of similar nature and gravity as the ones they are charged with had been or were about to be committed (see e.g. *Prosecutor v. Krnojelac*, ICTY Case No. Case No. IT-97-25-A, Appeal Judgment of 17 September 2003, para. 155). Superior responsibility in the context of the *ad hoc* tribunals does not entail strict liability. It has, nonetheless, been conceded that if 'had reason to know' is interpreted to mean that a superior has a duty to inquire further, on the basis of general information he has at hand, there would in fact be no essential material difference between 'had reason to know' and 'should have known' (see in this regard Delalic et al., *supra note 98*, para. 235).

109 See Decisions Taken by the ICC Preparatory Committee, UN Doc. A/AC.249/1997/L.5 Art. H (12 March 1997). This definition of knowledge is also enshrined in the general *mens rea* provision of the Rome Statute, Article 30(3).

Knowledge in this sense, also a prerequisite for superior responsibility under Article 7(3) ICTY and Article 6(3) ICTR, may be established through direct or circumstantial evidence.[110]

Conscious disregard of information putting the superior on notice of the need to investigate in order to ascertain whether subordinates have committed or are about to commit crimes, has been interpreted by the *ad hoc* tribunals on some occasions to amount to actual knowledge.[111] Such a conclusion, however, necessitates proof beyond reasonable doubt – through written evidence or testimony – that the superior was indeed directly made aware of the criminal activities of his subordinates or he himself indicated that he knew of such activities.

Constructive knowledge, on the other hand, may be established on the basis of circumstantial evidence that a superior could not have been unaware of the criminal activity of his subordinates. Thus even in the absence of directly indicative information regarding possible criminal activities made available to superiors, knowledge on their part may be presumed. Establishing constructive knowledge is essentially based on a 'must have known' standard. This does not, however, translate into negligence-type liability. Knowledge may not be presumed solely from a superior's position or the widespread nature and public notoriety of the crimes committed. There must also be other *indicia* present, such as e.g. the superior's relation to the persons implicated and the logistics involved, or the location of the superior at the time of the acts occurring.[112] In the end, in order to impute constructive knowledge to the superior there must be no logical conclusion in light of the evidence available other than that the superior must have known of the criminal activities of his subordinates.

The 'consciously disregarded information' standard of knowledge

This particular cognitive standard under Article 28(b) RS in effect amounts to 'wilful blindness'. To some extent it appears to share a similar meaning with the 'had reason to know' standard of Article 7(3) ICTY and Article 6(3) ICTR. Although limited, the similarity raises concerns, particularly in relation to the permissibility of liability for negligence under criminal law.

As will be recalled, the interpretation of 'had reason to know' in the case law of the *ad hoc* tribunals has on some occasions brought down the liability threshold dangerously close to the 'should have known' level of criminal negligence.[113] The resulting implication has been the liability of superiors who are in possession of sufficient information to be put on notice of subordinate criminal activity but are nevertheless genuinely ignorant as to any specific crime.[114] The information at the

110 Delalic et al., *supra note 9*, para. 386.
111 *Ibidem*, paras. 387-393.
112 *Idem*, para. 386.
113 See note 108 above.
114 I. Bantekas, *Principles of Direct and Superior Responsibility in International Humanitarian Law*, Manchester: Manchester University Press, 2002, p. 113.

superior's disposal need only be of a general nature, sufficient to engender suspicion of a criminal activity, rather than certainty as to the activity.[115] In addition, this information need only be made available to the superior; there is no corresponding requirement that the superior is explicitly requested to acquaint himself with the information thus provided.

Generally, 'wilful blindness' is regarded as a standard of advertent recklessness. If a superior is put on notice of suspicious information but takes no steps to investigate and remains deliberately ignorant of criminal activity, the culpability attached to his conscious choice not to gain knowledge does reasonably equate to culpability based on positive awareness. Liability is derived from the foreseeability of a criminal risk and the superior's conscious failure to inquire into the possible unlawful consequences. If, however, the superior fails to acquaint himself in a timely manner with information which could have put him on notice of criminal conduct, liability would then not be based on the superior's acceptance of a given risk. Instead culpability would appear to attach to a dereliction of duty (not reviewing available information in time) and a failure to perceive the probability of the risk. This in turn is reminiscent of inadvertent recklessness and crosses the line into *culpa* liability.

In this regard it must be noted that, apart from refuting the existence of a general duty to know on the part of superiors – civilian as well as military – the Appeals Chamber in *Delalic et al.* distanced itself from the *culpa*-type interpretation of 'had reason to know'. Failure to stay apprised of subordinate conduct at all times would not necessarily result in criminal responsibility.[116] The emphasis is placed on uncovering the superior's actual state of mind, rendering the question of whether he 'should have known' largely irrelevant. In *Bemba*, the ICC took a pointedly different stance with regard to military commanders. It upheld the existence of an obligation to actively seek to secure knowledge of the troops' conduct.[117] Although the decision did not discuss the cognitive standard enshrined in Article 28(b) with regard to civilian superiors, the Court would presumably adopt a much stricter approach. To the extent that a superior recognises and accepts the risk of a criminal activity but remains deliberately inactive, and is hence supportive or at least indifferent to the likelihood of unlawful subordinate behaviour, his liability may well be warranted.[118]

III.2.1c Activities within the effective responsibility and control of superiors

To incur liability for crimes committed by their subordinates, civilian superiors must also be shown to have exercised effective authority and control over the physical

115 Delalic et al., *supra note 98*, para. 393.
116 *Ibidem*, para. 226.
117 Bemba, *supra note 107*, para. 433.
118 For further discussion of the cognitive standard enshrined in Article 28(b) RS and the Court's reasoning in the *Bemba* Case, see Chapter 6.

perpetrators.[119] The determination of the 'effective authority' is made with a view to the superior's formal position within the chain of command, corresponding rights and *de facto* powers. As for the requirement of 'effective control', in their case law the *ad hoc* tribunals have interpreted it to comprise 'the material ability to prevent offences or punish the principal offenders'.[120] The issue of effective authority and control is thus closely connected to the existence of a superior-subordinate relationship and the question of whether the superior was under a duty to act in response to the crimes contemplated or committed by his subordinates. With respect to civilian superiors, however, the Appeals Chamber in *Bagilishema* has recognised that effective control will not necessarily be exercised, or established, in the same way as regards military commanders.[121]

Notably in relation to civilian superiors, Article 28(b) RS stipulates an explicit condition – sub-paragraph (ii) – which is lacking as such in the corresponding provisions on command responsibility in the Rome Statute and the Statutes of the *ad hoc* tribunals. This additional stipulation requires that the crimes for which the superior is held responsible concern subordinate activities which are also within the effective responsibility and control of the superior. Thus, Article 28(b) effectively sets forth an obligation on the part of the prosecution to establish a causal nexus between the behaviour of superiors and the criminal activities of their subordinates. Crimes committed outside the line of duty or unrelated to the activities of the organisation would therefore appear to fall outside the scope of Article 28(b).

On the one hand, the rationale behind the inclusion of this requirement is not difficult to comprehend considering the fundamentally different structures that paragraphs (a) and (b) seek to address. In the context of military formations, it is generally presumed that the chain of control functions properly and that commanders have stringently pre-defined, but also wide-ranging, powers and responsibilities in relation to informing, supervising and punishing subordinates. As regards non-military organisational units, however, a similar strict hierarchy may not exist or may not be equally reliable. To compensate for this looser power of command in the civilian environment, Article 28(b) provides that not only the physical perpetrators but also the activities they engage in are within the effective responsibility and control of the

119 Article 28(a) RS expounds the responsibility of military commanders for activities within their 'effective command and control'. The difference in formulation between paragraphs (a) and (b) of Article 28 is an explicit recognition of the difference in the nature of the control exercised by military and civilian superiors. The underlying assumption is that military commanders operate within a hierarchical structure based on a system of obedience. See K. Ambos, Superior Responsibility, in A. Cassese et al. (eds.), *The Rome Statute of the International Criminal Court: a Commentary*, Oxford: Oxford University Press, 2002, p. 858. Abidance by civilian orders may not be as forthcoming and automatic as it is generally presumed in the context of military chains of command.

120 See e.g. *Prosecutor v. Bagilishema*, Case No. ICTR-95-1A-A, Appeal Judgment of 3 July 2002, paras. 49-55; Delalic et al., *supra note 98*, paras. 196-198; Blaskic, *supra note 108*, para. 300-302.

121 Bagalishema, *supra note 120*, para. 55.

superior.[122] What constitutes 'effective responsibility and control' would depend on the circumstances of each particular case and may be difficult to calculate for non-military superiors. Among the determinant factors might be: the superior's *de jure* and *de facto* power of control, his responsibility for a particular group of subordinates, and his responsibility for the execution of a given activity (which led to the commission of the crime).

On the other hand, the additional condition featured in Article 28(b)(ii) has the propensity to overly restrict the scope of application of the superior responsibility doctrine in civilian settings. In a corporate context, particularly, confining liability to only those subordinate crimes which arise out of activities for which the superior bears direct responsibility, may allow senior officials to evade accountability. As will be discussed elsewhere,[123] middle management within corporate structures is generally delegated responsibility over groups of subordinates and their specific activities. It is also mid-level managers who possess both the authority and the effective power of control over individuals operating inside their sphere of responsibility. The complexities of the organisational environment, typified by numerous complex channels of information and fragmented task division, serve to distance the directors from the actual physical perpetrators. This in turn may help shield them from responsibility. The 'effective responsibility and control' over activities stipulation shifts the liability burden primarily onto the middle levels within the corporation.

III.2.1d The duty of superiors to act

Given that a superior has the requisite *mens rea* and effective control over his subordinates, he is to be held criminally responsible for any failure to use his authority to prevent or repress subordinate crimes from occurring or punish transgressions which have already materialised. This, however, does not amount to liability for a mere dereliction of duty with regard to the supervision of subordinates. The superior is also held culpable – albeit only indirectly – with regard to the crimes themselves.[124]

Legal commentators have challenged this particular trait of the superior responsibility doctrine in relation to specific intent crimes.[125] They have pointed out that, where the charges concern genocide and persecution, the liability of superiors is better described as liability for a breach of duty. A superior's authoritative duty to act is generally considered to encompass all measures within the superior's 'material

122 O. Triffterer, Causality, a Separate Element of the Doctrine of Superior Responsibility as Expressed in Article 28 Rome Statute?, 15 *Leiden Journal of International Law* 179 (2002) at 193.

123 See Chapter 6, section IV: The superior responsibility of corporate officials.

124 For a discussion of the *sui generis* nature of superior responsibility, see generally C. Meloni, Command Responsibility. Mode of Liability for the Crimes of Subordinates or Separate Offence of the Superior?, 5 *Journal of International Criminal Justice* 619 (2007).

125 E.g. D.L. Nersessian, *supra note 56*; W.A. Schabas, Mens Rea and the International Criminal Tribunal for the Former Yugoslavia, 37 *New England Law Review* 1015 (2003).

possibility',[126] also in circumstances of 'anticipated foreseeability'.[127] Thus, recklessness on the part of superiors with regard to certain character traits of their subordinates could be construed as a failure to act where those traits are deemed to constitute risk factors.[128] Such risk factors indicate the likelihood that a crime may be committed, and hence trigger the superior's authoritative duty. A failure of that duty results in liability for the offences perpetrated. It is precisely the incorporation of this *mens rea* standard into the superior responsibility doctrine that has prompted critics to allege that imposing upon superiors liability for *dolus specialis* crimes committed by subordinates, does not align with the principle of personal fault. In this regard, other authors have argued in favour of differentiating sentencing outcomes depending on the nature of the failure to act.[129]

The superior's duty to act within the meaning of Article 28(b) RS is threefold. It encompasses a duty to (1) control subordinates, (2) prevent or repress criminal activities and (3) once discovered, disclose the matter to the relevant authorities. The duty to control is the broadest in scope. According to its wording in the *chapeau* of Article 28(b), a superior is to be blamed for failing to sufficiently inform, educate, advise and supervise subordinates as to the benefit of the correct application of relevant laws.[130] The obligation, however, is effectively delimited by the conditions of having the requisite *mens rea* (Article 28(b)(ii)) and of taking 'all necessary and reasonable measures within his power to prevent or repress the commission of crimes' (Article 28(b)(iii)). These additional requirements, in fact, stipulate a dereliction of duty with respect to certain crimes only, i.e. when a superior knew or consciously disregarded a concrete threat to protected legal values but nevertheless failed to fully discharge his duty to act.[131]

Article 28(b) further requires a causal connection between the failure on the part of the superior to fulfil his duties and the crimes committed by his subordinates. It is the causality link interpreted in light of the *mens rea* prerequisites of Article 28 that has prompted Nerlich to conclude that superiors need not necessarily be punished as stringently as the physical perpetrators of crimes.[132] When established that the superior knew of the offences contemplated or committed, he can validly be blamed not only for failing to suppress or prevent them but also for the crimes themselves. However, a failure to punish *post factum* or to intervene in the absence of knowledge as to the subordinates' criminal activities appears to imply blameworthiness for a wrongful

126 E.g. Blaskic, *supra note 74*, para. 335; Delalic et al., *supra note 9*, para. 395.
127 Blaskic, *supra note 74*, para. 474.
128 Delalic et al., *supra note 98*, para. 238.
129 V. Nerlich, Superior Responsibility under Article 28 ICC Statute. For What Exactly is the Superior Held Responsible?, 5 *Journal of International Criminal Justice* 665 (2007).
130 Triffterer, *supra note 122*, p. 192.
131 *Ibidem*, p. 199.
132 Nerlich, *supra note 129*.

consequence mainly.[133] Thus although liability attaches to the failure to control as well as to the base crime, the difference in the nature of the culpability may warrant more nuanced sentencing.

IV CONCLUSION

The concept of superior responsibility and the 'common purpose' doctrine have undergone significant development since they were employed at Nuremberg. Continuous efforts to delineate the contours of potentially expansive liability modes are indicative of the inherent difficulty in squaring the peculiarities of collective crimes with the premise of personal guilt. The preoccupation with individual culpability, as discussed earlier,[134] is grounded in traditional domestic approaches to tackling ordinary transgression. Such approaches, however, are not necessarily suited for the reality of international crimes. While the requirements of due process must invariably remain imperative, the magnitude and complexities of those crimes necessitate accountability avenues that adequately reflect the true character and dynamics of deviance in group settings. The need to fight impunity, however, does not – neither should it – imply punishment at any cost. The cumulative development of international criminal law – from Nuremberg through the *ad hoc* tribunals' jurisprudence to the Rome Statute of the International Criminal Court – demonstrates the importance accorded to finding a fair balance when holding individuals liable for collective crimes.

The preceding exposition is relevant to the topic of corporate liability insofar as holding legal entities criminally responsible does not negate the prosecution and culpability of individual agents associated with those entities. Moreover, if political negotiations surrounding future revisions of the Rome Statute do not bring about an extension of the Court's jurisdiction beyond natural persons, individual liability for corporate representatives might be the only avenue for holding the business sector accountable for its involvement in grave human rights abuse. Culpability and punishment in this regard, however, must correspond to the degree of personal contribution to the crimes concerned. Existing liability modes should be carefully circumscribed, in keeping with some of the propositions expounded in this chapter.

Admittedly, perceptions of collective responsibility and mass punishment would be difficult to eliminate altogether. The reason lies in the nature of functional criminality which, like system criminality, is a form of group deviance, affecting individual behaviour and making personal culpability difficult to isolate from the collective context. Although predominantly, if not exclusively, employed with regard to political and military leaders, the doctrines of common purpose and superior responsibility are potentially applicable to corporate agents as well. They serve to

133 *Ibidem*, at 674-682.

134 See Chapter II.

demarcate the risk zone within which individual business actors may incur liability even for their indirect involvement in international crimes. At the same time, understanding the rationale behind the criticism targeting the doctrines' interpretation by the *ad hoc* tribunals eases the deduction of a number of general principles pertaining to the development of a viable approach to direct corporate criminal responsibility. While the tenet of personal guilt remains central to individual culpability, group deviance, whether of a systemic or corporate nature, necessitates recourse to innovative approaches to assessing blameworthy conduct.

CHAPTER 5
THE CRIMINAL LIABILITY OF CORPORATIONS WITHIN THE ROME STATUTE FRAMEWORK

I INTRODUCTION

Accountability, and accordingly the legal responsibility of individuals for their role in the perpetration of serious human rights violations, is a fundamental premise of international criminal law. While the moral responsibility of legal persons, MNCs in particular, for their involvement in international crimes has also been gaining in recognition, the legal dimension of this responsibility remains in the realm of controversy and speculation. Currently, the Rome Statute does not provide for jurisdiction over business enterprises. If the ICC jurisdiction *ratione personae* is extended to corporations in the future, prosecution is likely to stumble over the difficulty of effectively applying to organisations concepts essentially tailored for the individual as the subject of existing prohibitions. Domestic jurisdictions have struggled with the same predicament, seeking to devise avenues for squaring the subjective elements that attach to crimes with the collective, inanimate nature of economic entities.

The negotiations surrounding the adoption of the Rome Statute sought to adopt a moderate position by suggesting the ascription of corporate criminal responsibility via individual convictions. This was thought to circumvent the impossibility of fathoming the mental state of corporations *per se*. However, seeking to equate individual and corporate *mens rea* is a misplaced effort, both in perspective and implications. Whereas there are compelling reasons not to remove the subjective element from the discussion pertaining to the culpability and legal accountability of MNCs under criminal law (domestic or international), the peculiarities of organisational existence necessitate a different approach to the construction of the requisite *mens rea*.

This chapter begins by exploring the general objective and subjective stipulations, contained in the Rome Statute and elaborated upon in ICC case law thus far in relation to natural persons. Positing that existing modes of liability cannot adequately capture the institutionalised, economic perpetrators and facilitators of international crimes, it subsequently puts forward a *sui generis* model of corporate liability. The effort draws upon domestic as well as theoretical methods geared towards uncovering organisational fault. The drawbacks and comparative advantages of these methods are also critically discussed. The underlying assumption behind the choice of holistic approaches as best suited for the conceptualisation of fault and criminal responsibility on the part of MNCs, relates to the self-identity of corporations – a notion that was previously embraced in Chapter 2.

II The ambit of *actus reus* and *mens rea* in the Rome Statute

II.1 Acts and omissions

The drafters of the Rome Statute failed to include a definition of omission in a general provision pertaining to the *actus reus*,[1] prompting commentators to argue that only Article 28 can generate liability by omission.[2] Other legal scholars, however, have rejected both the rationale and the practicability of such a strict interpretation of the Statute. Van Sliedregt, for instance, has convincingly argued that complicity by omission extends beyond the criminal responsibility of superiors.[3] Noting that the legality principle relates to questions of jurisdiction rather than the scope of the applicable modes of liability,[4] she contends that interpreting ICC competencies as extending to crimes that entail positive acts only would exceedingly restrict the Court's jurisdiction *ratione materiae.* In this regard, the case law of the *ad hoc* tribunals has established that most of the offences within the tribunals' jurisdiction can be perpetrated either by acts or by omissions,[5] although the Statutes expressly codify criminal omission with respect to superior responsibility only. Most national legal systems also recognise passive behaviour that causes a criminal consequence, as punishable. Even those jurisdictions without an express provision on omission in their criminal codes, tend to construe liability from omission in certain circumstances.[6] The issue of whether omission constitutes a part of the *actus reus* of the crimes incorporated in the Rome Statute, has ultimately been left for the ICC to decide in its case law. There are compelling reasons and some indications that the outcome may favour a broader interpretation of the objective element. Existing articles refer to 'conduct' without mention as to what constitutes the culpable behaviour, i.e. an act or an omission. Early case law has, moreover, construed the ambit of Article 30 (stipulating the general mental aspect of the crimes codified in the Statute) with

---

1 UN Doc. A/CONF.183/2/Add.1, 14 April 1998. See also Report of the Working Group on General Principles of Criminal Law, 29 June 1998, UN Doc. A/CONF.183/C.1/WGGP/L.4/Add.1.

2 E. Wise, General Principles of Criminal Law, in: L.S. Wexler and M.C. Bassiouni (eds.), *Model Draft Statute for the International Criminal Court based on the Preparatory Committee's Text to the Diplomatic Conference, Rome, 15 June – 17 July 1998*, Pau: Eres, 1998, pp. 48-50.

3 E. van Sliedregt, *The Criminal Responsibility of Individuals for Violations of International Humanitarian Law*, The Hague: T.M.C. Asser Press, 2003, p. 55-56. See also M. Duttwiller, Liability for Omission in International Criminal Law, 6 *International Criminal Law Review* 1 (2006).

4 *Ibidem*, p. 66.

5 E.g. *Prosecutor v. Blaskic*, ICTY Case No. IT-95-14-T, Judgment of 3 March 2000, paras. 154, 186; *Prosecutor v. Kambanda*, Case No. ICTR 97-23-S, Judgment of 4 September 1998, para. 40.

6 P. Saland, International Criminal Law Principles, in: R.S. Lee (ed.), *The International Criminal Court. The Making of the Rome Statute. Issues, Negotiations. Results*. The Hague: Kluwer Law International, 1999, p. 212.

reference to acts *or* omissions which bring about (the risk of) certain consequences.[7] Thus, the Court appears prepared to acknowledge that both positive and 'omissive' conduct may give rise to liability, even outside the specific circumstances of superior responsibility.[8]

II.2 The *dolus directus* facet of Article 30 RS

As for the mental element of individual criminal responsibility, the Court has thus far interpreted it inconsistently. In line with the restrictive wording of Article 30, the requisite *mens rea* has been deemed to comprise at least two distinct levels of volition. In *Lubanga*, Pre-Trial Chamber I differentiated between *dolus directus* in the first degree and *dolus directus* in the second degree.[9] The former designates full intent and encompasses situations in which the defendant conducts himself with knowledge and willingness as to the objective elements of the offence. Accordingly, *dolus directus* in the first degree refers to behaviour which is intended to bring about a concrete result. The defendant means to engage in a particular conduct and means to cause specific consequences. *Dolus directus* in the second degree, on the other hand, indicates a mental state which emphasises the cognitive aspect of volition. While the behaviour of the individual is purposeful, he does not act with the concrete desire to bring about the consequence that eventually materialises. However, he is deemed to have possessed intent since he was aware that the consequence would be certain to occur as a by-product of his behaviour in the ordinary course of events.

The understanding of Article 30 as encompassing *dolus directus* in the first and second degree was subsequently affirmed in *Katanga*[10] and *Bemba*.[11] The distinction between intent to cause a particular consequence and more general intent to engage in an unlawful activity mirrors established principles of fault attribution in both civil and common law traditions.[12]

---

7 *Prosecutor v. Thomas Lubanga Dyilo*, Decision on the confirmation of charges, ICC-01/04-01/06-803-tEN, 29 January 2007, paras. 351-353; *Prosecutor v. Germain Katanga and Mathieu Ngudjolo Chui*, Decision on the confirmation of charges, ICC-01/04-01/07-717, 30 September 2008, paras. 227, 287, 310, 315, 357, 368-369; *Prosecutor v. Jean-Pierre Bemba Gombo*, Decision pursuant to Article 61(7)(a) and (b) of the Rome Statute on the Charges of the Prosecutor against Jean-Pierre Bemba Gombo, ICC-01/05-01/08-424, paras. 358-359.

8 Recently in the *Karadzic* Case, the ICTY Prosecution invoked the *Lubanga* and *Katanga* decisions on the confirmation of charges to substantiate its dismissal of the objections raised by the Defence in relation to the notion of liability for omission and its recognition in customary international law. It interpreted ICC case law as accepting liability for omission beyond the context of superior responsibility. See *Prosecutor v. Radovan Karadzic*, Prosecution Response to Preliminary Motion on Lack of Jurisdiction Concerning Omission Liability, IT-95-5/18-PT, 7 April 2009.

9 Lubanga, *supra note 7*, paras. 350-352.

10 Katanga, *supra note 7*, paras. 529-530.

11 Bemba, *supra note 7*, paras. 357-359.

12 For an overview of domestic gradations of intention in the Anglo-American, French, German and Dutch legal systems, see generally Van Sliedregt, *supra note 3*, pp. 43-48.

II.3 *Dolus eventualis* as a form of volition?

The status of *dolus eventualis* as a form of intent falling within the scope of Article 30 RS is more unsettled. In *Lubanga,* the Pre-Trial Chamber embraced – somewhat controversially – volition at the level of *dolus eventualis* as being prescribed by the Rome Statute and established in international criminal law.[13] *Dolus eventualis* was understood to encompass situations in which the defendant acts with awareness that a criminal consequence *might* occur. The consequence would not need to be certain but would have to be foreseeable. The accused would be deemed to have acted purposefully if established that he was conscious of the risk but nevertheless accepted the possible criminal result.[14]

According to the Bench, as long as the risk amounted to a substantial probability, *dolus eventualis* could be deemed to respect the outer limits of the 'will occur' stipulation of Article 30(2)(b).[15] In this regard Pre-Trial Chamber II in the *Bemba* Case adopted a pointedly different stance.[16] In *Lubanga,* the judges also extended the application of *dolus eventualis* to situations where the risk was foreseeable but nevertheless only minimal.[17] The perpetrator would be considered to have acted purposefully if he accepted the idea that his actions or omissions might result in the realisation of certain objective elements. Although such an approach finds support in the case law of the *ad hoc* tribunals,[18] it is clearly more difficult to reconcile with sub-paragraph 2b of Article 30.

---

13 *Dolus eventualis* is a civil law concept. It resembles the common law notion of recklessness although the two are not equivalent. Both generally denote the mental state accompanying behaviour which entails the risk of a criminal consequence occurring. The scope of recklessness in the common law is broader, however, in that it also encompasses inadvertent (i.e. *culpa*) conduct. See Van Sliedregt, *supra note 3*, p. 46. In their case law, the *ad hoc* tribunals have generally referred to *dolus eventualis* as the equivalent of advertent recklessness in common law. See *Prosecutor v. Tadic*, Case No. IT-94-1-A, Appeal Judgment of 15 July 1999, para. 220.

14 The Chamber differentiated between *dolus eventualis* and recklessness on the basis of the criterion of 'acceptance' understood as 'reconciliation' or 'manifest indifference'. It expounded that while the concept of recklessness required only that the perpetrator was aware of the existence of a risk that the objective elements of a crime might result from his or her actions or omissions, *dolus eventualis* was different in that it entailed the defendant reconciling himself or herself with the result. It thus considered recklessness a form of *culpa* (Lubanga, *supra note 7*, paras. 353-355). It must be noted here that scholarly and judicial opinion as to whether recklessness can, in some circumstances, be positioned at the same level as *dolus eventualis*, or is an entirely separate concept which is not encompassed within the meaning of intent, is divided. See e.g. G. Werle and F. Jessberger, 'Unless Otherwise Provided': Article 30 of the ICC Statute and the Mental Element of Crimes under International Criminal Law, 3 *Journal of International Criminal Justice* 35 (2005); *Prosecutor v. Stakic*, ICTY Case No. IT-97-24-T, Judgment of 31 July 2003, para. 587; *Prosecutor v. Blaskic*, ICTY Case No. IT-95-14-T, Judgment of 3 March 2000, para. 152.

15 Lubanga, *supra note 7*, para. 353.

16 Bemba, *supra note 7*, paras. 360-369.

17 Lubanga, *supra note 7*, para. 354.

18 See e.g. Stakic, *supra note 14*, para. 587.

In *Lubanga*, the Pre-Trial Chamber explicitly positioned *dolus eventualis* above the level of *culpa*. In criminal law, *culpa* is generally understood to denote blameworthiness for unintentional behaviour and hence may not necessarily translate into criminal liability.[19] In this regard, the Bench considered conscious negligence and gross negligence – both civil law notions designating *culpa* – as falling outside the scope of *dolus eventualis*.[20] While in principle this aligns with the understanding of domestic jurisdictions which recognise *dolus eventualis* as a form of intent, the judges' reasoning and the implications thereof remain unclear. In the Chamber's interpretation *dolus eventualis* revolved around the criterion of acceptance. Thus, only where there is awareness of a risk and reconciliation with that risk can the conduct be deemed to fall within the ambit of intentional behaviour. This might be fairly straightforward as long as the risk is substantial. However, in situations where the perceived risk is only minimal, *dolus eventualis* as defined in *Lubanga* does not exclude *culpa* behaviour from its scope as unequivocally as professed. On the one hand, the Chamber expressly held that, if the defendant was aware of some risk but thought he could avoid it, he could not be regarded as having acted intentionally, as he did not genuinely accept the consequences of taking the risk.[21] At the same time, however, the Bench ruled that awareness of a minimal risk combined with clear acceptance of that risk amounted to *dolus eventualis*. It did not account for the possibility of acceptance because the risk was only minimal and, therefore, the defendant misjudged it to be within his realm of control. In such a scenario, the defendant could be said to have accepted the risk,[22] however, according to the Chamber's own reasoning, if one perceives a risk and subsequently discounts it – for having considered the risk, one deems it highly unlikely to materialise or possible to avoid – then he cannot be said to have genuinely accepted that risk. In this sense, although in *Lubanga* the judges were quick to discount conscious negligence in relation to *dolus eventualis*, the definition of *dolus eventualis*

19 In civil law systems, which recognise *dolus eventualis* as a form of intent (e.g. Germany and jurisdictions influenced by the German legal tradition), *culpa* encompasses two distinct forms of negligence – conscious and non-conscious. Conscious negligence relates to situations in which the defendant acts despite his awareness of the risk of a criminal consequence because he misjudges either the risk or his ability to avoid it. In contrast, the cognitive element is irrelevant for non-conscious negligence. In common law jurisdictions, *culpa* refers to inadvertent recklessness and negligence (in the sense of a breach of duty). Some legal scholars regard the civil law concept of conscious negligence as corresponding to the common law standard of inadvertent recklessness. See G.P. Fletcher, *Rethinking Criminal Law*, Boston: Little, Brown & Co., 1978, p. 261. However, it must be noted that although generally considered a form of *culpa*, conscious negligence may in some circumstances be equated with *dolus*. See in this regard Van Sliedregt, *supra note 3*, p. 47. Jurisdictions of the civil law tradition take such an approach, for example, in cases involving gross criminal negligence. Common law systems, on the other hand, regard gross negligence as akin to inadvertent recklessness. See P. Cane, *Responsibility in Law and Morality*, Oxford: Hart Publishing, 2002, pp. 80-81.

20 Lubanga, *supra note 7*, para. 355.

21 Lubanga, *supra note 7*, footnote 437 in which the Chamber cites a classic example of conscious negligence, i.e. a driver speeding while trusting that nothing would happen because of his experience.

22 For a similar argument, see T. Weigend, Intent, Mistake of Law and Co-perpetration in the Lubanga Decision on Confirmation of Charges, 6 *Journal of International Criminal Justice* 471 (2008) at 483.

that they put forward somewhat blurred the distinction between the two concepts. Future case law must bring much needed clarification in this regard in order to dispense with concerns about *culpa*-type liability, particularly where other provisions of the Statute do not expressly provide for it.

Such clarification, however, will become a priority only if the Court does indeed lastingly adopt *dolus eventualis* as part of Article 30 RS. In the *Katanga* Case, Pre-Trial Chamber II pointedly refrained from ruling on a Defence Motion challenging the *Lubanga* findings in relation to *dolus eventualis*. The judges in *Katanga* rendered the contention moot since *dolus eventualis* did not form part of the particular indictment.[23] Subsequently, in *Bemba*, Pre-Trial Chamber II rejected *dolus eventualis* as inconsistent with a strict reading of Article 30 and the drafting history of the Rome Statute.[24]

It therefore remains to be seen to what extent the conclusions reached at the early stages of proceedings in the *Lubanga* Case will stand at trial and appeal. It is this author's view that anything short of awareness of a substantial risk coupled with acceptance of that risk stands at odds with the requirements of Article 30(2)(b) because of the latter's strict wording.[25] Moreover, the Statute's *travaux préparatoires* seem to indicate that the concept of *dolus eventualis* was considered during the drafting negotiations in Rome but was eventually abandoned in the final text.[26] This is not to deny, however, the general validity of *dolus eventualis* as a form of intent and the possibility for its proper application, as has been the case in domestic legal systems which rely on it. When sufficiently circumscribed and handled with care, *dolus eventualis* does not necessarily have a propensity for abuse.[27] Whether the definition of *dolus eventualis* espoused by Pre-Trial Chamber I in *Lubanga* generates the possibility for culpability to also be derived from inadvertent conduct, is critical for the position of the individual defendant. In this regard the challenge before the Court is not unique. The history of the international criminal tribunals from Nuremberg to The Hague has been a long sequence of troubled attempts to adjust the requisite *mens rea* for individual responsibility to both the peculiarities of group crimes and the

23 Katanga, *supra note 7*, para. 531.

24 Bemba, *supra note 7*, paras. 360-369.

25 As will be recalled, Article 30(2)(b) RS stipulates that a person has intent where in relation to a consequence, the person means to cause that consequence or is aware that it *will* [emphasis, *DS*] occur in the ordinary course of events.

26 In this regard, some legal commentators have contended that the reason for the removal of *dolus eventualis* from the text of the draft Rome Statute related to the fact that the concept did not appear in the final provisions defining crimes and therefore, it was not necessary to adopt a definition and incorporate it in Article 30 RS. See Werle and Jessberger, *supra note 14*, at 52 and W. Schabas, General Principles of Criminal Law in the International Criminal Court Statute, 4 *European Journal of Crime, Criminal Justice and Criminal Law* 400 (1998) at 420.

27 Favouring the inclusion of *dolus eventualis* in international criminal law doctrine, see F. Mantovani, The General Principles of International Criminal Law: The Viewpoint of a National Criminal Lawyer, 1 *Journal of International Criminal Justice* 26 (2003); G.G.J. Knoops, *Defences in Contemporary International Criminal Law*, New York: Ardsley Transnational Publishers, 2001.

requirements of due process. Particularly with regard to indirect contributions to collective criminality, such as participation in a criminal organisation/enterprise and failure to exercise superior duties of control, personal liability has been allowed to flow from divergent standards of intent and/or knowledge.[28] The *ad hoc* tribunals have further struggled with the criterion of *dolus eventualis*, according it a convoluted meaning. Such difficulties are not specific to international criminal justice. Domestic jurisdictions have also not been immune to the inherent complexity of separating attenuated forms of intent (*dolus*) from high degrees of carelessness (*culpa*). The implications of inconsistent interpretation and application of the mental element at the international level, however, are broader. They bear on the perceived legitimacy of existing courts through their potential to fuel mistrust in the functioning of a relatively underdeveloped penal system.

II.4 *Culpa*-type liability under the Rome Statute

Separate from the controversy surrounding *dolus eventualis* in the context of the Rome Statute, is the question of whether the Court can validly resort to other mental elements. Article 30 RS leaves room for the application of *culpa* standards, provided such standards are expressly stipulated elsewhere in the Statute. Thus, for instance, in laying out the responsibility of military commanders, Article 28(a) makes such an explicit reference to negligence. Negligence in the sense of a failure to perceive a risk has been excluded from the range of fault degrees deemed applicable by the *ad hoc* tribunals with regard to international crimes.[29] In contrast, the ICC has favoured the adoption of a purely objective standard for assessing individual blameworthiness in the circumstances of fiduciary relationships, in the military context specifically.[30] Moreover, the Court has already indicated that, while it does not consider the 'had reason to know' standard as negligence, this standard falls outside the scope of Article 30. It remains permissible, however, since it is provided for in Article 28(b) in relation to civilian superiors and it accords with the 'unless otherwise provided' stipulation of Article 30. Only strict liability is therefore clearly excluded from any application in the context of the Rome Statute.[31]

---

28 See in this regard Chapter 3, section II: The Nuremberg 'collective criminality' model and Chapter 4, section III.2.1b: The cognitive requirement for superior responsibility.

29 Generally, superior responsibility in the context of the *ad hoc* tribunals has been based on 'had reason to know' as the applicable cognitive standard. See Chapter 4, section III.2.1b: The cognitive requirement for superior responsibility.

30 Bemba, *supra note 7*, para. 433.

31 Since there is a requirement for a mental element to be proven in each individual case, the option of strict liability is not open. See A. Eser, Mental Elements – Mistake of Fact and Mistake of Law, in: A. Cassese et al. (eds.), *The Rome Statute of the International Criminal Court: a Commentary*, Oxford: Oxford University Press, 2002, pp. 902-903.

Understanding the Rome Statute framework is essential, for even if jurisdiction is not extended to business enterprises individual corporate agents remain within the ambit of the Court's prosecutorial reach. While some of the existing provisions (e.g. superior responsibility under Article 28(b)) may reveal some inherent limitations when transposed onto the MNC context,[32] this does not detract from the fact that, in principle, civilians who order, condone or otherwise facilitate the commission of an international crime may stand trial before the ICC. In the alternative, should the Rome Statute be amended to include corporations within the Court's jurisdiction *ratione personae*, the contours of the current framework provide an indication of what form corporate criminal responsibility could possibly assume. Such liability, moreover, need not bar individual prosecutions pursuant to the principles of attribution which have been laid out in already existing provisions and case law.

III Utilising the current Rome Statute provisions

The overarching *mens rea* stipulation of Article 30 RS and the various modes of liability enshrined in the Rome Statute were adopted with a view to the individual as the sole subject of ICC jurisdiction. Accordingly, this warrants an inquiry into their potential instrumentality with regard to corporations. Apart from the claim that individual criminal responsibility suffices, there is the related contention that the Statute is not entirely inoperative in respect of private business enterprises. On the one hand, an individual conviction of a corporate agent may indirectly implicate the entity in the commission of an international crime. On the other hand, there is the assertion that the notion of complicity enshrined in the Statute is transposable to corporations.

III.1 Indirectly implicating MNCs on the basis of individual convictions

A finding of personal culpability on the basis of any of the participation modes contained in Article 25 and Article 28(b) RS may indeed reverberate on the organisation. Depending on the particular circumstances of each individual case, it may create the perception of the entity itself having engaged in a blameworthy transgression. This is reminiscent of the Nuremberg judgments in the cases of *Farben* and *Krupp* where the USMT essentially deemed the corporations responsible for the utilisation of slave labour and the plunder of property in the occupied territories.[33] However, in light of the tribunal's jurisdictional limits, it was the individual corporate officials who were convicted in lieu of their respective organisations. The impression of *Farben* and *Krupp* as criminal instrumentalities has nevertheless persisted in time.

Conceivably, an individual conviction under the existing provisions of the Rome Statute may also yield financial repercussions for the business enterprise upon the

---

32 The application of the superior responsibility doctrine to corporate executives is extensively discussed in Chapter 6.

33 See Chapter 3, section III.3: The implicit denunciation of corporations as accessories to Nazi crimes.

sentencing of its individual agent. Article 77 RS provides among the applicable penalties for the forfeiture of proceeds, property and assets derived directly or indirectly from the commission of crimes. However, apart from concerns relating to its enforceability, Article 77 does not translate into a direct sanction on the organisation. Neither does it detract from the individual as the primary addressee of penal measures and the consequences (moral and material) that attach to them. Nevertheless, any financial effect that a company may come to bear as a result of the conviction of an agent for his involvement in an international crime, especially where the impugned conduct has materialised in the line of duty, may taint the corporate image and give the semblance of some form of responsibility imposed.

Such a perception may develop in the public eye following a finding of personal culpability even lacking any financial impact on the organisation itself. This is, perhaps, most probable in instances where the prosecution revolves around high-ranking management executives. However, the implication of the entity remains only indirect. Whether a 'tacit' assertion of corporate blameworthiness, and hence responsibility, can evince a plausible threat of reputational loss is moreover questionable. In any case, the deterrent effect (if any) would presumably be lower than that attaching to a finding of liability on the part of the entity itself.[34]

III.2 The notion of complicity as an avenue for corporate liability

Some scholars have attempted to link business involvement in grave human rights abuse with the notion of complicity as a mode of establishing legal responsibility.[35] The underlying assumption, supported by some empirical data,[36] is that corporations are rarely the material perpetrators of international crimes. Rather, economic actors provide political and (para)military groups with the opportunity and means to engage

---

34 This is assuming that corporate criminal responsibility has deterrent effects. The relationship between deterrence and criminal sanctions against corporations is further explored in Chapter 7.

35 E.g. International Commission of Jurists, *Corporate Complicity and Legal Accountability*, Report of the Expert Legal Panel on Corporate Complicity in International Crimes, 2008, at <www.business-humanrights.org/Updates/Archive/ICJPaneloncomplicity>; A. Clapham, Extending International Criminal Law beyond the Individual to Corporations and Armed Opposition Groups, 6 *Journal of International Criminal Justice* 899 (2008); A. Ramasastry, Corporate Complicity: From Nuremberg to Rangoon. An Examination of Forced Labour Cases and Their Impact on the Liability of Multinational Corporations, 20 *Berkeley Journal of International Law* 91 (2002); B. Stephens, The Amorality of Profit: Transnational Corporations and Human Rights, 20 *Berkeley Journal of International Law* 45 (2002); W.A. Schabas, Enforcing International Humanitarian Law: Catching the Accomplices, *International Review of the Red Cross*, No. 842 (2001).

36 A 2006 survey of the worst cases of reported corporate-related human rights harm, conducted by the UN Special Representative on Human Rights and Transnational Corporations, revealed that a significant fraction of the allegations involved companies being complicit in abuse perpetrated by states or non-state armed factions. See UN Doc. E/CN.4/2006/97. Another study, conducted by the Office of the High Commissioner for Human Rights, documented that 41% of human rights abuse allegations against companies concern indirect forms of involvement. See UN Doc. A/HRC/8/5/Add.2.

in mass human rights abuse. For instance, reports have accused MNCs of entering into joint ventures for the exploitation of natural resources with rogue governments and violent non-state armed factions.[37] Some of those ventures have allegedly entailed the exploitation of slave labour in diamond mines by the local partners or the forced deportation of populations from mineral-rich areas in circumstances that amount to war crimes or crimes against humanity. Seeking concessions and security, oil and mining companies have reportedly provided military forces with money, weapons and transport used for the torture and killing of civilians.[38] Business enterprises have also been alleged to sell dictatorial regimes electronic equipment and chemical substances used for the persecution and extermination of ethnic minorities.[39] MNCs thus tend to facilitate the principal perpetrators of international crimes, i.e. state organs and rebel groups, by supplying them with the goods and services they need in order to engage in human rights abuse. The contribution may be essential in enabling the realisation of the offence. Frequently, however, it serves to support or exacerbate already ongoing violations. The assistance typically transpires through legitimate commercial activities or transactions. Nonetheless, in penal as well as civil law the lawfulness of the conduct does not preclude liability where it brings about a criminal or harmful consequence.

The focus on complicity as a tool for capturing corporate involvement in international crimes has been prompted by a number of considerations. The UN Global Compact and similar initiatives have increasingly resorted to the notion,[40] as it is familiar to most national legal systems and operative in both civil and criminal law contexts.[41] The few attempts to prosecute corporate officials under international criminal law have also involved complicity as a mode of participation.[42]

However, the concept of complicity invoked in relation to human rights abuse and MNCs is an umbrella term which has no unitary meaning. Many of the civil cases brought against companies in the United States under the Alien Tort Claims Act concern allegations of complicity, although judicial opinion is divided as to its precise scope. Domestic criminal law standards of complicity in the form of aiding and

---

37 See Chapter 1, section I: Corporations, conflicts and human rights.

38 E.g. R. Dufresne, The Opacity of Oil: Oil Corporations, Internal Violence and International Law, 36 *New York University Journal of International Law and Politics* 331 (2004).

39 E. Black, *IBM and the Holocaust: The Strategic Alliance Between Nazi Germany and America's Most Powerful Corporation*, New York: Crown Publishers, 2001; M.J. Bazyler, Nuremberg in America: Litigating the Holocaust in United States Court, 34 *University of Richmond Law Review* 1 (2000).

40 For an overview of international 'soft-law' initiatives aimed at the regulation of corporate conduct in relation to human rights, see Chapter 1.

41 A. Ramasastry and R.C. Thompson, *Commerce, Crime and Conflict. Legal Remedies for Private Sector Liability for Grave Breaches of International Law*, FAFO Report, 2006, pp. 17-22, at <www.fafo.no/pub/rapp/536/536.pdf>.

42 See Chapter 3, section III.1: An overview of domestic military trials. Defendants at Nuremberg were charged with being leaders, organisers, instigators, or *accomplices*, in the formation or execution of a common plan or conspiracy to commit crimes against peace, war crimes and crimes against humanity. The tribunals were, however, vague in delineating the basis for each individual's conviction. See also *Prosecutor v. Musema*, Amended Indictment, ICTR Case No. ICTR-96-13-I, 19 April 1999.

abetting vary and even in international criminal law there are divergences among the existing tribunals.[43] In addition, the complicity notion has a non-legal pedigree. Advocates, victims and non-governmental organisations often condemn perceived business involvement in a wide range of human rights violations with reference to social expectations rather than actual legal standards.

Corporate complicity in international crimes is generally espoused to encompass three distinct forms of contribution.[44] This categorisation has also been embraced by the UN Global Compact.[45] Direct complicity refers to MNCs knowingly assisting states or other organised entities to commit violations of existing prohibitions. Such assistance may entail, for example, extending material support such as arms, military equipment or transportation to security forces engaged in violence against civilians in exchange for securing government concessions.[46] Indirect complicity, on the other hand, concerns instances of MNCs benefiting from international crimes although the business enterprises are not themselves directly involved in their perpetration.[47] Reaping the financial rewards of joint ventures with repressive governments, where the state authorities rely upon forced labour, abductions, torture and killings in the course of natural resource extraction, may be cited in this regard. Such 'beneficial' complicity is not seen as presupposing legal responsibility for the making of profit, since profit is essentially the corporate *raison d'être*. Instead blameworthiness is detected in the refusal to duly regard the (potentially) harmful effects of business activities on third parties and the company's acquiescence to human rights abuse for the sake of profit.[48] Attempts have also been made to extend the notion of corporate

---

43 Article 25(3)(c) RS stipulates a higher *mens rea* threshold for aiding and abetting than that established in the case law of the *ad hoc* tribunals. For a comparative analysis, see Van Sliedregt, *supra note 3*, pp. 87-94. The FAFO Report (*supra note 41*) further provides an overview of domestic standards with respect to complicity in the sense of aiding and abetting, ranging from 'shared intent' through *dolus directus* to various forms of *dolus eventualis* (pp. 18-20).

44 E.g. A. Clapham and S. Jerbi, *Categories of Corporate Complicity in Human Rights Abuses*, 2001, at <www.reports-and-materials.org/Clapham-Jerbi-paper.htm>. Also Ramasastry, *supra note 35*.

45 The UN Global Compact, Principle 2, at <www.unglobalcompact.org/AboutTheGC/TheTenPrinciples/Principle2.html>.

46 C. Forcese, Deterring 'Militarised' Commerce: The Prospect of Liability for 'Privatised' Human Rights Abuses, 31 *Ottawa Law Review* 171 (2000).

47 As pointed out by Ramasastry, indirect complicity may be a misnomer. In such circumstances, while the company does not directly (in the sense of knowingly) contribute to human rights violations, it benefits from profits generated from these same violations. Ramasastry, *supra note 35*, at 103.

48 In his 2008 report seeking to clarify the concept of corporate complicity, the UN Special Representative on Human Rights and Transnational Corporations expressly discounted mere profit gain as a basis for legal liability. See UN Doc. A/HRC/8/16, 15 May 2008 (para. 41). The Special Representative, however, referred to the findings of the South African Truth and Reconciliation Commission, which considered benefiting from abuse a relevant factor in determining the responsibility of companies for their involvement in apartheid. The Commission differentiated between directly profiting from activities promoting apartheid and indirectly benefiting by operating in apartheid society, linking only the former to the need for accountability. See SATRC Final Report at <www.polity.org.za/polity/

complicity to the so-called 'silent' involvement in international crimes. The understanding of silent complicity is based on the premise that corporations should not only refrain from contributing – directly or indirectly – to the violation of international norms but should also actively engage in denouncing human rights violations in host states. Even though such violations may be entirely unrelated to their activities, MNCs' mere presence on the territory of abusive states is perceived as acceptance of the states' policies of human rights abuse. As it gives rise to questions concerning the reach of MNCs' obligation to not only protect and respect but also promote human rights, silent complicity falls outside the discussion pertaining to corporate criminal responsibility. Imposing liability and punishment on business enterprises where the link between the companies' activities and the international crime is virtually non-existent, contradicts the very essence of criminal law. The issue of silent complicity therefore is better dealt with through self-regulation and 'soft' law, at the national or international level.

Since conduct that gives rise to serious human rights abuse often entails the violation of international criminal law, some commentators have sought to apply the complicity standard of that particular branch of law to the corporate context. In this regard, efforts directed at defining the risk zone within which a company may become exposed to liability under international criminal law have, in principle, recognised existing jurisdictional limitations. Arguments pertaining to the utility of various forms of accomplice responsibility have thus been put forward with reference to the individual defendant/corporate agent.[49]

Nevertheless, occasionally the contention has also surfaced that existing international standards for individuals may be extended – more or less mechanically – to corporate entities.[50] There are several potential fallacies that preclude the effective pursuit of such an approach. On the one hand, the scope of complicity in international criminal law is somewhat unsettled. There are considerable differences between the *ad hoc* tribunals and the Rome Statute in terms of the requisite objective and subjective elements.[51] On the other hand, if ICC provisions and case law are to be regarded as most authoritative since the Statute imposes certain obligations on States Parties, such a construction involves a predicament of another nature. Domestic jurisdictions vary in their respective culpability standards for complicity. Some may even not recognise modes of accomplice liability that are particular to international

---

govdocs/commissions/1998/trc/4chap2.htm>.

49 E.g. *Corporate Complicity and Legal Accountability*, Vol. II: Criminal Law and International Crimes, Report of the International Commission of Jurists Expert Legal Panel on Corporate Complicity in International Crimes, *supra note 35*; A. Reggio, Aiding and Abetting in International Criminal Law: The Responsibility of Corporate Agents and Businessmen for 'Trading with the Enemy' of Mankind, 5 *International Criminal Law Review* 623 (2005).

50 Special Representative on Human Rights and Transnational Corporations, UN Doc. A/HRC/4/35, 19 February 2007, para. 24.

51 See in this regard Chapter 4.

law. While States Parties that apply criminal law to corporations may choose to prosecute MNCs for international crimes even if the ICC jurisdiction remains bound to individuals only,[52] they are not obliged to adopt the Rome Statute elements of complicity (i.e. aiding and abetting) or other forms of accomplice liability. Ratifying States are required to give the Statute effect in their domestic legal orders. However, they enjoy a margin of appreciation in how to implement the treaty provisions. Whereas the obligation to criminalise and incorporate the elements of the crimes falling within the jurisdiction of the ICC is fairly straightforward, the existence of a similar prescription with regard to the modes of liability contained in the Rome Statute is doubtful. Such a prescriptive duty may promote the uniform application of international criminal law and perhaps guard against impunity gaps. However, it also entails the inherent danger of wide-ranging policy-implications and of rendering the principle of complementarity largely inoperative.

In case States Parties opt for the rather strict requirements of the Statute rather than more lenient national standards,[53] the question arises as to what extent adopting such a high culpability threshold with regard to corporations is warranted. The high *mens rea* stipulations of aiding and abetting and common purpose enshrined in the Rome Statute, have limitations when applied to allegations of corporate complicity. Creating the infrastructure for the commission of international crimes, e.g. through providing the financial and material means for human rights abuse in the course of legitimate business activity, entails a certain foreseeability of risk. Such foreseeability, however, is seldom likely to reach the knowledge threshold of sub-paragraphs 3c and 3d of Article 25 RS. 'Beneficial' complicity through negligence or even recklessness may furthermore not necessarily be captured by the participation modes incorporated in the Rome Statute. As will be seen below, domestic jurisdictions favour a much broader range of mental states with regard to corporate criminality. Moreover, constructing corporate criminal responsibility according to the principles of attribution applicable to individuals would compel the query of where to locate the requisite *actus reus* and *mens rea* necessary for a conviction. This in turn gives rise to concerns about the permissibility of equating individual to corporate fault.[54] Attempting to transpose existing standards from natural to legal persons thus leaves the question of how to construct the objective and subjective components of liability unanswered.

---

52 This might supposedly be the case in, e.g., the Netherlands. Whether by design or by oversight, legal persons have not been excluded from the scope of the 2003 War Crimes Act implementing the Rome Statute in the domestic legal order. In the Netherlands legal persons are subject to criminal prosecution (Article 51 of the Dutch Criminal Code).

53 For an illustration of the potentially divergent outcomes which may follow the domestic application of the international criminal law definition of complicity, albeit in relation to individual corporate officials, see H.G. van der Wilt, Genocide, Complicity in Genocide and International v. Domestic Jurisdiction Reflections on the Anraat Case, 4 *Journal of International Criminal Justice* 239 (2006).

54 See section IV.1.2 below: Liability along vicarious lines.

IV DIRECT CORPORATE CRIMINAL LIABILITY *SUI GENERIS*

The current Rome Statute framework is not tailored for application to non-natural persons. Neither does it appear suitable – for reasons previously discussed – to corporations *per se*. Should ICC jurisdiction be extended to business enterprises through a statutory revision in future, delegates may need to consider the practicability of a customised mode of liability. With a view to functionality, it might be advisable that such a provision has the capacity to sufficiently capture various forms of commercial involvement in international crimes, ranging from material perpetration (no matter how rare such occurrences might be) through knowing assistance to lesser forms of participation which, although not as blameworthy, nonetheless facilitate the commission of international crimes. Any attempt to design an effective form of corporate liability in international criminal law would also need to take into account inherent differences between natural persons and corporate entities, as well as the particular nature of organisational existence. The *sui generis* approach to the criminal responsibility of MNCs under the Rome Statute suggested hereafter, therefore entails the imposition of liability on corporations for their direct (intentional or knowing) as well as more indirect (beneficial) involvement in the gravest of human rights violations. Accordingly, blameworthiness is not inferred from individual convictions along the lines of indirect implication. Instead, findings of culpability and the corresponding punishments are intended to target the companies themselves, not only their individual agents.

Two closely inter-related issues underlie the inquiry into what might constitute direct corporate liability in international criminal law. On the one hand, there is the matter of the type of corporate fault that could justifiably trigger penal responsibility for a set of particularly serious offences, i.e. the 'core' crimes within the jurisdiction of the ICC. On the other hand, there is the question of how to construct the culpability threshold. The Rome Statute, although excluding corporations from its jurisdictional scope, does provide some space for manoeuvre. Extending the *actus reus* to conduct by omission and lowering the *mens rea* to *dolus eventualis* and beyond appear warranted and present some intriguing possibilities with regard to the prosecution of business enterprises.

IV.1 The criminal responsibility of corporations 'in the draft'

Although the Rome Conference did not result in the creation of a court with adjudicatory powers over legal persons,[55] the negotiations surrounding the drafting of

55 For an overview of the Rome Conference negotiations concerning legal persons, see Chapter 1, section IV.2: The International Criminal Court.

the Statute suggested some possible variants of constructing corporate criminal responsibility.

IV.1.1 Declarations of criminality

One of the approaches put forward and considered in the course of the consultation process was tailored after the Nuremberg concept of criminal organisations. It envisaged a power on the part of the Court to declare 'a group or organisation of every kind' criminal.[56] Declarations of criminality would follow the commission of a crime by a natural person 'on behalf of or with the assent of' the organisation. Once established, the criminal nature of the entity could not be questioned and the finding would be tied in with an obligation on the part of States Parties to take appropriate measures in response. Although the proposal resembled Article 10 of the Nuremberg Charter,[57] it did not envisage national prosecutions of individuals for membership of the organisations declared criminal. Conscious of the controversy surrounding the Nuremberg application of the criminal organisations concept as an avenue for ascribing individual responsibility,[58] the authors of the proposal were anxious not to encroach upon the presumption of innocence and the principle of personal guilt. The intended measures, potentially incumbent upon the domestic authorities to effectuate, therefore targeted the organisations *per se*. Among the penalties deemed applicable were fines, forfeiture of criminal proceeds, and reparation orders.

Despite the elimination of references to a crime of membership in a criminal organisation, the delegates conceded that the liability of natural persons prosecuted by national courts might not be disassociated completely from that of the organisation.[59] Even with safeguards in place, individual convictions would be difficult to divorce from perceptions of guilt by association. By endorsing the deduction of group criminality from the behaviour of a single individual operating from within or even outside the entity, the proposed approach was, furthermore, objectionable for its

56 UN Doc. A/CONF.183/C.1/L.3, 16 June 1998 in *Official Records of the United Nations Diplomatic Conference of Plenipotentiaries on the Establishment of an International Criminal Court*, Vol. III: Reports and Other Documents, at <untreaty.un.org/cod/icc/rome/proceedings/E/Rome%20Proceedings_ v3_e.pdf>.

57 Article 10 of the Nuremberg Charter read: 'In cases where a group or organisation is declared criminal by the Tribunal, the competent national authority or any Signatory shall have the right to bring individuals to trial for membership therein before national, military or occupation courts. In any such case the criminal nature of the group or organisation is considered proved and shall not be questioned.' *Trial of the Major War Criminals before the International Military Tribunal*, Nuremberg Germany (1947), Vol. I, pp. 10-18.

58 For a critical discussion of the concept of criminal organisations, as interpreted and applied at Nuremberg, see Chapter 2, section II.2: The concept of criminal organisations.

59 UN Doc. A/CONF.183/C.1/SR.1, 16 June 1998 in *Official Records of the United Nations Diplomatic Conference of Plenipotentiaries on the Establishment of an International Criminal Court*, Vol. II: Summary Records of the Plenary Meetings and of the Meetings of the Committee of the Whole, at <untreaty.un.org/cod/diplomaticconferences/icc-1998/docs/english/vol2/a_conf_183_c1_sr1.pdf>.

implication of collective guilt and collective punishment; it failed to specify the permissible contours of attributing liability from an individual to the organisation. In relation to profit-oriented enterprises in particular, as discussed elsewhere,[60] constructing liability via declarations of criminality would also not reflect the true nature of corporate involvement in international crimes. While a criminogenic culture that promotes unlawful or precarious conduct may exist within the entity, such an ethos or an isolated incident of involvement in an international crime does not necessarily render the company inherently criminal.

IV.1.2 Liability along vicarious lines

The deficiencies of the original French proposal compelled its refinement in the process of negotiations. Concerns about the necessary *mens rea* for individual convictions and the absence of a requisite link between the material perpetrator and the organisation prompted the strict separation of individual responsibility from corporate criminal liability. The latter became premised upon the unlawful conduct of agents or agencies,[61] thus precluding a finding of organisational culpability as a result of blameworthy individual behaviour which was neither endorsed nor within the control of the entity. The ambiguous formulation of the text, however, left open the question of whether corporate criminal responsibility would be based only upon personal or also group transgressions and how liability was to be constructed. It evidenced an inclination towards a vicarious type of liability. This position was subsequently solidified and the French delegation eventually put forward a construction of corporate criminal responsibility clearly premised on the identification principle. The final version of the proposed provision provided:

> [Without prejudice to any individual criminal responsibility of natural persons under this Statute, the Court may also have jurisdiction over a juridical person for a crime under this Statute.
>
> Charges may be filed by the Prosecutor against a juridical person, and the Court may render a judgment over a juridical person for the crime charged, if:
> a) The charges filed by the Prosecutor against the natural person and the juridical person allege the matters referred to in subparagraphs (b) and (c); and
> b) The natural person charged was in a position of control within the juridical person under the national law of the State where the juridical person was registered at the time the crime was committed; and

60 See Chapter 3, section II.3: A missed opportunity *vis-à-vis* corporate accountability?

61 Draft Article 23, paragraph 5, read: 'The Court shall have jurisdiction over legal persons, with the exception of States, when the crimes committed were committed on behalf of such legal persons or by their agencies or representatives.' See UN Doc. A/CONF.183/2/Add.1, p. 49.

c) The crime was committed by the natural person acting on behalf of and with the explicit consent of that juridical person and in the course of its activities; and
d) The natural person has been convicted of the crime charged.][62]

The prosecution of business entities was thus made dependant on the conviction of individuals who, by virtue of their position and power of control, could be regarded as personifying their respective organisations. The proposed approach reflected the nominalist method of ascribing criminal liability to corporations predominantly applied in domestic legal systems of common law orientation. This method encompasses two models of corporate criminal responsibility: the 'respondeat superior' principle and the identification doctrine. Both models refute the separate existence of corporations and hence ascribe to them a derivative form of liability which is necessarily vicarious in character.[63] The *actus reus* and *mens rea* for corporate criminal responsibility are uncovered in the conduct and mindset of certain agents within the organisation. Subsequently, the elements identified are artificially attributed to the company itself. The 'respondeat superior' construction extends liability to the corporation for unlawful acts committed by any employee. Its application is mostly limited to strict liability offences in the areas of, *inter alia*, consumer protection and environmental law.[64] With regard to *mens rea* crimes, national jurisdictions have generally recognised the need for additional conditionalities, including a requirement for the employee to have acted within the scope of his employment and with the authorisation of the organisation.[65] Compared to the method of 'respondeat superior', the identification doctrine is generally more restrictive. It equates the corporate entity with certain key personnel deemed to represent the entity's directing minds. Regarded as the physical alter ego of the organisation by virtue of their status and authority, these individuals' blameworthy behaviour is ascribed to the corporation, for the latter is considered incapable of existing independently of its agents.

Presumably, the choice of the identification doctrine as a means for constructing the liability of corporations under the Rome Statute was not an expression of overwhelming support for the nominalist perspective on corporations as possessing 'fictional' personality only. Rather, it seems to have been largely motivated by the

62 UN Doc. A/CONF.183/C.1/WGGP/L.5/Rev.2, 3 July 1998. Paragraph 6 of Article 23 further provided that: [The proceedings with respect to a juridical person under this article shall be in accordance with this Statute and the relevant Rules of Procedure and Evidence. The Prosecutor may file charges against the natural and juridical persons jointly or separately. The natural person and the juridical person may be jointly tried.]

63 For a general overview, see G.G.J. Knoops, The Transposition of (International) Criminal Liability Modes onto Private Corporations, in S. Adam, N. Colette-Basecqz and M. Nohoul (eds.), *Corporate Criminal Liability in Europe*, Brussels: La Charte, 2008.

64 E. Lederman, Models for Imposing Corporate Criminal Liability: From Adaptation and Imitation Toward Aggregation and the Search for Self-Identity, 4 *Buffalo Criminal Law Review* 641 (2001) at 653-654.

65 *Ibidem*, at 654-655. See also E. Colvin, Corporate Personality and Criminal Liability, 6 *Criminal Law Forum* 1 (1995) at 6-8.

perceived need to ensure that the primary jurisdictional focus remains on the individual. Moreover, the model of corporate criminal responsibility operative in France – whose delegation lobbied most actively for the extension of ICC jurisdiction to legal persons – was itself based on the 'directing mind' principle.[66]

The nominalist method of constructing corporate liability considered for adoption at the Rome Conference, exhibits several deficiencies. The ascription of corporate liability along vicarious lines does not reflect the *modus operandi* of MNCs as opposed to smaller businesses. In large organisations, characterised by multiple channels of communication and dispersed levels of control, the requisite *actus reus* and *mens rea* may not necessarily converge in a single individual. By inferring corporate blameworthiness from individual transgression, the nominalist approach also tends to distort the allocation of liability. The corporation may be insulated from liability even where corporate fault exists, because the finding of organisational culpability is made dependant on establishing the culpability of a particular agent. Alternatively, criminal responsibility for the entity and sanctions of collective impact may follow even in the absence of actual corporate fault. Revolving organisational liability around personal agency does not reflect the nature and dynamics of institutional structures. It ignores the impact that policies, culture and joint failures may have on individual behaviour. As evidenced in criminological literature on corporate deviance, processes of routinisation, rationalisation and socialisation serve to justify and conceal (potentially) criminal behaviour.[67] The implication of business in international crimes through legitimate transactions, often involving multipurpose goods whose end-use may not be apparent, further complicates matters. The peculiarities of corporate existence thus serve to disperse knowledge and responsibility. This is particularly relevant with regard to any attempts to couple the vicarious ascription of corporate liability with a requirement of 'explicit consent' on the part of the organisation. Had it been adopted in Rome, such a mechanism would have required proof of actual knowledge on the part of corporate governing bodies as a whole of the specific crimes committed by an individually culpable agent. While, in some circumstances, this could be indicative of corporate fault, it would not transcend the inherent difficulty of locating the requisite elements of culpability in a single individual.

66 G. Stessens, Corporate Criminal Liability: a Comparative Perspective, 43 *International and Comparative Law Quarterly* 493 (1994) at 496-497.

67 E.g. W. Huisman, Corporations and International Crimes, in A. Smeulers and R. Haveman (eds.), *Supranational Criminology: Towards a Criminology of International Crimes*, Antwerp: Intersentia, 2008; M. Punch, Suit Violence: Why Managers Murder and Corporations Kill, 33 *Crime, Law and Social Change* 243 (2000). See in this regard also Chapter 2.

IV.2 Domestic approaches to corporate criminal liability

Seeking to artificially transpose the combination of objective and subjective aspects that constitute the definition of a crime from an individual to the organisation, is a reflection of the deeply imbedded individualistic perception of society that typifies Western legal tradition. Hence, the rejection of the non-fictional character of corporations has been a hallmark of many legal systems in modern times.[68] Deriving corporate fault from personal culpability is, however, a misplaced manifestation of 19th century ideas about individual independence. Such ideas have, moreover, never been entirely divorced of the notion of collectivism. Both national and international law recognise the importance of the collective and the reality of human interdependence in relation to group crimes, whether institutionalised or not. As a result, and particularly with regard to corporate liability, a growing number of domestic jurisdictions have begun embracing elements of more holistic (as opposed to the strictly individualistic) views on the nature of corporations. Increasing recognition of the deficiencies of the nominalist approach has prompted growing domestic efforts to incorporate organisational theory in criminal law provisions pertaining to business enterprises. As will be seen below, holistic approaches vary. However they generally share the perception of corporations as having an existence of their own, separate from the existence of the individuals comprising them. This fundamental shift in perspective has broad repercussions for understanding how corporate fault materialises and accordingly what constitutes such fault.

IV.2.1 The principle of aggregation

Domestic legal systems of both individualist and more collectivist orientation in assessing corporate criminal liability, have resorted to aggregation as a means of capturing organisational transgression. The approach largely developed as a reaction to the inadequacy of the derivative models discussed above, which have the propensity to allow fatally harmful organisational 'sloppiness' to go unpunished.[69] It is, however,

68 Vicarious-type corporate liability has been embraced in e.g. South Africa (Criminal Procedure Act, No. 51 of 1977, § 332) and applied as a matter of common law by US federal courts (e.g. Western International Hotels Co. v. United States, 409 US 1125 (1973)). Variants of the identification principle have been espoused by legislators or courts in, *inter alia*, the UK (e.g. Tesco Supermarkets Ltd. v. Nattrass, AC 153 (1971); R. v. P&O European Ferries (Dover) Ltd., 93 Cr App R 72 (1990)), Canada (e.g. Canadian Dredge & Dock Co. v. R., 1 SCR 662 (1985)), Australia (Review of Commonwealth Criminal Law, Third Interim Report of Criminal Responsibility and Other Matters § 4BA (3)(a) 1990; and subsequently Model Criminal Code § 501.2 codified in the Criminal Code Act § 12.3 (2)(a)-(b)), Israel (Penal Law 1977 as amended in 1994, § 23 (a)(2) (3rd ed. 1999)), some US state courts (e.g. State v. Christy Pontiac-GMC Inc., 354 NW 2d 17, 19-20 (1984) and France (see Stessens, *supra note 66*, at 501).

69 A classic example, frequently cited in criticism of derivative corporate liability, is the *Herald of Free Enterprise* Case, which resulted in the acquittal of a ferry company for the infamous Zeebrugge disaster. The ferry capsized into open sea as due to a series of mistakes its doors were left open. The

not devoid of contention.[70] In general, the aggregation principle grounds the criminal liability of corporations on the combined acts or omissions of individual agents where each act or omission is in itself insufficient. Mental states and conduct on the part of different individuals are joined together and considered as a whole. The underlying rationale is that a combination of personal transgressions or minor failures might reveal a gross breach of duty on the part of the company, or collective awareness that warrants the entity's responsibility for a criminal consequence. Some jurisdictions have been hesitant to extend the application of aggregation to crimes requiring proof of intent as opposed to only knowledge.[71] Other legal systems have recognised the utility of the principle with regard to situations entailing recklessness and even gross negligence.[72] For instance, a Dutch court convicted a hospital trust for negligent homicide in failing to ensure that obsolete equipment was effectively disposed of in compliance with safety procedures. In the particular case, a patient died following the incorrect storage and subsequent use by an anaesthetist of the device. The combined acts and failures of the anaesthetist and senior management were deemed to constitute fault on the part of the organisation itself.[73]

Considering the conduct of different agents as a whole, helps uncover the existence of corporate fault which may otherwise remain hidden or go unpunished should the focus be on the subjective mental state of a particular individual. However, there is also the inherent risk of innocent individual conduct being regarded as indicative of corporate wrongdoing even in the absence of organisational failure pertaining to the implementation of proper policies and procedures.[74] Furthermore, matching the *actus reus* of one agent with the *mens rea* of another, particularly where the mental factor relates to intent, is somewhat awkward in its implications. The lack of concurrence between the physical and the subjective element is not in itself conceptually disturbing from the perspective of non-derivative approaches to constructing corporate criminal liability. The difficulty though lies in joining together conduct and mental states, which may have no connection to each other or to corporate fault. Lastly, the aggregation doctrine stands somewhat at odds with the notion of corporations having a separate existence and hence bearing legal and moral responsibility. On the one hand, the principle of aggregation recognises an independent corporate mental state.

---

accident resulted in the death of nearly two hundred passengers. The company managed to escape liability in part because the court could not find the requisite fault in a single individual for what was essentially a manifestation of 'organisational sloppiness'. R. v. P&O European Ferries (Dover) Ltd., 93 Cr App R 72 (1990).

70 For an overview of the criticism mounted against aggregation in domestic jurisdictions, see e.g. Lederman, *supra note 64*, at 661-677.

71 *Ibidem*, at 666. Attempts for recognition of the principle of aggregation in relation to knowledge as well as negligence have been made in Canada (Proposals to Amend the Criminal Code (General Principles) cl. 22 (1993).

72 Australian Criminal Code Act 1995 § 12.4(2).

73 *Ziekenhuis Leeuwarden*, District Court of Leeuwarden, 23 December 1987 (NJ 1988, 981).

74 Colvin, *supra note 65*, at 22-24.

On the other hand, however, it reduces that mental state to the mere collection of individual *mentes reae*, which are then vicariously transposed onto the corporation.

These abstract forewarnings demarcate the limitations of aggregation as a theoretical framework. They should not be read, however, as implying that aggregation cannot, or should not serve as a basis for corporate liability in national or international criminal law. When employed in combination with organisational theories pertaining to corporate fault, the aggregation principle is potentially instrumental in efforts to construct the corporate *mens rea*.[75]

IV.2.2 Proactive and reactive fault

Unlike the derivative models of corporate liability and the doctrine of aggregation, truly holistic approaches seek to locate culpability in genuine corporate fault. Whether the fault is proactive or reactive in nature, liability generally follows from a failure on the part of the organisation to exercise due diligence.[76] This failure reflects a breach of duty to ensure that adequate safeguards have been put in place capable of guarding against the (repeated) infliction of harm through corporate operations.

The weakness of the proactive and reactive models of corporate fault lies in the predominantly negligence-type liability that they seek to impose. On the one hand, the implementation of proper policies and procedures may not invariably prevent a crime from occurring. On the other hand, exclusive reliance on formal systems for internal supervision and control may serve to insulate the corporate entity from liability, particularly where a demonstration of due diligence is in itself allowed to negate responsibility.[77] The retrospective evaluation of rules and processes in the aftermath of a crime may also be prone to certain distortion.[78] In this regard, legal commentators have rightly contended that corporate criminal liability should not be allowed to flow

75 See section IV.2.4 below: Constructive corporate fault and section IV.3: The constructive method and international crimes.

76 See Comment, Developments in the Law – Corporate Crime: Regulating Corporate Behaviour through Criminal Sactions, 92 *Harvard Law Review* 1227 (1979) at 1257-1258, discussing corporate responsibility for failing to prevent the commission of a crime by instituting adequate policies and procedures. See also B. Fisse, Restructuring Corporate Criminal Law: Deterrence, Retribution, Fault and Sanctions, 56 *South California Law Review* 1141 (1983) at 1192-1205, expounding corporate attitude towards the offence *post factum* as a basis for organisational blameworthiness.

77 For an espousal of due diligence as a defence, see Fisse, *supra note 76*, at 1257-1258.

78 The argument that grounding liability on compliance programmes is a potentially ineffective approach has been put forward by, *inter alia*, R.G. Gruner, *Corporate Crime and Sentencing*, Charlottesville: Business Laws, Inc., 1994, pp. 276-277. He contends that corporations may produce 'window-dressing' programmes in order to insulate themselves from legal responsibility. For the opposing claim, postulating that the judicial ability to assess the adequacy of compliance programmes is greater than generally presumed, see V.S. Khanna, Corporate Liability Standards: When Should Corporations be Held Criminally Liable, 37 *American Criminal Law Review* 1239 (2000) at 1271-1274.

from a lack of adequate safeguards in combination with an objective result.[79] Rather, for fairness' sake, it ought to require some additional subjective factor.

The models of proactive and reactive fault have found some limited application in domestic jurisdictions.[80] Despite their shortcomings and if properly circumscribed, they may have a role to play in international criminal law as well.[81] The existence of a duty of care, and responsibility for breaches thereof, is recognised and operative in the context of the international courts in relation to individuals.[82] Nothing precludes the extension of a similar duty of care to corporations in the form of an explicit requirement to develop specific safeguards against organisational involvement in international crimes. Such safeguards may involve the unequivocal familiarisation of personnel with existing legal prohibitions and the integration of human rights policies as well as monitoring performance processes throughout the organisational structure. They may furthermore entail an obligation on MNCs to broaden the scope of their risk assessment practices and also give consideration to the human rights impact of their operations. MNCs' responsibilities with regard to due diligence, and the link between the latter and the prospect of legal liability for human rights violations, have increasingly been acknowledged by the United Nations.[83] For reasons delineated above, however, corporate liability, especially for the 'core' international crimes, is more sensibly rooted in a breach of duty where such a breach is coupled with additional factors.[84] Organisational attitude towards the necessity of – or potential requirement for – comprehensive internal systems for assessment and control in relation to the risk of human rights abuse may potentially reveal corporate recklessness

79 See A. Foerschler, Corporate Criminal Intent: Toward a Better Understanding of Corporate Misconduct, 78 *California Law Review* 1287 (1990) at 1306-1311, suggesting that corporate liability flows not only from the existence of a policy which could reasonably be deemed to create a risk for the violation of the law, but also from the adoption or acquiescence on the part of the corporation of individual agents' transgressions as a result of that policy. See also A. Ragozino, Replacing the Collective Knowledge Doctrine with a Better Theory for Establishing Corporate Mens Rea: The Duty Stratification Approach, 24 *Southwestern University Law Review* 423 (1995) at 448-457, who proposes that a requirement for corporate compliance programmes is coupled with international or knowing involvement in the crime on the part of either management or ordinary employees.

80 E.g. Proactive corporate fault has been incorporated into the United States Federal Guidelines for Sentencing Organisations (1 November 1991). The Guidelines provide for a reduction in fines should a corporation be convicted of a criminal activity, provided that the entity had put a comprehensive compliance programme in place. Ragozino, *supra note 79*, at 451-453.

81 See section IV.3.1b below: *Culpa* as a benchmark for corporate criminal responsibility.

82 See Chapter 4, section III: The concept of superior responsibility.

83 E.g. UN Doc. A/HRC/8/5, 7 April 2008; UN Doc. A/HRC/8/16, 15 May 2008. The UN Special Representative on Human Rights and Transnational Corporations has recently defined due diligence with regard to corporations in a broader sense as 'a comprehensive, proactive attempt to uncover human rights risks, actual and potential, over the entire life cycle of a project or business activity, with the aim of avoiding and mitigating those risks.' UN Doc. A/HRC/11/13, 22 April 2009 (para. 71).

84 See also section IV.3.1 below: Setting the subjective threshold of corporate liability.

or wilful blindness.[85] A failure to react adequately to an unwitting criminal transgression *post factum* may also translate into knowing contribution to an international crime. Proactive and reactive failings are an integral part of corporate fault but insufficient in themselves for criminal responsibility exceeding a mere breach of duty, since they essentially imply blameworthiness for organisational mismanagement rather than for a criminal consequence. Moreover, grounding liability on such failures would not necessarily align with specific intent offences.[86]

IV.2.3 The corporate ethos approach

The corporate ethos approach has emerged as a means of circumscribing the limitations inherent in basing corporate liability on a failure to implement formal policies and procedures.[87] It discerns corporate fault in the effect that organisational structure and culture produce on individual behaviour which results in the commission of a crime. Unlike the models of proactive and reactive fault, the theory of the corporate ethos seeks to focus on corporate intentionality (*dolus*) rather than mere negligence. It endeavours to impose criminal liability on corporations when an agent commits an illegal act as a result of either explicit or implicit endorsement by the corporation of a faulty operating system. Liability therefore follows when existing policies, structures or practices violate the law or when they encourage a corporate agent to engage in an illegal activity.

Recently, the corporate ethos method has been put forward for inclusion in the Australian Criminal Code. The proposal states that if intention, knowledge or recklessness is the fault element in relation to the offence, it must be attributed to the entity that expressly, tacitly or impliedly authorised or permitted the commission of the offence.[88] Such an authorisation or permission may be established by proving that a corporate culture existed within the organisation that directed, encouraged, tolerated or led to non-compliance with the law.[89]

The holistic models discussed above, *i.e.* proactive and reactive failure with regard to policy implementation and corporate ethos, are predominantly theoretical in nature. Since they tend to dispense with the *mens rea* element of crimes altogether, no jurisdiction has adopted them as leading principles for the attribution of criminal responsibility to corporations. However, as evidenced by the preceding paragraphs,

85 In this regard, some US courts, for instance, regard the inadequacy or non-existence of risk assessments on the part of corporations as an indication of recklessness.

86 W.S. Laufer and A. Strudler, Corporate Intentionality, Desert, and Variants of Vicarious Liability, 37 *American Criminal Law Review* 1285 (2000).

87 P.H. Bucy, Corporate Ethos: a Standard for Imposing Corporate Criminal Liability, 75 *Minnesota Law Review* 1095 (1991). For a discussion of corporate culture in relation to culpability, see generally P.A. French, *Collective and Corporate Responsibility*, New York: Columbia University Press, 1984.

88 Australian Model Criminal Code: General Principles (2004) § 12.3(1).

89 Australian Model Criminal Code: General Principles (2004) § 12.3(2)(c).

certain aspects of holistic approaches towards corporate fault have been gaining recognition. These pertain in particular to culpability for breaches of duty to guard against the commission of crimes and for sustaining a criminogenic organisational system. Even among domestic legal systems which have traditionally embraced the nominalist method, there is a trend in the direction of adopting more comprehensive liability schemes integrating vicarious-type liability with organisational theories of corporate fault. For example, Swiss law provides for the criminal responsibility of a business enterprise where the offence was committed in furtherance of corporate interests.[90] Although primarily relying on the doctrine of respondeat superior, Denmark and Finland also recognise corporate criminal liability for institutional or management failures.[91] Many countries have expanded legislative provisions to provide for crime resulting from organisational deficiencies and some have even introduced a rebuttable presumption of corporate liability.[92] There are, moreover, changes discernible in legal systems that have been particularly resistant to the departure from traditional approaches which require a finding of fault on the part of an individual corporate agent.[93]

IV.2.4 Constructive corporate fault

With the aim of overcoming the unease on the part of domestic jurisdictions with the idea of corporate fault entirely divorced from subjectivism as a feature of penal law, Laufer expounds a constructive approach that matches the requisite mental states of criminal offences with organisational peculiarities.[94] The model differentiates between various degrees of culpability but such culpability is not imputed to the corporation along traditional vicarious lines. Instead, corporate fault is discerned considering the unique aspects of the entity and its particular circumstances. Laufer's proposal thus accommodates for the central concerns in relation to other existing or theoretical methods. On the one hand, it recognises that corporations have a distinct existence which cannot be reduced to the (aggregation of) individual agents comprising them.[95] On the other hand, it also recognises the need for the attribution of corporate liability only where it is reasonable and fair to do so.[96]

---

90 S.S. Beale and A.G. Safwat, What Developments in Western Europe Tell Us About American Critiques of Corporate Criminal Liability, 8 *Buffalo Criminal Law Review* 89 (2005) at 113-115.

91 *Ibidem*, at 138.

92 Japan is cited as an example of a country where rebuttable presumption of liability exists in G. Heine, New Developments in Europe: Can Europeans Learn from the American Experience or Vice Versa? *St. Louis-Warsaw Transatlantic Law Journal* 173 (1998) at 182.

93 France with reference to negligence-based offences, Beale and Safwat, *supra note 90*, at 138.

94 W.S. Laufer, *Corporate Bodies and Guilty Minds: The Failure of Corporate Criminal Liability*, Chicago: University of Chicago Press, 2006.

95 *Ibidem*, pp. 70-71.

96 *Idem*.

Constructive corporate fault is thus detected in culpable corporate conduct coupled with a concurrent corporate mental state that corresponds to the *mens rea* element of the offence alleged. Conclusions in this regard may be drawn, according to Laufer, on the basis of reasonable inferences and evidence of actual awareness. Culpable conduct on the part of the organisation is identified on the basis of an objective test of reasonableness. The goal of the test is to determine whether 'given the size, complexity, formality, functionality, decision-making process, and structure of the corporate organisation',[97] it is reasonable to conclude that the physical elements of the offence may be validly attributed to the entity.[98] The purpose is to ensure that the organisation does not come to bear responsibility for isolated individual misconduct. Thus, under the proposed test the behaviour of agents who act outside the scope of their employment, contrary to explicit corporate policy and despite adequate due diligence safeguards, may not be attached to the entity itself.[99]

Objectivism also plays a role in constructing the corporate *mens rea* to the extent that the subjective requirement of an offence (i.e. intent, knowledge, recklessness or negligence) is uncovered through a method that is not entirely subjective.[100] The organisation is not judged against the objective standard of the reasonable man; there is an inquiry into its mentality. This enquiry is done with the assistance of reasonableness judgments. However, it also takes into account evidence of actual awareness.[101] Thus purposeful corporate transgression would be reflected in evidence of policies or practices which, given the features and circumstances of the particular organisation, appear to expressly or implicitly authorise, encourage or otherwise support the violation of the law. Knowledge would be deduced from actual awareness of the certainty of a risk and toleration of illegal conduct (considering the organisation as a whole). A finding of recklessness would follow the corporation's conscious

97 *Ibidem*, p. 72.

98 As Laufer explains, the objective test of reasonableness is different from the test of the reasonable man, in that it does not resort to 'objectivity as an external standard of behaviour'. The reasonableness test in the context of constructive fault is a 'non-subjective method for determining culpability'. It entails an appraisal of the corporation by reference to objective features (e.g. size, structure, formality), but does not involve judgment in relation to what the corporation ought to have reasonably done in the particular circumstances (*Idem*).

99 A similar approach was adopted by the Dutch Supreme Court in a judgment of 21 October 2003 (NJ 2006, 328). The Court concluded that an enterprise would be held criminally liable if the acts in question could be 'reasonably' attributed to it. The assessment of 'reasonableness' would depend on the circumstances of each individual case and include, *inter alia*, an inquiry into: the question of whether the acts took place within the sphere of the enterprise, whether the acts occurred in the ordinary course of business activities and whether the corporation benefited from those acts (LJN: AR7619, 29 March 2005, at <www.rechtspraak.nl>).

100 In this regard the constructive corporate fault method builds upon the subjective/objective model of liability put forward by G. Fletcher in: Theory of Criminal Negligence: a Comparative Analysis, 119 *University of Pensylvannia Law Review* 401 (1971) at 510.

101 Laufer, *supra note 94*, pp. 90-91.

disregard for a risk of harm. Negligence in turn would involve the corporation inadvertently creating the unjustifiable risk of a crime occurring.[102]

The constructive fault approach rejects a purely objective standard of negligence as the basis for corporate liability. A culpability standard judging the company against an external standard of fault, is deemed to 'strip the law of its moral meaning and render it indistinguishable from the civil law'.[103] At the same time, however, the model embraces the mental element of negligence. Such negligence is understood to be more subjective in nature, as it refers to a state of mind (or rather an attitude that reveals the blameworthiness of corporate behaviour). Since it is a method for uncovering organisational fault and tailored for the needs of the domestic prosecution of enterprises within an already existing legislative framework,[104] the constructive approach does not inquire into the justifiability of negligence as a standard of *mens rea* attaching to corporate criminal responsibility.[105] Nor does it examine the type of offences to which liability for criminal negligence attaches. In a sense, however, the incorporation of negligence in constructive corporate fault reflects growing acceptance of negligence as a yardstick for corporate conduct by domestic jurisdictions in recent decades. Since it constitutes the lowest threshold for culpability after strict liability, criminal law has been hesitant to recognise its relevance to situations other than statutory offences. Some legal commentators have even insisted on treating negligence as entirely separate from corporate *mens rea.*[106] Nonetheless, criminal negligence (i.e. gross negligence) has gradually become established as one of the mental elements required for conventional as opposed to strict liability offences.

Critics have predictably questioned the constructive corporate fault method for its emphasis on objectivism and its endorsement of negligence. There is a fear that it may project onto the discernment of individual mental states.[107] The method's propensity to facilitate the discovery of evidence and hence prosecution has also been condemned, for heightened criminal law enforcement should not necessarily be regarded as an end in itself.[108] Such criticism, however, is not entirely justified. The subjective foundation

102 *Ibidem*, pp. 78-87.

103 *Idem*, p. 87.

104 Laufer's classification of mental states attaching to corporate criminality into four broad categories, i.e. purpose, knowledge, recklessness and negligence, reflects a general hierarchy of culpable *mens rea* distinctions found in US state and federal law.

105 Neither do the other methods for constructing corporate fault previously discussed, e.g. the identification doctrine, aggregation, corporate ethos, although a preference for negligence as the basis of corporate liability is clearly discernible in some (e.g. proactive and reactive fault).

106 For a discussion of the justifications behind the separation of negligence from the *mens rea* element in criminal law, see R.A. Posner, *Economic Analysis of Law*, Boston: Little, Brown & Co., 1992, pp. 163-167, and more recently V.S. Khanna, Is the Notion of Corporate Fault a Faulty Notion?: The Case of Corporate Mens Rea, 79 *Boston University Law Review* 355 (1999).

107 Lederman, *supra note 64*, at 704-706.

108 *Ibidem*, at 702.

of criminal law has gradually been eroding even with regard to individuals.[109] Moreover, if objectivism has a role to play in criminal law, then it is precisely in relation to non-human entities. The utility of constructive fault is in its reliance on an adapted combination of holistic principles, such as aggregation, ethos and proactive/reactive duty of care, in uncovering corporate culpability. These principles are already operative – to one extent or another – in domestic jurisdictions. The constructive method, moreover, does not negate the role of entity-agent relationships as a traditional basis for the liability of business enterprises. Although it allows for reasonable inferences to be drawn from the interplay of organisational characteristics (i.e. structure, culture, policies, channels of communication and levels of control), it recognises that, in certain circumstances, criminal responsibility may be attributed to the entity somewhat along identification lines. This would be the case where the blameworthy conduct materialises with the exclusive or extensive participation of senior management.

IV.3 The constructive method and international crimes

Constructive fault as an avenue for uncovering corporate culpability under criminal law, transcends the limitations of other models – existing and theoretical. It acknowledges the true nature of corporate entities and reflects a developing trend in domestic jurisdictions towards adopting various organisational aspects when searching for the requisite *mens rea* on the part of business enterprises. Should it be incorporated in the Rome Statute, it may however need to be adapted to the peculiarities of international crimes.

IV.3.1 Setting the subjective threshold of corporate liability

Article 30 of the Rome Statute, as previously discussed, expressly leaves room for fault degrees other than those deemed to comprise knowledge and volition as the expression of intentional conduct. Although its compatibility with Article 30 is contentious, the ICC judiciary may nevertheless resort to the notion of *dolus eventualis* where the statutory provisions allow for it. As for *culpa* standards of liability, such are already present and operative in the context of Article 28 RS. If explicitly provided for in the *sui generis* provision pertaining to corporate criminal responsibility, the subjective criteria of *dolus eventualis* and *culpa* may have a role to play in relation to the culpability of companies too. This warrants an inquiry into their scope and justifiability with regard to international crimes.

109 C. Wells, *Corporations and Criminal Responsibility*, Oxford: Oxford University Press, 2005, pp. 67-69.

IV.3.1a The *dolus eventualis* standard of corporate misconduct

The unsettled status of *dolus eventualis* in international criminal law has primarily been due to its application in combination with the troubled notion of extended joint criminal enterprise.[110] The definition expounded by Pre-Trial Chamber I of the ICC in *Lubanga* also gives rise to some concerns.[111] In principle, however, *dolus eventualis* is a valid and acceptable standard for culpability, which many domestic jurisdictions have embraced with regard to individual participation in ordinary as well as international crimes. It is also an established fault degree pertaining to instances of corporate criminality in states that recognise business entities as subject to criminal prosecution and sanctions. Nothing precludes reliance on *dolus eventualis* in adjudicating the involvement of companies in grave human rights abuse as long as it does not negate the special intent requirement that attaches to certain offences. Nonetheless, there remains the uncertainty as to its precise scope. National legal systems vary in their interpretation of *dolus eventualis* as a basis for corporate culpability in criminal law. In common law jurisdictions it can translate into advertent recklessness and entails the conscious disregard of a substantial risk of a crime occurring. Civil law countries, where the term itself originates, generally understand *dolus eventualis* as indifference toward or acceptance of the chance that a proscribed result might occur. Although the risk need not be substantial, it must be more than negligible in order to be deemed genuinely accepted.[112] In *Lubanga,* the Chamber embraced the more extensive interpretation of *dolus eventualis* commonly accepted in Germany and German-influenced legal traditions in Europe and South America. The difficulty in this regard, in relation to both individual and corporate defendants, is how to establish awareness and acceptance, and how to demarcate the distinction between low levels of *dolus eventualis* and high degrees of *culpa.*

To this author's mind, uncovering corporate fault at the level of *dolus eventualis* through the constructive approach, would focus on the attitude that company behaviour can reasonably be said to have revealed in circumstances of risk. The inquiry into the mentality of the organisation would take into account evidence of actual awareness. Conclusions about the existence of such awareness would be drawn using the principle of aggregation. The challenge would be to ascertain whether, given

110 For a discussion of the doctrine of joint criminal enterprise and *dolus eventualis* (compared to advertent recklessness by the *ad hoc* tribunals) as a *mens rea* standard for individual responsibility in JCE context, see Chapter 4. Also K. Ambos, Amicus Curiae Brief on JCE in the Matter of the Co-Prosecutors' Appeal of the Closing Order Against Kaing Guek Eav 'Duch' Dated 8 August 2008, 20 *Criminal Law Forum* 353 (2009). As will be recalled, in *Lubanga*, the ICC sought to differentiate between *dolus eventualis* and recklessness. Lubanga, *supra note* 7, paras. 353-355.

111 See section II.3 above.

112 See e.g. F. de Jong, *Daad-Schuld* (Action-inferred Culpability. A Contribution to the Legal Theory of Action with Special Reference to the Normativisation of the Mental Element of Intent in Criminal Law), The Hague: Boom Legal Publishers, 2009.

the nature of the information available, the type of individual agents in whose possession it was and the peculiarities (structural and functional) of the given organisation, the corporation as a whole can be considered to have been aware of the risk of a criminal consequence. Depending on the meaning vested in *dolus eventualis* as a standard of corporate culpability and how it is linked to Article 30 RS, the awareness may not need to relate to the existence of a substantial risk. However, the risk would have to be foreseeable and it would have to be unjustifiable. The element of foreseeability is an essential component of the legality tenet, and sets criminal culpability for *mens rea* offences apart from strict liability.[113] The unjustifiability of the risk, on the other hand, serves to validate the prosecution of the business entity for the crime that has occurred. The constructive method would focus on the objective reasonableness of the risk. Liability would not follow a failure on the part of the entity to perceive what it ought to have perceived, i.e. an unjustifiable risk. Rather, corporate culpability would be derived from the awareness that the organisation – considered as a whole – had of the risk and how it chose to act with respect to the information it had at its disposal.

The constructive approach to corporate fault at the level of *dolus eventualis* would thus enquire whether there is evidence establishing that the company had reason to suspect a risk and consciously disregarded that risk. The emphasis would not be on whether a failure of due diligence prevented the corporation from perceiving a risk it should have or could have been aware of. Culpability would be set off where available information can be said to have sufficiently put the corporation on notice of the likelihood of a crime. The entity would come to bear criminal responsibility when the attitude displayed by it – through a collectivity of agents – reflects flawed formal procedures or informal practices that have been approved, encouraged or condoned at management level.

The 'had reason to know' standard has been given divergent interpretations by the international criminal tribunals in relation to individuals.[114] It has been positioned at levels ranging from 'must have known' to 'should have known' on the cognitive scale. The criterion, which has gained the most recognition in the case law of the ICTY and ICTR, entails a two-prong test. Liability is triggered when an individual who had a duty to exercise care disregarded general information that put him on notice of (the possibility of) a crime and that was sufficient to justify further inquiry. Although the ICC has not yet ruled on the meaning of 'had reason to know', the definition eventually adopted will presumably overlap with the stricter reading espoused by the *ad hoc* tribunals. The duty of care incumbent upon civilians in relation to international crimes is certainly less extensive than that of military personnel and, therefore, likely to revolve around the need to investigate suspicious information already at their

---

113 The importance of foreseeability with regard to individual criminal responsibility has been set out in e.g. *Prosecutor v. Milutinovic et al.*, Decision on Dragoljub Ojdanic's Motion Challenging Jurisdiction – Joint Criminal Enterprise, ICTY Case No. IT-99-37-AR72, 21 May 2003.

114 See in this regard Chapter 4, section III.2.1b: The cognitive requirement for superior responsibility.

disposal. In this sense, the 'had reason to know' standard would relate to recklessness rather than negligence.[115]

The reason for adopting 'had reason to know' as the subjective yardstick for *dolus eventualis* liability on the part of corporations, lies in the considerations expounded above. It recognises the obligation of companies to conduct themselves with due diligence, particularly in circumstances that entail the risk of involvement in international crimes. At the same time, it also acknowledges the inherent differences between profit-oriented business enterprises and military(-like) organisations.

Let us consider the hypothetical scenario of a corporation X trading in chemical substances. Some of its products, typically used in the pharmaceutical and agricultural sectors, are also potentially employable as components in the making of chemical weapons. A Ugandan company places an order for a large quantity of multipurpose material. Upon the review of the purchaser documentation designating the end use of the substance in agriculture, the transaction is completed and corporation X dispatches the delivery. At the time of the order, there is an ongoing conflict in Uganda, attracting considerable media attention. Government forces and rebel groups are engaged in protracted violence which purposefully or indiscriminately targets civilians. Several thousand have been killed on suspicion of supporting one or another of the warring parties; many more have been mutilated or raped. There are also widely publicised allegations that in a few remote areas the army is employing poisonous gas in combat operations against the rebels. No civilian casualties have been confirmed so far. An international NGO, monitoring the ban on chemical weapons, undertakes further investigation. In the meantime, it notifies the bigger chemical concerns in the world about the reports emerging out of Uganda and urges them to exercise greater caution when trading with business partners from the region.

The CEO, to whose attention the information is brought, trusts that there are formal policies and procedures put in place to satisfy regulatory requirements relating to the trade in dangerous chemical substances. At the same time, the department that examines the purchaser documentation detailing the order, is plagued by internal competition. There are substantial bonuses envisaged for those employees who complete the most transactions within a six-month period. The ordinary employee responsible for the transaction with the Ugandan company, has heard about the NGO report but, finding herself under pressure to perform, decides not to enquire into the links of the purchasing company with the Ugandan government. Had she done so, she would have discovered that the government owns more than a 50% share in the company concerned. The departmental manager who signs the transaction and authorises the dispatch of the delivery is also suspicious as to whether the large amount of the multipurpose chemical substance would indeed be used for agricultural

115 For further discussion in relation to individual corporate agents, see Chapter 6, section II.3.1b: Awareness.

purposes only. Having dealt with Ugandan business partners before, he is conscious of a discrepancy between the size of the Ugandan agricultural sector and the quantity of the order placed. Nevertheless, he disregards his concerns and completes the transaction. He is aware that other NGO reports have not been acted upon in the past since senior management is notoriously sceptical about such non-governmental attempts to interfere with business activities. Some time later, media and UN reports confirm that the Ugandan army has deployed chemical weapons against the opposition in a sizeable region of the country. As well as rebel fighters killed, several villages, with hundreds of civilian inhabitants each, have been wiped out. A UN investigative panel reveals that the poisonous gas contained the same substance sold by corporation X. Procurement instructions issued by the Ugandan government reveal that corporation X supplied at least 60% of the chemical used. Previously, other companies had also been used as suppliers, but the orders entailed considerably smaller quantities. Experts conclude that the material provided by corporation X must have been used in the manufacture of the chemical weapons concerned.

Clearly the transaction did not entail a purposeful or knowing involvement in an international crime. In light of the evidence, corporation X cannot be said to have completed the transaction with the certainty that a criminal consequence would inevitably occur. Nonetheless, can it reasonably be concluded that the enterprise acted with *dolus eventualis*? Awareness existed at various levels of the likelihood of an unjustifiable risk. The aggregation of information available and how it was dispersed throughout the organisation warrants the conclusion that corporation X as a whole was sufficiently put on notice of a risk. Moreover, it chose to disregard that risk and such disregard was manifested in a combination of acts and omissions. The indifference on the part of corporate agents – ordinary employees, middle management or senior directors – was either deliberate or advertently reckless. It reflected failings of due diligence coupled with a flawed corporate ethos which allowed and even encouraged certain practices to flourish unchecked.

IV.3.1b *Culpa* as a benchmark for corporate criminal responsibility

The status of *culpa*-type standards of responsibility for gross human rights violations is ambivalent in international law. With respect to individual criminal responsibility, the *ad hoc* tribunals have faltered on the line between negligence as *culpa* and gross negligence as comparable to *dolus*.[116] In general, however, liability for a failure to perceive a risk, in the absence of any indications pointing in the direction of that risk, has been refuted in the case law of the *ad hoc* tribunals.[117] As previously mentioned,

---

116 Van Sliedregt, *supra note 3*, pp. 46-47, 49, referring in particular to *Prosecutor v. Blaskic*, ICTY Case No. IT-95-14-T, Judgment of 3 March 2000 and the interpretation of *dol éventuel* as a form of *culpa* in French law.

117 *Prosecutor v. Delalic et al.*, ICTY Case No. IT-96-21-A, Appeal Judgment of 20 February 2001, para. 226.

in *Bemba* the ICC adopted a dissimilar stance. It postulated the existence of an active duty on the part of military commanders to stay apprised of subordinate conduct at all times.[118] In relation to civilian superiors, including corporate agents, the Rome Statute, however, clearly stipulates a higher *mens rea* threshold.[119] This has not precluded legal scholars from contending that there is room for gross negligence in international criminal law. In their view, culpable ignorance may validly give rise to criminal responsibility where there is an expectation to abide by certain standards or take specific precautions in addition to awareness of a risk and belief that the risk will not materialise.[120] The latter stipulation, i.e. awareness coupled with underestimation of the risk or overestimation of one's capabilities to prevent it from occurring, refers to the civil law concept of conscious negligence.[121] Negligence in relation to a duty to exercise due diligence is also relevant in the context of state responsibility for the unlawful conduct of its agents.[122] It must be noted, however, that such responsibility is not of criminal nature.

If *culpa* has a role to play in international criminal law, it is particularly relevant with regard to corporations. MNCs possess immense human, material and financial resources. Since the harm that may result through the use of the organisational structure is greater than it would be in the case of isolated individual conduct, national jurisdictions have long subjected companies to a reasonable expectation that they guard against the occurrence of harm in the course of their activities. Where a failure of due diligence[123] leads to a sufficiently culpable legal transgression, the corporation may be held criminally responsible for the harm. Due diligence is generally invoked where the (potential) harm affects an interest protected by the law. Such an interest may be laid out in a specific statutory provision. Alternatively, a duty of care may arise where the harm is foreseeable, and in particular stemming from the creation of a dangerous situation or being in charge of a dangerous item.[124]

To what extent reliance on negligence as a mental state is warranted with regard to corporate liability for international crimes, would largely depend on how due diligence is perceived. Several issues arise in respect of any attempt to hold negligent corporations responsible under international criminal law: (1) does a duty to act with

118 Bemba, *supra note 7*, paras. 432-433.

119 See Chapter 4, section III.2.1b: The cognitive requirement for superior responsibility.

120 A. Cassese, *International Criminal Law: Introduction*, Oxford: Oxford University Press 2003, p. 172.

121 See *supra note 19* for an explanation of the distinction between conscious and unconscious negligence and scholarly arguments contending that conscious negligence is comparable to inadvertent recklessness in common law.

122 R.P. Parnidge, *Non-State Actors and Terrorism. Applying the Law of State Responsibility and the Due Diligence Principle*, The Hague: T.M.C. Asser Press, 2007, pp. 4-6.

123 In principle the concept of due diligence is of civil law origin. In common law jurisdictions it is referred to as a duty of care. Herein the terms are used interchangeably.

124 Such is for instance the case at common law in Australia. See Callaghan v. R, 87 CLR 115, 123 (1952) and R. v. Taktak, 34 A Crim R 334, 343-344 (1988).

due diligence exist, (2) what does the duty entail, (3) how is the duty triggered, and (4) how is a failure of such a duty reconciled with the grave nature of the 'core' crimes?

Albeit not expressly stipulated as such, the requirement of due diligence is implicit in existing international law prohibitions with regard to violations of humanitarian law and the corporate obligation to refrain from becoming complicit in international crimes. In this regard, some may argue that the existence of a duty of care on the part of civilians in international criminal law, and the scope of that duty, is somewhat tenuous.[125] Others may point out that due diligence in international law is vested in states, as it is states that have the primary responsibility to ensure respect for human rights and safeguard against the occurrence of harm through corporate activities.[126] Indeed the status of economic entities' due diligence outside the context of municipal legal systems is unsettled.[127] The past decade has, however, witnessed a gradual shift towards imposing a more active duty on the part of corporations with regard to the observance of certain fundamental human rights standards, and in particular norms of *ius cogens* character.[128] Efforts to subject business enterprises to direct human rights obligations and to introduce a legal duty addressing the need to counteract corporate complicity in the 'core' international crimes, have been gaining recognition.[129] Whether such a duty has become established in practice is debatable for the time being. Nevertheless, just as domestic jurisdictions have come to acknowledge and apply due diligence obligations on the part of economic entities and with regard to human rights harm, so can a similar duty be extended at the international level, particularly in instances where the harm relates to 'the most serious' of crimes protected by existing legal prohibitions. It may be the case that such an interest with regard to corporations would ultimately need to be explicitly laid out in statutory provisions, such as those pertaining to the proposed liability of juridical persons under the Rome Statute.

There is also some uncertainty as to what the duty would entail and how it could be triggered. Efforts have been made to define the scope of due diligence with regard to human rights and extend traditional corporate risk assessment practices to include the so-called human rights impact assessment.[130] The need to exercise special care is

125 See e.g. A. Zahar, Command Responsibility of Civilian Superiors for Genocide, 14 *Leiden Journal of International Law* 591 (2001).

126 H. O'Connell, Due Diligence and the Power of Economic Players, in: C. Benninger-Budel (ed.), *Due Diligence and its Application to Protect Women from Violence*, Leiden/Boston: Martinus Nijhoff Publishers, 2008.

127 For an argument expounding due diligence as a basic principle of international law, applicable across diverse areas, albeit primarily in relation to states, see R.P. Barnidge, Jr., *Non-State Actors and Terrorism. Applying the Law of State Responsibility and the Due Diligence Principle*, The Hague: T.M.C. Asser Press, 2008.

128 See Chapter 1, sections II and III.

129 *Ibidem*.

130 Such a recommendation has already been put forward by the UN Special Representative on Human Rights and Transnational Corporations, UN Doc. A/HRC/8/5, 7 April 2008. An extensive guide to Human Rights Impact Assessment and Management, a joint initiative within the framework of the UN

particularly pressing where the company's operations, partners and/or products entail an inherent risk of serious human rights abuse. Indications of a heightened necessity for extra caution in discharging due diligence may include, *inter alia*, circumstances of ongoing civil war, a recent history of internal or cross-border violence or entering into a joint venture with a rogue business associate. The expectation to accommodate for the factor of human rights impact may also be said to legitimately arise in relation to a company's choice to trade in intrinsically dangerous products, such as e.g. arms, military equipment or substances potentially usable in the production of chemical weapons. In those circumstances and with regard to culpable negligence, the question would not be whether the enterprise could be regarded as having been sufficiently put on notice of the likelihood of a criminal consequence. It would in fact be irrelevant whether there existed, within the organisation, any realisation of the potential harm. A constructive approach to uncovering negligence – should negligence be adopted as a liability standard of corporate blameworthiness under the Rome Statute – would instead focus on the issue of whether the company inadvertently created the risk of a foreseeable and unjustifiable harm.

The inquiry, therefore, would entail an objective assessment of the foreseeability of the potential harm. Corporate involvement in international crimes, even where inadvertent (and hence falling within the realm of *culpa*), is not always entirely unconscious. The company is often, at the very least, cognisant of the circumstances in which it operates, e.g. exploiting natural resources in a time of civil conflict, selling weapons to a rebel group, setting up a joint venture with a repressive government. Although this may constitute a legitimate business activity in itself, it entails an inherent risk. For criminal liability to arise, the risk need not relate to a specific crime. Furthermore, the enterprise need not grasp the risk or deliberately expose itself to it. It is sufficient if the corporate conduct grossly deviates from what could be expected of the corporation in the particular circumstances. The risk may not be obvious, especially where the transaction involves multipurpose goods. Providing a financial incentive to a government, supposedly in support of a local development project, in exchange for mining concessions is one such example. The money may indeed be used for a valid purpose. However, it may also be employed for the construction of a detention centre where political dissidents are tortured and forcibly 'disappeared'. The company may not have at its disposal information indicating the likelihood of a criminal consequence. However, it can be expected – in situations requiring special care in relation to potential human rights impact – to actively take reasonable steps to ascertain or negate the likelihood of harm.

Global Compact, has also recently sought to translate general business obligations with respect to human rights into more meaningful, concrete requirements of due diligence. See J.F. Sherman, *Corporate Duty to Respect Human Rights: Due Diligence Requirements*, 2007, at <198.170.85.29/Sherman-Corporate-Duty-to-Respect-30-Nov-2007.pdf>.

This is not to say that corporations should bear responsibility for any injury that materialises through their activities because they happen to operate within a criminal system. There would in fact be no liability if the business entity could not have conceivably foreseen the risk. Reasonable foreseeability that a legitimate transaction or activity may facilitate an international crime must therefore always be established. Such foreseeability, however, need not be assessed from the perspective of what a reasonable corporation ought to have perceived in the given circumstances. Such an approach would entail judging the company against an external, purely objective standard. Instead, the constructive method of uncovering corporate fault in the form of culpable negligence would revolve around what the particular company concerned *could have* reasonably foreseen. Evidence of foreseeability may thus be uncovered in the geographical proximity of the enterprise to the international crimes it is alleged to have facilitated, as well as the nature, intensity and duration of its relationship with the material perpetrators (i.e. state authorities, rebel groups, etc.) The calculation of foreseeability in each individual case is thus inevitably bound to result in casuistic determinations.

In imposing liability, the critical issue would be the nature of the corporate response to the foreseeable risk (albeit not perceived by the enterprise itself), or rather the lack of a conceivable response. The inquiry into the company attitude would take into account the steps which the entity has taken to improve foreseeability. However, culpability would not be attached to mismanagement only. As stipulated earlier, shortcomings in corporate policy, employee supervision and control or monitoring of potential risks, which in principle fall within the ambit of due diligence that can reasonably be expected from a corporation, may be indicative of a company attitude.[131] Objective inferences from that attitude, as postulated by the constructive corporate fault approach, may serve to reveal the requisite mental element on the part of the business enterprise. Considering the limitations of deriving culpability from proactive and reactive fault,[132] there are nevertheless compelling reasons not to regard due diligence inadequacies relating to the putting of an internal compliance system in place as constituting a fault standard in itself. Negligent culpability on the part of the corporation would instead be deduced from an aggregation of acts and failures at different levels within the organisation and on the part of agents acting within the scope of their employment.

The need to consider *culpa*-type liability for corporate involvement in gross human rights violations finds support in social science research on organisational behaviour.[133] It is frequently presumed – and rightly so – that companies engage in

131 See section IV.2.2 above: Proactive and reactive fault.

132 *Ibidem.*

133 For a general overview of social science research on organisational behaviour and the effects of irrationality on corporate involvement in human rights abuse, see Note, Organisational Irrationality and Corporate Human Rights Violations, 122 *Harvard Law Review* 1931 (2009).

international crimes as a result of rational decisions to pursue profit regardless of the harm that might be inflicted through business operations. Much less attention, however, has been paid by legal scholars to the idea that organisations may also act irrationally to the detriment of their self-interest. This has possibly to do with the general unease that exists with regard to negligence as a standard in criminal law. To illustrate how corporations may become inadvertently engaged in human rights abuse, a recent note in the Harvard Law Review employed the example of an oil company relying on security forces to protect its local installations. Several biases may affect decision-making and preclude realisation of the risk of harm involved:

> '[Cognitive conservatism leads corporate agents] to interpret existing circumstances in a manner consistent with previously held attitudes. [...] [Thus individual employees might] underestimate the risk of conflict with the local population, perhaps because they are aware of a past operation of a similar nature that was successful. [An] optimism bias might lead the same group to overestimate the company's ability to deal with the risk that it had already downplayed [...]. Once the team has committed to a course of action on such flawed grounds, there could be increasing momentum to resist more negative information as it is subsequently attained. Finally [a] self-serving bias might colour inferences drawn at all three of these levels: the initial assessment of risk, the initial evaluation of capabilities, and the continuing reconsideration of both in light of new information.'[134]

At the same time the organisational environment may prompt the unconscious acceptance of certain choices and practices as aligning with the normal. The phenomenon of groupthink, on the other hand, may serve to distort reasonable conclusions and suppress dissent.[135] Structural difficulties within large organisations may furthermore impede communication and also 'minimise the ability to detect and stave off activities that deviate from normative standards and expectations'.[136]

Elaborating upon the example mentioned above and utilising the constructive method of uncovering corporate fault, what would render a business enterprise negligently culpable in relation to an international crime? For several years, company Y has profitably engaged in the extraction of crude oil in Angola. Prior to it setting up any operations in the country and while a civil war was still raging, government forces and rebel factions frequently fought for control over natural resources. On several occasions the UN reported that, in efforts to gain political and military advantage, the warring parties engaged in large-scale, deliberate or indiscriminate, violence against

134 *Ibidem*, at 1934-1936, referring to the work of D.C. Langevoort, Organised Illusions: a Behavioural Theory of Why Corporations Mislead Stock Market Investors (And Cause Other Social Harms), 146 *University of Pensylvannia Law Review* 101 (1997).

135 *Idem*, at 1936-1937.

136 *Idem*, at 1938, referring to D. Vaughan, The Dark Side of Organisations: Mistake, Misconduct, and Disaster, 25 *Annual Review of Sociology* 271 (1999) at 277.

civilians. Company Y initiated its business operations in Angola following a UN-mediated peace agreement. As part of the agreement a coalition government is instated, which gives leaders of the major rebel groups a share of the power and revenues accumulated through the exploitation of natural resources. Despite the country's violent history, for a number of years there are no reports of further humanitarian law violations against civilians.

Then, unsatisfied with his position within the government, a former rebel leader resigns from office and heads a united rebel movement comprising some of the smaller armed factions that have been excluded from the coalition. Subsequently, the rebels become engaged in protracted and increasingly violent clashes with the army forces, challenging the government's authority. They also seek to sabotage existing business operations and gain control over oil extraction sites. This would not only compel foreign oil companies functioning in Angola to negotiate terms with the rebels, but also weaken the financial and hence military capabilities of the government. Concerned about the attacks, company Y enters into an arrangement with the Angolan army forces. It provides them with money, arms and military equipment to protect its installations. Despite the changed political climate, it also sets in motion a project it has signed prior to the incidents of renewed violence. The contract entails the construction of a new extraction facility in a remote area by a local venture partner. Eventually the joint project results in the forceful relocation of nearly a thousand civilians. Men, women and children who allegedly sought to oppose the relocation and the destruction of their farmland, are killed. Hundreds are deployed as slave labour at the construction site. Company Y claims that it did not know, nor had reason to suspect, that its associates would commit such crimes. Since the peace agreement several years ago, there has been no reported grave human rights abuse against civilians. Senior management is not aware of violence on the part of the Angolan army forces used against the local population at any of the other extraction sites. The company furthermore has conducted an initial human rights impact assessment prior to initiating any operations in Angola and concluded that no immediate risk exists.

However, company Y fails to (properly) re-assess the situation and the accompanying risks in light of the new political climate. Since the renewed violence thus far has seemingly involved army and rebel forces only, the team responsible for carrying out the assessment does not consider that harm is likely to be inflicted on civilians. Directors do not doubt the conclusion in that regard, since information about possible excessive violence used against civilian protesters at one of the company's installation facilities has not reached them yet. However, they are aware of the initial impact assessment stipulating the need for continuous monitoring of potential human rights risks. At the same time, middle managers do not inquire into – or alternatively downgrade – the existence of links between the local venture partner in charge of the new construction project and the Angolan government. Therefore, they fail to consider the relevance of the fact that the government is a shareholder in company Y's business associate and has a substantial interest in the success of the project. The new oil extraction facility would provide the government with the opportunity to effectively evacuate an area which is believed to be one of the rebel movement's strongholds. It would also generate revenues, which could be subsequently used for the purchase of weapons and the enhancement of its military position *vis-à-vis* the rebels.

In those circumstances and depending on the evidence available, it might be reasonable to conclude that, had company Y acted with due diligence, it could have known that it was creating the risk of an unjustifiable harm. The constructive approach to uncovering corporate negligence would not focus on ascertaining what awareness various individual agents possessed. Instead the emphasis would be on the attitudes displayed towards business-related functions and duties. Jointly such attitudes, considered together with organisational peculiarities such as structure, culture and functionality, may preclude the corporation from grasping the (true extent of) risk involved in an otherwise lawful activity.

Admittedly, negligence would be a precarious ground of liability if the corporation were to be held responsible for crimes committed by others without any involvement on its part. However, it would not be unreasonable or unjust to impose criminal liability on entities for creating the necessary infrastructure for the perpetration of international crimes. Albeit inadvertent, such facilitation – particularly when essential and causally connected to the human rights abuse – entails moral responsibility. Although it might not render the company as blameworthy as in the circumstances of purposeful, knowing or reckless conduct, the punishment of negligent involvement in violations of humanitarian law is warranted by the serious nature of the harm involved. However, the question remains as to whether liability would attach to a crime itself or to a breach of duty.

Some domestic jurisdictions recognise negligence as an acceptable standard for corporate responsibility attaching even to crimes such as homicide.[137] In order to incur liability for the crime, however, the corporation must be established to have been grossly negligent. In principle, it must also be the material perpetrator of the offence. A constructive approach to corporate culpable negligence would consider the organisational conduct as a whole. It would take evidence of mismanagement into account but would primarily allow for the drawing of reasonable inferences from an aggregation of acts and omissions at different levels within the company. Liability would thus attach to positive as well as omissive conduct. Nevertheless, the notion of due diligence in relation to negligence as a liability standard cannot be entirely divorced from the perception that, should a company fail to safeguard against the occurrence of harm, it is then first and foremost responsible for a breach of a duty. With regard to individuals and the notion of superior responsibility revolving around the existence of a duty of care, the *ad hoc* tribunals have faltered on the idea of a

137 M.G. Welham, *Corporate Manslaughter and Corporate Homicide: a Manager's Guide to Legal Compliance*, London: Bloomsbury Professional, 2007.

dereliction of duty as a separate offence.[138] Article 28 RS generates liability for superior omissions and indirect culpability for subordinate criminal acts. Responsibility in this regard is justified by the nature of the relationship with the physical perpetrators. With respect to corporations reasoning along similar lines would be erroneous. Those who materially commit the human rights abuse using the infrastructure inadvertently created by business enterprises, are unlikely to be within the companies' effective sphere of influence and control. Although corporate liability would not be imposed for a failure to prevent the occurrence of a crime but for creating favourable conditions for the commission of the crime, it would be inextricably linked to due diligence shortcomings. Hence, it would only be fair if direct criminal responsibility on the part of the entity for negligent misconduct, and its corresponding consequences in terms of stigma and penalty – attach to a breach of duty rather than the offence that has materialised. Such an approach would also allow for negligence as a liability standard for corporations to align with the special intent requirement that attaches to certain international crimes.

IV.3.1c A word on *dolus specialis*

The *sui generis* approach to constructing corporate criminal responsibility, expounded above, does not dispense with the need to establish special intent if the entity is to be convicted for genocide or persecution. Instances where MNCs might engage in criminal conduct with the aim of destroying or discriminating against a racial, ethnic, national or religious group might be rare but not impossible to conceive. The question is how to uncover special intent where necessary for a conviction. The constructive method, with its holistic focus on corporate attitude as a manifestation of organisational *mens rea*, seems to adequately address this predicament. As correctly pointed out by Schabas, discussions pertaining to *dolus specialis* in the context of collectives tend to be 'distorted by our focus on individual culpability'.[139] He therefore questions the appropriateness of using the term 'special intent' in relation to organised entities and highlights the relevance of the element of policy in that regard. International courts have accepted that institutionalised groups can – in principle and acting through their agents – commit genocide and have sought to identify special intent in terms of policy. The ICJ in the Genocide Case[140] and, more recently, the ICC

138 Compare e.g. *Prosecutor v. Delalic et al.*, ICTY Case No. IT-96-21-A, Appeal Judgment of 20 February 2001 with *Prosecutor v. Hadzihasanovic et al.*, Decision on Joint Challenge to Jurisdiction, ICTY Case No. IT-01-47-PT, 12 November 2002.

139 W.A. Schabas, Discussion: Corporate Liability and State Criminality, *6 Journal of International Criminal Justice 947* (2008) at 964-965.

140 ICJ, Case concerning the Application of the Convention on the prevention and punishment of the crime of genocide (Bosnia and Herzegovina v. Serbia and Montenegro), Judgment (No. 91), 26 February 2007.

in relation to the arrest warrant against the Sudanese sitting Head of State,[141] have expounded that genocidal intent, i.e. a policy geared towards the destruction of a particular group as such, could be inferred through collectively assessing the conduct and attitudes of group members. The decisions did not concern the criminal responsibility of entities *per se* but nevertheless inquired into the existence of genocidal intent on the part of organised groups (e.g. state organs) as opposed to individuals.[142] However, they are indicative of the importance of safeguarding the *dolus specialis* component of certain international crimes in order not to detract from the moral approbation that attaches to them. They appear, furthermore, symptomatic of an understanding that the exclusively subjective approach to mental states where legal as opposed to natural persons are concerned, is ill suited. Special intent, however, is generally difficult to prove, even with regard to individuals. The constructive method, as outlined earlier, has the propensity to facilitate the discovery of evidence with regard to corporations. Nevertheless, it is unlikely that, as a result, a criminal court would be overly forthcoming in drawing conclusions about the existence of special intent on the part of business entities. Such conclusions must in principle be the *only* reasonable inference to be made in light of the available evidence.

IV.3.2 The scope of the objective element

The preceding discussion, pertaining to the requisite *mens rea* of direct corporate criminal responsibility, suggests the scope of the *actus reus* element with regard to the *sui generis* liability construction envisaged. As already stipulated, private business enterprises may, on occasion, infringe human rights directly though the commission of unlawful acts, i.e. acts, which violate international law, and are incompatible with the legitimate purpose for which the companies have been established. In reality, however, corporate involvement in war crimes, crimes against humanity and even genocide tends to be of more indirect nature. It generally entails various forms of assistance or contribution to crimes physically perpetrated by others, including providing the means for the crimes' commission. Such facilitation may involve, *inter alia*, extending logistical support, arms or military equipment as well as raw materials to serve as ingredients for the production of chemical or biological weapons by rogue

141 *Prosecutor v. Omar Hassan Ahmad Al Bashir ('Omar Al Bashir')*, Decision on the Prosecution's Application for a Warrant of Arrest against Omar Hassan Ahmad Al Bashir, ICC-02/05-01/09-3, 4 March 2009. The arrest warrant was issued on the same day. See *Prosecutor v. Omar Hassan Ahmad Al Bashir ('Omar Al Bashir')*, Warrant of Arrest for Omar Hassan Ahmad Al Bashir, ICC-02/05-09/1, 4 March 2009.

142 In *Nahimana et al.*, the ICTR also identified special intent with reference to organisational policy. In discussing the charges of genocide against the accused, the tribunal took into account not only evidence of personal statements but also the editorial policies of the media that the accused were associated with. It concluded that such editorial policies, reflected in writings and broadcasts, constituted evidence of genocidal intent on the part of the media (paras. 957-969). *Prosecutor v. Nahimana et al.*, Case No. ICTR-99-52-T, Judgment of 3 December 2003.

governments and insurgency groups. Assistance may also take the form of financial contributions to crimes, also generated as profit by joint ventures with repressive states and state-owned companies, or through bribery and bonuses aimed at securing concessions in the exploitation of natural resources. Typical of the indirect form of corporate involvement in international crimes is that the assistance rendered is often hidden behind the guise of legitimate business transactions or ambiguous industry methods. Furthermore, the contribution extended need not necessarily be in the form of tangible products or services. It may involve multipurpose goods, i.e. money and commodities whose end use is not always apparent.[143] It may well be manifested in encouragement or even inaction. The *actus reus* of direct corporate responsibility for involvement in international crimes, therefore, may be satisfied by 1) an unlawful act, 2) a lawful act which contributes to the commission of a crime, 3) moral support or 4) omission. Such an extensive interpretation of the requisite objective element is inevitably bound to raise some questions.

The situation of a MNC perpetrating grave human rights abuse itself is fairly straightforward. It is reminiscent of the Nuremberg cases of *Farben* and *Krupp,* prosecuted because the companies utilised, and actively sought to procure, slave labour in their production plants.[144] A constructive approach to corporate liability in those circumstances would strive to ascertain whether the impugned conduct is reasonably attributable to the organisation.[145] The inquiry would thus revolve around the question of whether the behaviour concerned – be it active or omissive – materialised in the course of employment duties and on the part of corporate agents related to one another in a way justifying the transposition of the aggregate conduct onto the entity. As already discussed elsewhere, omissions as manifestations of the *actus reus* are also operative in international criminal law outside the ambit of superior responsibility and there are indications that a similar position is being embraced by the ICC.[146] In the context of corporate liability, omissions would relate to failures of due diligence as well as conscious inaction. The focal point would not be whether the enterprise, personified in its directing minds, had the authority and actual control over the conduct of the physical perpetrators (where the latter are company employees). This follows to be determined in accordance with the principles of individual superior responsibility. With regard to the criminal liability of the corporation, the issue would

143 In this sense, the prosecution of corporations is likely to pose evidentiary challenges, albeit akin to those bound to plague investigation and proceedings against individual corporate agents. The difficulty inherent in ascertaining the goal and final use of financial contributions was apparent at Nuremberg in the cases of *Flick* and *Rasche*. See Chapter 3, section III.2: Synthesising the Nuremberg principles of individual criminal responsibility in relation to corporate officials. In this regard, Laufer contends that, by focusing on the peculiarities of the organisational form and by allowing the drawing of reasonable inferences, the constructive approach to corporate fault may facilitate the discovery of evidence. Laufer, *supra note 94*, p. 93.

144 See Chapter 3, section III: The Nuremberg prosecution of industrialists.

145 See section IV.2.4 above: Constructive corporate fault.

146 See section II.1 above: Acts and omissions.

be whether omissions to supervise and control as well as implement adequate policies and processes, or foster a law-abiding organisational culture, are causally linked to the commission of a crime or create the unjustifiable risk of a crime occurring.

Causation would be particularly pertinent in cases involving allegations of facilitation through material or moral contribution rather than physical perpetration on the part of the company itself. International criminal law has refuted causality *conditio sine qua non* as a prerequisite for individual culpability. Instead it favours the so called facilitation theory. The objective threshold varies depending on the liability mode concerned. While aiding and abetting, for instance, requires substantial contribution,[147] other forms of accomplice liability feature lower *actus reus* provisos.[148] The permissibility of grounding convictions on an objective element below the level of 'significant' has been heavily criticised, particularly in the context of JCE.[149] This is not to say, however, that less than substantial contribution cannot, or should not, give rise to criminal responsibility in other settings, also in relation to MNCs. Domestic jurisdictions of both the common law and the civil law orientation tend to interpret facilitation broadly.[150] Moreover, as pointed out by Reggio, substantial contribution is itself a concept of 'indeterminate' meaning.[151] In this sense, 'the determination of the relevant proximate causes' would largely depend on the particular circumstances of each individual case.[152] In an attempt to reconcile the facilitation theory with the requirement of 'substantial' applicable in relation to complicity under international criminal law, the International Commission of Jurists has extended a three-partite definition to facilitation. The latter has been deemed to encompass conduct 1) without which the abuse would not have occurred, 2) which aggravates the abuse, or 3) which alters the way in which the abuse is carried out.[153]

---

147 The requirement of 'substantial contribution' with regard to aiding and abetting has been firmly established in the jurisprudence of the *ad hoc tribunals*. E.g. *Prosecutor v. Krstic*, ICTY Case No. IT-98-33-A, Appeal Judgment of 19 April 2004, paras. 137-138; *Prosecutor v. Krnojelac*, ICTY Case No. IT-97-25-T, Judgment of 15 March 2002, paras. 88-90; *Prosecutor v. Aleksovski*, ICTY Case No. IT-95-14/1-A, Appeal Judgment of 24 March 2000, para. 163; *Prosecutor v. Akayesu*, Case No. ICTR-96-4-T, Judgment of 2 September 1998, para. 705.

148 As discussed in Chapter 4, Article 25(3)(d) RS sets the lowest objective threshold by criminalising 'any other way' in which an individual contributes to the commission of a crime by a group of persons sharing a common purpose.

149 See Chapter 4, section II.1.2: Jurisprudential attempts at counteracting the drawbacks of the JCE doctrine.

150 Facilitation is thus understood to refer to any assistance that renders the commission of the crime easier, irrespective of whether the crime would have materialised anyway. Reggio, *supra note 49*, at 670-671.

151 Reggio, *supra note 49*, at 671. For an overview of the different types of contribution considered sufficient in the jurisprudence of the *ad hoc* tribunals, see also H. Olasolo, *The Criminal Responsibility of Senior Political and Military Leaders as Principals to International Crimes*, Oxford: Hart Publishing, 2009, pp. 252-258.

152 Reggio, *supra note 49*, at 671.

153 *Corporate Complicity and Legal Accountability*, Vol. I: Facing the Facts and Charting a Legal Path, Report of the International Commission of Jurists Expert Legal Panel on Corporate Complicity in International Crimes, *supra note 35*, pp. 10-13.

As for moral support, or encouragement, such a form of contribution has also been acknowledged as a causation factor giving rise to individual culpability in national and international law. Intangible assistance on the part of corporations may also be manifested in tacit approval, which then serves to reinforce criminal practices. Such facilitation, however, would be exceedingly difficult to establish. In the context of complicity and with regard to natural persons, the *ad hoc* tribunals have sought to determine whether the status and presence of the defendant have had a legitimising effect on the actions of the physical perpetrators.[154] In relation to MNCs, the interpretation of moral support need not be strictly analogous. It might be regarded as providing those who materially commit international crimes with the impression that their behaviour is tolerated and even acceptable in general. 'Silent complicity' by mere presence in a criminal system cannot, however, give rise to criminal liability. At the same time, encouraging a rogue government to displace a population from an area believed to be rich in natural resources, with the promise of a share in future revenues, may warrant an inquiry into the responsibility of the business enterprise if the crimes actually materialise.

Furthermore, deducing the objective element of corporate misconduct from aggregate physical acts and omissions does not necessarily merit a differentiation in the types of corporate agents involved. Since liability is rooted in organisational fault, it is irrelevant whether the conduct is materially effectuated with the participation of individuals in positions of power, authority and control. In fact, the combined acts or omissions of any group of agents would suffice, as long as they are reasonably attributable to the corporation as a whole. Nonetheless, in reality, and particularly where responsibility arises in relation to failures of due diligence, omissions would have to be identified on the part of senior officials. As for the category of moral support as a form of *actus reus,* it would almost certainly have to be derived from corporate agents in a position of certain authority. Such authority would have to indicate a level of power and control capable of affecting the behaviour of the organisation. The absence of sufficient influence may render the causality link with the crimes tenuous.

V Conclusion

The preceding discussion on the possible form of direct corporate criminal responsibility in the context of the Rome Statute, draws heavily upon the constructive fault approach. At the same time, it has also sought to expand on it by elaborating on the instrumentality, underlying assumptions and implications of the constructive method when applied to the circumstances of international crimes. The model put forward is dictated as much by the character of corporate participation in international

154 E.g. *Prosecutor v. Kvocka*, ICTY Case No. IT-98-30/1-T, Judgment of 2 November 2001, para. 257; *Prosecutor v. Kunarac*, ICTY Case No. IT-96-23-T & IT-96-23/1-T, Judgment of 22 February 2001, para. 393; Akayesu, *supra note 147*, para. 705.

crimes as by the grave nature of the offences themselves. As seen, the need for constructing the liability of corporations *sui generis* is furthermore prescribed by the realisation that existing Rome Statute provisions cannot truly capture the scope of business participation in genocide, war crimes and crimes against humanity. Other approaches, suggested during negotiation rounds or operative at the domestic level, fail to adequately reflect genuine organisational fault and the extent of MNCs' moral blameworthiness.

The Rome Statute, nevertheless, provides sufficient room for manoeuvre, so that culpability and the construction of legal responsibility on the part of business enterprises need not be detached from the Statute's overall framework. The approach advocated above suggests the need for a broader interpretation of the requisite *mens rea* and *actus reus*, which may be justified by reference to the unique nature of corporations and their involvement in international crimes. It requires the judiciary to undertake an analysis similar to the one pertaining to the determination of individual responsibility in the context of collective criminality, albeit on a different level. Such an analysis would need to revolve around the perception of the corporation as a system and entail the evaluation of evidence and making of inferences with reference to group dynamics.

To some, such an approach may seem radical, particularly in light of recent trends to circumscribe overly broad liability doctrines applicable in international criminal law. It must be born in mind, however, that the suggested model allows for a differentiation of mental states and the corresponding type of liability. The nuanced appreciation of moral blameworthiness that it accommodates for warrants a distinction in levels of culpability. Accordingly, the extent of corporate responsibility for material perpetration or more indirect forms of participation revolving around *dolus* or *culpa,* must be duly reflected in sentencing.

CHAPTER 6
CULPABILITY BEYOND THE CONFINES OF THE CORPORATE FORM

I INTRODUCTION

In an increasingly deregulated and globalised commercial market, transnational corporations routinely structure their operations through intricate networks of subsidiaries and other affiliates. Deliberate configurations dispersing centres of control are primarily efficiency-motivated. At the same time, however, they also serve to minimise risk exposure in the pursuit of profit maximisation. The inherent complexities of organisational structure and functionality are thus not only an essential factor in constructing corporate criminal responsibility, they are also an impediment as well as a facet to be considered in the attempt to extend liability beyond the enterprise directly implicated in the commission of international crimes.

International criminal law has long recognised the notion that persons in positions of power and control have the duty to intervene where subordinates engage in the 'core' international offences. Operative with regard to individuals, the doctrine of superior responsibility, and in particular its underlying precepts, offer an intriguing avenue for narrowing the impunity gap in relation to corporate entities too. Albeit giving rise to a form of derivative liability, principles of superior duty and culpable failure to act are discussed hereunder in the context of direct criminal responsibility, since they relate to a genuine offence of omission attributable to parent corporations *per se*. It is thus not the conduct of the subsidiary company that is vicariously transposed onto the controlling entity. Blameworthiness is rather attached to the parent corporation's own faulty behaviour. Building upon the theoretical framework previously espoused, the constructive method of uncovering the requisite objective and subjective element has a role to play to this context too.

The criminal responsibility that may attach to MNCs – parent corporations as well as their affiliates – need not, however, preclude the liability of individual agents. While the inadequacies of prosecuting natural persons in lieu of organisations has prompted the present inquiry into direct corporate responsibility, the latter should not be seen as negating the need for accountability at the individual level. The notion of superior responsibility is potentially applicable in this regard too. However, in such cases, its interpretation must strictly align with established notions of individual culpability under international criminal law. A differentiation in approach, albeit with recourse to the same set of underlying principles, is warranted by the essentially different nature of natural and legal persons.

This chapter begins by highlighting the aptitude of traditional company law to insulate corporations from responsibility, and accordingly, puts forward a justification for seeking to transcend the restrictive principles of separate legal personality and limited liability. Focusing on direct, as opposed to vicarious, criminal responsibility, an attempt is made to define a number of criteria for the attribution of liability to parent corporations for their failure to ensure that they do not become involved in the commission of international crimes through their subsidiaries. Subsequently, the ascription of blame to purchasing companies in relation to criminal practices along the supply chain is briefly discussed. Last but not least, the implications of the respondeat superior concept, enshrined in Article 28(b) of the Rome Statute, is explored as to its application to individuals operating in a corporate context.

II Direct parent liability

The allocation of liability within corporate groups is among the most complex and controversial aspects of the law governing multinational operations. Domestic approaches vary, with outcomes often inconsistent and difficult to predict. The difficulty generally lies in the legal separation that has been accepted to exist between parent and subsidiary companies. Parent corporations could be held liable in their own right or jointly with affiliates for their respective (active) roles in the commission of international crimes.[1] Can a control relationship and a failure to intervene, however, justify the ascription of responsibility to the parent for the criminal transgressions of subservient entities?[2]

II.1 The intrinsic protections of the corporate form

Traditional company law is firmly anchored in the principles of separate legal personality and limited liability, which in effect serve to insulate the parent corporation from responsibility. While the separate personality concept dictates that each member of the corporate group is to be treated as a distinct juridical entity, the notion of limited liability transfers risks beyond the amount of the parent's investment to the subsidiaries. This strict separation between parent and subsidiary companies, however, is a predominantly artificial legal construction. It bears little semblance to economic reality and fails to meet the exigencies of multi-tiered multinational corporate groups in the modern world.[3] On the one hand, the parent-subsidiary relationship is frequently more closely-knit than the principle of separate legal existence generally

1 The construction of their criminal liability would then follow the principles previously espoused in Chapter 5.

2 The terms 'subsidiary', 'subservient' and 'affiliate' will be used interchangeably unless expressly specified otherwise. Thus 'subservient' should not be read to imply absolute control of the parent company over the subsidiary's management and operations. The substitution of 'affiliate' for 'subsidiary', on the other hand, should not be understood to connote belonging to separate corporate groups.

3 P.I. Blumberg, Accountability of Multinational Corporations: The Barriers Presented by the Concepts of the Corporate Juridical Entity, 24 *Hastings International and Comparative Law Review* 297 (2001) at 303.

acknowledges. With the rise and diversification of the multinational corporation in recent decades, has come the growing realisation that corporate groups are not necessarily aggregations of largely independent entities. More often than not, conglomerates comprise complex webs of deliberately interposed companies, with the parent entity controlling subsidiary operations.[4] On the other hand, the legal transposition of the distinct entity concept to corporate liability has been predominantly mechanical, as historically the concept was devised to protect individual investors from exposure to responsibility for company debts.[5] As a result, national legal systems have experienced a gradual shift in focus away from the principle of separate legal personality.[6] Instead, discussions pertaining to the attribution of responsibility within corporate groups have increasingly centred on the implications of the concept of limited liability.[7]

Generally, domestic courts rely on the limited liability doctrine to protect parent companies against the liabilities of their subsidiaries. Insulation from responsibility is, however, not absolute. In some instances, the interests of justice may dictate the attribution of liability to the parent despite its formal separation from subservient entities.[8] Such liability may be either direct – following the parent's own involvement in the impugned subsidiary acts – or vicarious in that the affiliate's conduct itself is ascribed to the parent company.[9] Vicarious liability arises when the legal contraption of the 'corporate veil' is lifted and the parent company is perceived as assuming the identity of its subsidiary. The practice of 'piercing the corporate veil' has developed as a natural response to the obstacles presented by thinly capitalised subsidiaries and multi-tiered limited liability in the context of the modern corporation. No uniform legal formula for effectively piercing the veil has emerged as yet, and it remains a contentious, cumbersome undertaking conceded as a remedy in rare circumstances only.[10] Common in tort and contract law, the corporate veil predicament is not entirely extraneous to criminal law. However, it is irrelevant when allocation of liability within

4 A. McGee, C. Williams and G. Scanlan, *The Law of Business Organisations*, Exeter: Law Matters Publishing, 2005, p. 105.

5 K. Amaeshi, O. Kingsley Osuji and P. Nnodim, *Corporate Social Responsibility in Supply Chains of Global Brands: a Bounderyless Responsibility? Clarifications, Exceptions and Implications*, p. 12, at <ssrn.com/abstract=947583>.

6 *Ibidem*, p. 11.

7 Blumberg, *supra note 3*, at 301.

8 P.T. Muchlinski, *Multinational Enterprises and the Law*, Oxford: Oxford University Press, 2007, p. 313; S. Joseph, *Corporations and Transnational Human Rights Litigation*, Oxford: Hart Publishing, 2004, p.130.

9 J. Zerk, *Multinationals and Corporate Social Responsibility*, Cambridge: Cambridge University Press, 2006, pp. 216-225.

10 For a general discussion of the corporate veil concept, see K.A. Strasser, Piercing the Veil in Corporate Groups, 37 *Connecticut Law Review* 637 (2005).

the corporate group is sought along direct lines.[11] In such a case, the responsibility that attaches to the parent corporation relates to its own misconduct and there is no need to transpose the subsidiary's identity. Hence, the intricacies of the 'corporate veil' predicament will not be explored any further here.

II.2 Justifying the attribution of criminal responsibility to parent companies

There are several reasons for attempting to attribute blame to parent corporations for their contribution to the human rights violations materialising through the activities of their foreign subsidiaries. There are limitations to the effective prosecution of affiliate companies in host states.[12] From a victims' perspective, the hierarchical extension of corporate liability may be rationalised, as in conditions involving, *inter alia*, legal obstacles, the parent enterprise is either the most appropriate or the only target available.[13] Ratner has also pointed out that extending compulsory regulation to parent entities has the propensity to encourage meaningful internal changes in terms of culture, policy, supervision and control throughout the corporate group.[14] Most importantly, and in relation to corporate liability under international criminal law, the prosecution and punishment of parent companies is warranted by the blameworthiness of their conduct when such conduct entails the commission or facilitation of a humanitarian violation by entities within their sphere of control. The imperative of justice and the need to preclude impunity dictate that parent enterprises not be allowed to abuse the corporate form in order to conceal their involvement in grave human rights abuse, or exploit the principle of separate juridical personality so as to evade responsibility.

Ability to satisfy reparation claims in circumstances where the subsidiary has insufficient capital is also a consideration to be factored in.[15] However, the latter is pertinent only insofar as it may affect the exercise of prosecutorial discretion regarding the strategic decision of whether to charge the parent corporation jointly with the affiliate or on its own. Availability of assets in relation to the capability of adequately meeting compensation claims by victims cannot in itself be a valid ground for attributing criminal liability to parent companies. Some form of participation in the impugned activities of the subsidiary must invariably be established.

---

11 See e.g. H. Ward, Securing Transnational Corporate Accountability Through National Courts: Implications and Policy Options, 24 *Hastings International and Comparative Law Review* 451 (2001) at 470; B. Stephens, Accountability: International Human Rights Violations Against Corporations in US Courts, in: M. Kamminga and S. Zia-Zarifi (eds.), *Liability of Multinational Corporations under International Law*, The Hague: Kluwer Law International, 2000, p. 223.

12 See in this regard Chapter 1, section III.1: Criminal liability.

13 Ward, *supra note 11*, at 463-464.

14 S.R. Ratner, Corporations and Human Rights: a Theory of Legal Responsibility, 111 *Yale Law Journal* 443 (2001) at 473-475.

15 As will be recalled, practical concerns about the ability of convicted individuals to satisfy victims' compensation claims underpinned proposals to include corporate criminal responsibility in the Rome Statute.

As stipulated earlier, while legitimate business enterprises may perpetrate international crimes themselves, typically they become involved in offences materially committed by others through the pursuit of lawful activities and transactions. In those instances, while their conduct is not criminal, it may nevertheless – advertently or inadvertently – bring about a criminal consequence. Whether the involvement – where sufficiently culpable – would give rise to the criminal responsibility of the entity concerned depends on the successful construction of the requisite corporate *actus reus* and *mens rea*.[16] Culpability would not be imposed purely along vicarious lines. Blameworthiness would instead be inferred from aggregate acts and due diligence omissions as well as organisational characteristics which reasonably indicate – when considered as a whole – genuine corporate fault. Likewise, the direct ascription of liability to a parent company would need to rest on a fault on the part of the parent itself. The behaviour of the subsidiary would not be transposed vicariously onto the central entity within the corporate group. Instead, the criminal responsibility of the parent would attach to acts and omissions which have occurred at the corporate headquarters and are causally related to the international crime that has materialised.[17] Fault may thus be discerned in the parent's contribution to its subsidiary's conduct. Alternatively, it may reflect a breach of duty to intervene as a result of which an international crime materialises.

II.3 The criteria for ascribing direct liability to parent corporations

It is not inconceivable that, in some instances, a parent entity may knowingly and/or intentionally engage in the commission of a humanitarian law violation by a subsidiary. Such involvement would entail culpability for the parent's active participation in the realisation of the offence, and accordingly responsibility for the crime effected. The parent company would thus be held liable – jointly with the subsidiary or separately on its own – in accordance with the principles of direct corporate criminal responsibility previously expounded. Purposefully and/or knowingly authorising or promoting criminal or risky behaviour on the part of the subsidiary are participatory modes, which may give rise to the parent's liability either as a principal or a secondary participant in the commission of the crimes.[18] Instructing an affiliate

16 For an extensive discussion of various avenues for constructing corporate culpability, see Chapter 5.

17 A similar argument has increasingly been relied upon in relation to the direct liability of parent corporations in domestic cases involving allegations of tortuous behaviour. For an overview of relevant US and UK jurisprudence and the attempted extension of liability test criteria in this regard to allegations of MNC human rights abuse under the ATCA, see Joseph, *supra note 8*, pp. 134-138 and Zerk, *supra note 9*, pp. 216-223.

18 For example, albeit not in relation to criminal liability, the contention in *Bowoto v. Chevron Texaco* was whether or not Chevron could be held liable for its participation in the impugned acts of its Nigerian subsidiary, Chevron Nigeria Ltd. The case, which arose under the Alien Tort Claims Act, concerned the deaths and injuries of protesters against the subsidiary's operations at the hands of the Nigerian military. The applicants alleged that Chevron Nigeria Ltd acted in concert with the Nigerian military.

to extend logistical support to a repressive military in the forced displacement of a local population with a view to securing land for the construction of an oil extraction site, exemplifies involvement in subsidiary conduct that may generate direct criminal liability on the part of the parent corporation.

Where the parent knew that a crime would occur or had reason to know that a given subsidiary activity might contribute to human rights abuse, liability may also be warranted. Awareness in this regard would be uncovered using the constructive method.[19] Culpability would attach to the company's choice not to intervene, irrespective of whether it was deliberate or the result of indifference. In any case, the attitude displayed by the parent would have to be causally linked to the affiliate's conduct entailing the material facilitation of an international crime. A failure to act on the part of the parent corporation may also reflect a negligent omission to foresee a reasonable and unjustifiable risk and/or notify its foreign affiliate of that risk. Could such a failure, however, give rise to liability?

In circumstances where the allegations against the parent do not concern affirmative action but omission, the question also arises as to whether liability is imposed for a crime or for a failure to prevent or safeguard against the risks of subsidiary operations. Some legal commentators have highlighted the relevance of the distinction between action and omission in relation to direct parent liability for negligent or reckless involvement in subsidiary acts. Referring to the *Unocal* Case and assuming that the company's subsidiary in Myanmar recklessly hired the army to perform project-related tasks which resulted in harm against civilians, Joseph reasons that:

> 'Unocal could be held liable for its *actions in promoting* its subsidiary's relationship with the Myanmar military, in reckless disregard of the likely human rights consequences of that relationship. However, it is unlikely that Unocal could be held liable for recklessly *allowing* its subsidiary to engage with the Myanmar government.'[20]

It must be noted in this regard that the case of *Unocal* arose under the ATCA and entailed liability for human rights abuse defined as tort. Accordingly, the criteria for establishing the liability of the parent company as a tortfeasor revolved first and foremost around the question of whether it owed a duty of care to the plaintiffs. In

---

Apart from finding sufficient evidence to conclude that Chevron Texaco had acted jointly with Chevron Nigeria Ltd, the court also held that the same facts could establish Chevron Texaco's liability as an aider and abettor to the actions of its subsidiary. Remarkably, the court also indicated that a failure to disavow the impugned acts could be interpreted as an attempt at cover-up and, accordingly, may render the parent corporation liable as principal. No C 99-2506 SI, 2004 US Dist LEXIS 4603 (2004), paras. 37-52.

19 See Chapter 5, section IV.3.1a: The *dolus eventualis* standard of corporate misconduct.

20 Joseph, *supra note 8*, p. 138. In March 2005, Unocal agreed to compensate the plaintiffs in a settlement that ended the lawsuit.

international criminal law, if an analogy were to be drawn between parent-subsidiary and superior-subordinate relationships, the issue of due diligence would also arise. The inquiry would, however, focus on the responsibility and power to control the impugned subsidiary conduct rather than the existence of a duty of care to the victims.

Undeniably the association between a parent company and its foreign affiliates is not necessarily the functional equivalent of the link that defines superiors and subordinates within a hierarchical structure. Having separate juridical personalities and management structures and practices, with which a higher authority (i.e. the parent company) may or may not effectively interfere, subsidiaries bear the primary responsibility for their conduct. Nevertheless, in some circumstances, the extension of liability can be validated by the nature of the control relationship that exists between the parent and the subsidiary. Determinations in this regard would invariably have to be made on a case-by-case basis.[21] Blameworthiness would attach to the parent's refusal to abide by a legal obligation and ensure that its conduct does not entail the commission of an international crime. Although the subsidiary might be the actual material participant, culpability on the part of the parent would be derived from its duty and ability to effectively intervene in the affairs of an entity within its sphere of control. Conclusions in this regard would be drawn on the basis of authority and control as the applicable standards. These criteria are firmly established in international criminal law with regard to the liability of individual superiors.[22]

As is the case with civilian superiors, extending liability to parent corporations should not be perceived to imply an absolute duty to stay apprised of subsidiary conduct at all times. Neither does it purport guilt and punishment along strict liability lines or an unconditional obligation to prevent, in any circumstances, subsidiary conduct that may involve the commission of an international crime. Given the criminal nature of the responsibility sought – and the social stigma and material consequences involved – the criteria attaching to the parent company's culpability must in fact be strictly circumscribed. Grounding criminal responsibility on a failure to intervene and raise awareness combined with a failure to exercise control over the subsidiary, as a result of which the subsidiary engages in the commission of an international crime, provides one possible approach. Such a construction roots liability in a fault on the part

---

21 Similarly, but in relation to the criminal responsibility of individual superiors, the *ad hoc* tribunals have ruled that the existence of authority and control over subordinate conduct is a matter of evidence rather than substantive law, and depends on the circumstances of each individual case. See e.g. *Prosecutor v. Halilovic*, ICTY Case No. IT-01-48-T, Judgment of 16 November 2005, para. 58; *Prosecutor v. Strugar*, ICTY Case No. IT-01-42-T, Judgment of 31 January 2005, para. 392; *Prosecutor v. Blaskic*, ICTY Case No. IT-95-14-A, Appeal Judgment of 29 July 2004, para. 69. The foregoing has recently been affirmed by Pre-Trial Chamber II of the ICC in *Prosecutor v. Jean-Pierre Bemba Gombo*, Decision pursuant to Article 61(7)(a) and (b) of the Rome Statute on the Charges of the Prosecutor against Jean-Pierre Bemba Gombo, ICC-01/05-01/08-424, 15 June 2009, para. 416.

22 For an overview of the international *ad hoc* tribunals' case law with regard to the criteria of authority and control in relation to superior responsibility, as well as Article 28(b) RS, see Chapter 4, section III.2: Superior responsibility under the Rome Statute.

of the parent itself. It furthermore draws upon the notions of awareness and control as the ground stones of liability in hierarchical settings, recognised and operative in international criminal law with respect to superior responsibility.

II.3.1 The duty to intervene

Failure to intervene as a component of direct parent liability presupposes a duty to intervene. This duty can be said to fall within the scope of due diligence that can reasonably be expected of corporations in relation to grave human rights violations. It relates to the obligation to ensure that the company does not – directly or indirectly – become involved in international crimes. Whether the requirement of due diligence to guard against risks through company activities may reasonably be extended to parent corporations when it is the subsidiary conduct that brings about a criminal consequence, would largely depend on a casuistic assessment of the nature of the relationship between a parent and its subsidiary in any particular situation. Where the separate legal personality of the foreign affiliate is merely a facade behind which the parent entity exercises dominant control over the subsidiary's management and decision-making, substantial due diligence expectations may justifiably attach to the controlling company. The obligation in this regard would be the same as that previously expounded with reference to business enterprises in general, i.e. take reasonable steps to ascertain that company operations do not inadvertently create an unjustifiable risk for human rights abuse. Under such conditions, the culpability inquiry would presumably focus predominantly, if not exclusively, on the parent corporation.[23]

In circumstances where the entities are not as interposed, a different reasoning is warranted. A parent entity, which has influence – albeit not prevailing – over its subsidiary, can still be expected to exercise some due diligence. Such due diligence, however, would not relate to a duty to proactively safeguard against subsidiary fault. The duty of care and blameworthiness for conduct the company could have foreseen, remain primarily vested with the subsidiary. However, given the influence that the parent may have and the serious nature of the crimes (potentially) entailed in the conduct of the affiliate entity, there arises a reasonable expectation to put the

---

23 In the present study, the inadvertent creation of an unjustifiable risk entailing an international crime, or in other words negligence as a standard for corporate criminal responsibility, is perceived as giving rise to liability for a breach of duty rather than the crimes that materialise. See Chapter 5, section IV.3.1b: *Culpa* as a benchmark for corporate criminal responsibility. In contrast, in ATCA-related case law, situations in which the subsidiary may be regarded as the 'alter ego' or 'agency' of the parent company, give rise to the parent's liability for the subsidiary's acts. Among the applicable criteria is the establishment of a close relationship or domination between the parent and the subsidiary. In *Bowoto v. Chevron*, for instance, the judge took into account the degree to which the parent corporation set or participated in setting policy, the directors and officers that the parent and subsidiary had in common, as well as the degree and content of the communication between the two entities concerning the incidents at issue. *Bowoto v. Chevron*, 312 F Supp 2d 1229 (2004), 1243.

subsidiary on notice of foreseeable risks. This does not imply a duty to gain foreseeability by evaluating the risks involved in the activities or transactions of subsidiary enterprises. Neither does it connote an obligation to continuously supervise the affiliates' conduct. Nevertheless, when the parent corporation is aware of the likelihood of a criminal consequence – irrespective of its substantiality – it has a duty to intervene, i.e. raise or verify awareness on the part of the subsidiary as to the (potentially) adverse human rights impact of its conduct. As explained above, the duty is inextricably linked to the authority that the parent company has over its affiliates.

II.3.1a Authority

Such authority need not relate to the parent's actual power of control over the subsidiary's activities. For the purpose of triggering the duty to intervene, it would suffice if the parent has influence over its affiliate. As stipulated previously, influence in this sense does not suggest an ability on the part of the parent corporation to unilaterally affect the course of subsidiary operations. In other words, the influence need not be essential in relation to the affiliate's decision-making process. However, the authority possessed by the parent must be such so as to entail an entitlement and/or capability to intervene in the subsidiary's overall management. The extent to which the parent corporation has chosen to exercise *effective* influence over the managerial affairs of its subservient entity would be irrelevant to the determination of whether or not there is a duty to intervene and alert the subsidiary to potential risks. As long as the parent enjoys formal or actual authority permitting it to partake in its affiliate's decision-making, a duty to intervene can be said to exist.

Clearly the aforementioned interpretation of 'authority' has been adapted to the peculiarities of the corporate context. The authority criterion as a factor underlying liability, however, is not entirely removed from the reality of international criminal law. Article 28(b) RS stipulates the individual responsibility of civilian superiors only in relation to subordinates who at the time of the impugned behaviour had authority over the subordinates involved.[24] Such authority is generally understood to denote a position of power, *de jure* or *de facto*.[25] The element of 'effective' allows for the application of the notion to relationships of indirect subordination too, particularly in relation to dispersed chains of command.[26] Furthermore, the condition of 'effective' in relation to authority must be viewed inseparably from the conjunctive factor of control. It is meant to ensure that only those individuals whose authority allowed them

24 See also Bemba, *supra note 21*, paras. 412-413, 418. It must be noted, however, that in the particular case, the Pre-Trial Chamber's reasoning concerned the meaning of 'authority and control' postulated with regard to military superiors in Article 28(a) RS.

25 E.g. *Prosecutor v. Delalic et al.*, ICTY Case No. IT-96-21-T, Judgment of 16 November 1998, para. 370. See also Chapter 4, section III.2.1: The components of superior responsibility as a mode of liability.

26 W.J. Fenrick, Article 28: Responsibility of Commanders and Other Superiors, in: O. Triffterer (ed.), *Commentary on the Rome Statute*, Nomos: Baden-Baden, 1999, p. 519.

to exercise a sufficient degree of control over their subordinates incur criminal responsibility.[27] A similarly strict conception of authority with regard to parent companies is unnecessary. The 'authority' stipulation in relation to the duty to intervene is herein understood to merely serve as a trigger of due diligence.

II.3.1b Awareness

Apart from the need to establish certain authority over the subsidiary, the duty to intervene would also be premised on the existence of some knowledge on the part of the parent as to a crime or a criminal consequence. The obligation to alert the affiliate would thus arise where the parent company is aware that a crime is occurring or might occur. It would not be necessary to demonstrate the parent's perception of the specific offence that eventually materialises in the course of the subsidiary's operations. It would suffice if there were an unjustifiable risk involved and the parent enterprise had foreseen that risk. Awareness in this regard is to be ascertained using the constructive method, i.e. on the basis of evidence of actual knowledge and reasonable inferences. The inquiry would revolve around the question of whether, given the size and functionality of the organisation, the nature of the information available and the type of individual agents in whose possession it was, the parent corporation can be said to have been aware of the risk. It must, therefore, at the very least be established that the parent had at its disposal information which put it on notice of potential risks entailed in subsidiary activities. Conclusions as to the existence of awareness on the part of the organisation as a whole would draw upon the principle of aggregation. However, as pointed out above, the aggregation of knowledge cannot be divorced from organisational characteristics. Although there may be no need to prove the foreseeability of a risk to senior management, it would not be enough if awareness were situated solely at the bottom of the parent company.

This interpretation of the cognitive standard underlying the duty to intervene, aligns with the subjective criteria applicable to the doctrine of superior responsibility in international criminal law. Those criteria have already been discussed elsewhere in the present study.[28] Nevertheless, it must be re-iterated here that the ICC has not yet ruled on the precise meaning of 'had reason to know' in civilian settings. In *Bemba*, Pre-Trial Chamber II emphasised the drafting history of Article 28 RS, indicating the intent of the drafters to introduce more stringent requirements for superiors who fall within the ambit of paragraph (b).[29] It hence implicitly rejected the existence of an active duty on the part of civilians to secure knowledge of their subordinates' activities, regardless of the information available at the time. Presumably, the 'had reason to know' standard would apply where the superior already had certain information at his or her disposal.

27 E. van Sliedregt, *The Criminal Responsibility of Individuals for Violations of International Humanitarian Law*, The Hague: T.M.C. Asser Press, 2003, pp. 183-185.

28 See Chapter 4, section III.2.1b: The cognitive requirement for superior responsibility.

29 Bemba, *supra note 21*, para. 433.

It remains unclear, however, what the implications of the additional factor of 'clearly indicating' might be. In their case law, the *ad hoc* tribunals have accepted that it is sufficient if the superior possessed general information indicating the need for additional inquiry into the subordinates' acts.[30] Somewhat ambiguously, Article 28(b) RS further stipulates that the available information clearly indicated that the subordinates were committing or about to commit crimes. Fenrick has contended that the cognitive standard in this regard would relate to awareness of a substantial risk.[31] Moreover, the question remains as to whether the information at the superior's disposal must be of more concrete nature, negating the expectation of further investigation in order to ascertain the risk.

With regard to corporations, considering their vast resources and the greater harm potentially intrinsic in the scale of their operations, it would be reasonable to interpret 'had reason to know' in the light of due diligence. Accordingly, the stipulation of 'clearly indicating' with regard to the information available would be understood to refer to the corporation having general notice of a crime or a risk. Such notice, however, must be sufficient to engender foreseeability, although it need not concern a concrete criminal consequence. With regard to parent corporations, the cognitive requirement may need to be interpreted more restrictively. Since the obligation to ascertain the existence and true extent of the risks involved is primarily vested with each separate subsidiary, the parent cannot be expected to investigate and verify suspicious information. Its duty to intervene extends only to communicating available suspicious information to its affiliate, which in turn is responsible for carrying out further inquiries. Thus, mere awareness of factual circumstances establishing the possibility of a criminal consequence, e.g. the subsidiary operating in a country ruled by a repressive military regime, cannot trigger a parent company's duty to intervene. The need to exercise special care is incumbent upon the business entity seeking to directly operate in the particular circumstances.

II.3.2 The power to intervene

Awareness and authority alone, or a breach of the duty to intervene (as described above), cannot serve as valid grounds for imposing direct criminal liability on parent corporations. As the UN Special Representative on Human Rights and Transnational Corporations has correctly pointed out, attributing responsibility to companies for the human rights impact of entities over which they may have only *some* leverage is a precarious approach.[32] Leverage in the sense of formal authority and/or a degree of influence does not necessarily entail power to intervene. The actual ability to prevent

30 E.g. Delalic et al., *supra note 25*, para. 393.
31 Fenrick, *supra note 26*, margin no. 21.
32 UN Doc. A/HRC/8/16, Clarifying the concepts of 'sphere of influence' and 'complicity', Report of the Special Representative of the Secretary-General on the issue of human rights and transnational corporations and other business entities, 15 May 2008, para. 13.

or suppress the behaviour that entails a criminal consequence is essential for the hierarchical extension of culpability. Accordingly, liability for the parent's own contribution to the subsidiary's impugned conduct, where such contribution is through omission rather than active participation, must be premised on the criteria of control and causation.

II.3.2a Control

The notion of control in both international and domestic law relates to legal competence as well as material ability to manage the (potentially) harmful or criminal behaviour of individuals or entities within one's realm of responsibility. In international criminal law, the control factor is critical to the determination of the liability of superiors for crimes committed by their subordinates. Article 28 RS in particular envisages criminal responsibility for superiors, military or civilian, when *subordinates* under their *effective control* commit crimes within the jurisdiction of the Court. The control requirement in this regard mirrors established case law of the *ad hoc* tribunals.[33] The power to intervene as a basis for liability where non-military superiors have control over the material perpetrators, also resonates in Nuremberg case law.[34]

Paragraph (b) of Article 28 RS furthermore stipulates that the subordinate crimes must concern *activities* which are within the superior's *effective control.* As Van Sliedregt explains, the aforementioned additional qualification of the requisite control threshold is not alien to national jurisdictions.[35] For instance, in the Netherlands, whose legal system allows for the prosecution of employers – natural and legal persons – for acts of their employees, criminal liability is premised on control over the acts and acceptance thereof.[36] Moreover, in a recent case concerning the alleged superior responsibility of a logging company owner for war crimes committed in Liberia between 2000 and 2002, the Hague Appeals Court invoked the issue of control in overturning the defendant's conviction at trial.[37] It held that Kouwenhoven's management powers, and hence control over the alleged material perpetrators, were not sufficiently established. According to the court, the available evidence also failed

33 E.g. *Prosecutor v. Blaskic*, ICTY Case No. IT-95-14-T, Judgment of 3 March 2000, paras. 302, 335; *Prosecutor v. Aleksovski*, ICTY Case No. IT-95-14/1, Judgment of 25 June 1999, para. 76-78; Delalic et al., *supra note 25*, para. 378.

34 E.g. The case of Pohl et al. Case, *Trials of War Criminals before the Nuremberg Military Tribunals under Control Council Law No. 10, October 1946 – April 1949 (TWC)*, Vol. V, Washington DC: Government Printing Office, 1949 – 1953, pp. 1052-1053 and Medical Cases, TWC, Vol. II, pp. 193-194. The Nuremberg judiciary, however, did not base convictions on the concept of superior responsibility as such. The judgments were, moreover, somewhat ambiguous as to the precise nature of the requisite control.

35 Van Sliedregt, *supra note 27*, pp. 200-201.

36 See also C.H. Brants and K.L.K. Brants, *De sociale constructie van fraude (The Social Construction of Fraud)*, Arnhem: Gouda Quint, 1991, pp. 223-253.

37 Kouwenhoven Case, LJN: BC7373, 10 March 2008, para. 9.21 (at <www.rechtspraak.nl>).

to substantiate the defendant's control over the deployment of the staff that supposedly committed the war crimes specified in the indictment. Also in relation to corporate rather than individual responsibility, and albeit not pertaining to criminal culpability, control over the impugned behaviour has been recognised in other domestic jurisdictions as essential for direct, as opposed to vicarious, parent liability.[38]

The element of control in the context of the international courts and tribunals has, furthermore, been relevant to the articulation of the conditions under which a person or an organised entity can be held to have acted as a *de facto* organ of a state. In this regard, the Appeals Chamber in *Tadic* has held that the requisite degree of control could vary depending on the circumstances of each separate case and the type of relationship involved.[39] In order to attribute to the state acts of private individuals – where the acts concerned are illegal or breach international law *ultra vires* – it has to be established that the state exercised *effective control* over the conduct of the physical perpetrators.[40] The attribution is thus grounded on the state instructing, endorsing or condoning specific actions. When the impugned conduct is performed by organised and hierarchically structured groups (e.g. military or paramilitary units) rather than private individuals, the applicable test favoured by the Appeals Chamber is somewhat different. In such circumstances, the test relates to the *overall control* of the state over the entity concerned. For the purpose of establishing overall control it is not necessary for the state to have directed or approved specific conduct. It suffices if the state has provided operational support and participated in the general planning of military or paramilitary activity.[41]

The aforementioned distinction between the criteria of effective and overall control was espoused by the ICTY for the purpose of adjudicating a jurisdictional issue raised in interlocutory appeal.[42] Consequently, it was deemed inapplicable by the Inter-

38 Albeit not yet tested in transnational human rights cases under the ATCA, such a control criterion has emerged out of US tort jurisprudence. As Joseph explains: 'The issue is not control by the parent over the subsidiary. Rather, the relevant control is that exercised by the parent over the conduct, which gave rise to the tort at issue. Thus, the relevant 'control test' focuses on the extent to which a parent is somehow in control of the causes of the tort, which will be linked to, but will not be the same as, the issue of a parent's control over its subsidiary.' Joseph, *supra note 8*, p. 136.

39 *Prosecutor v. Tadic*, ICTY Case No. IT-94-1-A, Appeal Judgment of 15 July 1999.

40 *Ibidem*, paras. 118-119, 141.

41 *Idem*, paras. 131, 137.

42 The Appeals Chamber was confronted with the question of whether the Prosecutor was right in challenging a Trial Chamber's judgment according to which the accused could not incur individual criminal responsibility for grave breaches under Article 2 of the ICTY Statute. According to the Defence, Article 2 applied to international armed conflicts only whereas the conflict, which the accused was involved in, was of an internal nature. Accordingly, in seeking to establish the nature of the conflict, the Appeals Chamber had to determine whether the Bosnian Serb military, which acted in armed opposition to Bosnian Muslim paramilitary units, could be regarded as a *de facto* organ of the Federal Republic of Serbia.

national Court of Justice in the context of state responsibility.[43] The attribution of responsibility to a state, according to the ICJ, could be based solely on the notion of *effective control*. The ICJ thus upheld the test enunciated earlier in the *Nicaragua* Case.[44] It envisages the responsibility of states for the unlawful conduct of organised groups only when the state has power to direct and enforce the specific crimes performed. Providing support in the form of training or financing, and participation in the overall coordination of activities would not suffice where the entity thus supported preserves some degree of independence.

The endorsement of the 'effective control' criterion by the ICJ has been criticised for being misguided.[45] According to Cassese, it not only creates an impunity gap by overlooking the very rationale behind the concept of state responsibility but also fails to properly reflect state practice.[46] Apart from its usefulness for assessing the blameworthiness of states which support secessionist or terrorist activity, 'overall control' has, furthermore, been recently embraced by the European Court of Human Rights in relation to the responsibility of international organisations.[47] Resonant and appealing as it might be, could such criticism of the 'effective control' stipulation be justifiably transposed onto the issue of corporate criminal liability?

Providing financial, logistical and organisational support to a group involved in the commission of an international crime may indeed suggest the existence of strong links between the state where the support originates and the entity engaging in humanitarian law violations. Accordingly, where it is established that the transgressions were performed under the overall authority of the state concerned, responsibility on the part of the state may be warranted. The circumstances of parent corporations implicated in international crimes through the conduct of their subsidiaries are, however, not comparable. As previously discussed, extending material assistance and services to the physical perpetrators of an international crime (e.g. a state army or a rebel group) may entail direct corporate responsibility. Awareness in that regard need not relate to a specific crime. It is sufficient if it involves a foreseeable and unjustifiable criminal consequence. Likewise, consciously financing or otherwise supporting a subsidiary in

---

43 ICJ, Case concerning the Application of the Convention on the prevention and punishment of the crime of genocide (Bosnia and Herzegovina v. Serbia and Montenegro), Judgment (No. 91), 26 February 2007.

44 ICJ, Case concerning Military and paramilitary activities in and against Nicaragua (Merits), 27 June 1986, paras. 105-115.

45 See e.g. A. Cassese, The Nicaragua and Tadic Tests Revisited in Light of the ICJ Judgment on Genocide in Bosnia, 18 *European Journal of International Law* 649 (2007).

46 *Ibidem*, at 654.

47 *Idem*, at 665-667, also discussing the ECHR cases of *Behrami and Behrami v. France* and *Saramati v. France, Germany and Norway*. The applicants in those cases alleged violations of Article 2 (the right to life) and Article 6 (the right to a fair trial) of the European Convention on Human Rights and Fundamental Freedoms. The Court concluded that the defendant states were not responsible for the conduct complained of, since the personnel who carried out the impugned acts were put under the overall authority and control of the UN.

the commission of human rights abuse may give rise to the direct criminal responsibility of the parent corporation for its active participation in the commission of the offence.

However, where the facilitation transpires through omission, or in other words, a failure to intervene and prevent or repress a crime or a foreseeable criminal consequence, any attempt to directly hold the parent culpable cannot be divorced from the issue of control. Such control, moreover, must be strictly construed. On the one hand, the economic and institutional ties between parent and subsidiary companies are substantially different to those between states and (para)military units. Thus, the drawing of incriminating inferences from evidence of overall control in the corporate context is likely to be tenuous. On the other hand, unlike the blameworthiness attached – explicitly or implicitly – to states or other entities by institutions such as the ICJ and the ECHR, the liability sought in the present study within the framework of the ICC is of a criminal nature. Hence, the mere existence of financial or organisational dependence on the part of a subsidiary company cannot be allowed, in itself, to give rise to the direct culpability of the parent. The criminal responsibility of parent enterprises for their failure to prevent or repress subsidiary involvement in international crimes must be premised on the parents' *actual power of control* over the impugned conduct.

In some cases, the subsidiary may be totally dependent on its parent corporation. Such dependence may be set out in formal controlling agreements or evidenced *de facto*, to the extent that the subsidiary can be deemed a mere alter ego of the parent or incapable of independent existence. The attribution of responsibility to the parent, therefore, would arise out of its effective control over the behaviour of the affiliate, irrespective of whether or not the control is coupled with a *de jure* authority to control. In some circumstances, a mere *de jure* relationship may suffice, provided that the parent corporation is thus endowed with the actual power to unilaterally affect the decision-making process of its subsidiary. In the latter instance, *de jure* and *de facto* power of control would in fact coincide. However, the existence of a *de jure* link, in the sense of the subservient entity being merely depicted within the organisational chart of its parent, could never suffice in itself.

In most cases subsidiaries are only partially dependent on their parent corporations. The parent may possess certain *de jure* or *de facto* authority and may partake in decision-making processes within its affiliates. This authority, however, may not necessarily translate into ability to actually control subsidiary operations. In such situations, it would be unjust to impose criminal responsibility on the parent company unless it is established that the parent had effective control over the specific activity impugned and thus can be said to have had the actual power to intervene. It is not inconceivable that, despite retaining a degree of independence, the subsidiary may be related to its parent in a manner which reveals a degree of actual dependence.

Assessing actual dependence in combination with formal authority is imperative so as to ensure that parent corporations do not evade liability by hiding behind the facades of their legally independent subsidiaries. The criterion of effective control, on the other hand, is critical for safeguarding against the unjustified attribution of criminal liability.[48] Invoking mere authority to control as a basis for criminal responsibility has in fact the propensity to implicate any parent corporation, irrespective of its material ability to control subsidiary actions. At the same time, overall involvement in the management and operations of a subservient entity cannot justify the imposition of liability either. The involvement must be such that it can actually affect the affiliate conduct constituting a sufficiently culpable transgression under international criminal law. The nature and amount of the requisite control would depend on the circumstances of each individual case. It may be evidenced by, *inter alia*, explicit controlling agreements, the extent of the parent's participation in the subsidiary's board of directors and the affiliate entity's actual dependence of existence or decision-making.

The effective control requirement has been criticised by the UN Special Representative on Human Rights and Transnational Corporations as too restrictive.[49] It could serve to release from liability parent corporations which do not actually control their subsidiaries but nevertheless substantially benefit from the subsidiaries' conduct.[50] While imposing criminal responsibility on companies for inadvertently creating the infrastructure for the commission of 'core' international crimes may be justified,[51] holding parent corporations liable in the absence of any involvement on their part or a power to intervene in the (potentially) criminal behaviour concerned, would be clearly erroneous. Fairness obliges that liability of the parent follows either direct participation in the impugned subsidiary activities, or a failure to control as a result of which human rights abuse materialises. Punishment for merely benefiting from the transgression of an affiliate entity would exceed what is permissible under penal law. The attribution of direct criminal responsibility must be rooted in genuine fault and reflect actual culpability on the part of the parent corporation.[52]

---

48 The 'authority to control' as opposed to the 'actual power to control' test has been rightly criticised for being overly broad. In relation to parent corporations' liability for the environmental violations of their subsidiaries under the United States Environmental Response, Compensation and Liability Act of 1980, Brown contends that the 'authority to control' test is 'so easy to meet, its application essentially obliterates the idea of limited liability for parent corporations. Normal activities of a parent with respect to its subsidiary without more ought not warrant an automatic finding of liability'. K.F. Brown, Parent Corporation Liability for Subsidiary Violations under Section 107 of CERCLA: Responding to United States v. Cordova Chemical Co., 1 *Brigham Young University Law Review* 265 (1998).

49 UN Doc. A/HRC/8/16, 15 May 2008, paras. 16-17.

50 A similar argument has been put forward in domestic jurisdictions grappling with the choice between 'authority to control' and 'actual power to control' as a prerequisite for parent liability. See Brown, *supra note 48*, at. 6.

51 See Chapter 5, section IV.3.1b: *Culpa* as a benchmark for corporate criminal responsibility.

52 In some circumstances, nevertheless, accruing profit through subsidiary operations might translate into liability, but not as the sole factor and only where a failure to intervene is coupled with conscious disregard or wilful blindness as to the effects of the affiliate's behaviour.

II.3.2b Causality

Closely related to the issue of control is causality as a requisite element underlying findings of culpability in penal law.[53] In the absence of a causal nexus between the impugned subsidiary conduct and the parent's failure to intervene, it would be unreasonable to attribute direct criminal responsibility to the parent corporation. If liability is to attach to the parent's own blameworthy conduct, then such conduct must be part of a chain of events sufficiently connected to the humanitarian law violation that transpires in the course of subsidiary activities. Although the element of causality need not be regarded as a *conditio sine qua non* for the occurrence of the human rights abuse,[54] it must, nevertheless, be established that the control breakdown contributed to the subsidiary involvement in an international crime.

Like the doctrine of superior responsibility in international criminal law, the liability of parent corporations would extend beyond direct causation.[55] Provided there is an actual power to intervene, a failure to take all necessary (and reasonable) measures to repress *post factum* the further commission of crimes which have already materialised, could be regarded as amply culpable to generate criminal blameworthiness. Depending on the factual links between the two companies, such a scenario may even translate into responsibility on the part of the parent itself for direct involvement in human rights violations, rather than liability for a failure to control (and thus only indirect engagement). Where the crimes occur despite the adequate efforts of the parent company, liability may still arise if the parent attempts to conceal its subsidiary's transgression.

As demonstrated by the foregoing discussion, direct parent liability may follow either active involvement in subsidiary activities, which facilitate the commission of 'core' international crimes, or a sufficiently culpable omission. Such an omission would not relate to a mere failure to supervise, i.e. gain awareness of a foreseeable risk. Criminal responsibility on the part of the parent corporation is premised on awareness of (the likelihood of) a crime or a criminal consequence and the existence of effective control over the impugned behaviour. Thus, blameworthiness does not attach to negligence

---

53 The central place assumed by the principle of causation in criminal law has also been emphasised in *Prosecutor v. Delalic et al.*, ICTY Case No. IT-96-21-A, Appeal Judgment of 20 February 2001, para. 398.

54 Also in *Delalic et al.*, and with regard to superior responsibility as a mode of liability, the Appeals Chamber has held that 'causation has not traditionally been postulated as a *conditio sine qua non* for the imposition of criminal liability on superiors [...] [At the same time, however], a recognition of a necessary causal nexus may be considered to be inherent in the requirement of crimes committed by subordinates and the superior's failure to take the measures within his powers to prevent them.' Delalic et al., *supra note 53*, paras. 398-399. Article 28 RS expressly codifies causality as a separate element. Paragraph (b) stipulates the criminal responsibility of civilian superiors for crimes committed by their subordinates *as a result of* the superiors' failure to exercise control properly.

55 Van Sliedregt, *supra note 27*, p. 190.

in foreseeing an unjustifiable risk arising out of subsidiary operations. Nevertheless, negligence in exercising control, where the parent has effective power over the impugned conduct, may result in the ascription of liability. This warrants the question of whether culpability in this regard concerns the attribution of crimes to the parent company or merely a failure to supervise in terms of timely and adequate intervention. The latter would seem to be the correct construction. On the one hand, it precludes the transformation of negligent omission into intentional criminality where special intent crimes are concerned.[56] On the other hand, it aligns with the contemporary interpretation of the superior responsibility doctrine. As explicitly emphasised in *Bemba*, 'where superior responsibility is concerned, an accused is not charged with the crimes of his subordinates but with his failure to carry out his duty as a superior to exercise control.'[57] Convictions would thus concern a lesser offence, and consequently, yield more lenient sentences. Allowing for the criminal responsibility of parent corporations in such circumstances, however, would also serve to narrow the impunity gap and acknowledge the moral blameworthiness of entities which have the material capability of controlling the material perpetrators or facilitators of international crimes. It would also contribute to efforts directed at ensuring the effective compensation of victims of grave human rights abuse.

III Direct criminal responsibility and supply chain dynamics

With the advent of the globalisation trend, demands for corporate accountability have also encroached on the relationship of business enterprises with their suppliers. Pressure for responsible supply chain management has begun to increasingly target companies' sourcing activities as well as the suppliers' exploitation of poor human rights conditions.[58] The Chief Prosecutor of the ICC has warned the business community of the liability risk intrinsic in the trade of blood diamonds, which are obtained through the commission of international crimes and serve to fuel conflicts in Africa.[59] Companies operating in other sectors have also been criticised for main-

56 Negligence as grounds for imposing superior responsibility for special intent crimes has been subject to extensive criticism by both legal scholars and practitioners. E.g. K. Ambos, Superior Responsibility, in A. Cassese (ed.), *The Rome Statute of the International Criminal Court: a Commentary*, Oxford: Oxford University Press, 2002; M. Damaska, The Shadow Side of Command Responsibility, 49 *American Journal of Comparative Law* 45 (2001); W.A. Schabas, General Principles of Criminal Law in the International Criminal Court Statute, 6 *European Journal of Crime, Criminal Law and Criminal Justice* 84 (1998).

57 Bemba, *supra note 21*, para. 415, referring to *Prosecutor v. Krnojelac*, ICTY Case No. IT-97-25-A, Appeal Judgment of 17 September 2003, para. 171, and Delalic et al., *supra note 53*, para. 198.

58 Amaeshi et al., *supra note 5*, p. 3.

59 Firms Face 'Blood Diamond' Probe, 23 September 2003, at <news.bbc.co.uk/2/hi/ business/3133108.-stm>.

taining business partnerships with suppliers that allegedly engage in torture and slave labour in the production process.[60]

As a reaction to the reputational threat of negative CSR publicity, a growing number of corporations have attempted to put in place systems of ethical standards agreements envisaging the severance of contractual links should suppliers be deemed to have breached pre-agreed codes of conduct.[61] Considerations pertaining to the actual effectiveness of such codes apart, the question arises as to whether it would be fair to also attribute to purchasing companies criminal liability for their suppliers' involvement in grave human rights abuse. The mere existence of ethical agreements cannot, and should not be allowed to, operate as a defence line against the ascription of legal responsibility and insulate corporations from liability for the commission of international crimes by their supply associates.[62] Moreover, severing a contractual relationship upon an external auditor uncovering the supplier's involvement in such crimes may – depending on the circumstances and the links between the entities concerned – not suffice as an adequate form of punishment. Legal sanctions, transgressing contract severance, might be necessary so as to reflect the serious nature of the impugned conduct. Such sanctions would need to emanate from an external authority and the obligation on the part of the purchasing company, where it has not been in a position to prevent or repress its supplier's behaviour, would therefore extend to submitting the matter for investigation and prosecution. In circumstances where the purchasing entity can be deemed to have been consciously involved in the supplier's criminal transgression, the ascription of liability beyond the material perpetrator (i.e. the supplier) might also be warranted. A lack of sanctions in this regard might be seen as contributing to impunity by encouraging business entities to engage in one-off contractual relationships of adverse human rights impact but great profit value.

Again, however, the ascription of criminal liability must invariably be grounded on genuine corporate fault. Along the lines of the proposed construction of culpability in the context of parent-subsidiary relationships, purchasing companies could incur criminal responsibility for either their direct involvement in crimes perpetrated by suppliers or a failure of duty with regard to such business affiliates. In both instances, liability would be derived from the purchasing company's own misconduct. Where it encourages or facilitates a crime committed by a supplier, the purchaser may be

---

60 *Corporate Complicity and Legal Accountability*, Vol. II: Criminal Law and International Crimes, Report of the International Commission of Jurists Expert Legal Panel on Corporate Complicity, 2008, p. 40, at <www.business-humanrights.org/Updates/Archive ICJPaneloncomplicity>.

61 At the same time, however, many MNCs prefer to adhere to purely voluntary initiatives. Most codes of conduct do not properly address the issue of corporate responsibility for the activities of suppliers or contractors. See Amaeshi et al., *supra note 5*, p. 4.

62 Likewise, as previously discussed, proactive due diligence in the sense of putting in place formal policies and procedures aimed at safeguarding against adverse human rights impact in the course of corporate operations, cannot in itself be permitted to serve as a defence and negate liability. See Chapter 5, section IV.2.2: Proactive and reactive fault.

prosecuted for its contribution to human rights abuse jointly with the material perpetrator or separately by itself. A failure of duty, i.e. a sufficiently blameworthy omission with regard to the supplier's behaviour, could also – in some circumstances – give rise to direct liability. The culpability construction in this regard, however, is bound to deviate from that applicable to parent-subsidiary relationships due to the rather different nature of the association between purchasers and their supply contractors.

The material ability to control affiliates' behaviour, and accordingly the duty to intervene and prevent or repress activities entailing a criminal consequence, arise out of the interposition between parent and subsidiary entities.[63] Given the relative independence of suppliers, the justifiability of a similar expectation with regard to purchasing companies is bound to be tenuous. However, aligning the scope of the expectation with the type of relationship characterising supply chain dynamics may validate the reasonable imposition of a certain duty. Such a duty would not relate to the purchasing company's power to control its suppliers, i.e. intervene in specific activities and eliminate the manifestations of criminal or risky behaviour. It would rather concern a responsibility to – at the very least – terminate the business association with the supplier concerned. This does not translate into an obligation for the purchaser to exercise any leverage that it might have in order to ensure that its supply contractors do not engage in international crimes. As in the case of subsidiaries, and perhaps even more so given their larger degree of independence, suppliers bear the primary responsibility for safeguarding against involvement in humanitarian law violations. The duty incumbent upon purchasing companies, therefore, does not imply an obligation to continuously supervise suppliers' activities or gain foreseeability of unjustifiable risks.

The duty to severe contractual links and submit the matter for further review to the relevant authorities would arise only where the purchaser becomes aware that a concrete supplier is involved in criminal or risky activities. Awareness in this sense may encompass actual and circumstantial knowledge, and be established with recourse to the constructive method. It may also include wilful blindness, which would be interpreted in line with corporate due diligence expectations. Accordingly, the cognitive standard would not be at variance with the criterion postulated earlier in the context of parent-subsidiary relationships.[64]

In any case, the duty to intervene (as defined above) must be regarded as applicable to immediate suppliers only. Relying on the proximity element as a trigger would ensure that the obligation to act is operative only in respect of purchasers who are sufficiently close to the crimes that materialise through their suppliers' activities. Thus responsibility would not be indefinitely extended along the supply chain. However, should an immediate supplier serve merely as a facade behind which a business enterprise seeks to hide its transactions with other providers formally situated further

63 See section II.3.2a above.
64 See section II.3.1b above.

down the supply chain, such a deceptive structural organisation should not prevent the attribution of responsibility beyond the sphere of the purchaser and its immediate suppliers. The interpretation of the proximity element would, therefore, be contingent upon the circumstances of each individual case.

The direct criminal liability on the part of the purchasing company for a failure to act would thus be based on the conditions of awareness and proximity. The failure would necessarily have to be assessed with reference to what the company could have reasonably been expected to do given its relationship with, and leverage over, the supplier concerned. In most instances, the failure would relate to the purchaser not terminating its business association with the supplying company involved in the commission of an international crime. In some circumstances, however, the omission may be connected to more stringent expectations, and therefore translate into culpability entailing greater sanctions. The latter scenario might arise out of conditions of economic integration between the purchasing enterprise and its suppliers. In such cases, the duty to intervene, and, accordingly, the failure to act, would assume somewhat broader dimensions. Liability would thus be incurred for breaches of the purchaser's power to control its affiliates and prevent or suppress their involvement in human rights abuse. Basing the direct criminal liability of purchasing companies on the criteria of awareness and proximity serves to safeguard against the unjustifiable extension of responsibility beyond the purchaser's *immediate* sphere of influence. It also ensures that blameworthiness attaches to genuine corporate fault only.

IV The superior responsibility of corporate officials

The inherent deficiencies of attributing liability to the corporation along purely nominalist lines, and in particular the divergence that may occur between individual culpability and corporate guilt, dictate that the construction of criminal responsibility on the part of MNCs follow a more holistic approach to the ascription of blame. Organisational blameworthiness, however, can never justify collective punishment.[65] Neither can it give rise to the mechanical imposition of vicarious responsibility on senior management echelons. Individual culpability is not negated by the group nature of the crimes committed, be it in a military, political or economic context. Thus, attaching criminal liability to a business entity does not preclude the prosecution of corporate agents implicated in offences arising out of company activities. The ascription of individual criminal responsibility, however, must always reflect the extent of personal involvement in the crimes concerned. While a position of authority

65 The criticism pertaining to the implications, real or perceived, of attaching culpability to an organised entity *per se*, is not novel. It has been raised with regard of the notion of 'criminal organisations', which was crafted and employed at Nuremberg. See Chapter 3, section II.2: The concept of criminal organisations. A similar critique resonates in discussions concerning the issue of direct corporate criminal responsibility, at the domestic or international level.

may entail a certain duty to supervise and control subordinate behaviour, superior status within civilian structures can validate the ascription of liability in very limited circumstances only. The application of the concept of superior responsibility to MNCs in particular poses some unique challenges.

In principle, there is nothing in the formulation of Article 28(b) RS that rules out the application of the doctrine of superior responsibility to corporate structures. The jurisprudence of the *ad hoc* tribunals has long recognised the warranted extension of the 'civilian superior' notion to business executives.[66] The liability of corporate managers for crimes committed under their authority has also been acknowledged by the post-Second World War military tribunals, although its construction has been controversial.[67]

While on some occasions the Nuremberg tribunals may have inferred guilt from a mere position of authority,[68] the subsequent development of the superior responsibility doctrine in international criminal law, and the *ad hoc* tribunals' emphasis on the element of effective control,[69] has diluted concerns that a judicial finding of a dereliction of duty would translate into a form of strict liability.[70] The *chapeau* of Article 28(b) RS envisages the criminal responsibility of superiors who fail to sufficiently inform, advise, supervise and control their subordinates. However, the implications of the *chapeau* are strictly circumscribed by the conditions stipulated in subparagraphs (i) to (iii). These conditions are, furthermore, linked to the preceding *chapeau* in a manner that establishes the requirement of a causal nexus between the

---

66 E.g. *Prosecutor v. Musema*, Case No. ICTR-96-13-A, Judgment and Sentence, 27 January 2000, paras. 135-148; Delalic et al., *supra note 25*, paras. 355-363.

67 In *Roechling et al.*, for instance, one of the defendants was found guilty for failing to alleviate abuses committed by Gestapo soldiers against forced labourers in the company's factory. Despite lacking formal authority to issue orders to Gestapo staff members, Herman Roechling was deemed to have had *de facto* influence over at least one of the physical perpetrators, as the latter was his son-in-law. The case of Roechling et al., *Law Reports of Trials of War Criminals (UNWCC)*, Vol. XIV, London: His Majesty's Stationary Office, 1949, Appendix B, p. 1075, para. 1092.

68 See in this regard Chapter 3, section III.2: Synthesising the Nuremberg principles of individual criminal responsibility in relation to corporate officers.

69 Delalic et al., *supra note 53*, paras. 256, 265-266. In *Kayishema and Ruzindana* (para. 220), later upheld in *Musema* as well (para. 141), the ICTR Trial Chamber concluded that powers of influence were sufficient to generate superior responsibility. See *Prosecutor v. Kayishema and Ruzindana*, Case No. ICTR-95-1-T, Judgment of 21 May 1999 and Musema, *supra note 66*. This approach, however, was expressly rejected by the Appeals Chamber in *Delalic et al.* It held that 'substantial influence as a means of control in any sense which falls short of the possession of effective control over subordinates, which requires the possession of material abilities to prevent subordinate offences or to punish subordinate offenders, lacks sufficient support in State practice and judicial decisions.' Delalic et al., *supra note 53*, paras. 265-266.

70 In *Akayesu* and *Musema*, the ICTR expressly rejected the view – essentially derived from the rule of strict liability – that superior responsibility is independent of criminal intent. *Prosecutor v. Akayesu*, Case No. ICTR-96-4-T, Judgment of 2 September 1998, para. 488 and Musema, *supra note 66*, para. 131.

omission on the part of the superior and the criminal acts of his subordinates.[71] A dereliction of proper control, as a result of which a crime is committed, would be punishable only when (1) there is knowledge or wilful blindness on the part of the superior about a situation involving the commission of crimes, and (2) there is a corresponding failure by the same superior to act within necessary and reasonable bounds.[72] As Triffterer explains, the potential danger inherent in a failure to control cannot, therefore, trigger either strict or vicarious liability. Superior responsibility in the meaning of Article 28(b) presupposes a continuation of the superior's inactivity after a given situation has started to endanger '*in concreto* legally protected values'.[73]

IV.1 Superior – subordinate relationships and the 'effective responsibility and control' test

The impugned failure to act may not be invoked *vis-à-vis* the conduct of anyone situated lower on the hierarchy ladder and within the civilian superior's scope of authority. Article 28(b) RS expressly stipulates that responsibility attaches to inactivity only when as a result of such inactivity (1) crimes are committed by *subordinates under* the superior's effective authority and control, and (2) the crimes concern *activities within* the superior's effective responsibility and control. The latter prerequisite operates as a safeguard against the reality of multiple control centres and weaker powers of authority characterising non-military structures.

Corporations are typically hierarchically organised entities, comprising numerous superior – subordinate relationships. Such relationships may be dispersed across various levels, areas of activity or even different enterprises within the corporate group. The decisive factor for establishing the existence of a superior – subordinate link within the meaning of Article 28(b), also in the corporate context, would be the superior's status entailing an inherent right to control, or rather the actual power of control, over the physical perpetrators.[74] While in the former instance authority emanates *de jure* from an official position and its corresponding rights, in the latter, influence is evinced by virtue of *de facto* control independent of formal status.[75] This, however, may pose certain difficulties in allocating superior responsibility in a

71 K. Ambos, Superior Responsibility, in: Cassese et al. (eds.), *The Rome Statute of the International Criminal Court: a Commentary*, Oxford: Oxford University Press, 2002.

72 O. Triffterer, Causality, a Separate Element of the Doctrine of Superior Responsibility as Expressed in Article 28 Rome Statute?, 15 *Leiden Journal of International Law* 179 (2002) at 199.

73 *Ibidem*.

74 In this regard, it would be immaterial whether or not the superior was formally insulated from the immediate perpetrators by a shield of intermediaries. *Prosecutor v. Oric*, ICTY Case No. IT-03-68-A, Appeal Judgment of 3 July 2008, para. 20.

75 Irrespective of formal authority, effective control must always be proven beyond reasonable doubt. In *Oric*, the Appeals Chamber held that '*de jure* authority is not synonymous with effective control. Whereas the possession of *de jure* powers may certainly suggest a material ability to prevent or punish criminal acts of subordinates, it may be neither necessary nor sufficient to prove such ability' (*supra note 74*, paras. 90-91).

corporate context. These difficulties become particularly evident where the role of persons from outside the immediate organisational structure of the material perpetrators comes to affect the determination of what constitutes a superior – subordinate relationship.

As mentioned above, sub-paragraph (ii) of Article 28(b) envisages the liability of civilian superiors only when they have effective responsibility and control over the subordinates' impugned acts. The superior's authority and power to intervene must, therefore, extend to the specific acts leading to the commission of a crime. While this strict requirement enshrined in sub-paragraph (ii) is intended – and rightly so – to safeguard against unwarranted extension of criminal liability in civilian settings, it overly circumscribes the scope of application of the superior responsibility doctrine to corporate structures.

The scenario of a company operating under dual decision-making authority is illustrative in this regard. Such a company is headed by an appointed executive director, who runs the day-to-day activities but, nonetheless, shares the overall decision-making power with the company's owner. Although the owner does not occupy a formal position within the organisational structure, his authority is effective, i.e. known to and abided by the company's employees. In such circumstances, the *de jure* authority of the appointed director may serve as a basis for his superior responsibility only if he had the actual competence to intervene in the acts of his subordinates and then only within his pre-defined field of responsibility and control. Even if his power of control were to be exceeded by that of the company's owner, he may, nevertheless, be held criminally liable for a failure to act and at least attempt to prevent or repress subordinate acts within his area of responsibility. For the most part, the culpability burden would, however, fall on the company's owner as the *de facto* authority in the organisational chain of command, provided his actual powers of control extend to the specific subordinate acts concerned. Accordingly, his lack of *de jure* control would not relieve him of individual liability.

The determination of superior – subordinate relationships in a multinational corporate context is bound to be considerably more complicated. A key issue in such cases would be the extent to which the parent entity's directing minds had the authority and power to exercise effective control over the acts of the subsidiary's employees. The nature and scope of inter-dependence between the parent and the subsidiary company would, therefore, have to be closely scrutinised. The degree to which subsidiary policies and activities are externally determined and supervised, and the type of involvement that the directing minds of the parent entity have in subsidiary operations, may be of critical importance. Ultimately, the allocation of superior liability may impinge on the directing minds of both the parent and the subsidiary entity, though in proportion to their respective degrees of actual control over the impugned conduct and then only if the conduct fell within their effective responsibility.

Clearly the difficulty lies in the practical application of the 'effective responsibility and control' stipulation, particularly where the attribution of criminal liability to corporate superiors is sought outside the confines of the immediate business entity employing the material perpetrators. The higher the superior – subordinate relationship extends and the further it transgresses organisational lines, the more actual authority and effective responsibility are likely to diminish. While this may pose an obstacle to the allocation of superior liability in any setting – military or civilian – it is particularly problematic with regard to large business enterprises. The structure and functioning of corporate enterprises are generally determined by efficiency considerations. Given the size of modern MNCs, such considerations often lead to the establishment of numerous control centres dispersed throughout the organisation or even spread across interposed entities within the corporate group. These control centres may not always be linked to each other in a strict hierarchy; instead, authority and responsibility may vary according to spheres of activity. One end result of the inherent complexity of corporations may thus be the insulation of senior executives (not only of the parent company but also of the entity whose agents engage in an international crime) from superior responsibility. The cause of this outcome would customarily lie in the division of labour, and corresponding powers and responsibilities, within the corporate structure. While the highest management is typically occupied with policy-making, it is the middle management that is responsible for the running of day-to-day operations. In such circumstances, the application of the dual 'effective responsibility and control' test, enshrined in Article 28(b) RS, appears to give rise to the superior responsibility of primarily the middle levels within the organisation. It is middle managers who are generally delegated the responsibility over groups of subordinates and the subordinates' specific activities. Hence, it is the level of middle management which possesses the authority, and at the same time, the actual power of control over the acts of those subordinates who fall within their pre-defined sphere of responsibility.

IV.2 The cognitive requirement and the corresponding failure to act

The cognitive requirement stipulated in sub-paragraph (ii) of Article 28(b) RS, is also prone to overly restrict the scope of application of the superior responsibility doctrine in the corporate context. The criminal responsibility of business executives, as civilians falling within the ambit of Article 28(b), would follow only where there is evidence of some knowledge on their part as to the (prospective) criminal involvement of their subordinates. Such knowledge (i.e. positive awareness or wilful blindness) would, however, rarely be present, or be exceedingly difficult to establish, at the level of the corporation's directing minds. Once again, the structural and functional convolution typifying modern business enterprises might serve to shield CEOs from liability.

Multiple networks of communication channels need not – and often do not – necessarily converge in senior executives. Awareness of (potentially) criminal activity by ordinary employees is generally likely to exist further down the corporate ladder and only rarely at the level of the highest management. While the highest echelon of directing minds is, in principle, responsible for the formulation of corporate policies and the overall management of the organisation and its operations, the implementation of those policies and the actual supervision of employees are usually delegated to the lower managerial levels. As a consequence of this fragmentation of tasks, should an employee become involved in the commission of an international crime, such involvement is bound to become known to the employee's immediate superiors first. The latter bear primary responsibility over corporate agents under their sphere of authority and have the duty to supervise, as well as the power to control, the activities of their subordinates. However, awareness on the part of middle managers of a crime or criminal consequence cannot be mechanically transposed to the organisation's CEOs.

In order to construct the superior responsibility of the corporation's directing minds, it would, therefore, have to be established that they have been either directly implicated in the specific employee activities concerned[76] or have been made aware of the employees' (potential) involvement in human rights abuse. Since Article 28(b) rejects the 'should have known' standard in relation to civilians, corporate executives need not be over-diligent in securing knowledge. They are not subject to an obligation to continuously monitor and actively inquire into subordinate conduct; a legitimate expectation arises only where they are sufficiently put on notice of a risk.

As already indicated above, difficulties are undoubtedly bound to arise in seeking to establish the requisite cognitive standard. The determination in each individual case would require a detailed examination of the structures comprising the corporate body, the formal and informal channels of communication on both horizontal and vertical level, the peculiarities of decision-making processes and the absolute and relative independence of various agents in implementing the decisions taken. The line of middle managers, serving as an intermediary link between senior executives and ordinary employees, would ultimately be critical for ascertaining the necessary *mens rea* on the part of the corporation's directing minds. Attempts to allocate superior responsibility to the directing minds of parent corporations would be further confounded by the need to examine the nature and extent of interdependence between parent and subsidiary entities.

76 It must be re-iterated here that superior responsibility within the meaning of the Rome Statute is only a complementary mode of liability. As it does not give rise to principal liability, superior responsibility would generally be pled in the alternative. Where the available evidence establishes the applicability of more than one mode of liability, and particularly where the impugned conduct relates to omission, the judges would be well advised to give preference to theories of commission rather than derivative forms of participation. The latter view has been advocated by e.g. H. Olasolo, *The Criminal Responsibility of Senior Political and Military Leaders as Principals to International Crimes*, Oxford: Hart Publishing, 2009, p. 109.

Assuming that the aforementioned high threshold of the requisite knowledge can be sufficiently established, the criminal liability of senior corporate executives would then also depend on their subsequent failure to act upon this knowledge. The duty to act entails an obligation on the part of the directing minds to take all necessary and reasonable measures within their material possibility to prevent, repress or punish subordinates. What would constitute necessary and reasonable measures would naturally depend on the circumstances of each particular case. The executive's duty to act, however, would extend only to the field of his actual authority, and effective responsibility and control. Once again, the principal personification of the superior duty postulated in Article 28(b) RS and the primary bearer of liability is thus likely to be middle management rather than the corporation's directing minds. The applicability of the superior responsibility doctrine to the CEOs of parent companies would, moreover, be circumscribed by the need to establish a high degree of subsidiary dependence and parent control.

V Conclusion

Complex patterns of economic integration have clear implications for the allocation of criminal liability within corporate groups and their affiliate networks. The interpretation and application of relevant legal principles must, therefore, be adjusted so as to reflect actual reality and narrow the accountability gap. At the same time, however, they must stay aligned with the fundamentals of criminal law. The ascription of responsibility must be allowed to transcend the limitations of the corporate form; nevertheless culpability should always remain firmly rooted in genuine fault. The latter holds true irrespective of whether organisational or personal failures are concerned. Such failures may not be mechanically transposed from the collective to the individual level and vice versa. Neither should they be seen, or sanctioned to give rise to strict liability or collective punishment. The construction of criminal liability expounded in this chapter has revolved around direct responsibility for conscious legal transgressions within areas of effective control.

As seen above, superior responsibility does not appear the most appropriate tool for constructing the culpability of MNCs' directing minds. Firmly rooted in the principle of complementarity, the ICC has been established to prosecute only those most responsible for the crimes falling within its jurisdiction. Intended to supplement, rather than supplant domestic legal systems, the drafters of the Rome Statute have explicitly recognised the primary responsibility of national courts to put on trial the multitude of individuals involved in the commission of international crimes. The Court will, therefore, step in only where domestic authorities are genuinely unwilling or unable to carry out the investigation or prosecution.[77] Even in such circumstances, a

77 Article 17(1) RS.

determination of insufficient gravity could render a case inadmissible.[78] A decision of Pre-Trial Chamber I in *Lubanga* has interpreted the applicable gravity threshold as extending to the category of most senior leaders only.[79] Given also the Court's limited resources, the prosecution may presumably opt for restraint in issuing indictments seeking to implicate middle managers of business enterprises pursuant to Article 28. In this regard, Article 25 RS appears to be a better-suited avenue for ensuring the accountability of corporate officials – from those who order the commission of crimes to those who merely facilitate the activities of groups with a common criminal purpose. The rather strict requirements that attach to the individual liability modes under Article 25, are not conducive to findings of culpability for failures of due diligence and faulty judgments either. International criminal law cannot, however, be expected to effectively resolve all potential loopholes without risking becoming too detached from its own principles.

Despite its circumscribed prospects in relation to individual corporate agents, the superior responsibility doctrine and its underlying concepts afford a functional approach to the construction of the criminal responsibility of business entities in relation to offences committed by their affiliates. Liability is premised on a failure to control as a result of which human rights violations materialise. Culpability is thus only indirectly linked to the crimes. Accordingly, the corresponding punishment warrants differentiation in terms of sentencing outcomes. Such an approach recognises that persons in a position of control – even if they are legal entities – have a certain responsibility towards those under their authority. It not only serves to address the impunity nurtured by the principle of separate personality, but is also cognisant of the fact that the best part of responsibility remains vested in the material perpetrators and participants more directly involved in the commission of international crimes.

78 Article 17(1)(d) RS.

79 *Prosecutor v. Thomas Lubanga Dyilo*, Decision on the Prosecutor's Application for a Warrant of Arrest, 10 February 2006, para. 63. This decision was included as an annex to the Decision Concerning Pre-Trial Chamber I's Decision of 10 February 2006, *Lubanga* (ICC-01/04-01/06-8-Corr), 24 February 2006. According to the Pre-Trial Chamber, the purpose of Article 17(1)(d) is to ensure that the ICC initiates cases only against the most senior leaders suspected of being the most responsible for the commission of crimes falling within the jurisdiction of the Court.

CHAPTER 7
CONCLUSION

I OVERVIEW

The desirability and feasibility of integrating corporate criminal responsibility within the Rome Statute of the International Criminal Court have been the central issues underpinning this research endeavour. In addressing the question of feasibility, the study traces the evolution of the collective criminality notion – in systemic as well as functional terms – from Nuremberg through the *ad hoc* tribunals' case law and the Rome Conference negotiations to the present-day ICC. It outlines repeated, but ultimately failed, attempts to align international penal regulatory mechanisms with the reality of corporate involvement in international crimes and highlights the impediments to extending criminal sanctions to business entities *per se*. In this regard, the study inquires into the level of recognition that the concept of corporate criminal responsibility in general has gained in domestic jurisdictions, and the objections on the part of the few remaining legal systems which reject the extension of criminal law provisions to legal persons on conceptual grounds.

In seeking to determine whether or not it is possible to construct the direct liability of corporations in the context of the ICC, the effort draws upon legal principles that are already operative in the Rome Statute. At times, however, the propositions admittedly exceed what is currently (and arguably) permissible under the ICC regime. Nevertheless, such propositions are not entirely removed from advances in legal practice and thinking at the national level. Largely theoretical, and discounting some of the more traditional domestic approaches to corporate criminal responsibility, the model put forward in this study is far from conventional. However, it also reflects an emerging trend, increasingly embraced by many legal systems, towards incorporating organisational theory in resolving matters of agency in criminal law. Organisational theory and the criminological perspective on corporate crime, outlined at the beginning of the research, are indispensable for understanding how functional deviance occurs and why individual prosecutions of corporate officials may not suffice to counteract corporate wrongdoing.

Cognisant of the tension between group criminality and individual criminal responsibility, this study further postulates the need for constructing the liability of natural and legal persons according to different sets of principles. While favouring strict adherence to personal fault for individuals, it advocates a broader interpretation and application of culpability criteria in relation to corporations, even suggesting the justifiability of a *culpa* standard in the context of international crimes. Considered against the backdrop of the existing regulatory gap with regard to corporate accountability for genocide, crimes against humanity and war crimes, the aforementioned alludes to the desirability of extending the jurisdiction *ratione personae* of the ICC to corporations. The record of MNCs' alleged involvement in grave human rights abuse worldwide and their role in perpetuating many a violent conflict, often revolving around the exploitation of natural resources, warrants attention to the issue of corporate criminal responsibility for the 'core' crimes as an avenue for promoting peace, stability and better protection of fundamental human rights.

This study thus provides a frame of reference on the topic of corporate criminal responsibility for international crimes. It does not incorporate an exhaustive comparative inventory of the domestic jurisdictions who are parties to the Rome Statute and who would be directly confronted with the challenge of tackling business involvement in instances of mass atrocity, should the Court's jurisdiction be extended beyond natural persons. The approach put forward, however, builds upon certain common denominators and notions familiar to both national and international criminal law. Subject to further developments in the field, it may have to be adapted and fine-tuned. It may even not materialise in the proposed form, if at all. In any case, its incorporation in the Rome Statute would not dispense with states' prerogative to determine – in line with their own legal traditions – the contours of the liability modes they would resort to in prosecuting corporate offenders for the 'core' international crimes. Nevertheless, the study will have served a broader social purpose if it revives debates about the need to include corporate criminal responsibility in the Rome Statute. It has demonstrated that there are no insurmountable legal difficulties in criminalising the involvement of business enterprises in genocide, war crimes and crimes against humanity, and has sought to outline what – in this author's view – the most appropriate avenue for addressing corporate criminality through the ICC might be.

Ultimately, the decision of whether or not to extend ICC jurisdiction to corporations would be a matter of political negotiations. In this regard, there are several concerns – of policy, practical as well as more theoretical orientation – that are prone to recur. These relate to the complementarity objection of states which refute the moral agency and responsibility of corporations, the effectiveness of criminal regulation, the implications of collective responsibility on individual punishment as well as the extent to which corporate liability can adequately serve the goals of international criminal justice. This chapter, therefore, seeks to revisit the main themes laid out in the introduction to this study. It considers critically the arguments put forward by delegates at the Rome Conference, as either grounds or obstacles, for incorporating the concept of corporate criminal responsibility in the Rome Statute, with a view to establishing their validity in more precise terms. In light of the propositions expounded in the present research, it also highlights the caveats of future attempts to include economic entities within the jurisdiction of the Court against the need to safeguard the position of the individual and maintain institutional legitimacy but also fight impunity and address existing regulatory deficiencies.

II Prospects along the Regulatory Continuum

The rise of the CSR movement, the erosion of the *societas delinquere non potest* principle and attempts to introduce more stringent regulatory mechanisms in relation to MNCs' and human rights at the international level, reflect growing recognition of the moral responsibility of business entities. This is symptomatic of the fluidity inherent in the notion of moral responsibility, which is continuously shaped by 'shifting views and beliefs in public opinion'.[80] Although the fixation on human agency tends to distort debates about moral blame in relation to culpability, a form of moral blameworthiness is increasingly at the heart of discussions pertaining to the desirability and feasibility of extending penal provisions to corporations. As a result, most domestic systems have gradually shifted their attention from the issue of moral personhood to the question of how to uncover fault on the part of legal persons. Nevertheless, the basic assumption that some form of moral responsibility must underpin criminal liability remains standing. Such moral responsibility – derived from the universal applicability of certain moral norms – is the yardstick by which to measure the wrongfulness of corporate conduct, albeit not in terms of the entity realising the moral blameworthiness of its actions and omissions.

There are, however, a few legal traditions which cannot reconcile themselves with the idea that culpability – even where legal as opposed to natural persons are concerned – can exist independent of moral agency. They espouse a predominantly deontological perspective of criminal law as a system operating on the premise of human conscience. As discussed in Chapter 2, however, even in moral philosophy this particular position has come under increasing challenge. Collectivists have put forward compelling arguments as to the plausibility of regarding corporations as identifiable entities, exceeding the mere collection of individuals comprising them. Rather than seeking to counter those who subscribe to the individualist and purist outlook on criminal law, this study has attempted to translate the theoretical contentions and empirical evidence of criminologists and organisational theorists into more practical terms. Nonetheless, the position of jurisdictions that reject corporate criminality on principle, and are likely to resist it in relation to the Rome Statute as well – and regardless of the question of moral agency as a prerequisite for culpability in criminal law – merits consideration on pragmatic grounds too. It is relevant to the issue of complementarity, which is often viewed as one of the bigger stumbling blocks precluding the extension of ICC jurisdiction beyond natural persons.

80 E. van Sliedregt, *The Criminal Responsibility of Individuals for Violations of International Humanitarian Law*, The Hague: T.M.C. Asser Press, 2003, p. 348.

II.1 The complementarity contention pertaining to 'inaction' and 'inability'

Lack of domestic legislation enabling the criminal prosecution of business enterprises for their involvement in (international) crimes can arguably be perceived in terms of 'inaction' under the ICC complementarity regime. However, as Kyriakakis explains, the complementarity regime in such circumstances cannot be said to have been affected itself, since the state that has remained inactive due to the peculiars of its legal culture *vis-à-vis* corporations, cannot question admissibility.[81] The refusal to recognise economic entities as falling within the scope of criminal law provisions can thus be regarded as precluding the exercise of jurisdiction, and hence the state's entitlement to challenge the admissibility of the case before the ICC and request deferral to the national courts.[82] Driven by state sovereignty considerations, national representatives and legal scholars may nevertheless discern in such a construction the threat of 'hidden discriminatory effect'.[83]

In postulating that the complementarity objection in this regard is not a legal assertion but a matter of competing policy perspectives, this author agrees with Kyriakakis. To the extent that the concept of complementarity is an attempt at reconciling two competing interests, i.e. national sovereignty with the goals of international criminal justice, the position that one assumes on the issue of corporate liability is inevitably pre-determined by one's personal conviction as to where the right balance lies. Far from seeking to undermine respect for the sovereignty of states and the importance of the principle of complementarity, it must be recognised that domestic jurisdictions have been accorded only 'conditional priority'[84] over the ICC. Apart from instances where national authorities are unable or unwilling to genuinely investigate and prosecute, the Court's intervention in cases of inactivity (due to the absence of enabling legislation) is necessitated by the need to fight impunity and narrow the existing regulatory gap. In this sense, the present study has been predicated upon a preference for placing the weight on the interests of international justice rather than the preservation of traditional state-centred archetypes.

Alternatively, a failure to recognise corporations as subject to criminal sanctions may be interpreted as 'inability' due to the total or substantial unavailability of the national judicial system.[85] Should the ICC jurisdiction be extended to business entities, declining to enact sufficient implementing legislation could arguably justify the Court's encroachment upon a state's prerogative to determine the scope of its domestic laws. The conscious decision not to adapt its legislation to the Rome Statute in terms

---

81 J. Kyriakakis, Corporations and the International Criminal Court: The Complementarity Objection Stripped Bare, 19 *Criminal Law Forum* 115 (2007) at 125-126.

82 Articles 18(2) and 19(2) RS.

83 Kyriakakis, *supra note 2*, at 126.

84 A. Eser, Towards an International Criminal Court: Genesis and Main Features of the Rome Statute, 20 *University of Tasmania Law Review* 1 (2001) at 18.

85 Article 17(3) RS.

of criminalising a certain category of offenders falling within the mandate of the Court, may be indicative of the state accepting 'the potentially discriminatory impact of the ICC's particular complementarity regime'.[86] Such an interpretative approach, however, gives rise to questions concerning the scope of the Court's power to require adequate amendments to existing domestic provisions so that they align with the essence and purpose of the Rome Statute.[87]

II.2 Alternatives to corporate criminal liability and the implications for the principle of complementarity

This study is clearly predicated on a preference for criminal regulation – at the national and international level – with regard to corporations involved in the commission of the 'core' international crimes.[88] The underlying rationale is pragmatic in part. Most private applications in jurisdictions which recognise human rights tort claims against MNCs as actionable, tend to fail.[89] Next to the predicament of *forum non conveniens* and other jurisdictional hurdles, civil regulation offers victims little incentive to seek redress. There are serious financial and other practical constraints on the part of plaintiffs associated with bringing civil claims against multimillion-dollar enterprises often incorporated outside the victims' domicile. At the same time, non-criminal proceedings afford business entities the possibility to seek out of court settlements. The commercial and reputational risks to companies of tort-based litigation confound precedent setting, and accordingly no transnational human rights case has yielded a merits decision as yet. Civil settlements are, furthermore, by and large confidential, thus precluding public admissions of responsibility.[90]

This is not to discard the value and record of non-criminal regulation at the domestic level or discount the moral agency contention of the principled opponents to corporate criminality. It is, moreover, doubtful whether the Rome Statute can oblige States Parties to accept the notion of corporate criminal liability and rely upon it where allegations of business participation in genocide, crimes against humanity and war crimes are concerned. Multilateral treaties adopted since the Rome Conference negotiations espouse a less rigid approach, endowing national authorities with a margin of appreciation in choosing the means for counteracting corporate misconduct which has been criminalised at the international level.[91] Not inconceivably, even in

86 Kyriakakis, *supra note 2*, p. 141.
87 See in this regard section II.2 below.
88 See also section V.2 below.
89 K.R. Jacobson, Doing Business With the Devil: The Challenges of Prosecuting Corporate Officials Whose Business Transactions Facilitate War Crimes and Crimes Against Humanity, 56 *Air Force Law Review* 167 (2005) at 216.
90 J. Clough, Not-So-Innocents Abroad: Corporate Criminal Liability for Human Rights Abuses, 11 *Australian Journal of Human Rights* 1 (2005) at 6, at <www.austlii.edu.au/au/journals/AJHR/2005/1.html>.
91 See Chapter 1, section IV.3: Some post-Rome developments.

those jurisdictions which have no conceptual objections to corporate criminal liability, governments may face significant pressure on the part of business to refrain from extending the concept to international crimes at the domestic level or to restrain prosecutorial initiative in opening criminal proceedings. As will be recalled, national legal systems that have been most forthcoming in the prosecution of MNCs for international crimes, prefer to settle for tort law litigation.[92]

An easy opt-out of the conundrum pertaining to the complementarity concerns of states which do not recognise corporate criminality on legal-philosophical grounds, could be to exempt such states from the extension of ICC jurisdiction to business enterprises. This, however, hides the risk of creating safe havens for corporate offenders. It would furthermore fail to address the position of states which prefer to have the option of regulating corporate misconduct through non-criminal means left open to them, and the issue of whether civil or administrative sanctions for corporations at the national level should be allowed to preclude the admissibility of a case before the Court. With regard to the latter, Haigh is inclined to answer in the positive. She advocates a nuanced 'exception-based' model, allowing for civil and administrative proceedings or alternatively individual criminal prosecutions as a bar to admissibility.[93] This may indeed constitute a compromise practicable enough to appease states and encompass most MNCs.

No solution, however, would be immune to criticism. On the one hand, seeking to extend to states a requirement to subject corporations to penal regulation is an aspiration that is prone to run into state sovereignty claims. On the other hand, while allowing for non-criminal sanctions at the national level might be the only viable avenue for resolving the complementarity stalemate, such an approach would not entirely dispense with sovereignty arguments either. While the Rome Statute regime should provide domestic jurisdictions with the tools and flexibility to exercise their discretion in tacking corporate wrongdoing in the context of international crimes, the ultimate authority to decide whether or not national authorities have adequately discharged their obligation in this regard remains vested with the Court. Repressive, albeit not penal, sanctions or individual prosecutions might preclude the admissibility of cases at the international level. Depending on the particular circumstances, however, the ICC might also consider such sanctions and prosecutions inadequate, and interpret them as reflecting unwillingness to respond to the illegality of corporate conduct. Although unlikely, such a scenario cannot be entirely discounted and may run into complications pertaining to *ne bis in idem*. Ultimately, the choice of how to best resolve complementarity concerns would be a matter of political negotiations.

---

92 See in this regard Chapter 1, section III.2: Liability through civil courts, outlining the difficulties surrounding the application of the US Alien Tort Claims Act.

93 K. Haigh, Extending the International Criminal Court's Jurisdiction to Corporations: Overcoming Complementarity Concerns, 14 *Australian Journal of Human Rights* 199 (2008) at 213.

II.3 Non-criminal regulation – a viable option for the ICC?

The preceding discussion also serves to address the contentions of those Rome Conference delegates who have advocated the desirability of non-criminal regulation of MNCs with regard to the 'core' international crimes at the ICC level.[94] It has been contended that the Court should consider the option of civil proceedings against corporations for two reasons. On the one hand, such an approach could provide a middle ground accommodating for the complementarity concerns of states who do not recognise the criminal liability of business entities on legal-philosophical grounds. On the other hand, it could constitute a necessary compromise, should political factors exclude corporate criminal responsibility as a feasible idea in the context of the ICC. In this regard, and on a more practical note, Amman has furthermore questioned the usefulness of criminal prosecution in relation to the goal of devising a workable reparatory regime for redressing victims of crimes within the jurisdiction of the Court.[95]

Indeed the benefits of civil regulation should not be easily discounted. The lower standard of proof and less rigorous procedural rules applicable to civil proceedings may serve to augment the efficiency of trials.[96] Moreover, the continuum of traditional sanctions in civil law in relation to corporations largely overlaps with the penalties envisaged in domestic and international criminal law.[97] In this sense, corporate prosecution under a civil or a criminal regulatory regime can be said to meet similar compensatory and incapacitatory goals. Given the essentially profit-oriented nature of business enterprises, fines, probation, license withdrawal, reparation orders and other such sanctions presumably also have the potential to exert a deterrent function regardless of the civil nature of the enforcement mechanism through which they may be imposed.

There are, however, several practical problems with seeking to subject corporations to non-criminal regulation through the Rome Statute. Apart from the question of

94 UN Doc. A/CONF.183/2/Add.1, 14 April 1998, Art. 23, para. 6, note 3.

95 D.M. Amman, Capital Punishment: Corporate Criminal Liability for Gross Violations of Human Rights, 24 *Hastings International and Comparative Law Review* 327 (2001).

96 Clough, *supra note 11*, at 9.

97 The feasibility and complexity of devising appropriate penalties for corporations is an extensive subject in itself, which has not been devoid of controversy. It has not been the purpose of this study to delve into the topic of corporate sanctions. Suffice it here to point out that national penal systems worldwide have come to recognise corporations as subjects of criminal law, irrespective of the form in which responsibility is incurred, and have come to apply a wide range of penalties. It is only reasonable to assume that international criminal law could draw upon this experience and similarly devise an appropriate set of sanctions. See, in this regard, Draft Article 76 concerning the penalties applicable to legal persons, discussed at the Rome Conference, UN Doc. A/CONF.183/2/Add.1. There was a broad-base agreement among delegates on what penalties could potentially apply to corporations. The sanctions envisaged included fines, forfeiture of proceeds, property and assets, closure of premises and prohibition of activities, dissolution of the corporation or orders for reparation. Some of those sanctions are not unfamiliar to domestic jurisdictions which subject corporations to civil liability.

whether the Court and its judiciary are sufficiently equipped to deal with the complexity of civil proceedings at the international level, there are also concerns pertaining to the need to negotiate and agree upon a separate procedural framework.[98] Flexibility in the choice of criminal or civil action – should such flexibility be deemed essential for ensuring that complementarity is operative with regard to all States Parties irrespective of their conceptual position on corporate criminality – may prompt allegations of disproportionate treatment on the part of corporate defendants. Moreover, although the penalties attaching to liability – whether criminal or civil – may be comparable, the social stigma and reputational loss in the eyes of the public are likely to amass in favour of criminal responsibility.[99]

III The pitfalls of collective criminality

In postulating the need and desirability of enhancing the legal accountability of business for its involvement in grave human rights abuse through penal law, this study has sought to demonstrate that there are compelling reasons to consider attaching direct liability to corporations rather than constructing culpability through individual corporate agents. Although MNCs are legitimate rather than criminal organisations, in reality they may – and sometimes do – become involved in international crimes. While the constituent elements of the offending conduct are by necessity physically realised by natural persons, it is the peculiarities of organisational existence that foster the deviant behaviour. They have the propensity to 'create a criminogenic environment that opens opportunities and rationalisations for rule-bending and rule-breaking.'[100] The size, complexity and differentiation of large organisations, as well as particular management styles, institutional cultures and group dynamics, may translate into poor control or communication, or unjustified risk-taking.[101] Such peculiarities are also often conducive to the infliction of harm through negligence or faulty judgment rather than conscious premeditation.[102]

The isolated prosecutions of individual agents cannot capture the true nature of corporate involvement in international crimes, nor effectively contain organisational wrongdoing. Convicting low-level employees for their personal contribution would allow the institution to become relatively easily detached from the crimes concerned. At the same time, the convictions of senior officials are likely to be difficult, sometimes even impossible to obtain.[103] While corporate policies, structure and culture

98 Haigh, *supra note 14*, at 210-211.

99 See section V.2 below: Deterrence, retribution and the expressive functions of (international) criminal law.

100 M. Punch, Suit Violence: Why Managers Murder and Corporations Kill, 33 *Crime, Law and Social Change* 243 (2000) at 274.

101 *Ibidem*.

102 *Idem*, at 252.

103 See in this regard Chapter 5, section IV.1.2: Liability along vicarious lines, and Chapter 6, section IV: The superior responsibility of corporate officials.

impact on individual behaviour, the facilitation of technical, human and financial resources, available by virtue of the organised entity, affect the degree of harm caused. Individual prosecutions may thus not necessarily reflect the egregious violations suffered through collective activity. Such prosecutions, furthermore, leave largely intact the incentive system for criminal behaviour that may exist within the corporation. The removal of only a few persons from the organisational structure is unlikely to have a significant impact on corporate conduct and may further encourage the designation of certain individuals as expendable, thus creating an additional line of defence in case of prosecution.[104]

In this regard, the present study has suggested that constructions of legal culpability need to accommodate for apparent differences between natural and legal persons. The model put forward in Chapter 5 thus expounds the suitability of uncovering corporate fault with recourse to objective inferences. Far from rejecting subjectivism as a cornerstone of criminal liability, especially with regard to individuals, it proposes a shift of perspective and approach – from seeking to expose the hidden mental state of a corporation to divining fault through the attitude displayed towards (the likelihood of) a criminal outcome. Conclusions in this regard would draw upon holistic models of corporate criminal liability, which seek to incorporate organisational theory in efforts to adequately capture corporate wrongdoing and which have gradually been gaining recognition even in domestic legal systems that have traditionally favoured the construction of corporate criminal responsibility along vicarious lines. Drawing upon the experience of national jurisdictions, Chapter 5 highlighted the propensity of nominalist theories, pertaining to the ascription of corporate fault, to distort the attribution of liability – at the organisational and individual level. While recognising that the impugned conduct necessarily materialises through individual agents, the effort has therefore been directed towards identifying an avenue which would not only ground corporate criminal responsibility on genuine organisational fault, but would also preclude findings of individual culpability transgressing the true extent of personal fault.

The latter is relevant insofar as there have been concerns – on the part of Rome delegates and others – that corporate criminal liability in the context of the Rome Statute might detract from the jurisdictional focus of the ICC on natural persons. To this author's mind, nothing precludes the prosecution of corporate agents, jointly with or separately from proceedings against the organised entity, as long as the individual criminal conviction does not follow mere group membership alone. If political negotiations do not bring about the extension of the Court's jurisdiction to corporations, individual prosecutions may be the only avenue for holding business accountable for its involvement in international crimes. In the alternative, should the

104 The side-effects of domestic individual prosecutions in the context of corporate criminality have been documented and discussed by, *inter alia*, J. Braithwaite, *Corporate Crime in the Pharmaceutical Industry*, London: Routledge & Kegan Paul Books, 1984, p. 308.

ICC jurisdiction *ratione personae* eventually incorporate profit-oriented enterprises, organisational features cannot, and should not be allowed, to negate the blameworthiness of individual transgressions. The actual effect of such transgressions and the true extent of culpability may become obvious only when considered against the backdrop of aggregate choices and behaviour. This is not to say, however, that individual responsibility in the corporate context cannot or need not align with the principle of personal fault. On the contrary, it must remain strictly circumscribed, although some reasonable concessions may have to be made in order to accommodate for individual participation in group crimes.

The inherent difficulties in effectively reconciling collective criminality with individual guilt, in a systemic or corporate context, serve to perpetuate a number of theoretical as well as more pragmatic concerns. At the national and international level the predicament has been inextricably linked to questions of due process. There is also the debate about the possible implications of attempts to tackle deviance in group settings in terms of collective punishment.

III.1 The imperative of aligning accountability with due process

Common purpose and superior responsibility, discussed in Chapter 4, delineate the outer limits of the permissible attribution of culpability to natural persons under the Rome Statute. Criticism addressed at how the doctrines have been applied by the *ad hoc* tribunals, serves to highlight substantive considerations pertaining to the unjustified extension of the principle of personal fault and forewarns the need for a more stringent interpretation in the context of the ICC. Such criticism is relevant to the topic of corporate criminal liability on different levels. On the one hand, the discussion of individual criminal responsibility modes in this study outlines the legal zone within which corporate officials – from senior managers to low-level employees – run the risk of prosecution for international crimes. On the other hand, it also points in the direction of certain shortcomings, which could circumscribe the modes' application and warrant consideration by prosecution teams in the process of formulating indictments.[105] The challenges inherent in putting up an effective defence not only in relation to potentially extensive participatory modes but also in the light of (arguably) the underprivileged position of defence counsel in international criminal proceedings are not to be discounted either.

With regard to corporate liability *per se*, due process issues of a different, but not entirely unrelated, sort are likely to arise. Even the opponents of the idea of subjecting business entities to compulsory criminal regulation recognise that extending jurisdiction beyond natural persons may alleviate certain evidentiary problems.[106] Domestic

105 See Chapter 6, section IV: The superior responsibility of corporate officials.

106 T. Weigend, Societas Delinquere Non Potest? A German Perspective, 6 *Journal of International Criminal Justice* 927 (2008) at 943.

jurisdictions have traditionally struggled with linking institutionalised decision-making with the harm resulting from corporate crime. In this regard, it has been argued that corporate criminal liability 'opens up wider possibilities and more powers of coercion for the competent authorities in carrying out their investigations into the alleged misconduct of corporations.'[107] As a by-effect of more effective inquiries, subjecting business to criminal regulation may also facilitate international cooperation.[108]

Weigend, however, questions the legitimacy of extending substantive criminal law provisions in order to assist the discovery of proof.[109] A similar argument can be put forward as criticism of constructive corporate fault, embraced by the present study, as a method of identifying corporate *mens rea*. It must be noted here, however, that criminal law has long accepted the drawing of reasonable inferences as a permissible method of evaluating evidence even in relation to individuals. As a matter of practicality, evidence of corporate fault is likely to be more forthcoming – provided that recourse is taken to the principle of aggregation, corporate ethos and other related approaches – than evidence of a single agent's mental state.[110] Solving evidentiary difficulties is moreover not the only, or even one of the more compelling, reasons for extending criminal law provisions to corporations. While the concept of direct corporate criminal responsibility may encourage prosecution, it clearly cannot secure convictions in itself. Prosecutors who are given recourse to 'unconventional' avenues for identifying corporate fault are still bound to face difficulties pertaining to the collection of evidence and defence challenges in this regard. The danger inherent in the making of inferences would, furthermore, be offset by the higher standard of requisite proof attaching to criminal proceedings.

The issue of evidence and how it is discovered is closely linked to the question of corporations' procedural rights in the criminal law process. Since there is currently no international institution enforcing the criminal responsibility of business entities, conclusions in this regard can be merely speculative. Domestic jurisdictions vary in the procedural rights they afford corporations subject to criminal prosecution. It is, however, generally accepted that the right to a fair trial should benefit legal persons as well as individuals although its application might be somewhat dissimilar. This includes the right to be sufficiently notified of the charges, to be heard by an independent and impartial tribunal, to have adequate time and facilities to prepare a defence, to have proceedings concluded within a reasonable period of time, etc. National courts have sometimes been criticised for subjugating due process to victims' interests and the needs of successful prosecution. There are ongoing debates

---

107 B. Swart, Discussion: International Trends towards Establishing Some Form of Punishment for Corporations, 6 *Journal of International Criminal Justice* 947 (2008) at 952.

108 *Ibidem*, at 953.

109 Weigend, *supra note 27*, at 943.

110 W.S. Laufer, *Corporate Bodies and Guilty Minds. The Failure of Corporate Criminal Liability*, Chicago: University of Chicago Press, 2006, p. 93.

concerning, for instance, the permissibility of discounting the prohibition on self-incrimination in relation to business enterprises and of compelling individuals to testify against their corporations.

At the international level, and provided corporations themselves are recognised as subject to penal sanctions, additional concerns are likely to surface. These include, but are not limited to, the question of whether or not corporate officials (and which ones) would need to be present at the trial and what interim measures may justifiably be imposed so as to possibly prevent the further commission of crimes or the defendants' interfering with evidence. Such issues need to be carefully considered in negotiations preceding a future amendment of the Rome Statute incorporating business enterprises within the Court's jurisdiction *ratione personae*. While other international judicial institutions have held that legal persons (including corporations) cannot legitimately claim the protection of as wide a range of substantive rights as are accorded to natural persons under existing regimes (i.e. ECHR, ECJ),[111] there is little disagreement about the basic protections afforded by procedural rights.[112]

The confidence that an international criminal court inspires in its commitment and ability to secure a fair trial is crucial for its legitimacy in the eyes of defendants and the general public. At the same, its capacity to accomplish its set goals in adjudicating each individual case is a key component for enhancing, *inter alia*, victims' perceptions of legitimacy. Effectively reconciling these concerns is a rather difficult task. In this regard, victim reparation and participation are issues that warrant more critical consideration than generally afforded. The prospect of reparations for victims has been traditionally heralded as one of the central arguments in favour of including corporations within the ICC jurisdiction. However, seeking to facilitate the Court's reparatory regime, cannot in itself be regarded as a justification for corporate criminal responsibility. Although victims have an interest in, and a right to, adequate redress, the prosecution of MNCs for their participation in international crimes should not give the semblance of a fundraising endeavour. The focus of attention must at all times remain on the corporate transgression, the breach of universally recognised principles of law and ethics. Although penal sanctions of corporations by the ICC may, and should, extend to reparation orders, this must not be permitted to blur the contours of the criminal law process or detract from the perceived legitimacy of the conviction. As

111 See Swart, *supra note 28,* at 953, pointing out that in a number of cases the European Court of Justice has held that corporations are entitled to the exercise of *some* convention rights. Also P. van Dijk, F. van Hoof, A. van Rijn and L. Zwaak (eds.), *Theory and Practice of the European Convention on Human Rights*, Antwerp: Intersentia, 2006, pp. 53, 59, referring to case-law of the European Court of Human Rights postulating that although corporations as legal persons are entitled to the same convention rights as natural persons, some substantive rights cannot apply to them, e.g. freedom of religion, freedom of conscience and the right not to be subjected to degrading treatment.

112 For instance, in a case of 1 June 1993 (NJ 1994, 52) the Netherlands Supreme Court ruled that Article 6 ECHR applied to natural as well as legal persons with regard to the right to appeal and the right to have a trial within reasonable time.

for the issue of victim participation, concerns have already been voiced in relation to the impact of overly broad participation on the length of proceedings before the ICC, defence rights and in particular the equality of arms tenet. Such questions remain pertinent irrespective of whether it is a natural or a legal person standing trial before the Court.

III.2 Collective punishment: effects on the 'innocent' bystander?

Apart from the more practical considerations detailed above, the idea of corporate criminal responsibility as an avenue for addressing organisational deviance, can never be entirely divorced of concerns relating to collective guilt, responsibility and punishment. The fixation of modern legal thinking on the individual serves to largely explain why we tend to perceive collective forms of responsibility as unjust, disproportionate and even incompatible with the criminal law process. In this regard, however, the moral and the legal aspect should be clearly distinguished. It must be borne in mind that they can exist independent of one another, although in practice they often coincide.

This study has rejected the acceptability of collective guilt in the legal sense, or of penalising individuals merely by dint of their membership in the corporate collectivity. Chapter 4 suggested the necessity for a strict interpretation and application of individual modes of liability geared towards the reality of deviance in group context. Although the Rome Statute is more circumscribed in its approach to the notions of common purpose and superior responsibility than the *ad hoc* tribunals have been in their practice, some uncertainties as to the scope of the requisite *mens rea* for convictions remain. In this regard, Chapter 5 delineated early ICC case law and the exhibited tendency on the part of the judiciary to stretch the contours of Article 30 RS, espousing a rather broad understanding of *dolus eventualis*. While the latter is a legitimate form of volition which should and arguably does (at least partly) have a place in the Rome Statute, the Court must take notice of the grey area where *dolus eventualis* may lapse into aggravated forms of *culpa*. *Culpa* behaviour, provided it is explicitly incorporated as punishable under the Rome Statute, is a reasonable and acceptable standard for corporate culpability. Chapter 5 sought to explain this with reference to the nature of corporations, the mechanics of organisational deviance and the idiosyncrasies of business involvement in international crimes. However, negligence-type liability has no place within the ICC statutory framework with regard to civilians. As Chapter 6 postulated, 'should have known' standards of culpability are not applicable outside the context of command responsibility.

In tracing the ongoing debates surrounding the notions of conspiracy, group membership liability, common purpose and superior responsibility from Nuremberg through the *ad hoc* tribunals' case law to the present-day ICC, the study has thus highlighted the controversy inherent in any attempt to square the reality of group crimes with the criminal law precept of personal fault. While allowing for the drawing of inferences from the individual to the corporate level on the basis of aggregate conduct and even knowledge, the present author nevertheless maintains that the criminal responsibility of corporations can be constructed so that it does not of necessity entail legal consequences for individual members. A finding of corporate fault need not preclude the prosecution of various agents, but convictions must correspond to the extent of their personal involvement.

Fears of collective punishment in the context of corporate criminal responsibility have, however, also broader connotations. They do not pertain solely to the legal effects of penalising organisations *per se* on those individuals who are personally (albeit remotely) involved in the group transgressions. It may also be contended that by holding the corporation criminally liable, third parties (i.e. employees and shareholders) may become affected and sanctioned for a wrongdoing in which they may not have participated at all. The transgressions of a handful of individuals are thus seen to serve as the basis for constructing the liability of a fictitious entity. This 'artificial' construction is then reversed so as to sweep within its reach anyone associated with the corporate entity, no matter how remotely or (presumably) innocent. Collective punishment may thus be understood not only as guilt (in the legal sense) by association but also in terms of generating consequences that affect (unjustifiably) individual rights on a large scale. Corporate sanctions, which may vary from punitive fines to the closure of premises, may presumably result in job losses. Employees of the corporation held liable, would thus in effect be collectively penalised for wrongdoings in which they may not have been personally involved. A similar argument may be put forward with regard to shareholders. It may be asserted that the financial consequences of criminal sanctions would in fact ultimately shift the burden of punishment onto innocent investors. In this regard, Wells has expressed concerns that dispersing the penalty among shareholders might actually diminish its deterrent effect,[113] presuming there is such an effect at all. Conceivably, it may even be suggested that corporate punishment is an ethically and economically unsound conception, as it would reduce foreign investments, affecting the jobs and general welfare of local populations in regions of the world where development needs are most urgent.

The utilitarian rationale of the latter contention is, however, disturbing if one were to consider its implications, particularly in the context of international crimes. It appears to condone impunity for the sake of economic and social development. By downplaying the need for retribution and the expression of condemnation in the case of blatant violations of 'core' universal norms, it inadvertently places a value on the loss of human life that is lower than the value of human life preserved. While there is some logic to this argument, its proponents would seem to overlook a number of important factors. On the one hand, if one considers the mass scale which generally typifies genocide, crimes against humanity and war crimes, the importance of the retributive rationale – and specifically its expressive function – takes on demanding

113 C. Wells, *Corporations and Criminal Responsibility,* Oxford: Clarendon Press, 1993, pp. 135-138.

undertones.[114] On the other hand, taking into account that it is often investment that is at the bottom of the crimes committed by MNCs, it would hardly seem unethical to disrupt the flow of such investment. Moreover, it remains to be empirically demonstrated whether the prospect of criminal prosecution and sanctions for involvement in international crimes would in fact result in any substantial reduction of investments in the developing world. It is also questionable whether by allowing investments of criminal impact to continue streaming into conflict zones unabated, development needs would be actually met. The revenues accumulated by governments in countries where (civil) wars rage, are generally consumed by military spending, the remainder used for the personal enrichment of a small elite of political and military leaders with a dubious human rights record. Not only is foreign investment rarely, if ever, used to subsidise economic and social development, but it also is something of an oxymoron to suggest that development can be meaningfully effectuated in times of violent conflict.

As regards the effects of corporate sanctioning on employees and shareholders in terms of job and profit losses, it is also disputable whether those effects are entirely unjustifiable. On the one hand, the nature of their association with the culpable corporation does not render them as guiltlessly innocent as they generally profess. Given the large scale of international crimes and the publicity generated by the media in this regard, the question remains as to whether employees and shareholders in fact lack any knowledge of the corporate involvement in the crimes alleged. Even in the lack of actual knowledge, their indirect burdening with corporate sanctions may be justified by their failure to inquire after any suspicions which may arise on their part because of the activities undertaken by the business enterprise. As voluntary agents within a democratic structure, and given sufficient forewarning about the consequences they may come to bear in case of corporate wrongdoing, employees and shareholders have considerable potential to effectuate corporate change. The prospect of dispersed sanctioning may trigger greater caution in decision-making and tighter control over the corporate governing bodies. Lastly, collective punishment in the sense of dispersed financial sanctions resulting from corporate criminal liability does not give rise to any issues or implications different from those relevant in the context of civil liability and the corresponding punishments for corporations. The array of sanctions potentially applicable to business entities (liable for 'core' international crimes) might in fact be better justified by reference to criminal rather than civil law, given the harshness of some of the measures envisaged.

The foregoing justifies dispersed sanctioning in the corporate context as a type of 'collateral damage' arising out of a democratic decision-making process. Admittedly, the internal structure and processes of some corporations which do not have shareholders exercising an additional level of control, may not necessarily be conducive to

114 See also section V.2 below.

employees interfering with, or disassociating themselves from, undesirable or illegal collective action. It may also be argued that the distribution of costs must invariably correspond to the distribution of guilt or that rationalisations of collective sanctioning are part of an unwelcome 'movement towards pragmatic instrumentalism' in the law.[115] By striving to advance the desired policy objectives of international criminal justice, this movement may arguably threaten the legitimacy of criminal law in general.[116] As this study has sought to demonstrate, however, corporate liability as a form of collective responsibility gives rise neither to collective (legal) guilt nor to collective sanctions. In this sense, the distribution of costs has no bearing on personal guilt.[117] While cognisant of the fact that collective action may not always be the outcome of (democratic) collective decision-making and, therefore of the moral guilt undertones of dispersed sanctioning, the present author postulates that the distribution of costs need not necessarily correspond to the distribution of guilt in the legal sense. This might be the inevitable fallout of corporate criminal responsibility.

IV Liability of MNCs in International Criminal Law: From Aspiration to Reality

The recognition of corporations as subjects of international criminal law can be rationalised as a response to changing social realities. Attempts to extend ICC jurisdiction beyond natural persons and critical discussions pertaining to liability modes in the context of collective criminality must, nevertheless, not be viewed through the prism of a panacea solution. Although the international courts and tribunals have not themselves aspired to personify such a perception, they have frequently failed (or have been accused of failing) to live up to their set goals or effectively contain public and victim expectations.[118]

Group criminality necessitates recourse to flexible, and somewhat unconventional, liability modes but also poses certain challenges in relation to individual culpability. While cognisant of inherent difficulties, this research advocates the desirability and (legal) feasibility of a form of collective responsibility, i.e. direct corporate responsibility. It attempts to narrow the impunity gap by suggesting the justifiable extension of notions which are already operative in international criminal law with regard to individuals, to business entities – not only those directly involved in human rights violations but also those which, in the pursuit of profit, allow for the commission of crimes by enterprises within their sphere of control. Propositions have

115 M. Damaska, Discussion: Blame and Punishment: Against an 'Instrumentalisation' of Criminal Law, 6 *Journal of International Criminal Justice* 947 (2008) at 966.

116 *Ibidem*, at 966.

117 See M. Waltzer, *Just and Unjust Wars*, New York: Basic Books, 1997, p. 297, postulating the same with regard to political guilt and collective responsibility.

118 For a critical overview of ICTY's efforts to meet and/or effectively contain victim and witness expectations, see e.g. E. Stover, *The Witnesses. War Crimes and the Promise of Justice in The Hague*, Philadelphia: University of Pennsylvania Press, 2005.

grounded the construction of corporate criminal liability on common denominators of blameworthy behaviour, thus adjusting it to the overall legal framework of the Rome Statute. Allowances for certain discrepancies have, nevertheless, been made with reference to the divergent nature of natural and legal persons. The model put forward builds upon domestic approaches, reflecting growing recognition of corporate criminality and the viability of taking recourse to more holistic and partly objective elements in relation to organisational culpability.

In this regard, critics may point out that the model does not align with more established methods of ascribing liability to corporations in national penal systems. A decade ago, the wide variety of existing domestic approaches was also perceived by Rome Conference delegates as an impediment to reaching a meaningful compromise. It must be noted here, however, that the model developed in this study is intended merely as a frame of reference, highlighting the comparative advantages and disadvantages of traditional as well as more innovative approaches applied or scrutinised at the national level. Although put forward as the most appropriate avenue for adequately capturing corporate wrongdoing in the context of the 'core' international crimes, this model is neither intended to, nor can it supersede domestic preferences unless national jurisdictions opt to align their relevant liability modes with international criminal law.

Motivated by the need to address regulatory deficiencies at the national level, close the existing void in international law and promote security and respect for the rule of law, the suggestions espoused by the present author are therefore an expression of hope. This research would have served its purpose if it contributes to the meaningful revival of the idea of corporate criminal responsibility in the context of the ICC and increases understanding of the various legal avenues for holding business accountable for its involvement in international crimes. Far from discounting the conceptual difficulties associated with penal liability for MNCs – which are not as insurmountable as professed by opponents – it must be recognised that the most critical impediment to incorporating private profit-oriented enterprises within the jurisdiction of the Court will ultimately be of political nature. State sovereignty, albeit arguably eroding, is a dearly treasured concept. For as long as states perceive a threat in extending jurisdiction to legal persons, in that penalising economic entities might be a step in the direction of encompassing state public bodies or a means for implicating states themselves in the commission of international crimes, they are likely to resist the requisite amendment of the Rome Statute.[119] Should political will, however, yield

119 E.g. H.G. van der Wilt, Het kwaad in functie (The Evil in Function), Amsterdam: Vossiuspers UvA, 2005, p. 17, doubting states' inclination to voluntarily subject themselves to criminal jurisdiction. See also A. Cassese, Boundary of Corporate Liability and the Nature of International Crimes: Between Individual Responsibility and State Criminality, in: Discussion, 6 *Journal of International Criminal Justice* 948 (2008) at 969, pointing out the political, rather than substantive, objections of states to the idea of state criminal responsibility.

acceptable compromises and broad-base support, the proponents and supporters of corporate criminal responsibility in the context of the ICC need not harbour unrealistic expectations. It must be acknowledged that pursuing the accountability of business entities through international criminal law will always remain only one element of a much more comprehensive strategy aimed at addressing the circumstances that give rise to grave human rights abuse.

V Corporate Accountability and the Goals of International Criminal Justice

The perceived need to ensure the censure and punishment of *any* category of offenders, whose conduct brings about or contributes to the commission of genocide, crimes against humanity and war crimes, has been a recurring assumption underpinning the discussion of whether or not international criminal law should extend penal sanctions beyond natural persons. The reality of MNCs' involvement in grave human rights abuse is well documented.[120] However, at the domestic level, cases targeting business entities *per se* for such crimes are rare. Although nearly every legal system around the world recognises the notion of corporate criminal liability, national authorities are generally resistant to the idea of subjecting business enterprises to penal regulation. Presumably this has as much to do with fears about the potential negative effects of excessive government involvement in economic activities, as with the fact that international criminal law is exclusively focused on natural persons. Frequently cited in this regard is the famous quote of the Nuremberg judgment, espousing that international crimes are committed by individuals and not by abstract entities.[121] In incorporating the Rome Statute in their domestic legal orders, some jurisdictions that recognise corporate criminality as a matter of principle, also in relation to *mens rea* offences, seem to have exposed business enterprises to the threat of liability for international crimes.[122] However, no prosecutions of corporations have been undertaken so far. It can be contended that this is a consequence of deeply ingrained reluctance – an offshoot of the influence of liberalism and the predominant focus on individualism typifying modern legal traditions – to accept that the most serious of crimes can be committed by 'fictitious' entities. Not inconceivably, however, it might also be the result of evidentiary difficulties in prosecuting corporations or of discretionary determinations that the purpose of particular trials would be better served by individual convictions.

120 See Chapter 1, section I: Corporations, conflicts and human rights and Chapter 3, section II.3: A missed opportunity *vis-à-vis* corporate accountability? for an overview of allegations against corporations from Nuremberg to present day.

121 *Trials of the Major War Criminals before the International Military Tribunal*, Vol. I, Nuremberg Germany 1947, p. 223.

122 E.g. the Netherlands in relation to the 2003 War Crimes Act.

The Nuremberg attempt at addressing business involvement in international crimes exemplified an early effort at the international level to tackle corporate delinquency. While recognising the collective nature of functional criminality, political considerations that were largely divorced of concerns about moral agency and corporations as subjects to criminal law, determined the tribunals' jurisdictional focus.[123] Nuremberg espoused the principle of individual responsibility for international crimes, refuting the 'acts of state' doctrine, which had traditionally served to preclude the accountability of state officials. However, Nuremberg did not deny that organised entities, such as states, could commit crimes as well.[124] Far from venturing into the topic of state criminal responsibility, which would have been as controversial then as it is today, the tribunals operated within their jurisdictional confines and convicted individuals only. Nevertheless, a retributive rationale underlined the perceived need to publicly pronounce the *Farben* and *Krupp* corporations as having committed international crimes, albeit through the instrumentality of their officials,[125] and declare certain (political, military and other repressive) organisations criminal.

The anticipation of deterrence nowadays also lies beneath proposals of corporate criminal responsibility for genocide, crimes against humanity and war crimes.[126] The Rome delegates perceived the possible extension of ICC jurisdiction to MNCs as a cautionary mechanism capable of inducing greater care in business decision-making and strengthening the existing obligation on the part of corporations to abide by universally recognised human rights norms. Fifty years after Nuremberg and with several international institutions geared towards consolidating the principle of individual criminal liability, there was the realisation that the prosecution of natural persons might not suffice. Allegations of corporate involvement in international crimes were mounting while the institutions for international criminal justice were seemingly lagging behind domestic jurisdictions, which had long provided avenues for the accountability of business. Eventually, economic entities were not included in the Court's jurisdiction although this may change in the future. The preamble to the Rome Statute espouses the determination of States Parties to 'put an end to impunity for the perpetrators of international crimes'. Recognising that 'such grave crimes threaten the peace, security and well being' of humanity, it thus assumes the lofty goal of con-

123 For a complete discussion, see W.A. Zeck, Nuremberg: Proceedings Subsequent to Goering et al., 26 *North Carolina Law Review* 350 (1948).

124 W.A. Schabas, Discussion: Corporate Liability and State Criminality, 6 *Journal of International Criminal Justice* 947 (2008) at 964.

125 *Law Reports of Trials of War Criminals (UNWCC)*, Vol. X, London: His Majesty's Stationary Office, 1949 (the cases of I.G. Farben and Krupp).

126 Generally corporate criminal liability, whether in national or international law, is justified by reference to its deterrent, retributive and compensatory function. E.g. S. Ratner, Corporations and Human Rights: a Theory of Legal Responsibility, 111 *Yale Law Journal* 443 (2002) at 478. For a discussion of the legitimation rationales of international criminal justice in general, see e.g. R. Henham, The Philosophical Foundations of International Sentencing, 1 *Journal of International Criminal Justice* 64 (2003), and M. Osiel, *Mass Atrocity, Ordinary Evil, and Hanna Arendt. Criminal Consciousness in Argentina's Dirty War*, New Haven: Yale University Press, 2001.

tributing to the prevention of genocide, war crimes and crimes against humanity. Naturally this evokes the question as to what extent corporate criminal responsibility, if incorporated in the Rome Statute, would align with, and serve, the goals of international criminal justice.

V.1 The 'problem' of plea bargaining

As discussed previously, given the reputational costs associated with publicly standing trial for international crimes, most corporations alleged to have participated in serious human rights violations have preferred to settle out of court. Whether MNCs would be as forthcoming with their admissions of criminal guilt before the ICC as they have been in domestic civil proceedings concerning gross human rights violations committed abroad, is a matter for speculation only. Nevertheless, the issue of guilty pleas and the extent to which the permissibility of plea-bargaining has the propensity to infringe upon the objectives of international criminal law, warrants some consideration.

There might be some justification to the argument that – just as with regard to individuals – negotiated justice for corporate offenders would fall short of providing adequate satisfaction to victims, effectively fighting impunity or affirming the rule of law at the international level.[127] These are legitimate concerns but they must also be considered against the backdrop of the legal process integrated in the Rome Statute. To the extent that plea agreements constitute a joint decision between the parties on whether or not to proceed to a full-blown trial, they can indeed be said to fit into the conflict-solving purpose of criminal proceedings.[128] Thus far no precedent exists to indicate the ICC's approach to guilty pleas. Article 65 RS appears to place considerable emphasis on 'the interests of justice, in particular the interests of the victims' envisaging the continuation of the trial, should the judges deem the complete presentation of facts necessary. The trial chambers are, moreover, not bound by any pre-existing agreements between the prosecution and defence about the modification of charges or the penalty to be imposed.[129] It is not inconceivable that, in accepting the form of any given plea agreement, the Court may be swayed by practical considerations.[130] The exact role of victims in proceedings following the submission of a

---

127 For a general overview of arguments in relation to plea bargaining, see e.g. N. Armoury Combs, Copping a Plea to Genocide: The Plea Bargaining of International Crimes, 151 *University of Pennsylvania Law Review* 1 (2002).

128 B. Swart, Damaska and the Faces of International Criminal Justice, 6 *Journal of International Criminal Justice* 87 (2008) at 105.

129 Article 65(5) RS.

130 In their practice, the *ad hoc* tribunals have generally accepted that guilty pleas may translate into a mitigated punishment. E.g. *Prosecutor v. Plavsic*, ICTY Case No. IT-00-39&40/1, Sentencing Judgment, 27 February 2003. In weighing the interests of all parties concerned, the ICC is presumably also bound to take into account the prospective costs of full-blown trials juxtaposed against the availability of only limited resources.

guilty plea remains, nevertheless, largely indeterminate for the time being. At the same time, however, and following in the tradition of the *ad hoc* tribunals, the judiciary is likely to emphasise the comparative 'substantive' advantages of guilty pleas as well. The most important of those self-professed benefits relate to the public acknowledgement of full responsibility and the facilitation of reconciliation through the creation of 'an accurate and accessible historical record' of events.[131] Although plea-bargaining is not devoid of drawbacks, its Rome Statute variant aligns with the policy implementing objectives of international criminal justice. In this sense, the danger of 'mismatches' between the goals set and the means through which these goals are pursued, is not imminent in the context of guilty pleas.[132] The legal process envisaged appears sufficiently accommodating for interests exceeding the pragmatic benefits of efficient conflict solving.

V.2 Deterrence, retribution and the expressive function of (international) criminal law

On a more general note, scholars of both legal and social science orientation have long queried the deterrence rationale of penal accountability with regard to individuals as well as corporations.[133] In international criminal justice, selectivity and indeterminacy are generally perceived as 'corrosive to the deterrent value of prosecution'.[134] There are only a few judicial institutions at the international level which can prosecute but a handful of perpetrators due to their limited resources. At the domestic level, criminal prosecutions for genocide, war crimes and crimes against humanity remain relatively rare even in relation to individuals, despite existing legislative provisions. Assessments of the prospect of detection and punishment cannot, therefore, be easily divorced from actual reality. While the aforementioned has, in principle, been posited in respect of natural persons, it holds true (and perhaps even more so) for corporations too. We cannot deny the somewhat justified expectation of MNCs that – because of the peculiarities of the justice process concerning instances of mass criminality and the protection afforded to them by the principle of separate legal personality – they may be able to avoid prosecution and criminal liability.

The effectiveness of deterrence as a penal strategy in both national and international law is, moreover, questionable for it is based on a misguided presumption of rationality. As Drumbl postulates, it is not self-evident that in circumstances of (ethnic) conflict 'the risk of punishment will deter [individuals] from engaging in violent

131 Swart, *supra note 49*, at 106, referring to the Obrenovic Sentencing Judgment, ICTY Case No. IT-02-60/ 2-S, 10 December 2003, paras. 111-116.

132 *Ibidem*, at 114.

133 For an overview of criminological research on criminal deterrence, see A. von Hirsch, A.E. Bottoms, E. Burney and P.O. Wikström, *Criminal Deterrence and Sentence Severity*, Oxford: Hart Publishing, 1999.

134 M.A. Drumbl, Collective Violence and Individual Punishment: The Criminality of Mass Atrocity, 99 *Northwestern University Law Review* 539 (2005) at 589.

behaviour that they, at the time, believe is morally justifiable and perhaps even necessary, if not downright gratifying'.[135] Since MNCs are generally not motivated by nationalist agendas, as is the case of political and military fanatics, the rationality argument in relation to deterrence assumes a different meaning in the corporate context. Explicit or implicit in the justification of corporate criminal liability is often the premise that MNCs are rational economic actors, who are concerned about costly guilty verdicts. Empirical criminological studies of corporate crime, and in particular existing domestic regulatory mechanisms for counteracting such deviance, however, have established that it is not the fear of criminal liability in terms of sanctions that tends to preclude transgressions of the law but rather the anxiety of reputational loss.[136] Moreover, an over-emphasis on the deterrent function of criminal law does not sufficiently consider organisational irrationality as a result of which MNCs may engage in human rights violations. Cognitive biases and structural difficulties that typify business entities serve to counterbalance the presumption that corporate involvement in international crimes and susceptibility to the threat of criminal sanctions are reducible to a simple cost-benefit analysis.[137]

The deterrence rationale of (international) criminal law with regard to corporations is, therefore, circumscribed. This is not to deny entirely the deterrent effect of (corporate) criminal liability. Despite the propensity of organisational decision-making to become skewed, concerns about profit-maximisation and reputational costs remain central to MNCs. In this sense, the value of criminal deterrence may be higher for corporations than it is for the euphoric individual participant in mass atrocity. Nevertheless, it is posited here that retribution remains the primary motivational factor for punishment in international criminal law.[138]

The theological notion of justice as regulatory vengeance can be detected in early judgments (i.e. Nuremberg). The more progressive Kantian conception of retributivism as 'just desserts' underlies more recent decisions. The international justice process, however, has diluted the meaning of retribution; punishment as a categorical imperative for those who deserve it – some have also argued – is 'neither an accurate [description] nor a realistic aspiration'.[139] Retribution as an objective act is particularly difficult to reconcile with proportionality concerns and the nature of international

---

135 *Ibidem*, at 591.

136 E.g. B. Fisse and J. Braithwaite, *The Impact of Publicity on Corporate Offenders*, Albany: State University of New York Press, 1983.

137 See Note, *Organisational Irrationality and Corporate Human Rights Violations*, 122 *Harvard Law Review* 1931 (2009).

138 J. Leinwand, Punishing Horrific Crime: Reconciling International Prosecution with National Sentencing Practices, 40 *Columbia Human Rights Law Review* 799 (2009); R. Henham, The Philosophical Foundations of International Sentencing, 1 *Journal of International Criminal Justice* 64 (2003) at 69, 72; D.B. Pickard, Proposed Sentencing Guidelines for the International Criminal Court, 20 *Loyola Los Angeles International and Comparative Law Review* 123 (1997) at 128-130.

139 Drumbl, *supra note 55*, at 587.

crimes. Scholars have consistently cast doubt on the relatively lenient nature of sentences imposed by existing international tribunals on convicted perpetrators.[140] There is the uncertainty as to whether criminal law, and in particular international criminal justice, can ever realistically be justified by reference to proportionality alone. In the end, no criminal punishment – irrespective of its severity – may compensate for the harm suffered by victims of mass crimes such as genocide.

The retributive discourse, however, has an expressive dimension too. The expressivist construction of retribution offers certain proportionality guidance.[141] More importantly, it also reveals the principal value of (international) criminal law where grave human rights violations are concerned. Expressivism recognises that criminal liability and punishment are not only about exacting a debt to society. Penal accountability has a strong symbolic significance; it is an authoritative demonstration of moral indignation and condemnation.[142] In international criminal law in particular, the expressive function of punishment – although not necessary identified explicitly as such by the judiciary – is evident from Nuremberg to present-day judgments.[143] It emanates from a set of social norms accepted as the bedrock of humanity.[144] Breaches of these norms evoke reprobation for they shock human conscience, trample individual dignity and threaten the very foundations of peaceful existence. Expressivism is not without its critics,[145] but at the same time it 'is not [nor need it be regarded as] a self-sufficient justification for punishment'.[146] However, it is an essential component of

140 E.g. S. Glickam, Victims' Justice: Legitimising the Sentencing Regime of the International Criminal Court, 43 *Columbia Journal of Transnational Law* 229 (2004) at 230, 247-248; A.M. Danner, Constructing a Hierarchy of Crimes in International Criminal Law Sentencing, 87 *Virginia Law Review* 415 (2001) at 488.

141 R.D. Sloane, The Expressive Capacity of International Punishment: The Limits of the National Law Analogy and the Potential of International Criminal Law, 43 *Stanford Journal of International Law* 39 (2007) at 81-85.

142 Sloane, *supra note 62*, pp. 69-71. See also J. Feinberg, *The Expressive Function of Punishment in Doing and Deserving*, Princeton University Press, 1970, p. 98.

143 D.M. Amman, Group Mentality, Expressivism and Genocide, 2 *International Criminal Law Review* 93 (2002) at 123.

144 The understanding of retribution as an expression of outrage at the brutal violation of commonly shared, universal human norms has also been increasingly reflected in judgments by the *ad hoc* tribunals. See e.g. *Prosecutor v. Aleksovski*, ICTY Case No. IT-95-14/1-A, Appeal Judgment of 24 March 2000, p. 185, in which the Appeals Chamber ruled that while it 'accepts the general importance of deterrence as a consideration in sentencing for international crimes, it concurs with the statement in *Tadic* that 'this factor must not be accorded undue prominence in the overall assessment of the sentences to be imposed on persons convicted by the International Tribunal.' An equally important factor is retribution. This is not to be understood as fulfilling a desire for revenge but as duly expressing the outrage of the international community at these crimes.' See also *Prosecutor v. Musema*, Case No. ICTR-96-13-T, Judgment and Sentence of 27 January 2000, para. 986; *Prosecutor v. Rutaganda*, Case No. ICTR-96-3, Judgment and Sentence of 6 December 1999, p. 456; *Prosecutor v. Furundzija*, ICTY Case No. IT-95-17/1-T, Judgment of 10 December 1998, para. 288.

145 E.g. Drumbl, *supra note 55*, at 592-596; I. Tallgren, The Sensibility and Sense of International Criminal Law, 13 *European Journal of International Law* 561 (2002) at 583.

146 Sloane, *supra note 62*, at 70.

criminal justice at the national and, perhaps even more so, at the international level. The expressive rationale enhances the operative value of both deterrence and retribution as justifications for criminal liability.

With regard to corporations, any attempt to ground their responsibility in criminal law may not be exclusively validated by reference to the efficient prevention of wrongdoing as an objective act. Deterrence plays a role to the extent that business enterprises respond to the threat of adverse publicity rather than the prospect of penal conviction. Criminal liability assumes an advantage over civil law and other less stringent mechanisms in that penal sanctions have stigmatising side effects.[147] The publicity alone of standing trial in the spotlight for international crimes carries unique censure. Subjecting corporations to criminal law regulation, particularly in relation to serious human rights abuse, serves to further uphold the universal validity of core social norms. Corporate criminal liability in this sense is an expression of solidarity on the part of the international community in the renunciation of double standards. It coveys the message that anyone who transgresses the law of nations, be it a natural or a legal person, must bear the consequences of the moral wrongfulness of their conduct. Criminal behaviour should not be allowed to thrive behind the disguise of organisational form and economic reasoning. The acceptance of penal accountability for MNCs reinforces the fundamental postulate that no one is above the law and everyone is equal before the law. Inherent in criminal liability is also the correction of the wrongdoer's denial of the victims' inherent worth.[148]

Holding corporations criminally liable for their involvement in genocide, crimes against humanity and war crimes, aligns with the broader goals of international criminal law. Provided it materialises in a future amendment to the Rome Statute, the concept of corporate responsibility for international crimes will reflect both historical and present-day reality. It will communicate recognition of the broader context of mass atrocity and the impact of transnational economic dynamics in nurturing environments that are conducive to the violation of human rights. The formal acknowledgement of the role played by private business enterprises in fuelling conflicts worldwide will also indicate appreciation for the suffering of a multitude of individuals who have fallen direct or indirect victims to corporate wrongdoing.

147 A. Ramasastry, Corporate Complicity: From Nuremberg to Rangoon. An Examination of Forced Labour Cases and Their Impact on the Liability of Multinational Corporations, 20 *Berkeley Journal of International Law* 91 (2002) at 153.

148 L. Friedman, In Defense of Corporate Criminal Liability, 23 *Harvard Journal of Law and Public Policy* 833 (2000) at 855.

SUMMARY

With the growing influence of multinational corporations (MNCs) and the profit-driven expansion of commercial activities to conflict-prone regions of the world, there have been mounting concerns about the corporate lack of accountability. Despite broad consensus that companies are bound by certain 'core' rules pertinent to all actors within the international domain, including the prohibition to engage directly or indirectly in genocide, war crimes and crimes against humanity, regulation remains piecemeal and largely deficient. While many domestic jurisdictions are reluctant or unable to vigorously pursue mandatory enforcement, the international system has not yet put in place any effective compliance mechanism. The International Criminal Court (ICC) presents a unique opportunity for the introduction of a sanctioning mechanism to offset – at least partially – existing regulatory deficiencies. This study explores the desirability and feasibility of subjecting business enterprises *per se* to regulation through international criminal law. It inquires into the permissibility and inherent challenges of extending penal provisions, and in particular the Rome Statute of the ICC, beyond natural persons.

Although most national legal systems nowadays recognise the notion of corporate criminal responsibility for domestic and/or international offences, there is the contention that penal law is a system operating on the premise of human conscience. This deontological perspective has been one of the objections raised to the idea of extending ICC jurisdiction to economic ventures. It translates into an anthropocentric view of the corporation as a mere collection of individuals, having no independent metaphysical existence of its own and, therefore, incapable of incurring culpability in terms of criminal law. However, even in moral philosophy this particular position has come under challenge. Collectivists have put forward compelling arguments as to the plausibility of regarding corporations as identifiable entities and morally responsible agents. Admittedly, the traditional fixation on human agency tends to distort debates about moral blame in relation to culpability even in those domestic jurisdictions that have shifted their focus from the issue of moral personhood to the question of how to uncover fault on the part of legal persons. Nevertheless, a form of moral blameworthiness – derived from the universal applicability of certain norms – is increasingly at the heart of discussions pertaining to corporate criminal liability. The idea that the ascription of culpability in relation to natural and legal persons is justifiably warranted on the basis of different sets of principles is gaining recognition. It postulates that although legal responsibility should not be entirely divorced from the morality paradigm, the culpability of corporations in penal law need not be grounded on the entity's realisation of the moral wrongfulness of its conduct, as is the case with individuals.

While the constituent elements of the offending behaviour are by necessity physically fulfilled by natural persons, it is the peculiarities of organisational existence that foster the deviant behaviour. The size, complexity and differentiation of large organisations, as well as particular management styles, institutional cultures and group dynamics, can translate into a criminogenic environment that is conducive to the infliction of harm through negligence and faulty judgment as well as conscious premeditation. Deficient internal processes (relating to supervision and control) and structural difficulties arising out of complex communication networks have the propensity to facilitate wrongful conduct. Bureaucratic routines, cognitive limitations and group socialisation also serve to promote behaviour which would be erratic when considered outside the context of the collective. Separated from the organisation, individuals do not generally have the same incentives, opportunities and means to engage in harmful activities. Neither can those activities reach the scale and impact that collective action and access to organisational resources bring about, particularly in the circumstances of the 'core' international offences. However, detecting blameworthiness for the transgressions of natural persons in the idiosyncrasies of the business form and, accordingly, attaching culpability to economic entities for fostering environments permissive to the commission of crimes, does not – and need not – exclude the responsibility of individuals to the extent of their personal misconduct. Should concerns related to the perceived threat of implicating states in international offences preclude the extension of ICC jurisdiction beyond natural persons, individual prosecutions may be the only avenue available for ensuring corporate accountability. Regardless of the direction which political negotiations surrounding future amendments to the Rome Statute with regard to the Court's *ratione personae* take, the question of how to construct individual liability in the context of group crimes inevitably arises.

The inherent difficulty in effectively reconciling the principle of personal fault with the collective nature of crimes (in systemic or institutional settings) is not novel. More than sixty years ago, cognisant of the challenges posed by group criminality, the Nuremberg tribunals embraced a model premised on the notions of conspiracy and criminal organisations. Pragmatic rather than dogmatic, the Nuremberg approach could not be easily divorced from concerns pertaining to guilt by association, mass punishment and strict liability. Despite the tribunals' caution in imposing criminal responsibility, the judgments tended to distort the contours of individual culpability and at times rendered the link with personal fault tenuous. The principles that emerged out of the judgments regarding political and military figures were subsequently relied upon also in relation to the prosecution of business officials for their involvement in Nazi crimes. Neither the IMT nor the Allies' domestic military courts had jurisdiction over legal persons. However, they sought corporate accountability within the constraints of their constitutive documents. Albeit inconsistent and somewhat deficient, the decisions rendered are notable in that they expressed recognition of the reality of corporate involvement in international crimes and the realisation that such criminality – being qualitatively different from individual deviance – warrants a distinct approach.

Although the Nuremberg model did not persist in time, the notions which formed its core, can be found in contemporary international law. The 'common design' and 'superior responsibility' doctrines have become firmly established as modes for incurring individual responsibility. Both extend culpability beyond the physical perpetration of crimes and are geared towards the reality of criminality in group settings. The limitations adopted in this regard in the context of the *ad hoc* tribunals and the ICC in particular, delineate the outer bounds for the permissible ascription of punishable individual culpability in present-day international criminal law. Understanding such limitations is pertinent to the discussion of corporate liability insofar as Articles 25 and 28 RS are capable of potentially capturing the contributions of individual business actors to the commission of international crimes. The magnitude and complexities of those crimes necessitate accountability avenues that adequately reflect the true character and dynamics of deviance in collective context – political, military or economic. The need to fight impunity, however, does not – neither should it – imply punishment at any cost. The cumulative development of international criminal law – from Nuremberg through the *ad hoc* tribunals' jurisprudence to the Rome Statute of the ICC – demonstrates the importance accorded to finding a fair balance when holding individuals responsible for group crimes. Within corporations, the actual effect of individual transgressions and the true extent of culpability may become obvious only when considered against the backdrop of aggregate choices and behaviour. This is not to say, however, that individual liability cannot or need not align with the principle of personal fault. On the contrary, it must remain strictly circumscribed, although some reasonable concessions may have to be made in order to accommodate for the element of collective criminality.

Although currently the ICC has no jurisdiction over legal persons, the negotiations surrounding the adoption of the Rome Statute entertained the idea of ascribing criminal responsibility to economic entities via individual convictions. This was thought to circumscribe the impossibility of fathoming the mental state of business enterprises *per se*. The isolated prosecutions of natural persons cannot, however, capture the true nature of corporate involvement in international offences, nor effectively contain organisational wrongdoing. The convictions of senior officials are likely to be difficult, sometimes even impossible to obtain. In large organisations, characterised by multiple channels of communication and dispersed levels of control, the requisite *actus reus* and *mens rea* may not converge in a single individual. Furthermore, while corporate policies, structure and culture impact on individual behaviour, the facilitation of technical, human and financial resources, available by virtue of the organised entity, affect the degree of harm caused. Individual prosecutions may thus not necessarily reflect the egregious violations suffered through group activity.

Seeking to artificially transpose the combination of objective and subjective aspects that constitute the definition of a crime from an individual to an organisation, is a misplaced effort, reflecting the deeply imbedded individualistic perception of society that typifies Western legal tradition. Corporate crime materialises through collective action or blameworthy inaction and cannot be detached from the institutional framework in which it takes place. Appropriate models for constructing the criminal liability of corporations must, therefore, take into account the peculiarities of organisational deviance. In this regard, a growing number of domestic jurisdictions have begun embracing elements of more holistic views on the nature of corporations. The models of aggregation, proactive or reactive fault, and corporate ethos are not entirely devoid of shortcomings. Nonetheless, they share the perception of corporations as having a separate existence, and overcoming the limitations of the nominalist method, they seek to ascribe culpability on the basis of genuine organisational fault.

The most advanced of the holistic models – that of constructive corporate fault – allows for reasonable inferences to be drawn from the interplay of institutional characteristics (i.e. structure, culture, policies, channels of communication and levels of control). Culpable conduct on the part of the organisation is identified on the basis of an objective test of reasonableness. The goal of the test is to determine whether 'given the size, complexity, formality, functionality, decision-making process, and structure of the corporate organisation', it is reasonable to conclude that the physical elements of the offence may be validly attributed to the entity. Far from rejecting subjectivism as the cornerstone of criminal liability, even in relation to legal persons, the model of constructive corporate fault proposes a shift in perspective – from seeking to expose the hidden mental state of a corporation to divining blameworthiness in the attitude displayed towards (the likelihood of) a criminal outcome.

Insofar as constructive fault appears to reflect most closely the true nature of corporations and is geared towards overcoming the drawbacks of other existing and theoretical approaches to ascribing corporate responsibility, it presents an intriguing possibility with regard to the criminal liability of economic entities under the Rome Statute. The provisions presently incorporated in the Statute have been drafted with a view to natural persons and are not suited for application to corporations. However, there is room for manoeuvre. Article 30 RS, for instance, allows for fault degrees other than those deemed to comprise knowledge and volition as the expression of intentional conduct. If explicitly provided for in a *sui generis* provision pertaining to corporate criminal responsibility, even *culpa* may serve as a basis for the culpability of companies. A constructive approach to uncovering negligence would focus on the question of whether the company inadvertently created the risk of a foreseeable and unjustifiable harm. Liability would revolve around what the entity concerned could have reasonably foreseen and the lack of a conceivable response evidenced from an aggregation of acts and failures at different levels within the organisation and on the part of agents acting within the scope of their employment.

If *culpa* has a role to play in international criminal law, it is particularly relevant with regard to corporations. Even where inadvertent, business involvement in the 'core' crimes is not always entirely unconscious. Companies are often, at the very least, cognisant of the precarious circumstances of the conflict zones in which they operate. Since the harm that may result through the use of the organisational structure is greater than it would be in the case of isolated individual misconduct, national jurisdictions have long subjected economic ventures to a reasonable expectation that they guard against the occurrence of harm in the course of their activities. The need to consider *culpa*-type liability for corporate participation in gross human rights violations finds also support in social science research on organisational behaviour. The institutional environment may distort reasonable conclusions, suppress dissent and impede communication. Corporate liability in this regard would be imposed for creating favourable conditions for the commission of crimes, and it would be inextricably linked to due diligence shortcomings. Hence, it would only be fair if direct criminal responsibility on the part of the entity for negligent misconduct attaches to a breach of duty rather than the actual offence that materialises.

A similar construction is warranted with respect to the liability of parent corporations for the criminal transgressions of subsidiary entities. In an increasingly deregulated and globalised commercial market, MNCs routinely structure their operations through intricate configurations of dispersed control, which often serve to minimise risk exposure in the pursuit of profit maximisation. However, the imperative of justice and the need to narrow the existing regulatory gap dictate that parent enterprises not be allowed to abuse the corporate form in order to conceal their involvement in grave human rights abuse, or exploit the principle of separate juridical personality so as to evade responsibility. In instances where a parent entity knowingly and/or intentionally engages in the commission of a humanitarian law violation by a subsidiary, culpability should attach to the parent's active participation in the realisation of the offence, and accordingly the responsibility incurred would be for the crime effected. A failure to act on the part of the parent corporation may also reflect a negligent omission to foresee a reasonable and unjustifiable risk and/or notify its foreign affiliate of that risk. In such circumstances, extending liability to parent corporations should not be perceived to imply an absolute duty to stay apprised of subsidiary conduct at all times. Neither does it purport guilt and punishment along strict liability lines or an unconditional obligation to prevent subsidiary conduct that may involve the commission of an international crime. Given the criminal nature of the responsibility sought, the criteria attaching to the parent company's culpability must be strictly circumscribed. Grounding liability on a failure to intervene and raise awareness combined with a failure to exercise effective control over the subsidiary, as a result of which the latter engages in a 'core' offence, provides one possible approach. Such a construction roots culpability in a fault on the part of the parent itself. It furthermore draws upon the notions of awareness and control as the ground stones of liability in hierarchical settings, already recognised and operative in international criminal law with regard to individuals.

Should the jurisdiction of the ICC be extended to profit-oriented business enterprises and a political agreement be reached on how culpability is to be ascribed, this would not dispense with the objections of states which do not recognise corporate criminal responsibility on legal-philosophical grounds or prefer to have the option of non-compulsory regulation left open to them. In this regard, the adoption of a nuanced 'exception-based' model, allowing for civil and administrative proceedings or alternatively individual criminal prosecutions, as a bar to the admissibility of cases before the ICC, may constitute the only practicable compromise capable of appeasing states and encompassing most MNCs. Without discarding the value and record of non-criminal regulatory means at the domestic level and while recognising that certain adjustments may have to be made in order to accommodate for the principle of complementarity, this study is nevertheless clearly premised on a preference for subjecting corporations to penal law provisions with regard to the 'core' international crimes. The expressive rationale of criminal liability and punishment carries a strong symbolic significance. Subjecting corporations to criminal law regulation, particularly in relation to serious human rights abuse, serves to uphold the universal validity of a set of social norms accepted as the bedrock of humanity. Provided it materialises in a future amendment to the Rome Statute, the concept of corporate responsibility for international crimes will, furthermore, acknowledge both historical and present-day reality. It will express recognition of the broader context of mass atrocity and the impact of transnational economic dynamics in nurturing environments that are conducive to the violation of human rights.

Samenvatting

De groeiende invloed van multinationale corporaties en de, door winstbejag gedreven uitbreiding van commerciële activiteiten naar conflictrijke gebieden in de wereld hebben geleid tot toenemende bezorgdheid over het gebrek aan verantwoording door zulke ondernemingen. Ondanks een brede consensus dat zij gebonden zijn aan bepaalde 'kernregels' die alle actoren in het internationale domein betreffen, waaronder het verbod direct of indirect betrokken te zijn of te geraken bij genocide, oorlogsmisdrijven en misdrijven tegen de menselijkheid, blijft regulering grotendeels achterwege, dan wel is zij lacuneus. Vele nationale jurisdicties zijn onwillig of niet bij machte om voor strikte verplichte handhaving te zorgen, en vooralsnog voorziet het internationale systeem niet in een effectief mechanisme om naleving af te dwingen. Het Internationale Strafhof (International Criminal Court – ICC) biedt een unieke gelegenheid om een sanctiemechanisme te introduceren waarmee bestaande gebreken in de regulering – ten minste gedeeltelijk – kunnen worden opgeheven. In deze studie worden de wenselijkheid en de mogelijkheden onderzocht om zakelijke ondernemingen *per se* aan de regels van het internationale strafrecht te onderwerpen. Daarbij wordt nagegaan in hoeverre het toelaatbaar zou zijn om de reikwijdte van bestaande strafrechtelijke bepalingen, en in het bijzonder die van het Statuut van het ICC, uit te breiden van louter natuurlijke personen naar tevens rechtspersonen, en welke bijzondere uitdagingen zich daarbij voordoen.

Hoewel de meeste nationale rechtssystemen tegenwoordig het concept van strafrechtelijke aansprakelijkheid van corporaties voor nationale en/of internationale misdaden erkennen, menen sommigen dat het strafrechtelijke systeem het menselijke bewustzijn als uitgangspunt heeft. Dit deontologische perspectief is als bezwaar naar voren gebracht tegen het idee dat de jurisdictie van het ICC zou moeten worden uitgebreid tot economische ondernemingen. Het laat zich vertalen als een antropocentrische zienswijze, waarbij de corporatie niet meer is dan een verzameling van individuen die geen eigen onafhankelijk metafysisch bestaan heeft en waaraan dus geen schuld in strafrechtelijke zin kan kleven. Zelfs in de moraalfilosofie echter wordt dit standpunt bestreden. Zogenaamde collectivisten hebben overtuigend beargumenteerd dat het plausibel is om corporaties als identificeerbare eenheden en moreel verantwoordelijke actoren te beschouwen. Toegegeven moet worden dat het debat over morele schuld in relatie tot de strafrechtelijke variant wordt gekleurd door de traditionele fixatie op de mens als actor, zelfs in die nationale jurisdicties waarin de focus van morele persoonlijkheid is verschoven naar de vraag hoe schuld bij rechtspersonen kan worden ontsluierd. Niettemin worden in toenemende mate discussies over de strafrechtelijke aansprakelijkheid van rechtspersonen gestuurd door een vorm van morele schuld die wordt ontleend aan de universele toepasselijkheid van bepaalde normen. Steeds vaker wordt erkend dat verschillende principes de toeschrijving van schuld aan natuurlijke dan wel rechtspersonen rechtvaardigen. Daarbij wordt aangenomen dat, hoewel juridische verantwoordelijkheid niet helemaal moet worden losgezien van het morele paradigma, de strafrechtelijke schuld van rechtspersonen niet, zoals bij natuurlijke personen het geval is, hoeft te worden gebaseerd op het bewustzijn bij de corporatie dat haar gedrag moreel verkeerd is.

Terwijl de constituerende elementen van dat gedrag noodzakelijkerwijs in fysieke zin door natuurlijke personen worden vervuld, zijn het de eigenaardigheden van het organisationele bestaan die deviantie onder hen bevorderen. De omvang, complexiteit en differentiatie van grote organisaties, evenals bepaalde stijlen van management, institutionele culturen en groepsdynamica, kunnen een criminogene omgeving produceren die bevorderlijk is voor de toebrenging van schade, niet alleen door bewust handelen maar ook door nalatigheid en verkeerde beoordeling. Gebreken in interne processen (met betrekking tot supervisie en controle) en structurele moeilijkheden vanwege complexe communicatienetwerken vergemakkelijken het ontstaan van onrechtmatig gedrag. Bureaucratische routines, cognitieve beperkingen en processen van groepssocialisatie bevorderen eveneens gedrag dat buiten de context van het collectief als deviant zou worden beschouwd. Los van de organisatie hebben individuen gewoonlijk niet dezelfde prikkels, mogelijkheden en middelen om schadelijke activiteiten te ondernemen. Noch hebben zulke activiteiten dezelfde omvang of invloed die het gevolg zijn van collectieve actie en de toegang tot organisationele middelen, zeker niet in de omstandigheden waarin de internationale 'kernmisdrijven' plaatsvinden.

Toch betekenen het situeren van verwijtbaarheid voor de overtredingen van natuurlijke personen binnen de eigenaardigheden van de ondernemingsvorm en, vervolgens, de toeschrijving van schuld aan economische eenheden wegens het bevorderen van een omgeving waarin het begaan van misdaden mogelijk wordt, niet – en ook niet noodzakelijkerwijs – dat individuen vrijuit gaan voor zover zij zich persoonlijk hebben misdragen. Wanneer een uitbreiding van de rechtsmacht van het ICC naar rechtspersonen onmogelijk zou blijken omdat daarmee de vrees dat in de toekomst ook staten als dader van internationale misdrijven zouden kunnen worden beschouwd dichterbij komt, blijft wellicht de vervolging van natuurlijke personen de enige mogelijkheid om verantwoording voor door corporaties gepleegde misdrijven te verzekeren. Bovendien, de vraag hoe individuele aansprakelijkheid in de context van groepsmisdrijven moet worden geconstrueerd, ongeacht de richting van de politieke onderhandelingen rond toekomstige herzieningen van het ICC Statuut met betrekking tot de *ratione personae* van het Hof, is onvermijdelijk.

De inherente moeilijkheid van effectieve overeenstemming tussen het beginsel van individuele schuld en de collectieve (systemische of institutionele) aard van misdrijven onder het internationale strafrecht is niet nieuw. In de wetenschap dat groepscriminaliteit een bepaalde uitdaging vormt, hebben de tribunalen van Neurenberg meer dan zestig jaar geleden een model omarmd gebaseerd op de concepten van samenzwering en van criminele organisaties. De Neurenberg-benadering, die eerder pragmatisch is dan dogmatisch, kon niet gemakkelijk worden losgezien van zorgen met betrekking tot schuld door associatie, collectieve bestraffing en risico-aansprakelijkheid. Hoewel de tribunalen voorzichtig waren in het toeschrijven van strafrechtelijke verantwoordelijkheid, werden door hun uitspraken de contouren van individuele schuld enigszins versluierd en was het verband met persoonlijke verwijtbaarheid niet altijd zonder meer duidelijk. De principes die uit die uitspraken tevoorschijn kwamen, en die betrekking hadden op politieke en militaire figuren, werden vervolgens gebruikt bij de vervolging van functionarissen in het zakenleven wegens hun betrokkenheid bij Nazi-misdaden. Noch het Internationale Militaire Tribunaal noch de nationale militaire tribunalen van de Geallieerden hadden rechtsmacht met betrekking tot rechtspersonen. Binnen de beperkingen van hun constituerende documenten hebben zij toch de aansprakelijkheid van corporaties trachten te construeren. Hoewel de uitspraken inconsistent zijn en enigszins gebrekkig, zijn zij opmerkelijk in de zin dat zij de realiteit van betrokkenheid van corporaties bij internationale misdrijven onderkennen, in het besef dat zulke criminaliteit – die kwalitatief anders is dan individuele misdaad – ook anders moet worden benaderd.

Hoewel het model van Neurenberg de tand des tijds niet heeft doorstaan, zijn de ideeën die de kern ervan vormen nog altijd aanwezig in het tegenwoordige internationale recht. De dogmatische concepten *common design* en *superior responsibility* zijn vast verankerd als de basis van individuele aansprakelijkheid. Beide breiden schuld uit tot voorbij het fysieke begaan van misdrijven en zijn gericht op de werkelijkheid van criminaliteit in een groepscontext. De beperkingen ervan die door de *ad hoc* tribunalen, en het ICC in het bijzonder, zijn aangebracht, markeren de buitenste grenzen van de toelaatbare toeschrijving van individuele schuld in het huidige internationale recht. Het begrijpen van zulke beperkingen is noodzakelijk in het debat over de aansprakelijkheid van rechtspersonen, nu de artikelen 25 en 28 van het ICC Statuut de bijdrage van individuele actoren uit de zakenwereld aan internationale misdrijven potentieel kunnen omvatten. De omvang en complexiteit van die misdrijven vereisen verantwoordingsmogelijkheden die een adequate weerspiegeling zijn van de ware aard en dynamiek van deviantie in een collectieve context – politiek, militair of economisch. De noodzaak om immuniteit in dit verband te bestrijden impliceert echter niet, mag ook niet impliceren, dat tot elke prijs moet worden gestraft. De cumulatieve ontwikkeling van het internationale strafrecht – van Neurenberg via de jurisprudentie van de *ad hoc* tribunalen tot het Statuut van het ICC – laat zien welk belang wordt gehecht aan een eerlijk evenwicht wanneer individuen verantwoordelijk worden gehouden voor groepscriminaliteit. Hoewel binnen corporaties het echte effect van individuele overtredingen en de ware aard van de schuld mogelijk pas duidelijk worden wanneer zij worden bezien tegen de achtergrond van een verzameling van keuzes en gedrag, wil dat niet zeggen dat individuele aansprakelijkheid niet volgens het principe van individuele schuld kan of moet worden vastgesteld. Integendeel, de grenzen van zulke aansprakelijkheid moeten strikt worden bewaakt, hoewel enkele redelijke concessies misschien noodzakelijk zijn om het element van collectieve criminaliteit mee te kunnen wegen.

Hoewel het ICC op dit moment geen rechtsmacht heeft met betrekking tot rechtspersonen, is tijdens de onderhandelingen rond de aanname van het ICC Statuut in Rome het idee wel geopperd om via individuele veroordelingen strafrechtelijke aansprakelijkheid aan corporaties toe te schrijven. Daarmee dacht men het probleem te vermijden dat de psychische gesteldheid van een onderneming *per se* onmogelijk kan worden vastgesteld. Geïsoleerde vervolgingen van natuurlijke personen kunnen echter de ware aard van de betrokkenheid van corporaties bij internationale misdrijven niet vatten, noch kunnen zij onrechtmatig organisationeel gedrag effectief beperken. Het veroordelen van topfunctionarissen zal allicht moeilijk, soms zelfs onmogelijk zijn. In grote organisaties, die worden gekenmerkt door meervoudige communicatiekanalen en verspreide niveaus van controle, zijn de vereiste fysieke en mentale elementen van strafbare feiten vaak verspreid over verschillende individuen. Bovendien, hoewel het beleid, de structuur en de cultuur van de corporatie het individuele gedrag beïnvloeden, is de omvang van de veroorzaakte schade vooral het gevolg van de technische, menselijke en financiële middelen die dankzij de georganiseerde eenheid aanwezig zijn. Het vervolgen van individuen weerspiegelt daarom lang niet altijd de gevolgen van schendingen die door groepsactiviteiten zijn veroorzaakt.

Proberen om op artificiële wijze de combinatie van objectieve en subjectieve aspecten, die de definitie van een misdrijf bepalen, van een individu naar een organisatie te vertalen, is een misplaatste poging die een diep gewortelde, en voor de Westerse rechtstraditie kenmerkende, individualistische perceptie van de samenleving weerspiegelt. De criminaliteit van corporaties manifesteert zich door collectief handelen of nalaten en kan niet worden losgekoppeld van het institutionele kader waarbinnen het plaatsvindt. Toepasselijke modellen om de strafrechtelijke aansprakelijkheid van corporaties te construeren moeten daarom rekening houden met de eigenaardigheden van organisationele deviantie. Wat dit betreft zoekt een toenemend aantal nationale rechtssystemen hun toevlucht tot elementen van meer holistische visies op de aard van de corporatie. Zulke modellen van aggregatie, proactieve of reactieve verwijtbaarheid, en corporatieve ethos zijn niet zonder tekortkomingen. Niettemin ligt er eenzelfde zienswijze aan ten grondslag, namelijk dat corporaties een eigen, apart bestaan hebben, en dat schuld moet worden toegeschreven op basis van daadwerkelijke organisationele verwijtbaarheid (waarmee de beperkingen van de nominalistische methode worden omzeild).

De meest vergaande van de holistische modellen – constructieve corporatieve verwijtbaarheid – laat het trekken van redelijke conclusies toe uit het samenspel van institutionele kenmerken (dat wil zeggen: structuur, cultuur, beleid, communicatiekanalen en controleniveaus). Het identificeren van verwijtbaar gedrag van de zijde van de corporatie vindt plaats op basis van een objectieve redelijkheidstoets. Doel daarvan is om te bepalen of het redelijk is, 'gegeven de omvang, complexiteit, formaliteit, functionaliteit, beslissingsprocessen en structuur van de organisatie', om te concluderen dat de fysieke elementen van het misdrijf aan de eenheid kunnen worden toegeschreven. Hiermee wordt echter subjectivisme als hoeksteen van strafrechtelijke aansprakelijkheid niet verworpen met betrekking tot rechtspersonen. Verre van. Het model van constructieve corporatieve verwijtbaarheid stelt een verandering van perspectief voor: van een poging de verborgen psychische gesteldheid van de corporatie te ontwaren naar het vaststellen van verwijtbaarheid op basis van de houding die wordt ingenomen ten aanzien van (de waarschijnlijkheid van) een strafbaar gevolg.

Voor zover constructieve verwijtbaarheid de meest getrouwe weerspiegeling lijkt te zijn van de ware aard van corporaties en bedoeld is om de tekortkomingen op te heffen van andere bestaande en theoretische benaderingen van het toeschrijven van verantwoordelijkheid aan corporaties, voorziet dit model in een intrigerende mogelijkheid om tot strafrechtelijke aansprakelijkheid van economische eenheden onder het ICC Statuut te komen. De huidige bepalingen van het Statuut zijn ontworpen met het oog op natuurlijke personen en zijn niet geschikt voor toepassing op rechtspersonen. Maar er is wel ruimte om te manoeuvreren. Zo laat artikel 30 bijvoorbeeld niveaus van verwijtbaarheid toe die niet zonder meer wetenschap en willen als uitdrukking van opzettelijk handelen vereisen. Wanneer een *sui generis* bepaling expliciet zou voorzien in de strafrechtelijke aansprakelijkheid van corporaties, zou zelfs *culpa* de basis kunnen zijn voor het toeschrijven van schuld aan ondernemingen. In een constructieve benadering van nalatigheid zou de nadruk dan liggen op de vraag of de onderneming onbedoeld het risico van een voorzienbaar en niet te rechtvaardigen gevolg heeft gecreëerd. De aansprakelijkheidsvraag betreft dan of, en in hoeverre de betreffende onderneming het gevolg redelijkerwijs had kunnen voorzien en al dan niet maatregelen heeft genomen ter voorkoming daarvan, gezien de aggregatie van handelen en nalaten op verschillende niveaus binnen de organisatie en van de zijde van actoren binnen de reikwijdte van hun betrekking.

Als voor *culpa* al een rol is weggelegd in het internationale strafrecht, dan is het in het bijzonder relevant met betrekking tot corporaties. Zelfs wanneer sprake is van onopzettelijke betrokkenheid van ondernemingen bij de kernmisdrijven, is er niet altijd totale onbewustheid. Op zijn minst zijn bedrijven vaak bekend met de hachelijke omstandigheden in de conflictgebieden waar zij opereren. Daar de mogelijke schadelijke gevolgen ernstiger zijn als gevolg van het gebruik van organisationele structuren dan wanneer sprake is van geïsoleerd individueel gedrag, worden in nationale rechtssystemen economische ondernemingen aan de redelijke verwachting onderworpen dat zij waken tegen het ontstaan van schade in de loop van hun zakelijke activiteiten. De noodzaak om een soort *culpa*-aansprakelijkheid te overwegen voor de betrokkenheid van corporaties in grove schendingen van mensenrechten vindt tevens steun in sociaal-wetenschappelijk onderzoek naar organisationeel gedrag. De institutionele omgeving kan het bereiken van redelijke gevolgtrekkingen in de weg staan, afwijkende meningen onderdrukken en communicatie verhinderen. Vanuit dit perspectief ontstaat strafrechtelijke aansprakelijkheid op basis van het creëren van omstandigheden waarin criminaliteit wordt bevorderd, en zij is onlosmakelijk verbonden met tekortkomingen in zorgplichten. Dientengevolge vereist de eerlijkheid dat schuld wegens nalatigheid alleen wordt toegeschreven voor de zorgplichtschending en niet voor het misdrijf dat het gevolg ervan is.

Een soortgelijke constructie is gerechtvaardigd met betrekking tot de aansprakelijkheid van moederondernemingen voor de strafbare overtredingen van dochtereenheden. In een toenemend gedereguleerde en geglobaliseerde markt, worden de operaties van multinationale corporaties gewoonlijk gestructureerd door middel van ingewikkelde constructies van verspreide controle, die vaak bedoeld zijn om risico's te minimaliseren met het oog op winstmaximalisatie. Rechtvaardigheidsoverwegingen en de noodzaak om de bestaande hiaten in de (internationale) regulering van corporatief handelen te dichten, vereisen echter dat moederondernemingen de corporatieve vorm niet mogen misbruiken om hun betrokkenheid bij mensenrechtenschendingen te verhullen, of om het principe van gescheiden juridische persoonlijkheden te gebruiken ten einde verantwoordelijkheid te ontlopen. In die gevallen waarin een moederonderneming bewust en/of opzettelijk door middel van een dochter het humanitaire recht schendt, betreft de verwijtbaarheid de actieve deelname van de moederonderneming in het misdrijf, zodat aansprakelijkheid voor het misdrijf zelf ontstaat.

Nalaten te handelen door de moederonderneming kan ook een weerspiegeling zijn van nalatigheid bij het redelijkerwijs moeten voorzien van een niet te rechtvaardigen risico, of nalaten een buitenlandse dochter op de hoogte te brengen van het bestaan van dat risico. Het uitbreiden van aansprakelijkheid tot de moederondernemingen moet in zulke gevallen niet worden opgevat als een absolute plicht altijd en onder alle omstandigheden op de hoogte te blijven van de handelwijze van een dochteronderneming. Evenmin worden hier schuld en straf volgens een principe van risicoaansprakelijkheid voorgesteld, of een onvoorwaardelijke plicht om de betrokkenheid van dochterondernemingen bij internationale misdrijven te voorkomen. Gegeven dat het hier om *strafrechtelijke* aansprakelijkheid gaat, is het noodzakelijk om de criteria die de schuld van de moederonderneming bepalen, streng te omschrijven. Een mogelijke benadering zou zijn om aansprakelijkheid te baseren op het nalaten te interveniëren en bewustzijn te creëren, gecombineerd met het nalaten effectieve controle uit te oefenen, als gevolg waarvan een dochteronderneming betrokken raakt bij een van de kernmisdrijven. In een dergelijke constructie is schuld gebaseerd op nalatigheid van de moederonderneming zelf. Bovendien bouwt zij voort op ideeën rond bewustzijn en controle als de hoekstenen van aansprakelijkheid in een hiërarchische context, die nu al worden erkend en gebruikt in het internationale strafrecht met betrekking tot individuen.

Wanneer de rechtsmacht van het ICC zou worden uitgebreid tot winstgeoriënteerde ondernemingen en politieke overeenstemming zou worden bereikt over hoe schuld moet worden toegeschreven, wordt hiermee nog niet tegemoetgekomen aan de bezwaren van staten die de strafrechtelijke aansprakelijkheid van corporaties om rechtsfilosofische redenen niet erkennen, of die de optie van niet-verplichtende regulering open willen houden. In dit verband vormt de adoptie van een genuanceerd 'exceptiemodel', waarbij civiele of administratieve rechtsgangen dan wel het vervolgen van individuen de rechtsmacht van het ICC stuiten, wellicht het enige mogelijke praktische compromis dat de meeste multinationale ondernemingen kan omvatten en staten toch tevreden kan stellen.

Zonder aan de waarde en mogelijkheden van niet-strafrechtelijke regulering op nationaal niveau af te doen, en in het besef dat bepaalde aanpassingen misschien nodig zijn om aan het complimentariteitsprincipe tegemoet te komen, wordt in dit onderzoek toch duidelijk gekozen voor strafrechtelijke bepalingen voor corporaties wanneer deze betrokken zijn bij de internationale kernmisdrijven. De expressieve functie van strafrechtelijke aansprakelijkheid en straf heeft een sterke symbolische betekenis. Het onderwerpen van corporaties aan het strafrecht, in het bijzonder in verband met ernstige mensenrechtenschendingen, heeft als doel de universele geldigheid van die sociale normen te onderstrepen die als het fundament van menselijkheid worden beschouwd. Wanneer het concept van corporatieve aansprakelijkheid voor internationale misdrijven in een toekomstig amendement van het ICC Statuut zou worden aangenomen, wordt bovendien zowel de historische als de huidige werkelijkheid onderkend. Het zou de erkenning zijn van de bredere context van massacriminaliteit en van de gevolgen van een transnationale economische dynamiek die een omgeving creëert waarin de schending van mensenrechten wordt bevorderd.

SELECTED LEGAL PROVISIONS

Article 21 RS
Applicable law

1. The Court shall apply:

   (a) In the first place, this Statute, Elements of Crimes and its Rules of Procedure and Evidence;
   (b) In the second place, where appropriate, applicable treaties and the principles and rules of international law, including the established principles of the international law of armed conflict;
   (c) Failing that, general principles of law derived by the Court from national laws of legal systems of the world including, as appropriate, the national laws of States that would normally exercise jurisdiction over the crime, provided that those principles are not inconsistent with this Statute and with international law and internationally recognised norms and standards.

2. The Court may apply principles and rules of law as interpreted in its previous decisions.

3. The application and interpretation of law pursuant to this article must be consistent with internationally recognised human rights, and be without any adverse distinction founded on grounds such as gender as defined in article 7, paragraph 3, age, race, colour, language, religion or belief, political or other opinion, national, ethnic or social origin, wealth, birth or other status.

Article 25 RS
Individual criminal responsibility

1. The Court shall have jurisdiction over natural persons pursuant to this Statute.

2. A person who commits a crime within the jurisdiction of the Court shall be individually responsible and liable for punishment in accordance with this Statute.

3. In accordance with this Statute, a person shall be criminally responsible and liable for punishment for a crime within the jurisdiction of the Court if that person:

   (a) Commits such a crime, whether as an individual, jointly with another or through another person, regardless of whether that other person is criminally responsible;

(b) Orders, solicits or induces the commission of such a crime which in fact occurs or is attempted;
(c) For the purpose of facilitating the commission of such a crime, aids, abets or otherwise assists in its commission or its attempted commission, including providing the means for its commission;
(d) In any other way contributes to the commission or attempted commission of such a crime by a group of persons acting with a common purpose. Such contribution shall be intentional and shall either:
 (i) Be made with the aim of furthering the criminal activity or criminal purpose of the group, where such activity or purpose involves the commission of a crime within the jurisdiction of the Court; or
 (ii) Be made in the knowledge of the intention of the group to commit the crime;
(e) In respect of the crime of genocide, directly and publicly incites others to commit genocide;
(f) Attempts to commit such a crime by taking action that commences its execution by means of a substantial step, but the crime does not occur because of circumstances independent of the person's intentions. However, a person who abandons the effort to commit the crime or otherwise prevents the completion of the crime shall not be liable for punishment under this Statute for the attempt to commit that crime if that person completely and voluntarily gave up the criminal purpose.

4. No provision in this Statute relating to individual criminal responsibility shall affect the responsibility of States under international law.

Article 28 RS
Responsibility of commanders and other superiors

In addition to other grounds of criminal responsibility under this Statute for crimes within the jurisdiction of the Court:

(a) A military commander or person effectively acting as a military commander shall be criminally responsible for crimes within the jurisdiction of the Court committed by forces under his or her effective command and control, or effective authority and control as the case may be, as a result of his or her failure to exercise control properly over such forces, where:
 (i) That military commander or person either knew or, owing to the circumstances at the time, should have known that the forces were committing or about to commit such crimes; and
 (ii) That military commander or person failed to take all necessary and reasonable measures within his or her power to prevent or repress their commission or to submit the matter to the competent authorities for investigation and prosecution.
(b) With respect to superior and subordinate relationships not described in paragraph (a), a superior shall be criminally responsible for crimes within the jurisdiction of the Court committed by subordinates under his or her effective authority and

control, as a result of his or her failure to exercise control properly over such subordinates, where:
(i) The superior either knew, or consciously disregarded information which clearly indicated, that the subordinates were committing or about to commit such crimes;
(ii) The crimes concerned activities that were within the effective responsibility and control of the superior; and
(iii) The superior failed to take all necessary and reasonable measures within his or her power to prevent or repress their commission or to submit the matter to the competent authorities for investigation and prosecution.

Article 30 RS
Mental element

1. Unless otherwise provided, a person shall be criminally responsible and liable for punishment for a crime within the jurisdiction of the Court only if the material elements are committed with intent and knowledge.

2. For the purposes of this article, a person has intent where:

(a) In relation to conduct, that person means to engage in the conduct;
(b) In relation to a consequence, that person means to cause that consequence or is aware that it will occur in the ordinary course of events.

3. For the purposes of this article, 'knowledge' means awareness that a circumstance exists or a consequence will occur in the ordinary course of events. 'Know' and 'knowingly' shall be construed accordingly.

Article 77 RS
Applicable penalties

1. Subject to article 110, the Court may impose one of the following penalties on a person convicted of a crime referred to in article 5 of this Statute:

(a) Imprisonment for a specified number of years, which may not exceed a maximum of 30 years; or
(b) A term of life imprisonment when justified by the extreme gravity of the crime and the individual circumstances of the convicted person.

2. In addition to imprisonment, the Court may order:

(a) A fine under the criteria provided for in the Rules of Procedure and Evidence;
(b) A forfeiture of proceeds, property and assets derived directly or indirectly from that crime, without prejudice to the rights of bona fide third parties.

Article 7 ICTY
Individual criminal responsibility

1. A person who planned, instigated, ordered, committed or otherwise aided and abetted in the planning, preparation or execution of a crime referred to in articles 2 to 5 of the present Statute, shall be individually responsible for the crime.

2. The official position of any accused person, whether as Head of State or Government or as a responsible Government official, shall not relieve such person of criminal responsibility nor mitigate punishment.

3. The fact that any of the acts referred to in articles 2 to 5 of the present Statute was committed by a subordinate does not relieve his superior of criminal responsibility if he knew or had reason to know that the subordinate was about to commit such acts or had done so and the superior failed to take the necessary and reasonable measures to prevent such acts or to punish the perpetrators thereof.

4. The fact that an accused person acted pursuant to an order of a Government or of a superior shall not relieve him of criminal responsibility, but may be considered in mitigation of punishment if the International Tribunal determines that justice so requires.

Article 6 ICTR
Individual criminal responsibility

1. A person who planned, instigated, ordered, committed or otherwise aided and abetted in the planning, preparation or execution of a crime referred to in articles 2 to 4 of the present Statute, shall be individually responsible for the crime.

2. The official position of any accused person, whether as Head of State or Government or as a responsible Government official, shall not relieve such person of criminal responsibility nor mitigate punishment.

3. The fact that any of the acts referred to in articles 2 to 4 of the present Statute was committed by a subordinate does not relieve his or her superior of criminal responsibility if he or she knew or had reason to know that the subordinate was about to commit such acts or had done so and the superior failed to take the necessary and reasonable measures to prevent such acts or to punish the perpetrators thereof.

4. The fact that an accused person acted pursuant to an order of a Government or of a superior shall not relieve him or her of criminal responsibility, but may be considered in mitigation of punishment if the International Tribunal for Rwanda determines that justice so requires.

Article 31 VCLT
General rule of interpretation

1. A treaty shall be interpreted in good faith in accordance with the ordinary meaning to be given to the terms of the treaty in their context and in the light of its object and purpose.

2. The context for the purpose of the interpretation of a treaty shall comprise, in addition to the text, including its preamble and annexes:

(a) any agreement relating to the treaty which was made between all the parties in connection with the conclusion of the treaty;
(b) any instrument which was made by one or more parties in connection with the conclusion of the treaty and accepted by the other parties as an instrument related to the treaty.

3. There shall be taken into account, together with the context:

(a) any subsequent agreement between the parties regarding the interpretation of the treaty or the application of its provisions;
(b) any subsequent practice in the application of the treaty which establishes the agreement of the parties regarding its interpretation;
(a) any relevant rules of international law applicable in the relations between the parties.

4. A special meaning shall be given to a term if it is established that the parties so intended.

Article 32 VCLT
Supplementary means of interpretation

Recourse may be had to supplementary means of interpretation, including the preparatory work of the treaty and the circumstances of its conclusion, in order to confirm the meaning resulting from the application of article 31, or to determine the meaning when the interpretation according to article 31:

(a) leaves the meaning ambiguous or obscure; or
(b) leads to a result which is manifestly absurd or unreasonable.

BIBLIOGRAPHY

Adam, S., Colette-Basecqz, N. and Nohoul, M. (eds.), *Corporate Criminal Liability in Europe*, Brussels: La Charte, 2008.

Amaeshi, K., Kingsley, O. and Nnodim, P., *Corporate Social Responsibility in Supply Chains of Global Brands: a Boundaryless Responsibility? Clarifications, Exceptions and Implications*, 2006 (at <papers.ssrn.com/sol3/papers.cfm?abstract _id=947583>).

Ambos, K., Amicus Curiae Brief on JCE in the Matter of the Co-Prosecutors' Appeal of the Closing Order Against Kaing Guek Eav 'Duch' Dated 8 August 2008, 20 *Criminal Law Forum* 353 (2009).

Ambos, K., Joint Criminal Enterprise and Command Responsibility, 5 *Journal of International Criminal Justice* 159 (2007).

Ambos, K., Superior Responsibility, in: Cassese, A., Gaeta, P. and Jones, J.R.W.D. (eds.), *The Rome Statute of the International Criminal Court: a Commentary*, Oxford: Oxford University Press, 2002.

Ambos, K., Article 25: Individual Criminal Responsibility, in: Triffterer, O. (ed.), *Commentary on the Rome Statute of the International Criminal Court*, Baden-Baden: Nomos, 1999.

Ambos, K., General Principles of Criminal Law in the Rome Statute, 10 *Criminal Law Forum* 1, Dordrecht: Kluwer Academic Publishers, 1999.

Amman, D.M., Group Mentality, Expressivism and Genocide, 2 *International Criminal Law Review* 93 (2002).

Amman, D.M., Capital Punishment: Corporate Criminal Liability for Gross Violations of Human Rights, 24 *Hastings International and Comparative Law Review* 327 (2001).

Arens, R., Nuremberg and Group Prosecution, *Washington University Law Quarterly* 329 (1951).

Armoury Combs, N., Copping a Plea to Genocide: The Plea Bargaining of International Crimes, 151 *University of Pennsylvania Law Review* 1 (2002).

Avery, C., Business and Human Rights in a Time of Change, in: Kamminga, M.T. and Zia-Zarifi, S. (eds.), *Liability of Multinational Corporations under International Law*, The Hague: Kluwer Law International, 2000.

Badar, M.E., Just Convict Everyone!: Joint Perpetration from Tadic to Stakic and Back Again, 6 *International Criminal Law Review* 293 (2006).

Bantekas, I., *Principles of Direct and Superior Responsibility in International Humanitarian Law*, Manchester: Manchester University Press, 2002.

Bantekas, I., The Contemporary Law of Superior Responsibility, 93 *American Journal of International Law* 573 (1999).

Barnidge, Jr., R.P., *Non-State Actors and Terrorism. Applying the Law of State Responsibility and the Due Diligence Principle*, The Hague: T.M.C. Asser Press, 2008.

Bassiouni, M.C., *Crimes against Humanity in International Criminal Law*, The Hague: Kluwer Law International, 1999.

Baumgartner, E., Aspects of Victim Participation in the Proceedings of the International Criminal Court, 90 *International Review of the Red Cross* 409 (2008).

Bazyler, M.J., Nuremberg in America: Litigating the Holocaust in United States Courts, 34 *University of Richmond Law Review* 1 (2000).

Beauchamp, T.L. and Bowie, N.E., *Ethical Theory and Business*, Englewood Cliffs: Prentice-Hall, 1993.

Benninger-Budel, C. (ed.), *Due Diligence and its Application to Protect Women from Violence*, Leiden/Boston: Martinus Nijhoff Publishers, 2008.

Betlem, G., Transnational Litigation against Multinational Corporations before Dutch Courts, in: Kamminga, M.T. and Zia-Zarifi, S. (eds.), *Liability of Multinational Corporations under International Law*, The Hague: Kluwer Law International, 2000.

Bittner, E. and Messinger, S.L. (eds.), *Criminology Review Yearbook*, Vol. II, Beverly Hills: Sage, 1980.

Black, E., *IBM and the Holocaust: The Strategic Alliance between Nazi Germany and America's Most Powerful Corporation*, New York: Crown Publishers, 2001.

Blumberg, P.I., Accountability of Multinational Corporations: The Barriers Presented by the Concepts of the Corporate Juridical Entity, 24 *Hastings International and Comparative Law Review* 297 (2001).

Borgwardt, E., Re-Examining Nuremberg as a New Deal Institution: Politics, Culture and the Limits of Law in Generating Human Rights Norms, 23 *Berkeley Journal of International Law* 401 (2005).

Borkin, J., *The Crime and Punishment of I.G. Farben: The Unholy Alliance between Hitler and the Great Chemical Combine*, New York: Barnes & Noble Books, 1979.

Boyd, K., The Inconvenience of Victims: Abolishing Forum Non Conveniens in US Human Rights Litigation, 39 *Virginia Journal of International Law* 41 (1998).

Braithwaite, J., *Corporate Crime in the Pharmaceutical Industry*, London: Routledge & Kegan Paul Books, 1984.

Brants, C.H., Gold Collar Crime. The Peculiar Complexities and Ambiguities of War Crimes, Crimes against Humanity and Genocide, in: Pontell, H.N. and Geis, G.L. (eds.), *International Handbook of White-Collar and Corporate Crime*, New York: Springer, 2006.

Brants, C.H. and Brants, K.L.K., *De sociale constructie van fraude* (The Social Construction of Fraud), Arnhem: Gouda Quint, 1991.

Brown, K.F., Parent Corporation Liability for Subsidiary Violations under Section 107 of CERCLA: Responding to United States v. Cordova Chemical Co., 1 *Brigham Young University Law Review* 265 (1998).

Bucy, P.H., Corporate Ethos: a Standard for Imposing Corporate Criminal Liability, 75 *Minnesota Law Review* 1095 (1991).

Callaghy, T.M., Kassimir, R. and Latham, R., *Intervention and Transnationalism in Africa: Global-Local Networks of Power*, Cambridge: Cambridge University Press, 2001.

Cane, P., *Responsibility in Law and Morality*, Oxford: Hart Publishing, 2002.

Cassese, A., Boundary of Corporate Liability and the Nature of International Crimes: Between Individual Responsibility and State Criminality, in: Discussion, 6 *Journal of International Criminal Justice* 948 (2008).
Cassese, A., The Nicaragua and Tadic Tests Revisted in Light of the ICJ Judgment on Genocide in Bosnia, 18 *European Journal of International Law* 649 (2007).
Cassese, A., *International Criminal Law: Introduction*, Oxford: Oxford University Press, 2003.
Cassese, A., Gaeta, P. and Jones, J.R.W.D. (eds.), *The Rome Statute of the International Criminal Court: a Commentary*, Oxford: Oxford University Press, 2002.
Clapham, A., Extending International Criminal Law Beyond the Individual to Corporations and Armed Opposition Groups, 6 *Journal of International Criminal Justice* 899 (2008).
Clapham, A. and Jerbi, S., *Categories of Corporate Complicity in Human Rights Abuses*, 2001 (at <www.reports-and-materials.org/Clapham-Jerbi-paper.htm>).
Clapham, A., The Question of Jurisdiction under International Criminal Law over Legal Persons, in: Kamminga, M.T. and Zia-Zarifi, S. (eds.), *Liability of Multinational Corporations under International Law*, The Hague: Kluwer Law International, 2000.
Clapham, A., *Human Rights in the Private Sphere*, Oxford: Clarendon Press, 1993.
Clinard, M.B. and Yaeger, P.C., *Corporate Crime*, New York: Free Press, 2000.
Clough, J., *Not-So-Innocents Abroad: Corporate Criminal Liability for Human Rights Abuses*, 2005 (at http://www.austlii.edu.au/au/journals/AJHR/2005/1/html).
Coffee, J.C., No Soul to Damn, No Body to Kick: an Unscandalised Inquiry into the Problem of Corporate Punishment, 79 *Michigan Law Review* 386 (1981).
Cohen, D.V., Ethics and Crime in Business Firms: Organisational Culture and the Impact of Anomy, 6 *Advances in Criminological Theory* 183 (1995).
Colvin, E., Corporate Personality and Criminal Liability, 6 *Criminal Law Forum* 1 (1995).
Comment, Developments in the Law – Corporate Crime: Regulating Corporate Behaviour through Criminal Sanctions, 92 *Harvard Law Review* 1227 (1979).
Cooper, D., Collective Responsibility, 'Moral Luck' and Reconciliation, in: Jokic, A. (ed.), *War Crimes and Collective Wrongdoing: a Reader*, Oxford: Oxford University Press, 2001.
Cooper, D.E., Collective Responsibility, 43 *Philisophy* 258 (1968).
Corlett, J.A., Collective Punishment and Public Policy, 11 *Journal of Business Ethics* 207 (1992).
Dalton, M., *Men Who Manage*, New York: John Wiley & Sons, Inc., 1959.
Damaska, M., Blame and Punishment: Against an 'Instrumentalisation' of Criminal Law, in: Discussion, 6 *Journal of International Criminal Justice* 947 (2008).
Damaska, M., The Shadow Side of Command Responsibility, 49 *American Journal of Comparative Law* 45 (2001).
Danner, A.M. and Martinez, J.S., Guilty Associations: Joint Criminal Enterprise, Command Responsibility and the Development of International Criminal Law, 93 *California Law Review* 75 (2005).
Danner, A.M., Constructing a Hierarchy of Crimes in International Criminal Law Sentencing, 87 *Virginia Law Review* 415 (2001).
Darcy, S., *Collective Responsibility and Accountability under International Law*, Leiden: Martinus Nijhoff Publishers, 2007.

De George, R.T., *Business Ethic*, New York: Macmillan, 1986.
Dijk, P. van, Hoof, F. van, Rijn, A. van and Zwaak, L. (eds.), *Theory and Practice of the European Convention on Human Rights*, Antwerp: Intersentia, 2006.
Drumbl, M.A., Collective Violence and Individual Punishment: The Criminality of Mass Atrocity, 99 *Northwestern University Law Review* 539 (2005).
Dufresne, R., The Opacity of Oil: Oil Corporations, Internal Violence and International Law, 36 *New York University Journal of International Law and Politics* 331 (2004).
Duttwiller, M., Liability for Omission in International Criminal Law, 6 *International Criminal Law Review* 1 (2006).
Eaton, J., The Nigerian Tragedy. Environmental Regulation of Transnational Corporations and the Human Right to a Healthy Environment, 15 *Boston University International Law Review* 261 (1997).
Eltringham, N., *Accounting for Horror: Post-Genocide Debates in Rwanda*, London/Virginia: Pluto Press, 2004.
Ermann, M.D. and Lundman, R.J. (eds.), *Corporate and Governmental Deviance: Problems of Organisational Behaviour in Contemporary Society*, New York: Oxford University Press, 1978.
Eser, A., Mental Elements – Mistake of Fact and Mistake of Law, in: Cassese, A., Gaeta, P. and Jones, J. R. W. D. (eds.), *The Rome Statute of the International Criminal Court: a Commentary*, Oxford: Oxford University Press, 2002.
Eser, A., Towards an International Criminal Court: Genesis and Main Features of the Rome Statute, 20 *University of Tasmania Law Review* 1 (2001).
Feinberg, J., *The Expressive Function of Punishment in Doing and Deserving*, Princeton: Princeton University Press, 1970.
Fenrick, W.J., Article 28: Responsibility of Commanders and Other Superiors, in: Triffterer, O. (ed.), *Commentary on the Rome Statute of the International Criminal Court*, Baden-Baden: Nomos, 1999.
Fisse, B., Restructuring Corporate Criminal Law: Deterrence, Retribution, Fault, and Sanctions, 56 *South California Law Review* 1141 (1983).
Fisse, B. and Braithwaite, J., *The Impact of Publicity on Corporate Offenders*, Albany: State University of New York Press, 1983.
Fletcher, G.P., Collective Guilt and Collective Punishment, 5 *Theoretical Inquiries in Law* 163 (2004).
Fletcher, G.P., Liberals and Romantics at War: The Problem of Collective Guilt, 111 *Yale Law Review* 1499 (2002).
Fletcher, G.P., *Rethinking Criminal Law*, Boston: Little, Brown & Co., 1978.
Fletcher, G.P., Theory of Criminal Negligence: a Comparative Analysis, 119 *University of Pennsylvania Law Review* 401 (1971).
Foeschler, A., Corporate Criminal Intent: Toward a Better Understanding of Corporate Misconduct, 78 *California Law Review* 1287 (1990).
Fombrun, C., *Reputation: Realising Value from the Corporate Image*, Cambridge: Harvard Business School Press, 1996.
Forcese, C., ATCA's Achilles Heel: Corporate Complicity, International Law, and the Alien Tort Claims Act, 26 *Yale Journal of International Law* 487 (2001).

Forcese, C., Deterring 'Militarised' Commerce: The Prospect of Liability for 'Privatised' Human Rights Abuses, 31 *Ottawa Law Review* 171 (2000).
Freeman, R.E. and Werhane, P.H., Business Ethics: The State of the Art, 1 *International Journal of Management Reviews* 1 (1999).
French, P. and Wettstein, H. (eds.), *Shared Intentions and Collective Responsibility*, Boston: Blackwell Publishing, 2006.
French, P., The Corporation as a Moral Person, in: May, L. and Hoffman, S. (eds.), *Collective Responsibility: Five Decades of Debate in Theoretical and Applied Ethics*, New York: Rowman and Littlefield, 1991.
French, P., *Collective and Corporate Responsibility*, New York: Columbia University Press, 1984.
Friedman, L., In Defense of Corporate Criminal Liability, 23 *Harvard Journal of Law and Public Policy* 833 (2000).
Friedman, M., The Social Responsibility of Business is to Increase its Profits, in: Beauchamp, T.L. and Bowie, N.E. (eds.), *Ethical Theory and Business*, Englewood Cliffs: Prentice-Hall, 1993.
Frulli, M., Jurisdiction Ratione Personae, in: Cassese, A., Gaeta, P. and Jones, J.R.W.D. (eds.), *The Rome Statute of the International Criminal Court: a Commentary*, Oxford: Oxford University Press, 2002.
Gedicks, A., *Resource Rebels: Native Challenges to Mining and Oil Corporations*, Cambridge: South End Press, 2001.
Geis, G. and Meier, R.F. (eds.), *White-Collar Crime*, New York: Free Press, 1977.
Gilbert, M., *Sociality and Responsibility: New Essays in Plural Subject Theory*, Oxford: Rowman and Littlefield, 2000.
Ginsberg, G. and Kudriavtsev, V.N. (eds.), *The Nuremberg Trial and International Law*, Dordrecht/Boston: Martinus Nijhoff Publishers, 1990.
Glickam, S., Victims' Justice: Legitimising the Sentencing Regime of the International Criminal Court, 43 *Columbia Journal of Transnational Law* 229 (2004).
Global Witness, *A Crude Awakening: The Role of the Oil and Banking Industries in Angola's Civil War and the Plunder of State Assets*, 1999 (at <www.globalwitness.org/reports/show.php/en.00016.html>).
Goldhagen, D.J., *Hitler's Willing Executioners: Ordinary Germans and the Holocaust*, London: Abacus, 1996.
Greenwood, C., Command Responsibility and the Hadzihasanovic Decision, 2 *Journal of International Criminal Justice* 598 (2004).
Gruner, R.G., *Corporate Crime and Sentencing*, Charlottesville: Business Laws Inc., 1994.
Gustafson, K., The Requirement of an 'Express Agreement' for Joint Criminal Enterprise Liability: a Critique of Brdjanin, 5 *Journal of International Criminal Justice* 134 (2007).
Haigh, K., Extending the International Criminal Court's Jurisdiction to Corporations: Overcoming Complementarity Concerns, 14 *Australian Journal of Human Rights* 199 (2008).
Hart, H.L.A., *Punishment and Responsibility. Essays in the Philosophy of Law*, Oxford: Clarendon Press, 1968.

Heine, G., New Developments in Europe: Can Europeans Learn from the American Experience or Vice Versa?, *St. Louis-Warsaw Transatlantic Law Journal* 173 (1998).
Helihy, E.D. and Levine, T.A., Corporate Crisis: The Overseas Payment Problem, in: Bittner, E. and Messinger, S.L. (eds.), *Criminology Review Yearbook*, Vol. II, Beverly Hills: Sage, 1980.
Henham, R., The Philosophical Foundations of International Sentencing, 1 *Journal of International Criminal Justice* 64 (2003).
Hirsch, A. von, Bottoms, A.E., Burney, E. and Wikström, P.O., *Criminal Deterrence and Sentence Severity*, Oxford: Hart Publishing, 1999.
Hood, J., *The Heroic Enterprise: Business and the Common Good*, New York: Free Press, 1996.
Huisman, W., Corporations and International Crimes, in: Smeulers, A. and Haveman, R. (eds.), *Supranational Criminology: Towards a Criminology of International Crimes*, Antwerp: Intersentia, 2008.
Huisman, W., *Between Profit and Morality. Background Factors of Regulatory Compliance and Violation by Corporations*, The Hague: Boom Legal Publishers, 2001.
Human Rights Watch, *Some Transparency, No Accountability*, 2004 (at <hrw.org/sites/default/files/reports/angola0104.pdf>).
International Commission of Jurists, *Corporate Complicity and Legal Accountability. Report of the Expert Legal Panel on Corporate Complicity in International Crimes*, 2008 (at <www.business-humanrights.org/Updates/Archive/ICJPaneloncomplicity>).
Isaacs, T., Collective Moral Responsibility and Collective Intention, in: French, P. and Wettstein, H. (eds.), *Shared Intentions and Collective Responsibility*, Boston: Blackwell Publishing, 2006.
Jackson, R.H., Report of the United States Representative to the International Conference on Military Trials, Doc. XIII, XVII, XVIII and XX, Washington, 1949.
Jacobson, K.R., Doing Business With the Devil: The Challenges of Prosecuting Corporate Officials Whose Business Transactions Facilitate War Crimes and Crimes against Humanity, 56 *Air Force Law Review* 167 (2005).
Jägers, N., *Corporate Human Rights Obligations: In Search of Accountability*, Antwerp: Intersentia, 2002.
Jamieson, K., *The Organisation of Corporate Crime*, Thousand Oaks: Sage, 1994.
Janis, I.L., *Victims of Groupthink*, Boston: Houghton Mifflin Company, 1972.
Jaspers, K., *The Question of German Guilt* (translated by E.B. Ashton with a new introduction by W. Koterski), New York: Fordham University Press, 2000.
Jenkins, R., *Corporate Codes of Conduct: Self-Regulation in a Global Economy*, United Nations Research Institute for Social Development, 2001 (at <www.natural-resources.org/ minerals/cd/docs/other/jenkins.pdf>).
Jokic, A. (ed.), *War Crimes and Collective Wrongdoing: a Reader*, Oxford: Oxford University Press, 2001.
Jong, F. de, *Daad-Schuld* (Action-Inferred Culpability), The Hague: Boom Legal Publishers, 2009.
Jørgensen, N.H.B., A Reappraisal of the Abandoned Nuremberg Concept of Criminal Organisations in the Context of Justice in Rwanda, 12 *Criminal Law Forum* 371 (2002).

Joseph, S., *Corporations and Transnational Human Rights Litigation*, Oxford: Hart Publishing, 2004.

Kamminga, M.T. and Zia-Zarifi, S. (eds.), *Liability of Multinational Corporations under International Law*, The Hague: Kluwer Law International, 2000.

Khanna, V.S., Corporate Liability Standards: When Should Corporations be Held Criminally Liable?, 37 *American Criminal Law Review* 1239 (2000).

Khanna, V.S., Is the Notion of Corporate Fault a Faulty Notion?: The Case of Corporate Mens Rea, 79 *Boston University Law Review* 355 (1999).

Kittichaisaree, K., *International Criminal Law*, Oxford: Oxford University Press, 2001.

Knoops, G.G.J., The Transposition of (International) Criminal Liability Modes onto Private Corporations, in: Adam, S., Colette-Basecqz, N. and Nohoul, M. (eds.), *Corporate Criminal Liability in Europe*, Brussels: La Charte, 2008.

Knoops, G.G.J., *Defences in Contemporary International Criminal Law*, New York: Ardsley Transnational Publishers, 2001.

Kramer, R.C., Corporate Crime: an Organisational Perspective, in: Wickam, P. and Daley T. (eds.), *White-Collar and Economic Crime. Multidisciplinary and Cross-National Perspectives*, Lexington: Lexington Books, 1982.

Kyriakakis, J., Corporations and the International Criminal Court: The Complementarity Objection Stripped Bare, 19 *Criminal Law Forum* 115 (2007).

Langevoort, D.C., Organised Illusions: a Behavioural Theory of Why Corporations Mislead Stock Market Investors (and Cause Other Social Harms), 146 *University of Pennsylvania Law Review* 101 (1997).

Laufer, W.S., *Corporate Bodies and Guilty Minds: The Failure of Corporate Criminal Liability*, Chicago: University of Chicago Press, 2006.

Laufer, W.S. and Strudler, A., Corporate Intentionality, Desert, and Variants of Vicarious Liability, 37 *American Criminal Law Review* 1285 (2000).

Lawson, B., *Collective Intentionality and Agency*, a paper presented at the 'Agency and Identity' conference held at the University of Toronto on 18 – 20 May 2007 (at <www.chass.utoronto.ca/gpsu/conference/2007/papers/lawson.pdf>).

Lee, R.S. (ed.), *The International Criminal Court. The Making of the Rome Statute. Issues, Negotiations, Results*, The Hague: Kluwer Law International, 1999.

Lederman, E., Models for Imposing Corporate Criminal Liability: From Adaptation and Imitation toward Aggregation and the Search for Self-Identity, 4 *Buffalo Criminal Law Review* 641 (2001).

Leinwand, J., Punishing Horrific Crime: Reconciling International Prosecution with National Sentencing Practices, 40 *Columbia Human Rights Law Review* 799 (2009).

Lippman, M., War Crimes Trials of German Industralists: The Other 'Schindlers', 9 *Temple International and Comparative Law Journal* 173 (1995).

Lippman, M., Nuremberg: Forty Five Years Later, 7 *Connecticut Journal of International Law* 1 (1991).

Luban, D.J., War Crimes: The Law of Hell, in: May, L. (ed.), *War. Essays in Political Philosophy*, Cambridge: Cambridge University Press, 2008.

Mantovani, F., The General Principles of International Criminal Law: The Viewpoint of a National Criminal Lawyer, 1 *Journal of International Criminal Justice* 26 (2003).

Marres, R., *In Defence of Mentalism: a Critical Review of the Philosophy of Mind*, Amsterdam: Rodopi, 1989.

May, L. and Hoffman, S. (eds.), *Collective Responsibility: Five Decades of Debate in Theoretical and Applied Ethics*, New York: Rowman and Littlefield, 1991.

McGee, A., Williams, C. and Scanlan, G., *The Law of Business Organisations*, Exeter: Law Matters Publishing, 2005.

Meloni, C., Command Responsibility. Mode of Liability for the Crimes of Subordinates or Separate Offence of the Superior?, 5 *Journal of International Criminal Justice* 619 (2007).

Mettraux, G., *International Crimes and the Ad Hoc Tribunals*, Oxford: Oxford University Press, 2005.

Moore, M., The Moral and Metaphysical Sources of the Criminal Law, in: Pennock, J.R. and Chapman, J.M. (eds.), *Criminal Justice,* New York: New York University Press, 1985.

Morris, H., George Fletcher and Collective Guilt: a Critical Commentary on the 2001 Storrs Lectures, 78 *Notre Dame Law Review* 731 (2003).

Muchlinski, P.T., *Multinational Enterprises and the Law*, Oxford: Oxford University Press, 2007.

Muchlinski, P.T., *Multinational Enterprises and the Law*, Oxford: Blackwell, 1995.

Nerlich, V., Superior Responsibility under Article 28 ICC Statute. For What Exactly is the Superior Held Responsible?, 5 *Journal of International Criminal Justice* 665 (2007).

Nersessian, D.L., Whoops, I Committed Genocide! The Anomaly of Constructive Liability for Serious International Crimes, 30 *SUM Fletcher Forum of World Affairs* 81 (2006).

Nollkaemper, A. and Wilt, H.G. van der, *System Criminality in International Law*, Cambridge: Cambridge University Press, 2009.

Note, Organisational Irrationality and Corporate Human Rights Violations, 122 *Harvard Law Review* 1931 (2009).

O'Connell, H., Due Diligence and the Power of Economic Players, in: Benninger-Budel, C. (ed.), *Due Diligence and its Application to Protect Women from Violence*, Leiden/ Boston: Martinus Nijhoff Publishers, 2008.

Olásolo, H., *The Criminal Responsibility of Senior Political and Military Leaders as Principals to International Crimes*, Oxford: Hart Publishing, 2009.

O'Rourke, A., Joint Criminal Enterprise and Brdjanin: Misguided Overcorrection, 47 *Harvard International Law Journal* 307 (2006).

Osiel, M., *Mass Atrocity, Ordinary Evil, and Hanna Arendt. Criminal Consciousness in Argentina's Dirty War*, New Haven: Yale University Press, 2001.

Parnidge, R.P., *Non-State Actors and Terrorism. Applying the Law of State Responsibility and the Due Diligence Principle*, The Hague: T.M.C. Asser Press, 2007.

Pennock, J.R. and Chapman, J.M. (eds.), *Criminal Justice*, New York: New York University Press, 1985.

Pickard, D.B., Proposed Sentencing Guidelines for the International Criminal Court, 20 *Loyola Los Angeles International and Comparative Law Review* 123 (1997).

Pomorski, S., Conspiracy and Criminal Organisations, in: Ginsberg, G. and Kudriavtsev, V.N. (eds.), *The Nuremberg Trial and International Law*, Dordrecht/Boston: Martinus Nijhoff Publishers, 1990.

Pontell, H.N. and Geis, G.L. (eds.), *International Handbook of White-Collar and Corporate Crime*, New York: Springer, 2006.

Posner, R.A., *Economic Analysis of Law*, Boston: Little, Brown & Co., 1992.

Powles, S., Joint Criminal Enterprise. Criminal Liability by Prosecutorial Ingenuity and Judicial Creativity?, 2 *Journal of International Criminal Justice* 606 (2004).

Prakash Sethi, S., *Setting Global Standards. Guidelines for Creating Codes of Conduct in Multinational Corporations*, New York: John Wiley & Sons, Inc., 2003.

Punch, M., Suite Violence: Why Managers Murder and Corporations Kill, 33 *Crime, Law and Social Change* 243 (2000).

Quinney, R., The Study of White-Collar Crime: Toward a Reorientation in Theory and Research, in: Geis, G. and Meier, R.F. (eds.), *White-Collar Crime*, New York: Free Press, 1977.

Ragozino, A., Replacing the Collective Knowledge Doctrine with a Better Theory for Establishing Corporate Mens Rea: The Duty Stratification Approach, 24 *Southwestern University Law Review* 423 (1995).

Ramasastry, A. and Thompson, R.C., *Commerce, Crime and Conflict. Legal Remedies for Private Sector Liability for Grave Breaches of International Law. A Survey of Sixteen Countries*, 2006 (at <www.fafo.no/pub/rapp/536/536.pdf>).

Ramasastry, A., Corporate Complicity: From Nuremberg to Rangoon. An Examination of Slave Labour Cases and Their Impact on the Liability of Multinational Corporations, 20 *Berkeley Journal of International Law* 91 (2002).

Ramasastry, A., Secrets and Lies? Swiss Banks and International Human Rights, 31 *Vanderbilt Journal of Transnational Law* 325 (1998).

Ratner, S.R., Corporations and Human Rights: a Theory of Legal Responsibility, 111 *Yale Law Journal* 443 (2001).

Reggio, A., Aiding and Abetting in International Criminal Law: The Responsibility of Corporate Agents and Businessmen for 'Trading with the Enemy' of Mankind, 5 *International Criminal Law Review* 623 (2005).

Reno, W., *Warlord Politics and African States*, London: Lynne Rienner Publishers Inc., 1998.

Robinson, D., *The Identity Crisis of International Criminal Law*, a working paper, 2008 (at <papers.ssrn.com/sol3/papers.cfm?abstract_id=1127851>).

Saland, P., International Criminal Law Principles, in: Lee, R.S. (ed.), *The International Criminal Court. The Making of the Rome Statute. Issues, Negotiations, Results*, The Hague: Kluwer Law international, 1999.

Salo, R.S., When the Logs Roll Over: The Need for an International Convention Criminalising Involvement in the Global Illegal Timber Trade, 16 *Georgetown International Environmental Law Review* 127 (2003).

Schabas, W.A., Corporate Liability and State Criminality, in: Discussion, 6 *Journal of International Criminal Justice* 947 (2008).

Schabas, W.A., Mens Rea and the International Tribunal for the former Yugoslavia, 37 *New England Law Review* 1015 (2003).

Schabas, W.A., Enforcing International Humanitarian Law: Catching the Accomplices, *International Review of the Red Cross*, No. 842 (2001).

Schabas, W.A., *Genocide in International Law: The Crime of Crimes*, Cambridge: Cambridge University Press, 2000.

Schabas, W.A., General Principles of Criminal Law in the International Criminal Court Statute (Part III), 6 *European Journal of Crime, Criminal Law and Criminal Justice* 84 (1998).

Sherman, J.F., *Corporate Duty to Respect Human Rights: Due Diligence Requirements*, 2007 (at <198.170.85.29/Sherman-Corporate-Duty-to-Respect-30-Nov-2007.pdf>).

Sherman, L., *Scandal and Reform*, Berkeley: University of California Press, 1978.

Silver, D., A Strawsonian Defence of Corporate Moral Responsibility, 42 *American Philosophical Quarterly* 279 (2005).

Sliedregt, E. van, System Criminality at the ICTY, in: Nollkaemper, A. and Wilt, H.G. van der, *System Criminality in International Law*, Cambridge: Cambridge University Press, 2009.

Sliedregt, E. van, Joint Criminal Enterprise as a Pathway to Convicting Individuals for Genocide, 5 *Journal of International Criminal Justice* 184 (2007).

Sliedregt, E. van, *The Criminal Responsibility of Individuals for Violations of International Humanitarian Law*, The Hague: T.M.C. Asser Press, 2003.

Sloane, R.D., The Expressive Capacity of International Punishment: The Limits of the National Law Analogy and the Potential of International Criminal Law, 43 *Stanford Journal of International Law* 39 (2007).

Smeulers, A. and Haveman, R. (eds.), *Supranational Criminology: Towards a Criminology of International Crimes*, Antwerp: Intersentia, 2008.

Smis, S. and Borght, K. van der, Legislation, Belgium: Act Concerning the Punishment of Grave Breaches of International Humanitarian Law, 38 *International Legal Materials* 918 (1999).

South African Truth and Reconciliation Commission, Final Report, 1998 (at <www.polity.org.za/polity/govdocs/commissions/1998/trc/4chap.htm>).

Stephens, B., The Amorality of Profit: Transnational Corporations and Human Rights, 20 *Berkeley Journal of International Law* 45 (2002).

Stephens, B., Accountability: International Human Rights Violations against Corporations in US Courts, in: Kamminga, M.T. and Zia-Zarifi, S. (eds.), *Liability of Multinational Corporations under International Law*, The Hague: Kluwer Law International, 2000.

Stessens, G., Corporate Criminal Liability: a Comparative Perspective, 43 *International and Comparative Law Quarterly* 493 (1994).

Stokes, R.G., *Divide and Prosper: The Heirs of the I.G. Farben under Allied Authority, 1945-1951*, Berkeley: University of California Press, 1988.

Stover, E., *The Witnesses. War Crimes and the Promise of Justice in The Hague*, Philadelphia: University of Pennsylvania Press, 2005.

Strasser, K.A., Piercing the Veil in Corporate Groups, 37 *Connecticut Law Review* 637 (2005).

Strawson, P.F., *Freedom and Resentment and Other Essays*, Oxford: Methuen & Co. Ltd., 1974.

Sun Beale, S. and Safwat, A.G., What Developments in Western Europe Tell Us About American Critiques of Corporate Criminal Liability, 8 *Buffalo Criminal Law Review* 89 (2002).

Sutherland, E.H., *White Collar Crime: The Uncut Version*, New Haven: Yale University Press, 1983.
Swart, B., Damaska and the Faces of International Criminal Justice, 6 *Journal of International Criminal Justice* 87 (2008).
Swart, B., International Trends towards Establishing Some Form of Punishment for Corporations, in: Discussion, 6 *Journal of International Criminal Justice* 947 (2008).
Tallgren, I., The Sensibility and Sense of International Criminal Law, 13 *European Journal of International Law* 561 (2002).
Telford, T., *Final Report to the Secretary of the Army on the Nuernberg War Crimes Trials under Control Council Law No. 10*, Washington, 1949.
Triffterer, O., Causality, a Separate Element of the Doctrine of Superior Responsibility as Expressed in Article 28 Rome Statute?, 15 *Leiden Journal of International Law* 179 (2002).
Triffterer, O. (ed.), *Commentary on the Rome Statute of the International Criminal Court*, Baden-Baden: Nomos, 1999.
Tuinstra, J.T., *Defence Counsel in International Criminal Law*, The Hague: T.M.C. Asser Press, 2009.
United Nations Panel of Experts, *Report on the Illegal Exploitation of Natural Resources and Other Forms of Wealth of the Democratic Republic of the Congo*, 2002 (at <www.nisat.org/sanctions%20reports/DR%20Congo/UN%202002-10-16%20DR%20 Congo.pdf>).
United Nations Panel of Experts appointed pursuant to UN Security Council Resolution 1306, *Report in relation to Sierra Leone*, 2000 (at <www.un.org/Docs/sc/ committees/SierraLeone/SlselectedEng.htm>).
United Nations Panel of Experts established by the UN Security Council pursuant to Resolution 1237, *Final Report on Violations of Security Council Sanctions against UNITA*, 2000 (at <www.un.org/News/dh/latest/angolareport_eng.htm>).
Vaughan, D., The Dark Side of Organisations: Mistake, Misconduct, and Disaster, 25 *Annual Review of Sociology* 271 (1999).
Vaughan, D., *Crime Between Organisations*, Columbus: Ohio State University Press, 1979.
Wagner, M., *Corporate Criminal Liability: National and International Responses*, a background paper for the Reform of Criminal Law 13th international conference 'Commercial and Financial Fraud: a Comparative Perspective', Malta, 8 – 12 July 1999 (at <www.icclr.law.ubc.ca/publications/reports/corporatecriminal.pdf>).
Waltzer, M., *Just and Unjust Wars*, New York: Basic Books, 1997.
War Crimes Research Office, American University Washington College of Law, *Victim Participation at the Case Stage of Proceedings*, 2009 (at <www.wcl.american.edu/ warcrimes/icc/documents/WCROReportonVictimParticipationattheCaseStageofProc eedingsFebruary2009.pdf?rd=1>).
Ward, H., Securing Transnational Corporate Accountability through National Courts: Implications and Policy Options, 24 *Hastings International and Comparative Law Review* 451 (2001).
Weigend, T., Societas Delinquere Non Potest? A German Perspective, 6 *Journal of International Criminal Justice* 927 (2008).

Weigend, T., Intent, Mistake of Law and Co-perpetration in the Lubanga Decision on Confirmation of Charges, 6 *Journal of International Criminal Justice* 471 (2008).
Welham, M.G., *Corporate Manslaughter and Corporate Homicide: a Manager's Guide to Legal Compliance*, London: Bloomsbury Professional, 2007.
Wells, C., *Corporations and Criminal Responsibility*, Oxford: Oxford University Press, 2005.
Wells, C., *Corporations and Criminal Responsibility*, Oxford: Oxford University Press, 2001.
Werle, G. and Jessberger, F., Unless Otherwise Provided: Article 30 of the ICC Statute and the Mental Element of Crimes under International Criminal Law, 3 *Journal of International Criminal Justice* 35 (2005).
Wexler, L.S. and Bassiouni, M.C. (eds.), *Model Draft Statute for the International Criminal Court based on the Preparatory Committee's Text to the Diplomatic Conference, Rome, 15 June – 17 July 1998*, Pau: Eres, 1998.
Wickam, P. and Daley T. (eds.), *White-Collar and Economic Crime. Multidisciplinary and Cross-National Perspectives*, Lexington: Lexington Books, 1982.
Williams, R., *The Long Revolution*, Harmondsworth: Penguin, 1965.
Wilt, H.G. van der, Joint Criminal Enterprise. Possibilities and Limitations, 5 *Journal of International Criminal Justice* 91 (2007).
Wilt, H.G. van der, Genocide, Complicity in Genocide and International v. Domestic Jurisdiction Reflections on the Anraat Case, 4 *Journal of International Criminal Justice* 239 (2006).
Wilt, H.G. van, *Het Kwaad in Functie* (The Evil in Function), Amsterdam: Vossiuspers, 2005.
Wise, E., General Principles of Criminal Law, in: Wexler, L.S. and Bassiouni, M.C. (eds.), *Model Draft Statute for the International Criminal Court Based on the Preparatory Committee's Text to the Diplomatic Conference, Rome, 15 June – 17 July 1998*, Pau: Eres, 1998.
Zahar, A., Command Responsibility of Civilian Superiors for Genocide, 14 *Leiden Journal of International Law* 591 (2001).
Zeck, W.A., Nuremberg: Proceedings Subsequent to Goering et al., 26 *North Carolina Law Review* 350 (1948).
Zerk, J., *Multinationals and Corporate Social Responsibility*, Cambridge: Cambridge University Press, 2006.
Zimmerman, M.J., Sharing Responsibility, 22 *American Philosophical Quarterly* 115 (1985).
Zuppi, A., Slave Labour in Nuremberg's I.G. Farben Case: The Lonely Voice of Paul. H. Herbert, 66 *Lousiana Law Review* 495 (2006).

TABLE OF CASES

ICC

Germain Katanga and Mathieu Ngudjolo Chui
ICC-01/04-01/07-717, Decision on the confirmation of charges, 30 September 2008.

Jean-Pierre Bemba Gombo
ICC-01/05-01/08-424, Decision pursuant to Article 61(7)(a) and (b) of the Rome Statute on the charges of the Prosecutor against Jean-Pierre Bemba Gombo, 15 June 2009.

ICC-01/05-01/08-388, Decision adjourning the hearing pursuant to Article 61(7)(c)(ii) of the Rome Statute, 3 March 2009.

Omar Hassan Ahmad Al Bashir
ICC-02/05-01/09-3, Decision on the Prosecution's application for a Warrant of Arrest against Omar Hassan Ahmad Al Bashir, 4 March 2009.

Thomas Lubanga Dyilo
ICC-01/04-01-06/1401, Decision on the consequences of non-disclosure of exculpatory materials covered by Article 54(3)(e) agreements and the application to stay the prosecution of the accused, together with certain other issues raised at the Status Conference on 10 June 2008, 13 June 2008.

ICC-01/04-01/06-803-tEN, Decision on the confirmation of charges, 29 January 2007.

ICC-01/04-01/06-8-Corr, Decision on the Prosecutor's application for a Warrant of Arrest, 10 February 2006, annexed to Decision concerning Pre-Trial Chamber I's decision of 10 February 2006, 24 February 2006.

The cases are also accessible via <www.icc-cpi.int>.

ICTY

Aleksovski
Case No. IT-95-14/1-A, Appeal Judgment of 24 March 2000.
Case No. IT-95-14/1, Trial Judgment of 25 June 1999.

Blaskic
Case No. IT-95-14-A, Appeal Judgment of 29 July 2004.
Case No. IT-95-14-T, Trial Judgment of 3 March 2000.

Brdjanin
Case No. IT-99-36-A, Appeal Judgment of 3 April 2007.
Case No. IT-99-36-A, Amicus Curiae Brief of the Association of Defence Counsel, 5 July 2005.
Case No. IT-99-36-T, Trial Judgment of 1 September 2004.
Case No. IT-99-36-A, Decision on Interlocutory Appeal, 19 March 2004.
Case No. IT-99-36-T, Decision on Motion for Acquittal Pursuant to Rule 98bis, 28 November 2003.
Case No. IT-99-36-T, Decision on Motion by Momir Talic for Provisional Release, 28 March 2001.

Delalic
Case No. IT-96-21-A, Appeal Judgment of 20 February 2001.
Case No. IT-96-21-T, Trial Judgment of 16 November 1998.

Furundzija
Case No. IT-95-17/1-T, Trial Judgment of 10 December 1998.

Hadzihasanovic
Case No. IT-01-47-AR72, Decision on Interlocutory Appeal in Relation to Command Responsibility, 16 July 2003.
Case No. IT-01-47-PT, Decision on Joint Challenge to Jurisdiction, 12 November 2002.

Halilovic
Case No. IT-01-48-A, Appeal Judgment of 16 October 2007.
Case No. IT-01-48-T, Trial Judgment of 16 November 2005.

Karadzic
Case No. IT-95-5/18-PT, Prosecution Response to Preliminary Motion on Lack of Jurisdiction Concerning Omission Liability, 7 April 2009.

Krajisnik
Case No. IT-00-39-T, Trial Judgment of 27 September 2006.

Krnojelac
Case No. IT-97-25-A, Appeal Judgment of 17 September 2003.
Case No. IT-97-25-T, Trial Judgment of 15 March 2002.

Krstic
Case No. IT-98-33-A, Appeal Judgment of 19 April 2004.

Kunarac
Case No. IT-96-23-T & IT-96-23/1-T, Trial Judgment of 22 February 2001.

Kvocka
Case No. IT-98-30/1-A, Appeal Judgment of 28 February 2005.
Case No. IT-98-30/1-T, Trial Judgment of 2 November 2001.

Milutinovic
Case No. IT-99-37-AR72, Decision on Dragoljub Ojdanic's Motion Challenging Jurisdiction, 21 May 2003.

Obrenovic
Case No. IT-02-60/2-S, Sentencing Judgment, 10 December 2003.

Oric
Case No. IT-03-68-A, Appeal Judgment of 3 July 2008.

Plavsic
Case No. IT-00-39&40/1, Sentencing Judgment, 27 February 2003.

Simic
Case No. IT-95-9-T, Trial Judgment of 17 October 2003.

Stakic
Case No. IT-97-24-T, Trial Judgment of 31 July 2003.

Strugar
Case No. IT-01-42-T, Trial Judgment of 31 January 2005.

Tadic
Case No. IT-94-1-A, Appeal Judgment of 15 July 1999.

Vasiljevic
Case No. IT-93-32-A, Appeal Judgment of 25 February 2004.

The cases are also accessible via <www.icty.org>.

ICTR

Akayesu
Case No. ICTR-96-4-T, Trial Judgment of 2 September 1998.

Bagambiki
Case No. ICTR-99-46-T, Trial Judgment of 25 February 2004.

Bagilishema
Case No. ICTR-95-1A-A, Appeal Judgment of 3 July 2002.
Case No. ICTR-95-1A-T, Trial Judgment of 7 June 2001.

Gacumbitsi
Case No. ICTR-2001-64-A, Appeal Judgment of 7 July 2006.

Kambanda
Case No. ICTR-97-23-S, Trial Judgment of 4 September 1998.

Karemera
Case No. ICTR-98-44-AR72.5, Decision on Jurisdictional Appeals: Joint Criminal Enterprise, 12 April 2006.

Kayishema and Ruzindana
Case No. ICTR-95-1-T, Trial Judgment of 21 May 1999.

Musema
Case No. ICTR-96-13-A, Appeal Judgment and Sentence, 27 January 2000.
Case No. ICTR-96-13-I, Amended Indictment, 19 April 1999.

Nahimana
Case No. ICTR-99-52-T, Trial Judgment of 3 December 2003.

Ntakirutimana
Case No. ICTR-96-10-A, Appeal Judgment of 13 December 2004.

Rutaganda
Case No. ICTR-96-3, Trial Judgment and Sentence, 6 December 1999.

The cases are also accessible via <www.ictr.org>.

NUREMBERG

IMT Judgment
Trial of the Major War Criminals before the International Military Tribunal, Vol. I, Nuremberg Germany, 1947, pp. 171-367.

Altstötter et al.
Trials of War Criminals before the Nuremberg Military Tribunals under Control Council Law No. 10, Nuremberg (TWC), Vol. III, Washington 1949-1953, pp. 3-1201.

Brandt et al.
Trials of War Criminals before the Nuremberg Military Tribunals under Control Council Law No. 10, Nuremberg (TWC), Vol. II, Washington 1949-1953, pp. 1-336.

Flick
Law Reports of Trials of War Criminals (UNWCC), Vol. IX, London: His Majesty's Stationary Office, 1949, pp. 1-54.

Franz Holstein et al.
Law Reports of Trials of War Criminals (UNWCC), Vol. VIII, London: His Majesty's Stationary Office, 1949, pp. 22-32.

I.G. Farben
Law Reports of Trials of War Criminals (UNWCC), Vol. X, London: His Majesty's Stationary Office, 1949, pp. 1-67.

Krupp
Law Reports of Trials of War Criminals (UNWCC), Vol. X, London: His Majesty's Stationary Office, 1949, pp. 69-177.

Otto Sandrock et al.
Law Reports of Trials of War Criminals (UNWCC), Vol. I, London: His Majesty's Stationary Office, 1949, pp. 35-45.

Pohl et al.
Trials of War Criminals before the Nuremberg Military Tribunals under Control Council Law No. 10, Nuremberg (TWC), Vol. V, Washington 1949-1953, pp. 195-1256.

Roechling et al.
Lauterpacht, H. (ed.), Annual Digest and Reports of Public International Law Cases 1948, London: Butterworth & Co., 1953, pp. 410-412.

Rudolf Hoess
Law Reports of Trials of War Criminals (UNWCC), Vol. VII, London: His Majesty's Stationary Office, 1949, pp. 11-66.

Weizsaecker et al.
Trials of War Criminals before the Nuremberg Military Tribunals under Control Council Law No. 10, Nuremberg (TWC), Vol. XIV, Washington 1949-1953, pp. 1-1002.

Zyklon B
Law Reports of Trials of War Criminals (UNWCC), Vol. I, London: His Majesty's Stationary Office, 1949, pp. 93-103.

ICJ

Bosnian Genocide
Case concerning the Application of the Convention on the prevention and punishment of the crime of genocide, Judgment (No. 91), 26 February 2007.

Nicaragua
Case concerning Military and paramilitary activities in and against Nicaragua (Merits), 27 June 1986.

The cases are also accessible via <www.icj-cij.org>.

ECHR

Agim Behrami and Bekir Behrami v. France, Application No. 71412/01
Ruzdi Saramati v. France, Germany and Normay, Application No. 78166/01
(Joined cases (2007) 45 EHRR SE10)

The cases are also accessible via <www.echr.coe.int>.

DOMESTIC CASES

Australia
Callaghan v. R., 87 CLR 115 (1952).
R. v. Taktak, 34 A Crim R 334 (1988).

Canada
Canadian Dredge & Dock Co. v. R., 1 SCR 662 (1985).

The Netherlands
Kouwenhoven, LJN: BC 7373 (2008).
Van Anraat, LJN: BA 4676 (2007).
Ziekenhuis Leeuwarden, NJ 1988, 981 (1987).
Daderschap: LJN: AR 7619 (2005).

United Kingdom
Tesco Supermarkets Ltd. v. Nattrass, 1972 AC 153 (1971).
R. v. P&O European Ferries (Dover) Ltd., 93 Cr App R 72 (1990).

United States (ATCA-related)
Abebe-Jira v. Negewo, 72 F 3d 844 (1996).
Beanal v. Freeport-McMoran Inc., 969 F Supp 362 (1997).
Bowoto v. Chevron Texaco Corp., 312 F Supp 2d 1229 (2004).
Doe II (Unocal), 395 F 3d 932 (2002).
Doe v. Unocal Corp., 963 F Supp 880 (1997).
Estate of Ferdinand Marcos Human Rights Litigation Hilao v. Estate of Marcos, 25 F 3d 1467 (1994).
Iwanowa v. Ford Motor Co., 67 F Supp 2d 424 (1999).
Kadic v. Karadzic Doe I II, 70 F 3d 232 (1995).
Presbytarian Church of Sudan v. Talisman Energy, 244 F Supp 2d 289 (2003).
Tel-Oren v. Lybian Arab Republic, 726 F 2d 774 (1984).

United States (other)
Western International Hotels Co. v. United States, 409 US 1125 (1973).
State v. Christy Pontiac-GMC Inc., 354 NW 2d 17-20 (1984).

TABLE OF UN AND OTHER DOCUMENTS

UN Special Representative on Human Rights and Transnational Corporations

UN Doc. A/HRC/11/13, Report of the Special Representative of the Secretary-General on the issue of human rights and transnational corporations and other business enterprises. Business and human rights: towards operationalising the 'protect, respect and remedy' framework, 22 April 2009.

UN Doc. A/HRC/RES/8/7, Human Rights Council Resolution 8/7, Mandate of the Special Representative of the Secretary-General on the issue of human rights and transnational corporations and other business enterprises, 18 June 2008.

UN Doc. A/HRC/8/5, Report of the Special Representative of the Secretary-General on the issue of human rights and transnational corporations and other business enterprises, 23 May 2008.

UN Doc. A/HRC/8/5/Add.2, Addendum to the Report of the Special Representative of the Secretary-General on the issue of human rights and transnational corporations and other business enterprise. Corporations and human rights: a survey of the scope and patterns of alleged corporate-related human rights abuse, 23 May 2008.

UN Doc. A/HRC/8/16, Report of the Special Representative of the Secretary-General on the issue of human rights and transnational corporations and other business enterprises: Clarifying the concepts of 'sphere of influence' and 'complicity', 15 May 2008.

UN Doc. E/CN.4/2006/97, Interim Report of the Special Representative of the Secretary-General on the issue of human rights and transnational corporations and other business enterprises, 22 February 2006.

UN Doc. E/CN/4/RES/2005/69, UN Commission on Human Rights, Human Rights Resolution 2005/69: Human Rights and Transnational Corporations and Other Business Enterprises, 20 April 2005.

See <www2.ohchr.org/english/issues/trans_corporations/reports.htm>.

UN Conference of Plenipotentiaries on the Establishment of an International Criminal Court

UN Doc. A/CONF.183/C.1/WGGP/L.5/Rev.2, 3 July 1998.

UN Doc. A/CONF.183/C.1/WGGP/L.4/Add.1, 29 June 1998.

UN Doc. A/CONF.183/C.1/L.3, 16 June 1998.

UN Doc. A/CONF.183/C.1/SR.1, 16 June 1998.

UN Doc. A/CONF.183/2/Add.1, 14 April 1998.

UN Doc. A/AC.249/1997/L.5, 12 March 1997.

See <untreaty.un.org/cod/icc/rome/proceedings/contents.htm>.

Other

European Council Regulation nr. 864/2007, on the law applicable to non-contractual obligations, O.J. 2007, L199/40, 11 July 2007.

European Council Regulation nr. 44/2001 on jurisdiction and the recognition and enforcement of judgments in civil and commercial matters, O.J. 2001, L12/1, 22 December 2000.

Council of Europe Convention on the Protection of the Environment through Criminal Law (1998).

Council of Europe Convention on the Protection of Children against Sexual Exploitation and Sexual Abuse (2007).

ILO Tripartite Declaration of Principles Concerning Multinational Enterprises and Social Policy, (1978) 17 ILM 422.

Kofi Annan's Global Compact (1999), at <www.globalcompact.org>.

OECD Guidelines for Multinational Enterprises, (1976) 15 ILM 969.

Second Protocol to the European Convention on the Protection of the European Communities Financial Interests (1997).

UN Doc. E/CN.4/Sub.2/2003/38/Rev.2, Commentary on the Norms on the Responsibilities of Transnational Corporations and Other Business Enterprises with regard to Human Rights (2003).

UN Convention against Transnational Organised Crime (2000).

UN Convention against Corruption (2000).

UN Convention for the Suppression of Financing of Terrorism (1999).

INDEX

CURRICULUM VITAE

Desislava Stoitchkova (1981) holds a Bachelor of Arts degree (*summa cum laude*) in Social Sciences, with a focus on law and politics, and a Masters degree (*cum laude*) in international and European law, both obtained at Utrecht University. As a doctoral researcher at the Willem Pompe Institute for Criminal Law and Criminology (2006-2010), she taught courses on international criminal law, acted as an ICC correspondent for the Netherlands Quarterly of Human Rights and was a supervisor in the Utrecht Law School Clinic on Conflict, Human Rights and International Justice. In addition, she published on topics of human rights law and international criminal law and procedure, including as a contributor to the Annotated Leading Cases of the International Criminal Tribunals series. Previously she worked at the Netherlands Institute of Human Rights (2004-2006) and was involved in a human rights training programme for magistrates and public prosecutors in Bulgaria. She also provided specialised legal advice to defence lawyers litigating ECHR-related cases before domestic courts at the district and appellate level, and extended consultancy services in relation to international human rights law to non-governmental organisations operating both in the Netherlands and abroad.

SCHOOL OF HUMAN RIGHTS RESEARCH SERIES

The School of Human Rights Research is a joint effort by human rights researchers in the Netherlands. Its central research theme is the nature and meaning of international standards in the field of human rights, their application and promotion in the national legal order, their interplay with national standards, and the international supervision of such application. The School of Human Rights Research Series only includes English titles that contribute to a better understanding of the different aspects of human rights.

Published titles within the Series:

1 Brigit C.A. Toebes, *The Right to Health as a Human Right in International Law*
ISBN 90-5095-057-4

2 Ineke Boerefijn, *The Reporting Procedure under the Covenant on Civil and Political Rights. Practice and Procedures of the Human Rights Committee*
ISBN 90-5095-074-4

3 Kitty Arambulo, *Strengthening the Supervision of the International Covenant on Economic, Social and Cultural Rights. Theoretical and Procedural Aspects*
ISBN 90-5095-058-2

4 Marlies Glasius, *Foreign Policy on Human Rights. Its Influence on Indonesia under Soeharto*
ISBN 90-5095-089-2

5 Cornelis D. de Jong, *The Freedom of Thought, Conscience and Religion or Belief in the United Nations (1946-1992)*
ISBN 90-5095-137-6

6 Heleen Bosma, *Freedom of Expression in England and under the ECHR: in Search of a Common Ground. A Foundation for the Application of the Human Rights Act 1998 in English Law*
ISBN 90-5095-136-8

7 Mielle Bulterman, *Human Rights in the External Relations of the European Union*
ISBN 90-5095-164-3

8 Esther M. van den Berg, *The Influence of Domestic NGOs on Dutch Human Rights Policy. Case Studies on South Africa,Namibia, Indonesia and East Timor*
ISBN 90-5095-159-7

9 Ian Seiderman, *Hierarchy in International Law: the Human Rights Dimension*
ISBN 90-5095-165-1

10 Anna Meijknecht, *Towards International Personality: the Position of Minorities and Indigenous Peoples in International Law*
ISBN 90-5095-166-X

11 Mohamed Eltayeb, *A Human Rights Approach to Combating Religious Persecution. Cases from Pakistan, Saudi Arabia and Sudan*
ISBN 90-5095-170-8

12 Machteld Boot, *Genocide, Crimes Against Humanity, War Crimes: Nullum Crimen Sine Lege and the Subject Matter Jurisdiction of the International Criminal Court*
ISBN 90-5095-216-X

13 Corinne Packer, *Using Human Rights to Change Tradition. Traditional Practices Harmful to Women's Reproductive Health in sub-Saharan Africa*
ISBN 90-5095-226-7

14 Theo R.G. van Banning, *The Human Right to Property*
ISBN 90-5095-203-8

15 Yvonne M. Donders, *Towards a Right to Cultural Identity?*
ISBN 90-5095-238-0

16 Göran K. Sluiter, *International Criminal Adjudication and the Collection of Evidence: Obligations of States*
ISBN 90-5095-227-5

17 Nicola Jägers, *Corporate Human Rights Obligations: in Search of Accountability*
ISBN 90-5095-240-2

18 Magdalena Sepúlveda, *The Nature of the Obligations under the International Covenant on Economic, Social and Cultural Rights*
ISBN 90-5095-260-7

19 Mitsue Inazumi, *Universal Jurisdiction in Modern International Law: Expansion of National Jurisdiction for Prosecuting Serious Crimes under International Law*
ISBN 90-5095-366-2

20 Anne-Marie L.M. de Brouwer, *Supranational Criminal Prosecution of Sexual Violence: The ICC and the Practice of the ICTY and the ICTR*
ISBN 90-5095-533-9

21 Jeroen Gutter, *Thematic Procedures of the United Nations Commission on Human Rights and International Law: in Search of a Sense of Community*
ISBN 90-5095-557-6

22 Hilde Reiding, *The Netherlands and the Development of International Human Rights Instruments*
ISBN 978-90-5095-654-3

23 Ingrid Westendorp, *Women and Housing: Gender Makes a Difference*
ISBN 978-90-5095-669-7

24 Quirine A.M. Eijkman, *We Are Here to Serve You! Public Security, Police Reform and Human Rights Implementation in Costa Rica*
ISBN 978-90-5095-704-5

25 Antoine Ch. Buyse, *Post-conflict Housing Restitution. The European Human Rights Perspective with a case study on Bosnia and Herzegovina*
ISBN 978-90-5095-770-0

26 Gentian Zyberi, *The Humanitarian Face of the International Court of Justice. Its Contribution to Interpreting and Developing International Human Rights and Humanitarian Law Rules and Principles*
ISBN 978-90-5095-792-2

27 Dragoş Cucereanu, *Aspects of Regulating Freedom of Expression on the Internet*
ISBN 978-90-5095-842-4

28 Ton Liefaard, *Deprivation of Liberty of Children in Light of International Human Rights Law and Standards*
ISBN 978-90-5095-838-7

29 Laura van Waas, *Nationality Matters. Statelessness under International Law*
ISBN 978-90-5095-854-7

30 Jeroen Denkers, *The World Trade Organization and Import Bans in Response to Violations of Fundamental Labour Rights*
ISBN 978-90-5095-855-4

31 Irene Hadiprayitno, *Hazard or Right? The Dialectics of Development Practice and the Internationally Declared Right to Development, with Special Reference to Indonesia*
ISBN 978-90-5095-932-2

32 Michał Gondek, *The Reach of Human Rights in a Globalising World: Extraterritorial Application of Human Rights Treaties*
ISBN 978-90-5095-817-2

33 Jeff Handmaker, *Advocating for Accountability: Civic-State Interactions to Protect Refugees in South Africa*
ISBN 978-905095-910-0

34 Anna Oehmichen, *Terrorism and Anti-Terror Legislation: The Terrorised Legislator? A Comparison of Counter-Terror Legislation and Its Implications on Human Rights in the Legal Systems of the United Kingdom, Spain, Germany and France*
ISBN 978-90-5095-956-8

35 Simon Walker, *The Future of Human Rights Impact Assessments of Trade Agreements*
ISBN 978-90-5095-986-5

36 Fleur van Leeuwen, Women's Rights Are Human Rights. The Practice of the Human Rights Committee and the Committee on Economic, Social and Cultural Rights
ISBN 978-90-5095-980-3

37 Eva Rieter, *Preventing Irreparable Harm. Provisional Measures in International Human Rights Adjudication*
ISBN 978-90-5095-931-5

www.ingramcontent.com/pod-product-compliance
Ingram Content Group UK Ltd.
Pitfield, Milton Keynes, MK11 3LW, UK
UKHW051922100926
8556IPUK00021B/1321

9 789400 000247